Newberry County, South Carolina

DEED ABSTRACTS

VOLUME II
Deed Books C, D-2, and D
1794–1800 [1765–1800]

By

Brent H. Holcomb

SCMAR
2000

HERITAGE BOOKS
2019

HERITAGE BOOKS

AN IMPRINT OF HERITAGE BOOKS, INC.

Books, CDs, and more—Worldwide

For our listing of thousands of titles see our website
at
www.HeritageBooks.com

Published 2019by
HERITAGE BOOKS, INC.
Publishing Division
5810 Ruatan Street
Berwyn Heights, Md. 20740

Library of Congress Catalog Card Number: 98-75025

International Standard Book Numbers
Paperbound: 978-0-7884-5869-9

INTRODUCTION

Newberry County was formed in 1785 as a county of Ninety Six District. It remained in Ninety Six District through the year 1799 for higher court cases. A small corner of Newberry County (near present-day Chapin) was a part of Orangeburgh District until 1788. In the year 1800 with the end of the county court system, Newberry County became Newberry District. In the colonial period the area of Newberry County was considered part of Craven County or Berkeley (sometimes spelled Barkley) County in South Carolina. Prior to the border surveys of 1764 and 1772, the area was included in the North Carolina counties of Anson, Mecklenburg, and Tryon. For this reason a few grants and deeds from North Carolina are referenced in the Newberry County deeds. Land grants from North Carolina are frequently referred to as "north patents." The South Carolina deeds prior to 1785 were recorded in Charleston and in some cases a few years later. The Charleston deeds have been abstracted and published through the year 1788, those from 1773-1788 by the writer. The deeds of the aforementioned North Carolina counties have also been abstracted and published. Volume 1 of this series included deeds recorded in Newberry County 1785-1794. The deeds in this volume were recorded 1794-1800. As is common, there are deeds recorded from a much earlier time period. The earliest deed included in this work dates from 3 & 4 September 1765 and is found in Deed Book D, pages 22-26. With this work, the deed abstracts for the Newberry County area are now in print from the beginning through the year 1800. Researchers should find this work unusually helpful, as the Newberry deed indices contain references only to those instruments which are transfers of real property. Depositions, deeds of gift and bills of sale for slaves and other personal property are not included in the index available at the Newberry County Court House and on microfilm. For that reason many of these records, containing valuable genealogical information, have gone undetected by many researchers. The instruments in this volume have been abstracted from LDS microfilm and South Carolina Archives microfilm, using the original deed books in Newberry when necessary.

The Quaker community in Newberry County is apparent in deeds included in this volume, recognizable by their "affirmations" instead of oaths and in the language such as "the fifth day of the fourth month called April." Other early settlers in the Newberry County area were German Protestant immigrants, some Germans from Pennsylvania, and Irish Protestant immigrants, many of whom settled in the area in and around the present town of Prosperity. As indicated in some of the deeds, there were also settlers from North Carolina. Migration from Newberry County to other areas of South Carolina is indicated in deeds as well.

My thanks to Mr. James D. McKain for preparing the excellent index.

Brent H. Holcomb
January 7, 1999

C, 1-3: 30 Aug 1794, John Blalock of Newberry County to William Taylor (lately from Ireland) of same county, for £80 sterling, 100 acres on waters of Indian Creek, call'd or known by the name of Gilders Creek between Broad and Saluda Rivers, formerly granted to Jacob Gilder 12 Dec 1768, recorded in Book 3D, page 16, vacant on all sides when granted but now adj. Hugh Boyd, James Shearer, widdow Renwick, John Huston. John Blalock (seal), Wit: Ptk Lowry, Arch'd McMullin, Wilson Crozar Glasgow. Proved in Newberry County by the oath of Patrick Lowry 17 Nov 1794 before John Speake, J.P. Recorded 25 Nov 1794.

C, 4-9: Lease and release. 1 & 2 Jan 1789, Joseph Cambell and Sarah his wife of Newberry County to Alexander McKie of same, for £100, 350 acres granted 2 May 1770 to Joseph Campbell on waters of Little River adj. David Hambrea, Henry Pitts, John Monk, George Goggans, Daniel Goggans. Joseph Campbell (X) (Seal), Sarah Cambell (S) (Seal), Wit: Bartlett Satterwhite, Dudly Brooks. Proved in Newberry County by the oath of Dudly Brooks 3 July 1789 before William Caldwell, J.P. Recorded 29 Nov 1794.

C, 10-11: 19 May 1792, Obadiah Roberts, sadler, of Newberry County, Ninety Six District, to Isaac Evans, planter, for £45 sterling, 150 acres on both sides Hedley Creek, a small branch of Indian Creek, granted to Henry Roberts in 1769 adj. land of Jacob Pennington, John Johnson, Thomas Evans, John Evans. Obadiah Roberts (Seal), Wit: John H. Bush, John Teer, John Evans (X). Proved in Newberry County by the oath of John Evans 26 July ____ before P. Williams, J. P. Recorded 8 Dec 1794.

C, 12: 30 Oct 1794, Sabra Badger, late of County of Newberry, to Henry Criek of same, negro man named May about 35 years of age. Sabra Badger (mark, Wit: John Coate, Sneed Davis (mark). Recorded 15 Dec 1794.

C, 12-14: 1 Aug 1794, Philemon Waters Senr of Newberry County to Rachel Waters, his wife, for love and affection, 100 acres in the fork between Saluda River & Bush River, being the land whereon the above Philemon Waters Sen: now lives, convenient to the dwelling house and plantation where said Philemon now lives, adj. Daniel Parkins, Cullen Lark. Philemon Waters (Seal), Wit: Wm. Satterwhite, B. H. Saxon. Recorded 15 Dec 1794.

C, 14-18: Lease and release. 11 & 12 Nov 1793, John Harmon of Newberry County to William Wright of same, for £30 sterling, 50 acres on waters of Saluda River granted to Margret Reich 25 May 1774 and by her and her lawful husband John Cummerlander conveyed to said John Harmon 4 & 5 Jan 1785, in all 100 acres. John Harmon (Seal), Wit: William Blair, Thomas McNeese, David Blair. Proved in Newberry County by the oath of Thomas McNeese 18 Sept 1794 before Peter Julien, J.P. Recorded 18 Dec 1794.

C, 19: John Blalock of Newberry County for £100 sterling to James Shearer of same county, one negro wench named Lish and child, 21 April 1788. Wit:

Wm Webster, Wm Wilson. Proved in Newberry County by the oath of William Webster 16 Dec 1794 before John Speake, J.P. Recorded 30 Dec 1794.

C, 20-24: Lease and release. 26 Nov 1791, Joshua Inman Sen:, planter, of Newberry County, to John Marbutt, planter, of same, for £40 sterling, 50 acres on waters of Bush River adj. Frederick Burtz, John Inman, Mercer Babb, Esqr., half of 100 acres granted to Rufus Inman 10 June 1774 and conveyed by him to Joshua Inman Senr 14 & 15 Oct [year not indicated]. Joshua Inman, Wit: Aaron Coppock, James Barrett. Proved 26 Nov 1791 by the oath of Aaron Coppock before Mercer Babb, J.P. Recorded 5 Jan 1795.

C, 25: Benjamin Butler of Newberry County to Willis Butler of same, three feather beds & furniture, one roan mare, one bay horse, five head of cattle, 12 head of hoggs, 50 bushels of corn & one Iron pott, & half dozen plats, two basons, one shovel plow, 14 March 1794. Benjamin Butler (X) (Seal), Wit: John Butler, Wm. Butler. Proved in Newberry County by the oath of William Butler 9 March 1794 before Pro. Williams, J.P. Recorded 6 Jan 1795.

C, 26: South Carolina, Newberry County. Personally appear'd before me Charity Mills & Makes oath that about two years & ten months ago her husband lost a number of hoggs, estray'd away amongst which was an old black sow marked with a crop & slit in each ear, also a number of other hoggs same mark, others not marked at all, 10 Dec 1794. Charity Mills (X), before Peter Julien, J.P.

Rebekah Mills makes oath that her father marked with a crop & slit in each & particular remembers there loosing the black saw mentioned within.

Thomas W. Waters makes oath he took up seven hogs, six of which had the above mark & believes them to be the same. Thos. W. Waters.

Peter Lester makes oath that he was one of the appraisers that valued such hoggs for said Waters & they valued them at Eleven dollars. Peter Lester (X). Recorded 6 Jan 1795.

C, 27-28: South Carolina, Ninety Six District. 19 Oct 1794, James Virden & Sarah his wife of Newberry County to Charles Hewit of same, for £120 sterling, 200 acres on south side Enoree River adj. Isaac Pennington, Edeniah Virden, granted 5 June 1786. James Verden (X) (Seal), Sarah Verden (mark) (Seal), Wit: W. Kelly, William Nabours, James Cater. Proved in Newberry County by the oath of Ja's Cato 30 July 1794 before John Speake, J.P. Recorded 6 Jan 1795.

C, 29: Rachel Waters of Newberry County for natural love and affection to my son Dennis Lark, one negroe girl named Anica about 8 years old, 15 Nov 1794. Rachel Waters (Seal), Wit: Cullen Lark, M. W. Moon. Proved 20 Nov in Newberry County by the oath of Cullen Lark before Mercer Babb, J.P. Recorded 6 Jan 1795.

C, 30-31: 21 Feb 1794, Charles Griffin and Mary his wife of Newberry County to Reuben Griffin of same, for £68 sterling, 130 acres originally granted to Jonathan Mote 20 Jan 1773 adj. land of Jacob Gray, Michael Rey, James Griffin, Wm Johnson, and land for the meeting house. Charles Griffin (Seal), Mary Griffin (X), Wit: Alexander Simpson, John Gray (X), Frankey Griffin (X). Proved by the oath of Alexander Simpson 2 May 1794 before Providence Williams, J.P. Recorded 7 Jan 1795.

C, 32-33: 21 Feb 1794, Charles Griffin and Mary his wife of Newberry County to Reuben Griffin of same, for £68 sterling, 100½ acres on west side and north side of the Quaker Branch, part of 350 acres originally granted 12 Dec 1768 to James Griffin deceased, adj. land granted to Jonathan Mote. Charles Griffin (Seal), Mary Griffin (X), Wit: Alexander Simpson, John Gray (X), Frankey Griffin (X). Proved by the oath of Alexander Simpson 2 May 1794 before Providence Williams, J.P. Recorded 7 Jan 1795.

C, 34-37: Lease and release. 14 & 15 March 1794, Joseph Coppock of Newberry County, planter, to Thomas Coppock, blacksmith, of same, for £100 sterling, 250 acres, part of 400 acres on Bush Creek, granted to John Ridgedell 22 March 169 and conveyed in part, viz 250 acres to Joseph Coppock 12 Oct 1784. Joseph Coppock (Seal), Wit: David Miles, Thomas Haskit, John Coppock. Proved 24 Nov 1794 by the oath of Thomas Haskit before Mercer Babb, J.P. Recorded 16 Jan 1795.

C, 38-40: Lease and release. 13 & 14 Oct 1794, Enoch Smith of Pendleton County, SC, to Azariah Pugh of Newberry County, for £80 sterling, 205 acres on waters of Bush River granted to Enoch Smith 4 Dec 1786, recorded in Book PPPP, page 251, adj. Joseph Scott, John Mills, land formerly of Azariah Pugh Senr, and William Aspinell. Enoch Smith (Seal), Wit: Samuel Looper, Joseph Looper, Moses Smith. Proved in Newberry County 17 Oct 1794 by the oath of Moses Smith before Mercer Babb, J.P. Recorded 19 Jan 1795.

C, 41-42: 1 Dec 1794, Samuel Proctor Senr of Newberry County, for natural love and affection to son in law Joseph White, part of 350 acres granted to said Samuel Proctor 13 May 1768 on Pages Creek, waters of Mudlick Creek, to be divided: to son Philip Proctor 50 acres, to son Edward 50 acres, to nephew Samuel Adams, 50 acres, the remainder of 200 acres to Joseph White. Saml Proctor Senr (mark) (Seal), Wit: Thos Wm. Fakes, Stephen Vetito, John Proctor. Proved by the oath of Stephen Vetito 7 Jan 1795 before James Mayson, J.N.C. Recorded 21 Jan 1795.

C, 43-45: Lease and release. 9 & 10 Oct 1794. Henry Coate & his wife Mary of Newberry County to Francis Atkins of same, for £15 sterling, 57 acres on waters of Scotch Creek, a branch of Bush River, adj. Benjamin Atkins, Francis Atkins, Joseph Scott, William Jenkins, Little John Coate, granted to Henry Coate 29 Oct 1794. Henry Coate (Seal), Mary Coate (X) (Seal), Wit: George Goggans, Thomas Atkins, John Coate. Proved by the oath of John Coate 13 Oct 1794 before Peter Julin, J.P. Recorded 21 Jan 1795.

C, 46-47: 4 June 1794, Henry Counts Senr of Newberry County to John Eigleberger of same, for £20 SC money, 10 acres in Berkley County adj. Daniel Ebb, John Fellers, Jacob Singley, part of 300 acres granted to Herman Nuffer 9 Jan 1755, recorded in Book LN, page 155, 11 March 1752. Henry Counts (H) (Seal), Wit: Philip Sligh (PS, Joseph Whyer (M). Proved by the oath of Philip Slight 10 Jan 1795 before William Houseal, J.P. Recorded 21 Jan 1795.

C, 48-50: Lease and release. 3 & 4 Aug 1774, William Gilleland of Ninety Six District and wife Elenor to Jacob Chandler of same, for £300 SC money, 100 acres in the fork of Broad and Saluda Rivers, part of 250 acres granted to Jeremiah Lewis 27 Nov 1770, conveyed by him to William Gilleland 20 & 21 Dec 1771. William Gilliland (Seal), Elenor Gilliland (Seal), Wit: Oliver Lyttle, Simeon Quinn, Thos Nicholson (X). Recorded 22 Jan 1795.

C, 51-55: Lease and release. 30 Nov 1791, John Ellemon of Newberry County, executor of the estate of Enos Ellemon of Newberry County, deceased, to William Ellemon of same, planter, for £50 sterling, 150 acres on north side Saluda River on a branch called the Beaver Dam, adj. land of William Weeks, John Ellemon, granted to Joshua Griffin 13 July 1770 and conveyed by him to Enos Ellemon, and another tract adj. it of 131½ acres, 150 acres granted to Thomas Dodd, all of which land is settled by his will and leaving his wife and his oldest son the said John Ellemon, and granted to said William Ellemon, part of his own dowry and part as purchased. John Ellemon, Susannah Ellemon, wit: Benjamin Pearson, William Weeks. Proved by the oath of Benjamin Pearson 12 Nov 1794 before Mercer Babb, J. P. Recorded 22 Jan 1795.

C, 56-58: Lease and release. 23 & 24 Jan 1794, Mercer Babb Esqr., of Newberry County, and Samuel Gilbert of the State of Pensylvania, to John Crumley, planter, of said county, for £51 6/8 SC money, 200 acres on waters of Saluda River, on a branch called Beaver Dam, part of tract granted to Josiah Buckman [sic] 18 May 1771 and conveyed by him to William Weeks 18 June 1771, and the above Mercer Babb, Esquire, exr. of the estate of William Weeks deceased hath conveyed the same unto Samuel Gilbert agreeable to a bond formerly given unto Joshua Gilbert by the said Weeks. Samuel Gilbert (Seal), Wit: Robert Richardson, Onslow Barrett, Samuel Crumley. Proved by the oath of Samuel Crumley 21 Aug 1794 before Mercer Babb, J.P. Recorded 23 Jan 1795.

C, 59-60: 8 April 1794, Thomas Hollinhead to John Livingston, both of Newberry County, for £30, 299 acres (except 81 acres belonging to Boston Cook), 218 acres in the fork of Broad and Saluda Rivers on a branch of Campin Creek and streams of Williams Creek granted to said Hollinhead 6 Jan 1794, recorded in Book K. No 5, page 53. Thomas Hollinhead (X) (Seal), Mary Hollinhead (X) (Seal), Wit: William Young, Andrew Swan. Proved by the oath of Andrew Swan 4 Oct 1795 before Peter Julin, J.P. Recorded 27 Jan 1795.

C, 61-63: 1 Dec 1793, Samuel Lindsey & Jacob Frost, both of Newberry County, planters, to Peter Braselman of same, merchant, for 508 shillings, 9 pence sterling, 5 acres on a branch of Kings Creek, part of 209 acres sold by John Lindsey to Jacob Frost. Samuel Lindsey (Sal), Jacob Frost (Seal), Wit: Charles Crenshaw, John Ellis, Rob't Powell. Proved by the oath of Robert Powell 9 Jan 1795 before Edward Finch, J.P. Recorded 27 Jan 1795.

C, 63: Thorowgood Chambers of Newbery County for £60 sterling to Peter Brasilman of same, one negro named Dick about 17 years of age, 16 Jan 1794. Thorowgood Chambers (Seal), Wit: Peter Stalley, Robt Powell. Proved by the oath of Robert Powell 9 Jan 1795 before Edward Finch, J.P. Recorded 27 Jan 1795.

C, 64-66: Lease and release. 20 & 21 Jan 1791, Mercer Babb Esqr., of Newberry County, to Samuel Gilbert of the State of Pensylvania, for £1, 200 acres on waters of Saluda River, on a branch called Beaver Dam, part of tract granted to Joseph Buchanan 18 May 1771 and conveyed by him to William Weeks 18 June 1771, and the above Mercer Babb, Esquire, exr. of the estate of William Weeks deceased hath conveyed the same unto Samuel Gilbert agreeable to a bond formerly given unto Joshua Gilbert by the said Weeks, Samuel Gilbert, right heir of Joshua Gilbert deceased. Mercer Babb (Seal), Wit: William Wright, Thomas Haskitt. Proved by the oath of Thomsa Haskit 9 Oct 1794 before Providence Williams, J.P. Recorded 27 Jan 1795.

C, 67-69: Lease and release. 22 Jan 1794, Jariot Campbell & his wife Srah of Newberry County to Daniel McKie of same, for £200 sterling, 50 acres, the remainder of a tract granted to Jooseh Campbell for 350 acres 2 May 1770 and devolved to Jariot Campbell by heirship, on a small branch of Little River claled Rocky Creek, adj. Land of Francis Davenport, Daniel McKie, John Waldrop, Alex'r McKie, and land whereon Hamilton Murdock now lives. Jariot Campbell (Seal), Sarah Campbell (X) (Seal), Wit: J. Brown J. N. C., Drury Satterwhite, William Smith (mark). Reocrded 27 Jan 1795.

C, 70: 11 Dec 1794, Samuel Benjamins of Newberry County to SAmuel Lindsey of same, for £20 sterling, one negro woman named Mary, one horse, one mare and all my household furniture, etc. Samuel Benjn (Seal), Margaret Benjamin (X) (Seal), Wit: Wm Satterwhite, Sneed Davis (mark). Proved by the oath of William Satterwhite 8 Jan 1795 before John Speak, J.P. Recorded 27 Jan 1795.

C, 71-74: Lease and release. 25 & 26 Aug 1794, Clement Davis of Ninety Six District, SC, to Samuel Teague of same, for £10 sterling, 108 acres on a small branch of Bush River called Reedy branch, part of 200 acres adj. Marmiduke Coats. Clement Davis (mark) (Seal), Wit: John Furnas, Abraham Teague, Daniel Johnston. Porved by the oath of John Furnas 23 Dec 1794 before Mercer Babb, J.P. Recorded 29 Jan 1795.

C, 75-77: 19 Sept 1776, John Neil and Lydda his wife of Ninety Six District, Newberry County, to David Boyd of same, for £200 SC money, 200 acres in Berkley County in the fork between Broad and Saluda Rivers, on a small branch of Kings Creek called Lick branch, waters of Enoree River, granted 11 Aug 1775 to Jered Smith and conveyed to John Neil 25 July 1776. John Neil (Seal), Lidda Neil (X) (Seal), Wit: James Wilson, John Wilson, John Boyd (X). Proved in Ninety Six District 10 Oct 1783 by the oath of John Wilson before John Lindsey, J.P. Recorded 29 Jan 1795.

C, 78-82: Lease and release. 24 & 25 July 1776, Jered Smith, carpenter, of Ninety Six District, to John Neil, farmer, for £225 SC money, 200 acres in Berkley County in the fork between Broad and Saluda Rivers, on a small branch of Kings Creek called Lick branch, waters of Enoree River, granted 11 Aug 1775 to Jered Smith. Jered Smith (X) (Seal), Wit: Wm. Woodall, Elisa Lindsey, Thomas Lindsey. Proved in Ninety Six District 25 July 1776 by the oath of William Woodall before Benjamin Tutt, J.P. Recorded 30 Jan 1795.

C, 83-86: Lease and release. 15 & 16 Nov 1783, David Boyd of Ninety Six District, to Isaac Palmore of same place, and settlement of Kings Creek, by grant dated 11 Aug 1774 to Jered Smith, 200 acres in Berkley County in the fork between Broad and Saluda Rivers, on a small branch of Kings Creek called Lick branch, waters of Enoree River, now conveyed for £500 SC money. David Boyd (Seal), Wit: Thomas Lindsey, Richard Speake, John Doyel (O). Proved 29 Dec 1784 in Ninety Six District by the oath of Richard Speake before John Lindsey, J.P. Recorded 3 Feb 1795.

C, 87-89: 5 Feb 1787, John Satterwhite Senr of Newberry County to Bartlett Satterwhite Junr of same, for £100 sterling, 185 acres on Mudlick Creek adj. John Satterwhite, John Satterwhite Junr, William Menneweather [sic], part of 600 acres granted to William Thompson, 2 Aug 1768 and conveyed by said Thompson to John Satterwhite 7 & 8 May 1769. John Satterwhite Senr (Seal), Frances Satterwhite (mark) (Seal), Wit: William Mereweather, Sterling Dickson, James Altom (mark). Proved by the oath of William Menneweather 18 Feb 1787 before William Caldwell, J.P. Recorded 3 Feb 1795.

C, 90-93: Lease and release. 16 Jan 1772, James Coate of Berkley County, SC, to John Crumley of same, for £350 sterling, 250 acres adj. land of Samuel Kelly, Joseph Currey, granted to James Coate 4 May 1771. James Coate (Seal), Rebekah Coate (O) (Seal), Wit: David Rees, Nathaniel Haworth, William Coate. Proved by the oath of Nathaniel Haworth in Newberry County 20 June 1794 before Mercer Babb, J.P. Recorded 4 Feb 1795.

C, 93-95: 15 Oct 1791, John Tune, planter, of Newberry County, to Thomas Peterson of same, for £25 sterling, 55 acres on waters of Saluda River adj. Widow Turner, James Dugall, granted to said John Tune 6 March 1786. John Tune (Seal), Wit: Thadeus Owen, James Owen, Alexander Stewart (A). Proved 13 Sept 1794 by the oath of Alexander Stewart before Mercer Babb, J.P. Recorded 4 Feb 1795.

C, 96-99: Lease and release. 8 & 9 Oct 1794, Jennet Stewart of newberry County to Joshua Stewart of same, for £62 s10 sterling, 125 acres, part of 250 acres granted to Jennet Stewart 10 Jan 1771 adj. said Jennet Stewart, John Glenn. Jennet Stewart (I) (Seal), Wit: Robert Speer, William Stewart (X), Robert Stewart. Proved 10 Oct 1794 bey the oath of William Stewart (X) before Mercer Babb, J.P. Recorded 4 Feb 1795.

C, 99-102: Lease and release. South Carolina, Ninety Six District, Newberry County. 10 & 11 Oct 1789, Michael Burtz, planter, of district above mentioned, to Frederick Burtz, planter, of same, for £15, 150 acres on waters of Bush River originally granted to Michael Burtz 6 June 1785, recorded in Book DDDD, page 294. Michael Burtz (X) (Seal), Wit: Joshua Inman, James Barrett, Jehu Inman. Proved 5 Jan 1790 by the oath of James Barrett before Mercer Babb, J. P. Recorded 6 Feb 1795.

C, 103-104: 6 March 1794, John Johnston to James Johnston, both of Newberry County, for seven shillings sterling, 119 acres on the south side of Indian Creek, part of tract granted to John Garret 24 March 1756, recorded in Book QQQ, page 172. John Johnston (Seal), Wit: Uriah Conner, Charles Johnston. Proved 6 July 1794 by the oath of Uriah Conner before Providence Williams, J.P. Recorded 6 Feb 1795.

C, 105-108: Lease and release. 4 & 5 June 1792, Phillemon Waters Senr of Newberry County, planter, to John Waits of same, vulcan, for £100 sterling, 200 acres on north side Great Saluda known by the name of Camp Hill, part of grant to William Mazyck 7 Sept 1771 of 500 acres, and by William Mazyck's sons William and Isaac Mazyck to Col. Phillimon Waters 27 Oct 1790, adj. Allin Robison, Henry Criek, William Musgrove. P Waters (Seal), Wit: Lidia Richardson (mark), David Richardson. Proved by the oath of David Richardson 5 June 1792 before John Julin, J.P. Recorded 16 Feb 1795.

C, 109-112: Lease and release. 13 & 14 Nov 1773, Richard Dowd of Berkley County, SC, to Isaiah Pemberton, planter, of same, for £150 SC money, 150 acres granted to said Richard Dowd 3 Nov 1771 in the fork between Broad and Saluda Rivers on a small branch of Bush River called Williams Beaverdam branch, adj. land granted to Joseph Evans, Samuel Cumpton, Providence Williams, recorded in Book FFF, page 405. Richard Dowd (mark) (Seal), Wit: John Hookey, Joseph Evans, Thos Wadlington Junr. Proved in Ninety Six District by the oath of John Hookey 16 Nov 1773 before Jonathan Downs, j.P. Recorded 16 Feb 1795.

C, 113-116: Lease and release. 13 & 14 Nov 1773, Joseph Evans of Berkley County to Isaiah Pemberton of same, for £100 SC money, 100 acres granted to Joseph Evans 28 Aug 1767 in the fork between Broad and Saluda Rivers on a small branch of Bush River called Beaverdam branch, recorded in Book BBB, page 271. Richard Dowd (mark) (Seal), Wit: John Hookey, Richard Dowd (mark), Thos Wadlington Junr. Proved in Ninety Six District by the oath of John Hookey 16 Nov 1773 before Jonathan Downs, j.P. Recorded 16 Feb 1795.

C, 117: John James Breeding Hammons of Newberry County, planter, bound to Jesse Anderson of same, planter, in the sum of £500 sterling, 8 March 1794, to obey the award, arbitrament and determination of Thomas Gordon, Micajah Harris and Levi Anderson, arbitrators, 10 March 1794. John James B. Hammons (X) (Seal), Wit: Eliza Gordon (mark), Adam Glazier. Proved in Newberry County 6 Aug 1794 by the oath of Adam Glazier before Edward Finch, J.P. Recorded 21 Feb 1795.

C, 118: South Carolina, Newberry County. We the arbitrators chosen by Jesse Anderson, admr. on the estate of Henry Anderson decd., and John James Breeding Hammons to settle all disputes and controversies between them, do award that after the payment of the judge Debts the administrator shall make an equal division of the balance of the personal estate of the deceased amongst the legatees, and determine that the plantation purchased from Richardson by Ruth Hammons during her widowhood shall for the ensuing year be rented out at the rate of £3 sterling in trade at cash price to be paid on demand by the person renting the said place, which sum shall be paid to the said Hammons, and order that at the expiration of one year, be sold at a credit of 8 years, the purchase giving bond and security, the bond to have interest from the date and to be annually paid for the schooling of the three legatees hereafter mentioned, and at the end of nine years, the plantation shall be equally divided among or between Josiah Anderson, Jacob Anderson, and Henry Anderson, sons & legatees of said Henry Anderson, deceased, with such interest as may be due them from the administrator. Thos Gordon, Micajah Harris, Levi Anderson. Recorded 21 Feb 1795.

C, 119: 20 Dec 1794, James Strawther of Newberry County to Sims Brown of same, in consequence of said Sims Brown being security for £4295 s17 d5, the full amount of the estate of Jacob Anderson deceased, mortgage to said Sims Brown, 11 head of cattle, 36 head of hoggs, four feather beds and furniture, three pots and one skillet, one brown bay mare, one gray horse. James Strawther (Seal), Wit: William McCrackin, Perry Anderson. Recorded 21 Feb 1795.

C, 120: 1 January 1795. Received of James Strawther and Sims Brown, £24 s17 d6, it being in full of all the estate of Jacob Anderson deceased, my father, is indebted to me. Nathan Anderson. Wit: Perry Anderson.

1 January 1795. Received of James Strawther and Sims Brown, £24 s17 d6, it being in full of all the estate of Jacob Anderson deceased, my father, is indebted to me. Perry Anderson. Wit: Nathan Anderson.

1 January 1795. Received of James Strawther and Sims Brown, £24 s17 d6, it being in full of all the estate of Jacob Anderson deceased, my father, is indebted to me. Mary Anderson (X). Wit: Perry Anderson.

1 January 1795. Received of James Strawther and Sims Brown, £24 s17 d6, it being in full of all the estate of Jacob Anderson deceased, my father, is indebted to me. Rebekah Anderson (X). Wit: Perry Anderson.

C, 121-122: John Barlow, planter, for £80 sterling, to Andrew Smyth Junr and Elizabeth Ann Smyth, his wife, three negro children: one little negro boy named Santa Croix about 5 years old, one little negro girl named Harriet about 2½ years old, one little negro child named Ireland, about 3 months old, 28 Feb 1795. John Barlow (Seal), Wit: John MacCary, Josiah Gates. Proved by the oath of John MacCary 2 March 1795 before Charles Griffin, J. P. Recorded 2 March 1795.

C, 122-123: John Barlow, planter, of Newberry County, for £65 sterling, to Andrew Smyth Junr and Elizabeth Ann Smyth, his wife, of same, three negro children: one negro man named George about 20 years old, 8 Dec 1794. John Barlow (Seal), Wit: David Speers, Wm Craig. Proved by the oath of Wm Craig 2 March 1795 before Charles Griffin, J. P. Recorded 2 March 1795.

C, 124-125: South Carolina, Newberry County. John Adolph Lagrown of county aforesaid for love to my grandson Frederick Lagrown, a tract of 200 acres, part of 450 acres granted to Lawrence Lagrown, which I order to remain in the possession of Ann Mary Lagrown, my wife, during her life, 19 Sept 1794. Jno Adolph Lagrown (Seal), Wit: John Reasor, Elizabeth Cappleman, Philip Gruber. Proved in Newberry County by the oath of John Rice [sic] 28 Feb 1795 before John Speak, J.P. Recorded 10 March 1795.

C, 126: South Carolina, Newberry County. Nicholas Latner of said county bound to John Eigleberger, Andrew Cromer and Philip Gruber, mortgage of a tract of 124 acres in the fork of Saluda & Broad River adj. land of John Voluntine Lattiner, for payment of £9 s17 s6 sterling with interest before 21 March 1796, dated 21 March 1795. Nicholas Latener (L) (Seal), Wit: Michael Keebler, Mary Lagrown (X), Barbary Eiglebarger (+). Recorded 23 March 1795.

C, 127: William Gilliam of Newberry County bound to Benjamin Evans of same, blacksmith, in the sum of £64 for the payment of £32 on or before 3 Sept 1796. William Gilliam (Seal), Wit: Sam. Kelley Senr, George Latham, John Kelly Senr. Recorded 24 March 1795.

C, 128-130: 2 & 3 Sept 1794, William Gilliam of Newberry County, farmer, to Benjamin Evans of same, blacksmith, mortgage of 165 acres granted to said Gilliam 15 Feb 1769 on Bush Creek, adj. heirs of William Taylor decd, William McDowal, James Wadlington, the successors of Jacob Brooks, Benjamin Evans, James Commack, for payment of £64. William Gilliam (Seal), Wit: Sam. Kelley Senr, George Latham, John Kelly Senr. Proved by the oath of John Kelly 28 Feb 1795 before Edw'd Finch, J.P. Recorded 24 March 1795.

C, 131-132: 29 Aug 1794, James Buchanan, planter, and Suckey his wife, of Ninety Six District, to Alexander Bookter, planter, of same, for £50 sterling, 200 acres in Newberry County on south side Broad River. James Buchanan (Seal), Suckey Buchanan (X) (Seal), Wit: John Mink, Edmond Kelley, James Kelley. Proved by the oath of John Mink 19 Dec 1794 before Reuben Sims, J.P. Recorded 25 March 1795.

C, 133-136: Lease and release. 22 & 23 Sept 1794, Robert Creswell to James Creswell, both of Newberry County, for £150 sterling, 100 acres granted to Joseph White on Saluda River adj. land of James Creswell, John Caldwell; also 200 acres, being the one third of undivided moiety granted to Robert Cunningham, which were given to Robert Creswell as his portion of his father's land. Robert Creswell (Seal), Wit: R. Watts, E. Creswell, James Hill. Recorded 25 March 1795. Plat included, pursuant to the tenor of the will of James Creswell deceased dated 26 May 1778, 200 acres on Saluda River, plat dated 1 Sept 1794. W. Anderson, Ex'r.

C, 137-140: Lease and release. 5 & 6 March 1779, James Wadlington of Ninety Six District, planter, and Margaret his wife, to William Strawther, late from Virginia, for £2260 SC money, 200 acres, part of 400 acres granted to Jacob Duckett on the diving ridge comprehending several draughts leading from Kings Creek & Indian Creek, conveyed by Jacob Duckett to Thomas Wadlington decd, and the said Thomas Wadlington did transfer the said 400 acres to his two sons Thomas Wadlington and James Wadlington. James Wadlington (Seal), Margaret Wadlington (Seal), Wit: James Ford, George Gray, Francis Strawther. Recorded 27 March 1795.

C, 141-144: Lease and release. 7 March 1780, William Strawther of Berkley County, SC, planter, and Susannah his wife, to James Ford of same, for £9750 SC money, 200 acres, part of 400 acres granted to Jacob Duckett on the diving ridge comprehending several draughts leading from Kings Creek & Indian Creek, conveyed by Jacob Duckett to Thomas Wadlington decd, and the said Thomas Wadlington did transfer the said 400 acres to his two sons Thomas Wadlington and James Wadlington, conveyed by James Wadlington to William Strawther 5 & 6 March 1779. William Strawther (Seal), Susannah Strawther (mark) (Seal), Wit: Francis Ford, Williamson Liles, Bolden Ford. Proved 4 April 1780 by the oath of Thomas Ford before John Lindsey, J.P. Recorded 30 March 1795.

C, 145: Benjamin Long of Newberry County to Elizabeth Turner of same, for £85 sterling, one negro fellow named Monday, 26 Feb 1790. Benjamin Long (Seal), Wit: Thomas Waters. Proved by the oath of Thomas Waters 2 March 1795 before Edw'd Finch, J.P. Recorded 30 March 1795.

C, 146: Gabriel Friday of Orangeburgh District, SC, to Alexander Bookter of Ninety Six District, for £50 sterling, one negroe man slave called Sizar, about 22 years of age, 15 Aug 1794. Ga'l Fridig (Seal), Wit: Thomas Rogers, Wm.

T. Linton. Proved in Newberry County by the oath of William T. Linton 26 Feb 1794 before Reuben Sims, J.P. Recorded 31 March 1795.

C, 147-148: John Barlow of Newberry County for £1500 sterling to Andrew Smyth Jun'r and Elizabeth Ann Smith his wife, planter, 400 acres between the forks of Mudlick Creek and Little River, granted to John Andrews and by Samuel Andrews, son of said John, conveyed to John Barlow; also 12 negroes, viz, four negro men: Wigdon about 25 years old, Tom about 25 years old, Major about 28 years old, Jacob about 40 years old; Bob about 60 years old, a boy Thomas about 10 years old, two wenches named Mary Ann about 50 years old and Susannah about 27 years old, and Susannah's children Fortune about 7 years old, Santa Croix about 5 years old, and Harriet nigh three years old, dated 27 Feb 1795. John Barlow (Seal), Elizabeth Barlow, Wit: John MacCary, Josiah Gates. Proved 2 March 1795 by the oath of John MacCary before Charles Griffin, J.P. Recorded 31 March 1795.

C, 148-149: 10 Dec 1794, Alexander McKie of Newberry County to Daniel McKie of same, for £130 sterling, 200 acres, part of 350 acres granted 2 May 1770 to Joseph Campbell and conveyed by Joseph Campbell and Sarah his wife to Alexander McKie 1 & 2 Jan 1789, adj. Henry Pitts, John Monk, George Goggans, James Campbell. Alexander McKie (Seal), Wit: Benj'a Long, John Satterwhite, B. Satterwhite. Proved 27 Feb 1795 by the oath of John Satterwhite before J. R. Brown, J.N.C. Recorded 2 April 1795.

C, 150: South Carolina, Ninety Six District. The legatees of the estate of Robert Johnson, late of Caswell County, North Carolina, appoint our trusty friend and related John Gates, admr. to the said estate, our lawful attorney 5 Jan 1795. Angus Campbell (Seal), James Gates (Seal), Thomas Crimmins (Seal), Peter Smith (Seal), Simpson Warren (Seal), Wit: J. R. Brown, J.N.C. Recorded 2 April 1795.

C, 151-152: 13 Dec 1794, James Odell of Newberry County to John Odell Jun'r of same, in consideration of the said John Odell's right in the real estate of his father John Odell of Newberry County, deceased, 196 acres of land in Newberry, County, part of 302 acres on a ranch of Enoree River adj. Joseph Duckett, Basil Robinson, James Duncan, John Duncan, granted to said James Odell and Joseph Duckett in partnership 3 March 1794. James Odell (Seal), Wit: Joel Whitten, Henry Hill (X), John Pearson. Proved 10 Jan 1795 by the oath of Joel Whitten before Levi Casey, J. N. C. Recorded 2 April 1795.

C, 153-156: Lease and release. 27 & 28 Sept 1791, Solomon Lynch of Ninety Six District, planter, to Joseph Reagan, blacksmith, for £15 SC money, 50 acre, pat of two tracts. Solomon Lynch (Seal), Sarah Lynch (X) (Seal), Wit: William Wright, David Jay, Moses Arnold. Proved 21 Oct 1791 by the declaration of David Jay before Elisha Ford, J.P. Recorded 2 April 1795.

C, 157-158: Daniel Rogers of Newberry County to Thomas Chappel of same, for £125 sterling, one sorrel mare branded HH, one black mare branded AC,

11 head of black cattle, 5 head of hoggs, three feather beds & furniture, with sundry household goods, 1 Jan 1795. Daniel Rogers (Seal), Wit: Rees Harris, John Thomas S. M. Proved by the oath of Rees Harris 2 March 1795 before Robert Gilliam, J.P. Recorded 3 April 1795.

C, 159-162: Lease and release. 14 & 15 Dec 1792, James Yeldall of Edgefield County, SC, to Reason Reagan of Newberry County, for £50 sterling, 100 acres in Newberry County on waters of Bush River adj. land of Isaac Mills Reason Reagan, John Dawbins, recorded in Book EEE, page 253, granted to Henry Glass 28 July 1769 and left by will to Ralph McDugall and by said Ralph McDugall conveyed to James Yeldall decd 15 Aug 1770 and fell to present James Yeldall as heir to said James yeldall deceased. James Yeldall (Seal), Wit: Mathias Elmore, Eliz'a Yeldall (mark), Isaac Elmore. Proved in Newberry County by the oath of Matthias Elmore 3 March 1794 before Peter Julin, J.P. Recorded 3 April 1795.

C, 163-166: Lease and release. 26 & 27 Jan 1795, Henry Pitts Junr and Elizabeth his wife of Newberry County for £25 sterling to John Floyd of same, 50 acres, part of 100 acres granted to William Anderson and conveyed by him to Henry Pitts Junior 31 July & 1 Aug 1787 on a small branch of Saluda called Sandy Run, adj. Robert Johnson, Henry Butler. Henry Pitts (X) (Seal), Elizabeth Pitts (X) (Seal), Wit: Daniel McDaniel (X), James Alton (X), John Butler. Proved 28 Feb 1795 by the oath of Daniel McDaniel before John Speake, J.P. Recorded 3 April 1795.

C, 167-171: Lease and release. 25 Dec 1794, Little Berry Harris and Mosely Harris, exrs. of the will of Nathaniel Harris of Newberry County, to William Caldwell of same, for £25 sterling, 64 acres, part of tract granted to the late Nathaniel Harris on Mill Creek, adj. William Caldwell, William Farrow. Little B. Harris, Mosely Harris (Seal), Saml Harris (Seal), Clough Harris (Seal), Jemima Gilliam (Seal), Wit: Bartlett Brooks (X). Abel Pearson, James Roach (X). Proved by the oath of Bartlett Brooks 2 March 1795 before Providence Williams, J.P. Recorded 3 April 1795.

C, 172-175: Lease and release. __ Dec 1794, Samuel Harris, Little Berry Harris, Mosely Harris, and Jemima Gilliam, to Clough Harris, all of Newberry County, for £25 sterling, 75 acres on waters of Mill Creek, adj. William Farrow. Little B. Harris, Mosely Harris (Seal), Saml Harris (Seal), Clough Harris (Seal), Jemima Gilliam (Seal), Wit: Bartlett Brooks (X). Abel Pearson, James Roach (X). Proved by the oath of Bartlett Brooks 2 March 1795 before Providence Williams, J.P. Recorded 3 April 1795.

C, 176-177: 4 May 1794, Thomas Johnson and Elizabeth his wife to Thomas Gary for £56, 150 acres on north side Saluda River granted to said Thomas Johnson 23 April 1785. Thomas Johnson (seal), Elisy Johnson (X) (Seal), Wit: Jehu Johnston, Daniel Johnston. Proved 11 Aug 1794 by the oath of Daniel Johnston before Providence Williams, J.P. Recorded 9 April 1795.

C, 178-179: 20 Jan 1795, John Sparks and Margaret his wife of Newberry County to William Calmes of same, for £10, 100 acres between Broad and Saluda Rivers on the south side of Enoree, 100 acres part of tract granted to John Sparks adj. Mary Foster, Francis Wafer, adj. land granted to Isaac Pennington now belonging to said Calmes. John Sparks (Seal), Margaret Sparks (Seal), Wit: Levi Johnson, John Wadlington, James Vardiman. Proved by the oath of John Wadlington 2 March 1795 before John Speake, J.P. Recorded 9 April 1795.

C, 180-181: 5 March 1795, Jesse Anderson of Newberry County to Samuel Muffet [Maffet] of same, for £25 s16 sterling, 100 acres on a small draught of Second Creek adj. Samuel Lonam, Jeremiah Williams. Jesse Anderson (Seal), Wit: Robert Rutherford, Benjamin Johnson, James Brown, John Pope. Proved by the oath of John Pope 5 March 1795 before J. R. Brown, J.N.C. Recorded 9 April 1795.

C, 182-183: 9 Feb 1795, Mathias Quattlebaum and Rachel his wife of Newberry County to John Yans of same, for £50 sterling, 100 acres on Sleepy (otherwise Rockey) Creek, a branch of Turkey Creek, adj. land of Margaret Rachel Derrin (alias Quaddlebum on Bounty) recorded in Book LL, page 384. Mathias Quaddlebum (X) (Seal), Rachael Quaddlebum (Seal), Wit: Peter Quaddlebum, Jacob Robtogal, George Long (GL). Proved in Newberry County by the oath of Peter Quaddlebum 21 Feb 1795 before Wm Houseal, J.P. Recorded 9 April 1795.

C, 184-185: 11 March 1794, William Thomas Linton of Newberry County to John Maxedon of same, for £100 sterling, 100 acres in the fork of Enoree and Broad Rivers, formerly granted to John Robinson Senr and conveyed to John Robinson Junr and from him to Thadeus Shirly. Wm T. Linton (Seal), Wit: Mark Robinson, John Maxedon Junr, Martha Maxedon. Proved by the oath of John Maxedon 17 March 1795 before Reubin Sims, J.P. Recorded 9 April 1795.

C, 186-187: 10 Nov 1794, Thomas Jones, exr. of the will of Paul Townsend of Charleston, to Reuben Sims of Newberry County, for £130 sterling, 450 acres laid out to Thomas McElduff, John Stewart, Benjamin Anderson, Sarshall Grasty & James Liles, land formerly laid out to William Case and John ONeal by patents. Thos Jones (Seal), Wit: Jacob Seibles, Peter C. Graff. Proved in Orangeburgh District by the oath of Jacob Seibles 11 Dec 1704 before William Fitzpatrick, J.P. Recorded 11 April 1795.

C, 188-189: 15 Jan 1795, Abraham Larrowe, planter, of Newberry County, to John Gorrie Senr, planter, of same, for £50, 119 acres on north side Enoree River. Abraham Larrour (Seal), Sarrah Larrour (X), Wit: John Gorrie Junr, Noah Bonds. John Larrour. Proved by the oath of John Gorree Junr 17 Feb 1795 before Reuben Sims, J.P. Recorded 13 April 1795.

C, 190-191: 27 May 1793, Levi Casey of Newberry County to Joseph Herndon of Wilkes County, North Carolina, for £10 SC currency, 50 acres on waters of Duncan Creek, granted to Levi Casey 6 Aug 1792, recorded in Book E No. 5, page 338. Levi Casey (Seal), Wit: Samuel Dogan, John Linvell Hendrix, Thomas Graw. Proved 3 March 1795 by the oath of Samuel Dogan before Edward Finch, J.P. Recorded 13 April 1795.

C, 192-195: Lease and release. 8 & 9 Jan 1795, William Stewart, alias Little William Stewart, son of William Stewart decd, with Mary his wife of Edgefield County, and William Stewart, son of Alexander Stewart deceased, to Joseph Reagan, blacksmith, of Newberry County, for £60 sterling, 200 acres on south side of Beaver Dam Creek, waters of Saluda, adj. land of Saml Brown, Joseph Reagan, part of 400 acres granted to William Stewart deceased 22 Jan 1769. William Stewart (Seal), Mary Stewart (mark) (Seal), William Stewart (Seal), Wit: John Thomas S. M., Robert Speir, John Reagan. Proved in Newberry County by the oath of John Reagan 2 March 1795 before Peter Julin, J.P. Recorded 13 April 1795.

C, 196-198: 29 Dec 1794, Joel Whitten and Sarah his wife of Lawrence County, to Eleanor Odell of Newberry County, for five shillings, 18 acres, part of Newberry County and part in Laurance County on SW side Enoree River adj. land of John Odell deceased, part of 184 acres granted to said Joel Whitten 7 April 1794. Joel Whitten (Seal). Sarah Whitten (Seal), Wit: Rignal Odell, James Odell, Abel Pearson. Proved in Newberry County by the oath of Rignal Odell 29 Dec 1794 before L. Casey, J.N.C. Recorded 13 April 1795.

C, 199-200: 26 Nov 1790, Edward Finch of Newberry County to Henry Gaines of same, for £140 sterling, 150 acres in the fork between Broad and Saluda Rivers on a branch of Broad River called Cannons Creek, granted to James Murphy 30 Oct 1767, recorded in Book BBB, page 312. Edward Finch (Seal), Wit: Charles Crenshaw, John Ellis, William Ragland. Acknowledged by Edward Finch 2 April 1759 before John Speak, J.P. Recorded 14 April 1795.

C, 201-202: 3 March 1795, Richard Wright of Newberry County to John Stewart of same, for £10 sterling, 150 acres on south side Broad River on waters of Cannons Creek, adj. Jacob Bouzart, Samuel McConnel, recorded in Auditor Generals Office in Book M No. 14, page 132. Rich'd Wright (Seal), Wit: John B. Mitchell, Joseph Chapman, John Livingston. Proved 3 March 1795 by the oath of John Mitchell before Edward Finch, J.P. Recorded 20 April 1795.

C, 203: 10 Dec 1794, Francis Davenport of Newberry County to Isaac Davenport of same, for £50 SC currency, one negro fellow named Cage, about 21 years old. Francis Davenport (Seal), Wit: John Kenneday, David Davinport, William Margin (X). Proved by the oath of David Davinport 3 March 1795 before Robert Gilliam, J.P. Recorded 20 April 1795.

C, 203-205: 28 March 1795, Israel Gaunt Senr to Joseph Mooney, planter, both of Newberry County, for £50 sterling, 200 acres on a branch of Youngs fork on waters of Bush River, adj. Thomas Mills, Alex'r Mills, William Summers & Timothy Thomas. Israel Gaunt (Seal), Hannah Gaunt (Seal), Wit: Thomas Smith, Jacob Gaunt, William Aspenel (O). Proved in Newberry County by the oath of Thomas Smith before Thos W. Waters, J.P. Recorded 20 April 1795.

C, 205: South Carolina, Ninety Six District. Henry Graves and Ralph Graves of Granville County, North Carolina, executors of the estate of John Williams Jun'r deceased, appoint Capt. John Wallice of Newberry County, SC, being the trustee named in the said John Williams' will to transact certain matters, authorise him to transact the said matter, 17 March 1795. Henry Graves (Seal), Ralph Graves (Seal), Wit: J. R. Brown J.N.C., John Satterwhite Senr. Recorded 20 April 1795.

C, 206-209: Lease and release. 31 Oct & 1 Nov 1794, Mathew Harbinson of Chester County, Pinckney District, SC, to John Glenn of Newberry County, Ninety Six District, for £20 sterling, being half of 200 acres granted 8 July 1774 to Susannah Wade and conveyed by her in 1776 to said Mathew Harbinson, deceased, and from him unto Henry Harbinson, son and heir at law, on north side Saluda River. Mathew Harbinson (Seal), Wit: Robert Speer, James Glenn, William Speer. Proved in Newberry County by the oath of Robert Speer 2 March 1795 before Peter Julin, J.P. Recorded 20 April 1795.

C, 210-211: William Petti Pool of Newberry County to William Turpin and Thomas Wadsworth, merchants, of same, mortgage of one negro wench Moll about 30 years of age, Patience about 30 years old, Hannah about 12 years of age, Lin about 11 years of age, Violet nine years of age, Esther seven years of age, and George three years of age, sold in open market to secure payment of £87 s12 d2¼, 1 Jan 1795. Wm Pettipool (Seal), Wit: Dan Symmes. Recorded 21 April 1795.

C, 212-216: Lease and mortgage. 1 January 1795, William Petti Pool of Newberry County to William Turpin and Thomas Wadsworth, merchants, of same, mortgage of 147 acres on waters of Mudlick of Little River of Saluda, adj. Thomas Turner, Robert Gaudy, granted to Hamilton Murdock and by him conveyed to Daniel McKie. Wm Pettipool (Seal), Wit: Daniel Symmes, John Garvin. Recorded 21 April 1795.

C, 217-218: 20 Feb 1795, George Hart and Delilah Hart his wife of Rutherford County, North Carolina, to John Cary Royston of Newberry County, SC, for £150 sterling, all the estate of the late Solomon Nichols deceased. George Hart (mark) (Seal), Delilah Hart (mark) (Seal), Wit: William Wilson, Robt Royston. Proved in Newberry County by the oath of William wilson 10 April 1759 before Edward Finch, J.P. Recorded 26 April 1795.

C, 219: 1 January 1795, Moses Lindsey, planter, of Ninety Six District, SC, to David Boyd of same, one negro boy named Dan for £53 sterling. Moses Lindsey (Seal), Robert Caldwell (mark), Samuel Morris. Recorded 27 April 1795.

C, 220-221: 14 Feb 1795, Thomas Spray of Newberry County to David Boyd of same, for £40 sterling, 100 acres, part of 293 acres on waters of Bush River granted to James Lindsay in 1786 and conveyed to Benjamin Berry and then to Thomas Spray, adj. Clement Davis. Thomas Spray (Seal), Wit: John Turner, Elijah Teague, James Caldwell (X). Proved by the oath of James Caldwell 5 March 1795 before J. R. Brown, J.N.C. Recorded 27 April 1795.

C, 222-223: 23 Feb 1794, Joshua Reeder of Newberry County to David Boyd of same, for £20 sterling, 100 acres granted to aid Joshua Reeder 29 April 1768 on waters of Guiders Creek. Joshua Reeder (Seal), Wit: Joseph Caldwell (mark), James Caldwell (mark), John Caldwell (X). Proved by the oath of James Caldwell 5 March 1795 before J. R. Brown, J.N.C. Recorded 27 April 1795.

C, 224-227: Lease and release. 15 & 16 Jan 1795, Charles Burton of Newberry County to John Swan of same, for £28 sterling, 100 acres, part of 200 acres granted to said Charles Burton 9 Nov 1774 surveyed 18 Jan 1773, recorded in the Auditor Generals Office, Book M. No. 13, page 473 in the fork between Broad and Saluda Rivers, adj. Robert Dunnon and David Griffin, recorded in Book TTT, page 362. Charles Burton (Seal), Grizy Burton (mark) (Seal), Wit: Robert Drennen (mark), Jno B. Mitchell, Edward Finch, J.P. Acknowledged 3 March before Edward Finch, J.P. Recorded 27 April 1795.

C, 228-229: James Wilson of Logan County, Kentucky, appoints friend Mathew Wilson of Newberry County, SC, his attorney, 10 Nov 1794, to dispose of tract on waters of Indian Creek on Long Branch, granted to James Wilson deceased, 300 acres which fell to me said James Wilson by the death of his eldest brother William Wilson decd. James Wilson (Seal), Wit: Thomas Davis, John Boyd (mark), Prov. Williams. Proved in Newberry County by the oath of Providence Williams, J.P. 21 April 1795. Recorded 26 April 1795.

C, 229-231: Lease and release. 3 & 4 April 1795, John Wright, son of Joseph Wright decd, of Newberry County to Isaac Elmore of same, for £10 sterling, 50 acres granted to my father Joseph Wright (whose only son and heir I am), 5 Dec 1786 on waters of Bush River adj. Mathias Elmore, Abner Elleman, Saml McKinny. John Wright (Seal), Wit: David Pugh, Richard Thomson, James Johnson. Proved by the oath of Jas Johnson 4 April 1795 before Thos W. Waters, J.P. Recorded 28 April 1795.

C, 232: Daniel McKie of Newberry County bound to Ann Floyd, widow of same in the sum of £1000 sterling, 12 March 1794, surety against Isaac Teasdale of Charleston, tract of 750 acres whereon said Anne Floyd now lives, by note dated 7 Dec 1790. Daniel McKie (Seal), Wit: George Goggans,

Thomas Leverett (X). Proved by the oath of George Goggans 18 April 1795 before Charles Griffin, J.P. Recorded 11 May 1795.

C, 233-234: John Millhous, Millwright, for love and affection to Thomas Wilkinson Furnas (a minor under 21 years), son of John Furnas of Bush River, brewer, 50 acres granted to said John Millhous 29 April 1768 on waters of Bush River, adj. John Furnas Esquire, dated 1 April 1769. Jno Millhous (Seal), Wit: Thomas Cheek, Stephen Elmore, Samuel Kelly. Proved by the oath of Saml Kelly Senr before Elisha Ford, J.P., 2 May 1795. Recorded 11 May 1795.

C, 235: 30 Nov 1794, Thomas Lindsey & Lidda his wife of Newberry County to daughter Polley Wells and her husband George Wells of same, for love and affection, one negro girl named Betty. Thomas Lindsey (Seal), Lyda Lindsey (X) (Seal), Wit: Michael Gore, Isaac Guilder (mark). Proved by the oath of Michael Gore 6 May 1795 before Edward Finch, J.P. Recorded 12 May 1795.

C, 236-237: 16 June 1794, John Coats of Newberry County to James Campbell and Samuel Lindsey of same, for £100 sterling, 1½ acres in Newberry village being in six lotts, each ¼ acre, two name by the name of Cobbs lots, the other four numbers 27, 28, 29, and 30, on Market Street and Union Street. John Coate (Seal), Susanah Coate (Seal), Wit: Thomas Lindsey, John Crick, Henry Crick, Fred Nance. Proved 16 June 1794 by the oath of Thomas Lindsey before John Speak, J.P. Recorded 12 May 1795.

C, 238-242: Lease and release. 12 & 13 Dec 1794, Daniel McKie of Newberry County to Thomas Reeder of same, for £130 SC money, 180 acres on waters of Little River, part of 350 acres granted to Joseph Campbell 2 May 1770, conveyed to Alexander McKie by Joseph Campbell and Sarah his wife 2 Jan 1789. Daniel McKie (Seal), Fanny McKie (seal), Wit: George Goggans, John Patterson, Jerrat Campbell. Proved by the oath of George Goggans 10 Jan 1795 before Providence Williams, J.P. Recorded 12 May 1795.

C, 243-245: 1 & 2 Oct 1791, Samuel Edwards of Ninety Six District, for £10 sterling, 190 acres on waters of Halls branch of Bush River, adj. James Dobbins, William Mills, Peter Hawkins, Edward Finch, granted to Samuel Edwards 6 June 1775. Samuel Edwards (mark) (Seal), Hannah Edwards (mark) (Seal), Wit: Proved by the oath of James Johnson 30 Jan 1795 before Peter Julin, J.P. Recorded 12 May 1795.

C, 246-247: 7 Feb 1795, John Kershaw of the Town of Camden, SC, Esquire, to Lewis and Thomas Dinkins of same place, innkeepers, whereas James Kershaw, John Kershaw, and Joseph Kershaw, exrs. of the will of Joseph Kershaw, esquire, late of Camden, deceased, in February Term 1793 obtained a judgment against Joshua Dinkins in the county court of Kershaw for the sum of £85 s13 d6 sterling with costs, and there is now due on said judgment the sum of £65 sterling, and said Joseph Kershaw deceased did on 21 Feb 1790, by indentures assigned all his property unto William Ancrum, Edward Darrel,

James Fisher, Robert h. Henry and James Kershaw, five of the creditors of said Joseph Kershaw deceased in trust, now said John Kershaw as attorney for said trustees, to make over to said Lewis and Thomas Dinkins the said judgment and all money due. John Kershaw (Seal), Wit: Geo Brown. Proved in Kershaw County by the oath of George Brown 19 March 1795 before Francis Boyakin, J.P. Recorded 13 May 1795.

C, 248-249: Christopher Hogle, late of Ninety Six District, Broad and Saluda Rivers, but now of Hallifax, Nova Scotia, yeoman, appoint George Gray and William Dawkins Lane, no or late of district and state aforesaid, my lawful attorney, 6 Nov 1787. Christopher Hogle (Seal), Wit: Wm Morris, D. McKetchen. Province of Nova Scotia in North America: Gerrald Fitzgerrald, notary public, certifies that Christopher Hogle signed the power of attorney, 26 Nov 1787. Recorded 16 May 1795.

C, 250-251: 3 Aug 1792, George Gray Junr of Newberry County to Daniel Davalt of same, for £10 s16 d6 sterling, 100 acres, which was willed from Daniel Davalt decd to his son Peter Davalt and willed from Peter Davalt deceased to said George Gray Junr, and is part of a tract granted to Barnard Livingston in 1749. George Gray Junr (Seal), Wit: Henry Boozer, Peter Gray. Proved by the oath of Henry Boozer 19 Feb 1793 before David Ruff, J.P. Recorded 16 May 1795.

C, 251-252: 23 Jan 1795, Frederick Gray of Newberry County to Daniel Davalt of same, for three guineas, 25 acres, granted to Fredk Gray 6 May 1793, being part of 71 acres. Frederick Gray (Seal), Wit: William Shepherd, Michael Long, James Shepherd. Proved by the oath of James Shepheard 11 May 1795 before David Ruff, J.P. Recorded 16 May 1795.

C, 253-254: 8 May 1795, William Dawkins Lane of Union County, SC, farmer, as attorney for Christopher Hogle, to Daniel Davalt of Newberry County, for £40 currency, 200 acres, part of 300 acres granted to John Frederick Hogle, being the whole of said survey except for 100 acres adj. land of Robert Neill, Zimmerman. Wm. D. Lane atty for Christopher Hogle (Seal), Wit: James Baird, James Shepherd, Margaret Heller (X). Proved in Newberry County by the oath of James Shepherd 11 May 1795 before David Ruff, J.P. Recorded 16 May 1795.

C, 255-257: 11 Nov 1787, John Newton, cabinet maker, to Thomas Peterson of same, for £30 sterling, tract on waters of Little River. John Newton (Seal), Wit: Robert Tate, James Foster, Baxter Simpson (mark). Proved by the oath of James Foster 11 Dec 1789 before Thos W. Waters, J.P. Recorded 6 May 1795.

C, 258: William Caldwell and Joseph Williams bound to Samuel Henderson, and James Waldrop Senr, in the sum of £460 s16 d8, 28 Jan 1795, for William Caldwell and Joseph Williams, exrs. of Maj. John Williams decd, to make title to said Samuel Henderson and James Waldrop to 350 acres, agreeable to platt certified by Jacob Roberts Brown, D. S., on south side Mudlick Creek by 12 Jan next. William Caldwell (Seal), Joseph Williams (Seal), Wit: John Simpson, William Ross. Recorded 29 May 1795.

C, **259-260**: South Carolina, Ninety Six District, Lawrence County. 28 March 1795, Daniel Williams Senr., planter, of said county, planter, to James Waldrop and Samuel Henderson of same, mortgage of one negro fellow Harry and one negro Moses, one negro wench Jude and her two children George and Lena, one negro girl Sarah, for the payment of £400 sterling. Daniel Williams (Seal), Wit: William Caldwell, William Caldwell, John Simpson. Recorded 29 May 1795.

C, 260: Newberry County, Guilders Creek. Hugh Boyd's mark recorded: right eat a swallow fork and the left ear a hole. Recorded 29 May 1795.

C, 261: Christian Algire of Newberry County to Anna Barbara his wife, 100 acres on Cannons Creek adj. land of John Cannon, Ephraim Cannon, 9 Aug 1793. Christian Algire (Seal), Wit: Wm. Houseal, John Kinard. Proved by the oath of John Kinard 24 Nov 1792. Recorded 29 May 1795.

C, 262-263: 16 Dec 1794, John Lake of Kershaw County, SC, to John Hunter of Newberry County, for £50 sterling, 100 acres on two small streams called Buzzard branch and Peters Creek, waters of Tyger River, adj. Hardies, Campbell, David Ferguson, Noland. John Lake (Seal), Wit: James Waters, Moses Hunter, Andrew Hunter. Proved in Newberry County 13 May 1795 by the oath of Moses Hunter before Reuben Sims, J.P. Recorded 4 June 1795.

C, 264-265: 12 March 1784, Levi Anderson, planter, to Jacob Anderson, cordwiner, for £50 sterling, tract in Newberry County on a branch of Enoree River called Indian Creek adj. Henry Anderson, Robert Mars, Thomas Gordon, Levi Anderson, Jacob Anderson, Gabriel Anderson, Robert Dugan. Levi Anderson (Seal), Wit: Robert Johnston, Nathan Anderson. Proved in Newberry County by the oath of Nathan Anderson 18 May 1795 before Providence Williams, J.P. Recorded 4 June 1795.

C, 266-267: 31 May 1794. John Liles of Newberry County to Williamson Liles of same, planter, for £50 sterling, 250 acres on waters of Enoree River, granted to John Liles 23 June 1774 adj. William Liles, Richard Bonds, David Lake. John Liles (Seal), Wit: Arromanos Liles, John Volentine. Proved by the oath of John Volentine 18 May 1759 before Reuben Sims, J.P. Recorded 4 June 1795.

C, 268-272: Lease and release. 24 & 25 March 1795, Francis Davinport Sr. and Mary Davinport of Newberry County to Francis Davinport Junr of same, for £50 SC currency, 100 acres, part of 350 acres in Berkley County on waters of Little River granted to Francis Davinport Senr 2 May 1770 adj. David Emry, Henry Pitts, John Monk, George Goggans, Daniel Goggans. Francis Davenport (Seal), Mary Davenport (mark) (Seal), Wit: Daniel McKie, Isaac

Davenport, Martha Davenport (X). Proved by the oath of Isaac Davenport 18 May 1795 before Charles Griffen, J.P. Recorded 4 June 1795.

C, 273: Articles of agreement between Francis Davenport and Mary Turner of Newberry County, in case they should marry that said Mary Turner not to request any of the said Davenport's estate that his former wife hath gotten, 20 Sept 1794. Francis Davenport (Seal), Mary Davenport (mark) (Seal), Wit: Isaac Davenport, Martin Chester. Proved by the oath of Isaac Davenport 18 May 1795 before Charles Griffen, J.P. Recorded 4 June 1795.

C, 274: 8 May 1795, Francis Davinport Sr. and Mary Davinport of Newberry County to Francis Davinport Junr of same, for £20 sterling, one negro man slave named Anthony, about 18 years old. Francis Davenport (Seal), Wit: John Thomas S. M., Isaac Davenport, Ann Thomas (mark). Proved by the oath of Isaac Davenport 18 May 1795 before Charles Griffen, J.P. Recorded 4 June 1795.

C, 275: 4 April 1795, James Williams of Newberry County appoints Providence Williams Senr of same, his attorney to convey tract of 133 acres on the waters of Bush River. James Williams (Seal), Ann Williams (Seal), Wit: John Williams, Providence Williams. Proved by the oath of Providence Williams 4 April 1795 before John Speak, J.P. Recorded 5 June 1795.

C, 276-279: Lease and release. 10 & 11 May 1795, Henry Metzker, mechanic, of St. Bartholomews Parish, SC, to Phillemon Waters Senr of Newberry County, for £100 sterling, 200 acres on the south fork of Indian Creek, granted to Barbara Farleren 21 Jan 1761, recorded in Grant Book 10, page 70, which descended to said Henry Metzker by heirship, being the grandson of Barbara Farlaren and son of Margaret Metzker. Henry Metzker (Seal), Wit: John Riley, Adam Culliatt. Proved 7 May 1795 by the oath of Adam Culliatt before Mathew Driscoll, Q.U. of Charleston District. Recorded 5 June 1795.

C, 280-285: Lease and release. 4 & 5 Dec 1768, William Beg of Charleston to James Williams of Berkley County, on Bush River, planter, for £50 SC currency, 100 acres granted to William Beg 24 Nov 1767 in the fork of Broad and Saluda Rivers in Berkley County. William Beg (Seal), Wit: William Grayham, Daniel Monro. Proved in Berkley County by the oath of Daniel Monro 28 Oct 1771 before John Troup, J.P. Recorded 5 June 1795.

C, 286-290: Lease and release. 13 & 14 April 1795, Providence Williams, Esquire, of Newberry County, attorney for the late James williams, to Thomas Clark of settlement of Beaverdam, waters of Bush River, for £57 s10 sterling, 169 acres adj. Daniel Williams, John Belton, Thomas Clark, part of two grants, one granted to William Beg for 100 acres 13 May 1768, recorded in Book DDD, page 213, and conveyed to James William deceased 5 Dec 1768, the other granted to James Williams for 300 acres 14 Sept 1771, recorded in Book III, page 272, the said James Williams being heir at law of said James Williams deceased. James Williams (Seal), Ann Williams, Providence Williams atty. Wit: Isaac Cannon, Job Colvin, James Lindsey. Proved 28 May 1795 by the oath of James Lindsey before John Speak, J.P. Recorded 6 June 1795.

C, 291-292: 29 July 1794, James Goggans of Newberry County to Daniel McKie of same, for £50 sterling, 25 acres, part of tract of 350 acres granted to Joseph Campbell deceased 2 May 1770, on north side of Jerred Campbell's spring branch, adj. Daniel McKie, Francis Davenport. James Goggans (Seal), Wit: George Goggans, B. Satterwhite, William Smith (X). Proved by the oath of George Goggans 4 March 1795 before Peter Julin, J.P. Recorded 6 June 1795.

C, 293-294: _____ 1794, James Strawhon of Newberry County to Moses Strawhon his father of same, for £20 SC money, 50 acres, the westward end of tract which George Heep conveyed to said James Strawhon, granted to Robert Johnson 3 July 1786 adj. John Sunford, Richard Fowler, James Young. James Strawhon (mark) (Seal), Wit: John Speak J.P., Gassaway Rogers, Richard Bennett. Recorded 6 June 1795.

C, 294-295: State of North Carolina, Granville County. Daniel Williams Senr of state and county aforesaid for £15 Virginia currency to John Williams (son of Daniel) and John Williams Senr, both of Newberry County, 27 negroes named Phil, Jack, Will, Kyzer, Moses, Harry, Jacob, Jude, Isbell, Ruth, Easter, Rose, Aggy, Aron, John, Davie, Frankey, Suckey, Sarah, Edom, Little Fill, Solomon, George James, Lett, Winney & Morris, 23 July 1792. Daniel Williams (seal), Wit: Howell Moss (X), Daniel Williams Junr, jurat. Proved in Granville County NC by the oath of Daniel Williams Junr 28 March 1793 before Samuel Smith, J.P. Proved in court, November 1792, Granville County N.C., A. Henderson, C.C. Recorded in Lawrence County, SC, Book D, page 356. Recorded in Newberry County 8 June 1795.

C, 296-297: Whereas by a deed dated 23 July 1792, my brother Daniel Williams of North Carolina, did convey to me and a certain John Williams Junr 27 negroes [same as in above deed, but ages also recorded here], and we the said John Williams S. D. and John Williams Jun'r did not buy nor contract to pay any money or consideration for the said negroes, but the said deed was made on a secret trust that we should hold said negroes, 20 April 1793. John Williams (Seal), Wit: Charles J. Colcock, Stephen Heard. Proved in Abbeville County 22 April 1793 by the oath of Charles Colcock before Julius Nichols Junr, J.P. Recorded 8 June 1795.

C, 298-299: Whereas by a deed dated 23 July 1792, Daniel Williams, late of North Carolina, did convey to his brother John Williams S. D. and to John Williams Junr 27 negroes deceased, in secret trust, and John Williams S. D. did on 20 April 1793 perfect a general release and quit claim, and said John Williams Junr deceased in his life time appointed me as his atty or Trustee to settle the said business aforesaid, I, John Wallace, as the trustee and the said Daniel Williams to avoid the trouble and expence of Law here mutually consented and agreed to leave al the said disputes to the final ending and determination of John Satterwhite and James Caldwell, 25 March 1795. John Wallace trustee (Seal), Wit: R. Brown, J.N.C. Recorded 8 June 1795.

C, 299-305: Lease and release. 21 & 22 June 1787, John Milhous of Orangeburgh District, planter, to the lawful heirs of John Kelley, late of Wateree in Camden District, deceased, for £107 SC currency, 250 acres in Newberry County, Ninety Six District, on a branch of Saluda River called Bush Creek, recorded in Book WW, page 153, granted to Barbara Echard 7 Oct 1762; and a tract granted to John Milhous 3 Dec 1766, recorded in Book FFF, page 152; and another grant to John Milhouse 29 April 1768 recorded in Book CCC, page 76. John Milhouse (Seal), Wit: Saml Gaunt, George Latham, Saml Kelley Senr. Proved by the oath of George Latham 19 May 1795 before Peter Julien, J.P. Recorded 9 June 1795.

C, 306-309: Lease and release. 22 & 23 Jan 1779, Sarah Duncan of Ninety Six District, Sc, to her son Samuel Duncan, of same, planter, for £10 SC money, 150 acres on a small branch of Bush Creek now commonly called Bush River, part of 350 acres granted to said Sarah Duncan 19 Sept 1770. Sarah Duncan (mark) (Seal), Wit: Enos Elleman, John Duncan, James Hall (H). Proved in Newberry County by the oath of James Hall 9 March 1795 before Prov. Williams, J.P. Recorded 9 June 1795.

C, 310-313: Lease and release. 22 Sept 1794, William Gilreath of Newberry County to James Hall, planter, of same, for £100 sterling, 200 acres in Berkley County in the fork between Broad and Saluda Rivers on a small branch of Kings Creek adj. James Murphy, granted to William Wadlington 2 April 17773, recorded in Book OOO, page 473, conveyed by him to said William Gilreath 7 & 8 Jan 1788, recorded 18 May 1789 in Deed Book A, page 642. William Gilreath (Seal), Mary Gilreath (mark) (Seal), Wit: Thomas Hall, Samuel Maffet, John Littler Jones. Proved by the oath of John Little Jones 13 Dec 1794 before Edward Finch, J.P. Recorded 10 June 1795.

C, 314-317: Lease and release. 17 & 17 Dec 1794, Philemon Waters Esqr. of Newberry County to Thomas Willoughby Waters, for £300 sterling, 800 acres at the mouth of big creek, along a tract of land said Philimon Waters conveyed to Isaac Elmore. adj. Wallice Jones, Parkins' corner formerly said to be Simmons, Morehead, William Musgrove, granted to John Musgrove Senr deceased, but now to Peter Lester, William Taylor, across a path that leads from where Jesse Pugh lives to Taylors. P. Waters (Seal), Wit: Wm. Thomson, Philimon Waters. Recorded 10 June 1795.

C, 318: 9 Jan 1795. George Ruff, merchant, of Newberry County, for love and affection to his loving daughter Elizabeth Rutherford, 300 acres of land: 200 acres granted to Daniel Horsey, 66 acres granted to George Ruff and 340 acres granted to Daniel Horsey, also one negro fellow Peter, one negro girl Hagar. Geo Ruff (Seal), Wit: Conrod Rahm, Adam Epting. Proved by the oath of Conrod Rahm 9 Jan 1795 before David Ruff. J.P. Recorded 10 June 1795.

C, 319: Thos W. Waters, William Summers, and Peter Julin Esquire, bound to the judges of Newberry County in the sum of £1000 sterling, 21 March 1795, bond for Thomas W. Waters as tax collector. Thos W Waters (Seal), William Summers (Seal), Peter Julin (Seal), Wit: South Bradshaw, William Day, R. Brown, J. N. C. Recorded 12 June 1795.

C, 320-321: 21 March 1795, Thos W. Waters of one part and William Summers and Peter Julin Esquire, of the other part, said Thomas W. Waters has given his bond to Newberry County, now mortgages to William Summers and Peter Julin Esquire, plantation on Saluda River, 850 acres (excepting 225 acres Jesse Pugh has my bond for a title for), one negro wench called Hanna, one mill containing upwards of 100 gallons bought of Col. Robert Rutherford, other items including horse bought of David Jay, one sorrel mare in the possession of James Johnson, one cow got from William Pearson, a cow I gave at George Gibsons and one at David Pughs, a cow and calf at Thomas Butlers, two yearlings at Cullen Lark's place, two cows and two yearlings at Mrs. Lark's, a note of hand said Waters has from Elijah Botner, quantity of leather at Joseph Thomsons with 100 bushels of salt at home, the balance at William Hilburns. Thos W Waters (Seal), Wit: South Bradshaw, Wm Day, before R. Brown, J. N. C. Recorded 12 June 1795.

C, 322-324: 22 Nov 1777, Elijah Teague, yeoman, of Ninety Six District, to Robert Gilliam, planter, of same, for £125 SC money, 125 acres, part of 250 acres granted to Elijah Teague, on beaver dam branch of Bush River. Elijah Teague (Seal), Ailse Teague (X) (Seal), Wit: Saml Kelly, Samuel Teague. Proved by the affirmation of Saml Kelley __ May 1795 before Providence Williams, J.P. Recorded 12 June 1795.

C, 325-327: 5 Feb 1781, Robert Gilliam, planter, of Ninety Six District, to James Hall, planter, of same, for £100, 125 acres, part of 250 acres granted to Elijah Teague, on beaver dam branch of Bush River, conveyed by him to Robert Gilliam 22 Nov 1777. Robert Gilliam (Seal), Phebe Gilliam (Seal), Wit: John Thomas, Henry Littlejohn (H), Amos Duncan. Proved by the affirmation of Amos Duncan 5 May 1795 before Elisha Ford, J.P. Recorded 12 June 1795.

C, 328-330: 6 Jan 1795. James Hall, farmer & Sarah his wife, of Newberry County, to John Furnas, blacksmith, for £85 SC money, 125 acres, part of 250 acres granted to Elijah Teague, on beaver dam branch of Bush River, conveyed by him to Robert Gilliam 22 Nov 1777, conveyed to James Hall 5 Feb 1781 [see preceding deeds]. James Hall (H), Sarah Hall (Seal), Wit: John Williams, John Sloan, William Hall. Proved by the oath of John Williams 8 May 1795 before Providence Williams, J.P. Recorded 12 June 1795.

C, 331-333: 12 May 1795, Henry Summers of Lexington County, SC, planter, to John Weadiman, for £50 sterling, 100 acres granted to Henry Summers 2 Oct 1786, recorded in Grant Book OOOO, page 79, on waters of Broad River adj. William Stone, Mathias Hair. Heinrich Somer [German signature] (Seal),

Wit: John Kinard (big) (K), Joseph Clapp (mark), John Kinard (little). Proved by the oath of John Kinard (little) 19 June 1795 before William Houseal, J.P. Recorded 29 June 1795.

C, 334-337: Lease and release. 9 & 10 Sept 1789, Patrick McMichael of Newberry County, weaver, and Elizabeth his wife, to William Aspinell of same, for £30 SC money, 50 acres, part of 150 acres granted to Patrick McMichael 7 March 1775 on waters of Bush River, adj. McCleland, Gaunt. Patrick Carmichael (Seal), Elizabeth Carmichael (mark) (Seal), Wit: Giles Chapman, Thomas Reagan, William Thomson. Proved by the affirmation of Giles Chapman 22 June 1795 before Peter Julin, J.P. Recorded 30 June 1795.

C, 338-339: 27 Aug 1792, Abraham Thomson, planter, of Newberry County, to Robert More of same, planter, for £20 sterling, 200 acres, part of 300 acres granted to Abraham Thomson 3 May 1775, recorded in Book XXX, page 425, on waters of Cannons Creek, adj. Charles Thomson, John Barlow, Thomas McNeel, John Inlow. Abraham Thomson (mark) (Seal), Wit: Thomas McNure, Charles Burton, John Moore. Proved by the oath of Thomas McNure 1 July 1795 before Peter Julin, J.P. Recorded 6 July 1795.

C, 340-341: 20 Dec 1790, Frederick Fraser of Charleston District, to James Waldrop of Ninety Six District, for 10 shillings, 550 acres in Craven county on south side Enoree River adj. Joseph Waldrop, James Hall, joseph Patterson, Luke Waldrop, granted to William Williamson decd 2 April 1773 and conveyed by him to Frederick Fraser 20 & 21 Dec 1790. Fredk Fraser (Seal), Wit: E. Rutledge Junr, Solomon Waldrop, Samuel Waldrop. Recorded 13 July 1795.

C, 342-343: Henry Caston of Newberry County to John Walker of Laurence County, SC, for the valuable sum to which the said John Walker hath already paid and stands liable by his being surety, I mortgage to him the tract whereon I now live, with one horse, saddle and bridle, bed and furniture, etc., 30 Jan 1795. Henry Caston (Seal), Wit: Thomas Johnson, Thos Johnson Senr, John Johnson. Proved by the oath of John Johnson 21 July 1795 before Prov. Williams, J.P. Recorded 22 July 1795.

C, 344-345: Mary Leonard, widow, of Newberry County, relict and admx. of Laughlin Leonard deceased, appoint John Leonard and Jacob Crosswhite, my son and son in law, of the aforesaid place, my attorneys, whereas some time about 25 years since in Culpepper County, Virginia, division was made of the personal estate of Walter Leonard decd, between his widow Catharine Leonard, his daughter Phoeby wife of John Neel and Laughlin Leonard, his son my decd husband, and whereas the said John Neil and Phoeby his wife have six negroes given them in full consideration of full claim and demand against the said estate, and all the remainder of the said estate due at the death of his mother Catharine Leonard was to devolve to him the said Laughlin Leonard, negroes, one negro wench called Milley, one negro girl called Rachael, one negro man called Ben, one negro man called Isaac, one negro man called Jacob, 20 July 1795. Mary Leonard (Seal), Wit: R. Brown, J. N. C. Recorded 29 July 1795.

C, 346-347: Hannah Crumly, extx. and Joshua Inman and Robert Richardson, exrs. of the estate of John Crumly deceased, all of Newberry County ,appoint Thomas Horner of same, attorney to receive sums of money owing, especially of David Lupton the sum of £100 with interest and Robert Bull the sum of £200, 29 July 1795. Hannah Crumley (Seal), Joshua Inman (Seal), Robert Richardson (Seal), Wit: R. Brown. Recorded 31 July 1795.

C, 348-353: Lease and release. 25 & 26 March 1794, Robert Brooks of Ninety Six District, Newberry County, to Asa Garrett of same, for £50 sterling, 125 acres, part of 205 acre tract granted to said Robert Brooks 5 Feb 1787, recorded in Book PPPP, page 643, adj. land of Uriah Conner, William Gray, William Simpson, Richard Brooks, William Speakman, John Gary, William Wilson, on Indian Creek. Robert Brooks (Seal), Mary Brooks (mark) (Seal), Wit: Uriah Conner, Nancy Brooks (X), James Lindsey. Proved by the oath of James Lindsey 9 July 1795 before Prov. Williams, J.P. Recorded 4 Aug 1795.

C, 354-359: Lease and release. 25 & 26 May 1794, Richard Brooks of Ninety Six District, Newberry County, to Asa Garrett of same, for £50 sterling, 50 acres, part of 200 acres granted to said Richard Brooks __ Feb 1768 on a small branch of Indian Creek, recorded in Book BBB, page 521, adj. land of Richard Brooks. Richard Brooks (X) (Seal), Wit: James Bonds (X), Sarah Brooks (X), James Lindsey. Proved by the oath of James Lindsey 29 July 1795 before Providence Williams, J.P. Recorded 4 Aug 1795.

C, 360-363: 13 & 14 May 1795, John Wilkinson Senr of Newberry County, Ninety Six District, to Thomas Reid of same, planter, for £40 SC money, 60 acres on the branch of Scotch Creek, waters of Bush River, adj. Enoch Pearson, John Wilkinson, part of 200 acres granted to said John Wilkinson. John Wilkinson (mark) (Seal), Wit: Edwd Benbow, Thomas Reid, Rosannah Russell (X). Proved by the affirmation of Edward Benbow 18 July 1795 before Frederick Nance, J.P. Recorded 18 Aug 1795.

C, 364: Ambrose Hudgens of Newberry County for £10 sterling, to Charles Pitts of same, one feather bed and furniture, cattle, one chest and flax wheel, one check reel, plows, etc., and part of the corn this present year on the premises whereon I now live and tobacco that is made. Ambrose Hudgens (Seal), Wit: William Dodgen, William Young, Rachael Young (mark). Acknowledged before R. Brown, J.N.C. Recorded 18 Aug 1795.

C, 365-367: 4 Aug 1795, Francis Davenport Senr of Newberry County to my children Isaac Davenport, William Davenport, David Davenport, Sarah Beeks and Abigail Davenport; to my son Isaac Davenport, a negro man named Peter, one negro man named Coy and one negro man named Mingo, one negro girl named Rachel & 20 acres of land, adj. Mr. Daniel McKie, six cows and calves, & one two year old heifer & a two year old steer, sixty head of hoggs and 16 head of sheep, all marked with a swallow fork in the left ear & the right ear a sharp, 3 horses and one more and yearling colt & all my plantation tools and household furniture; to my son William Davenport, one negro boy named Dick; to my loving son David Davenport, 200 acres of land, one negro boy named Oliver, one father bed and one mare and colt; to my loving daughter Sarah Beeks, one negro boy named Tom; to my loving daughter Abigail Davenport, one negro girl named Nan and one feather bed. Francis Davinport (Seal), Wit: Ezekiel Waldrop, Edward Turner, George Goggans. Proved by the oath of Ezekiel Waldrop 5 Aug 1795 before Charles Griffin, J.P. Recorded 18 Aug 1795.

C, 367-368: 4 Aug 1795, Francis Davenport Senr of Newberry County, planter to my daughter Patty Waldrop, one negro girl named Patience. Francis Davinport (Seal), Wit: Isaac Davinport, Edw'd Turner, Elizabeth Towling. Proved by the oath of Isaac Davenport 5 Aug 1795 before Charles Griffin, J.P. Recorded 18 Aug 1795.

C, 369-370: 1 Aug 1795, Francis Davenport Senr of Newberry County, planter to Nancy Waldrop, for natural love and affection, one negro girl named Eliza. Francis Davinport (Seal), Wit: David Davinport, Edward Turner, William Morgan (M). Proved by the oath of David Davenport 1 Aug 1795 before Charles Griffin, J.P. Recorded 18 Aug 1795.

C, 371-375: Lease and release. 19 Sept 1787, David Caldwell of Newberry County, Ninety Six District, to Isaac Dison of same, for £200 sterling, 255 acres on waters of Saluda River, adj. land of Henry Hazel, William Furlow, John Caldwell, John Wallice, Robert Williams, granted to said David Caldwell 1 Jan 1785. David Caldwell (Seal), Philadelphia Caldwell, Wit: James Caldwell, D. Dyson. Proved by the oath of Daniel Dyson 28 July 1795 before Robert Gillam, J.P. Recorded 19 Aug 1795.

C, 376-381: Lease and release. 12 & 13 May 1795, Robert Gillam Senr and Mary his wife of Ninety Six District, Newberry County, to Robert Gillam Junr of same, for £200 sterling, 627 acres on waters of Pages Creek and Saluda River, adj. Thomas Wadsworth, Isaac Mitchell, William Burges, Robert Gilliam Senr, granted to Edmond Ellis 2 May 1770 and conveyed by him to Robert Gilliam 9 & 10 Sept 1776, and the remainder granted 27 Nov 1770 to said Robert Gillam Senr. Robert Gillam Senr (Seal), Mary Gillam (X) (Seal), Wit: Daniel Towles, Timothy Goodman, James Forrest. Proved by the oath of Daniel Towles 9 July 1795 before Robert Gillam, J.P. Recorded 19 Aug 1795.

C, 382-387: Lease and release. 4 & 5 June 1787, Samuel Proctor, planter, of Fairfield County, Camden District, to James Wilson, weaver, of Newberry County, for £50 s5 sterling, 250 acres granted to Saml Proctor 1 Sept 17860 on a small branch of Enoree River called Kings Creek in Ninety Six District adj. Charles King, John Furnas. Samuel Proctor (Seal), Wit: Jeremiah Williams, Hugh Garmany, Thos Parrott Junr. Proved in Newberry County by the oath of Jeremiah Williams 8 Dec 1789 before John Lindsey, J.P. Recorded 19 Aug 1795.

C, 388-393: Lease and release. 16 & 17 March 1795, Adam Killer of Newberry County, planter, to George Killer of same, planter, by grant dated 19 March 1768 to Johannes Setzler, 400 acres in the fork between Broad & Saluda Rivers, adj. Michael Lominack, Michael Suber, recorded in Book PPP, page 73, conveyed 4 & 5 July 1770, now for £100 SC money, 150 acres, part of said tract. Adam Killer (mark), Wit: John Dawkins, Christian Ruff, Michael Dickert Senr. Proved by the oath of John Dawkins 29 July 1795 before R. Brown, J.N.C. Recorded 20 Aug 1795.

C, 395-398: Lease and release. 12 & 13 Nov 1775, Richard Lewis of Ninety Six District, to John Davis of same, for £300 SC money, 100 acres on north side Saluda River adj. Richard Pendall, granted to Stephen Lewis 4 Nov 1757 descended by the decease of said Stephen to Richard Lewis eldest son and heir at law. Richard Lewis (Seal), Wit: Chesley Davis, Chesley Davis Junr (X), Jesse Davis (X). Proved in Newberry County by the oath of Jesse Davis 2 June 1794 before Peter Julin, J.P. Recorded 20 Aug 1795.

C, 399-401: 17 Jan 1795, Herman Davis of Newberry County, planter, to Reason Davis of same, for £50 sterling, 75 acres, part of 200 acres granted to said Herman Davis 26 April 1766, recorded in the Auditors Office, Book H. No. 8, page 147, and in the Secretaries office Book AAA, page 235. Herman Davis (Seal), Wit: Hermon Davis, William Dunlap, Josiah Elliot. Proved by the oath of Herman Davis 29 July 1795 before Providence Williams, J.P. Recorded 22 Aug 1795.

C, 401-402: Isaac Dyson of Cumberland County, North Carolina, for £60 sterling to John Dyson of Newberry County, SC, one negro slave about 20 years of age named Jess, 27 July 1795. Isaac Dyson, Wit: Danl Dyson, James Dyson. Proved by the oath of Daniel Dyson 28 July 1795 before Robert Gillam, J.P. Recorded 22 Aug 1795.

C, 402-403: William Largent of Edgefield County, SC, Ninety Six District appoint my friend James Lindsey of Newberry County, my attorney, 2 December 1794. William Largent (M) (Seal), Wit: Abraham Beach, Benjamin Wood (mark). Proved by the oath of Abraham Beach 29 March 1795 before Prov. Williams, J.P. Recorded 22 Aug 1795.

C, 404-406: South Carolina, Laurence County. 1 Oct 1792, Samuel Saxon, Sheriff of Ninety Six District, to Henry Wilson, whereas Joacim Bulow of Charleston, lately in the court of common pleas at Cambridge obtained judgment against Richard Strawther of Newberry County in the sum of £98 s8, by writ of fieri facias dated 16 Nov 1791, to levy of the goods and chattles of Richard Strawther, now for £41 sterling, sells 200 acres upon the Spring place and 150 acres in the fork between Broad and Saluda Rivers adj. Mr. Pallor, Jacob Oxner, Ulrage Eaynes, originally granted to Jacob Fulger (alias Feilger) and conveyed by him to Jacob Felker Junr and from him to Richard Strawther. S. Saxon (Seal), Sheriff 96 Dist, Wit: Mathew Ramsey, Jno Trotter. Proved in Abbeville County by the oath of Mathew Ramsey 3 Aug 1795 before John Trotter, J.P. Recorded 24 Aug 1795.

C, 407-409: 17 Aug 1795, Richard Watts, Sheriff of Newberry County, to Thomas Farrow of same, whereas Joshua Dinkins of Kershaw County was seized of tract of 150 acres in Newberry County on waters of Saluda, Mudlick Creek, and John Kershaw, James Kershaw & Joseph Kershaw, exrs. of the esate of Joseph Kershaw decd, at a court held for Kershaw County, Camden District, February term 1793, obtained judgment for the sum of £85 s13 d2 sterling, by writ of fieri facias, sells said 150 acres. Drury Satterwhite DS for R. Watts (Seal), Wit: Fredk Nance, J.P., B. Satterwhite, Wm Satterwhite. Recorded 24 Aug 1795.

C, 410-411: 15 July 1795, Henry Caston, cordwiner, of Ninety Six District, Newberry County, to Joseph Greer of Laurence County, for 10 shillings, 30 acres in Newberry County on waters of Indian Creek, on Headley Creek, granted to Peter Brasilman and thence conveyed to Francis Davis to Henry Caston, adj. Thomas Johnston, John Lindsey, to Ninety Six Waggon road, William Davis. Henry Caston (Seal), Martha Caston (O), Wit: Thomas Johnston Senr, Thomas Johnston Junr, James Johnston. Proved by the oath of Thomas Johnston Junr 28 July 1795 before Fred Nance, J.P. Recorded 24 Aug 1795.

C, 412: Adrine West of Newberry County for love and affection to son Andrew West, one chesnut sorrel stud colt two years old not branded, known by the name of the Red Deer, also one sorrel gelden known by the name of Lightfoot, 29 June 1795. Adrine West (mark) (Seal), Wit: Jer. McDaniel, John McDaniel. Proved by the oath of John McDaniel 4 July 1795 before Peter Julin, J.P. Recorded 28 Aug 1795.

C, 413-418: Lease and release. 26 & 27 May 1795, John Thomas and Isaac Thomas of Newberry County, to Stephen Elmore, taylor, for £0 sterling, 55 acres, part of 150 acres granted to Isaac Thomas 21 Jan 1787, on waters of Bush River, recorded in Book SSSS, page 462. Isaac Thomas, Mary Thomas (X), John Thomas (Seal), Ann Thomas (Seal), Wit: James Weeks, Mathias Elmore. Proved by the oath of both witnesses 29 June 1795 before Fred Nance, J.P. Recorded 31 Aug 1795.

C, 419-426: Lease and release. 7 & 8 Nov 1794, John Dominick Senr of Newberry County, planter, to John McDaniel, planter, of same, for £25 sterling, 200 acres (except 50 acres sold to Michael Weet) granted to John Dominick Senr recorded in Auditors Office Book M. No. 12, page 68, 15 Jan 1774, on north side Saluda River adj. Jacob Brown, Jacob Moury, Peter Hare, Conrad Neis. John Dominick Senr (X) (Seal), Wit: Jer McDaniel, Michael Wett (X). Proved by the oath of Jeremiah McDaniel 2 Feb 1795 before Peter Julin, J.P. Recorded 1 Sept 1795.

C, 426-428: 14 Feb 1795, Jacob Counts and his wife of Lexington County, SC, to Jeremiah McDaniel for £50 sterling, 100 acres in Craven county now Newberry County on south side Broad River adj. Michael Dickert, Jacob Moury, granted to Peter Hare Senr 13 March 1772 for 200 acres, recorded in Book L. No. 11, page 37, now 100 aces was left to John Hare by his father Peter Hare's will 25 Sept 1773. Jacob Counts (Seal), Susanah Counts (X) (Seal), Wit: Thomas Hughs, John McDaniel. Proved in Newberry County by the oath of John McDaniel 4 July 1795 before Peter Julin, J.P. Recorded 1 Sept 1795.

C, 429-434: Lease and release. 16 Dec 1789, William Caldwell, Esquire, of Newberry County to Charles Crumley of same, planter, for £50 sterling, 300 acres on waters of Bush River adj. John Crumly, James Coates, John Johnson, one Lonam, recorded in Book BBBB, page 490. William Caldwell (Seal), Wit: James Abernathy, Thomas Crumley, John Crumley. Proved by the oath of James Abernathy 1 Aug 1794 before Mercer Babb, J.P. Recorded 2 Sept 1795.

C, 434-436: 2 March 1795, Henry Tate and Ann his wife of Newberry County to Christopher Weadingham of same, for £40 sterling, 147 acres on north side Big Saluda on a branch thereof, adj. John Waits, Henry Crieks, Beverly Borroums, Christopher Cains, granted to Nehemiah Rotan. Henry Tate (Seal), Ann Tate (O) (Seal), Wit: Beverly Bourrum, Ann Pope, Elizabeth King (X). Acknowledged by Henry Tate 6 March 1795 before Peter Julin, J.P. Recorded 2 Sept 1795.

C, 436-440: Lease and release. 9 & 10 Jan 1787, Elizabeth Brown of settlement of Kings Creek, Newberry County, to Robert Brown her son, of same, for £20 sterling, 150 acres, granted to said Elizabeth Brown 25 May 1774, recorded in Book FFF, page 283, on south side Enoree River on waters of Kings Creek adj. Jerred Smith, John Wilson, Robert Brown, Clement Davis. Elizabeth Brown (mark) (Seal), Wit: Richard Tear, William Riley (X), James Lindsey. Proved 31 Jan 1787 by the oath of James Lindsey before John Lindsey, J.P. Recorded 2 Sept 1795.

C, 441-443: 7 May 1794, Robert Brown, planter, of Newberry County, to James Wilson of same, farmer, for £60 sterling, 150 acres granted to Elizabeth Brown 25 May 1774 and conveyed to Robert Brown 9 & 10 Jan 1787 [see preceding deed] adj. Sims Brown, Jerred Smith, Jane Wilson. Robert Brown (Seal), Wit: Samuel McCreary, John Park, Samuel Ragland. Proved by the oath of John Park 3 March 1795 before Edward Finch, J.P. Recorded 2 Sept 1795.

C, 444-445: John Coate, planter, of Newberry County to George Latham, merchant, for five shillings, quit claim of 42 acres on waters of Bush River, adj. John Coate, Reed, William McGlameries, Hugh Creighton, 29 Sept 1794. John Coate (Seal), Wit: Saml Kelley Senr, John Kelley Senr, James Daugherty. Proved by the affirmation of John Kelley Senr 29 July 1795 before Elisha Ford, J.P. Recorded 5 Sept 1795.

C, 446-448: 31 Aug 1795, Nathan Anderson of Newberry County to samuel Lindsey of same, mortgage of 150 acres granted to Jacob Anderson, one negro man named Joe about 22 years old, one horse, saddle, and bridle, for payment of bond for £150 sterling, by bond dated 15 May 1795. Nathan Anderson (Seal), Wit: Daniel Clary J.P., Caleb Lindsey, Fred Nance, J.P. Recorded 25 Sept 1795.

C, 448-453: Lease and release. 9 & 10 June 1775, Jacob Harling of Ninety Six District, SC, planter, to Philip Sligh of same, planter, for £100 SC money, 100 acres granted to Jacob Harling 25 May 1774 on waters of Kings Creek adj. Robert Brannon, James Wilson. Jacob Harling (mark) (Seal), Wit: Martin Singley, George Hartell. Proved by the oath of Martin Singley 10 June 1775 before William Houseal, J.P. Recorded 25 Sept 1795.

C, 454-458: Lease and release. 25 & 26 Jan 1785, Philip Sligh of Ninety Six District, planter, to James Wilson of same, weaver, for £200 SC money, 100 acres granted to Jacob Harling 25 May 1774 on waters of Kings Creek adj. Robert Brannon, James Wilson, recorded in Book FFF, page 354, conveyed 9 & 10 June 1775 to Philip Sligh Jacob Harling (mark) (Seal), Wit: Jeremiah Williams, William Houseal. Proved by the oath of Jeremiah Williams 12 Feb 1778 before William Houseal, J.P. Recorded 25 Sept 1795.

C, 459-464: Lease and release. 1 & 2 April 1793, John Woodall Senr, planter, of Pendleton County, Washington District, SC, planter, to James Wilson of Newberry County, planter, for £100 sterling, 150 acres in the fork of Broad and Saluda Rivers on a small branch of Enoree called Kings Creek adj. John Brown, Thomas Morgan, Isaac Parner, Charles King, Simon Reeder, recorded in Book FFFF, page 68. John Woodall (Seal), Wit: Penington King, John Yeargan, Josiah Eliot. Proved in Newberry County by the oath of John Yeargan 24 Jan 1794 before Edward Finch, J.P. Recorded 26 Sept 1795.

C, 465-468: Lease and release. 3 & 4 Feb 1791, Jesse Tate of Ninety Six District, to Samuel Lindsey and William Waddleton, of same, for five shillings, 396 acres on north side Saluda river adj. William Anderson. James Tate (Seal), Wit: James Tate Junr, Samuel Tate, Caleb Lindsey. Proved 28 Sept 1795 by the oath of Caleb Lindsey before Fred Nance, J.P. Recorded 2 Oct 1795.

C, 468-469: South Carolina, Newberry County. Ann Floyd, widow, for love and affection to her daughter Margaret Davinport, wife of Joseph Davinport, one negro woman Lucy and one negro girl called Lucy, 1 Oct 1795. Ann Floyd (mark) (Seal), Wit: J. R. Brown, J.N.C. Recorded 14 Oct 1795.

C, 469-470: South Carolina, Newberry County. Ann Floyd, widow, for love and affection to son William Floyd, one negro man Peter, 1 Oct 1795. Ann Floyd (mark) (Seal), Wit: J. R. Brown, J.N.C. Recorded 14 Oct 1795.

C, 470-471: South Carolina, Newberry County. Ann Floyd, widow, for love and affection to son Robert Floyd, one sorrel gelding called Jack and one negro boy Charles, and one negro woman Nan, 1 Oct 1795. Ann Floyd (mark) (Seal), Wit: J. R. Brown, J.N.C. Recorded 14 Oct 1795.

C, 471-472: Thomas Johnston of Newberry County to Jehu Johnston of same, for £20, one negro woman Hagur, about 30 years old, 29 Sept 1794. Thomas Johnston (Seal), Wit: Daniel Johnson, Mary Johnston (X). Proved 29 Sept 1795 by the oath of David Johnson before Charles Griffin, J.P. Recorded 25 Oct 1795.

C, 472-474: 13 Sept 1795, Thomas Johnston of Newberry County to Daniel Johnston of same, for natural love and good will, 83 acres on waters of Bush River, part of 250 acres granted to Thomas Johnston 14 Dec 1754, adj. John Johnston, Jehu Johnston. Thomas Johnston (Seal), Wit: Thomas Goggans, William Goggans. Proved 23 Sept 1795 by the oath of Thomas Goggans before Charles Griffin, J.P. Recorded 25 Oct 1795.

C, 475-476: 16 Sept 1795, William Burton to John Justis, both of Newberry County, for £12 sterling, one black horse natural trotter about 13 hands 3 inches high, one hind foot white and a small star in his forehead, branded IK, one sorrel mare, branded HP. William Burton (Seal), Wit: John Davis, James Burton. Proved 29 Sept 1795 by the oath of James Burton before Fred Nance, J.P. Recorded 15 Oct 1795.

C, 476-477: South Carolina, Newberry County. Ann Floyd, widow, for love and affection to daughter Temperence Liverett, wife of Thomas Liverett, one negro boy Carolina and one negro wench Milley, 1 Oct 1795. Ann Floyd (mark (Seal), Wit: J. R. Brown, J.N. C. Recorded 14 Oct 1795.

C, 477-478: South Carolina, Newberry County. Before the Court of the County aforesaid, Daniel Clary Esq'r deposeth that some time in October 1780 three negroes to wit Sam, his wife Tamer, and her daughter Lydia, as he understood was the property of John Hampton were brought to the house of this deponant by Mr. Daniel Parkins which said negroes were by the British Commandant at that time at Ninety Six ordered to be kept by this deponant till further ordered. That some time in the latter end of the year 1780 or the beginning of 1781 an armed party came to the house of this deponant among whom were Francis Prince, John McElhaney and others who took said negroes and carried them all away... at the same time Godfrey Adams appeared in the said court & made oath that he saw the above named negroes in the possession of the said Clary and knew them to be the said Hampton's property. Proved in Open Court 20 October 1795. Test Fred Nance. C.N.C. Danl Clary, Godfrey Adams. Recorded 3 Nov 1795.

C, 478-481: 10 April 1795, Olleman Dodgen of Newberry County to Nathan Thomas of same, for £40 sterling, 124 acres in Newberry County on Sandy Run and Little River adj. David Emry, Robert Gowdy, Thomas Green,

William Burton, part of 300 acres granted to William Dodgen 12 April 1711. Olleman Dodgen (Seal), Sarah Dodgen (mark) (Seal), Wit: Jesse Palmer, Susanah Osborne (X), James Redins (M). Proved by the oath of Jesse Parmer 28 Aug 1795 before Charles Griffin, J.P. Recorded 21 Nov 1794.

C, 481-484: 17 May 1787, Hugh Marshall, planter, and Mary his wife to Ninety Six District to William McMorris Jun'r of Camden District, planter, 536 acres granted 15 Oct 1784 on Bush River, a branch of Saluda, adj. William Reeder, John Gray, Charles Gray, Samuel Newman decd, Jacob Chandler, Robert Lewis. Hugh Marshall, Mary Marshall (mark), Wit: John Turner, Alexander Turner, John Turner. Proved by the oath of John Turner 22 May 1789 before John Lindsey, J.P. Recorded 2 Dec 1795.

C, 485-489: 9 Oct 1795, John Adkison Junr to John Adkison Senr, both of Newberry County, mortgage of 300 acres granted to William Hudgeons, by debt of £210. John Adkison (X) (Seal), Wit: Bt. Satterwhite Senr, Dudley Brooks, Zach Smith Brooks. Proved by the oath of Dudley Brooks 19 Oct 1795 before Fred Nance, J.P. Recorded 28 Dec 1795.

C, 490: 9 Oct 1795, John Atkinson Senr of Newberry County to Grace Atkinson of same, for £29 s5 sterling, one negro girl Amy about 7 years old, one feather bed. John Atkinson (X) (Seal), Wit: Bt. Satterwhite Senr, Dudley Brooks. Proved by the oath of Dudley Brooks 19 Oct 1795 before Fred Nance, J.P. Recorded 28 Dec 1795.

C, 491: 24 Jan 1794, James Spearman and Thomas Spearman of Newberry County to Zachariah Smith Brooks for £140 sterling, four negroes: Judy, Dinah, Letty & Barnet. James Spearman (Seal), Thos Spearman (Seal), wit: Bt. Satterwhite, Joseph Burges (X). Proved by the oath of Bartlett Satterwhite Sr 6 Aug 1759 before Daniel Clary, J.P. Recorded 28 Dec 1795.

C, 492: 9 Oct 1795, John Atkinson Senr of Newberry County to John Atkinson Junr of same, for £71 sterling, one negro man Tom about 40 years old, one negro woman Jude about 20 years old, one negro woman Beck about 15 years old, one negro woman named Cate about 23 years old, one negro girl about one year old, one negro girl about one year old and one negro boy about one year old, named Hannah, Darkis and Elisha. John Atkison (X) (Seal), Wit: Bt. Satterwhite Senr, Dudley Brooks. Proved by the oath of Dudley Brooks 19 Oct 1795 before Fred Nance, J.P. Recorded 28 Dec 1795.

C, 493: 9 Oct 1795, John Atkinson Senr of Newberry County to John Atkinson Junr of same, for £193 s1 d4 sterling, one wagon and four horses, one bay filley, five head of sheep, 90 hoggs, 19 head of cattle, four feather bed and furniture, 100 bushels of barley. John Atkison (X) (Seal), Wit: Bt. Satterwhite Senr, Dudley Brooks. Proved by the oath of Dudley Brooks 19 Oct 1795 before Fred Nance, J.P. Recorded 28 Dec 1795.

C, 494-498: Lease and release. 4 & 5 March 1784, Robert Moore, planter, of Ninety Six District, to William Shepherd, taylor, of same, for £5 s14 s3 sterling, 50 acres adj. Robert Moore, David Glenn, James Shepherd, part of 200 acres granted to George Gray 26 Sept 1772 and conveyed by him to William Moore 17 & 18 March 1776 on waters of Cannons Creek adj. William Moore, James Shepherd Senr, Barnet Mountz, Mr. Gray, David Martin, recorded in Secretary's Office Book MMM, page 78. Robert Moore (Seal), Elizabeth Moore (X) (Seal), Wit: Lewis Caursey, James Shepherd, Adam Glazier. Proved in Ninety Six District by the oath of James Shepherd 4 Sept 1785 before Geo Ruff, J.P. Recorded 28 Dec 1795.

C, 499: South Carolina, Newberry County. John Coate of county aforesaid manumits a negro man named Jesse, about 26 years of age. John Coate (mark) (Seal), Wit: Richard Thomson, Daniel Richardson, Wright Coats. Proved by the oath of Richard Thomson 18 Oct 1795 before Elisha Ford, J.P. Recorded 29 Dec 1795.

C, 500-501: 6 July 1795, William Tenant, Sheriff of Ninety Six District, to James Tinsley of Newberry County, by virtue of a writ of fieri facias from the court of common pleas at the suit of William Caldwell against Joseph Griffin & Mary his wife, sells for £11, 150 acres on waters of Mudlick Creek, adj. Pinckney, Benjamin Collier, Thomas Gill, the property of Joseph Griffin. Wm Tenant S 96 D (Seal), Wit: S. Saxon, Wm. Mayson. Recorded 29 Dec 1795.

C, 502-503: 3 Dec 1794, David Shelton of Fairfield County for 15 s1 d7 sterling in gold and silver and £20 s15 s2 which I was in due[?] the store of Alexander Bookter & Co., one negro boy named Ben about 15 years old. David Shelton (Seal), Wit: George Dawkins, Andrew Crooks, John Mink. Proved in Newberry County by the oath of George Dawkins 10 March 1795 before David Ruff, J.P. Recorded 30 Dec 1795.

C, 504: South Carolina, Newberry County. Personally appeared George Goggans and makes oath that he wrote a bond on 12 March 1795 which bond by mistake was dated 1795 and signed by William McKie and given to Ann Floyd, which bond has since been recorded in the Clerks Office, Newberry County, 5 May 1795 in Deed Book C, page 232. George Goggans before Thos W. Waters, 20 Oct 1795. Personally appeared Thomas Liverett (X) and makes oath that he was a witness to the above bond.

C, 505-506: Personally appeared Isaac Mitchell Senr before Jacob Roberts Brown, Esquire, and made oath that in 1771 John Newton purchased of William Ellis 100 acres on the north side of Little River, granted to John Dooly and conveyed by said Dooly to William Ellis, and that he was one of the witnesses to the said titles and that in 1781 a party of the Torys or British Adherents came to his this deponants plantation and then and there burnt his house and destroyed all the said titles, and that the said titles were only probated and not recorded, dated 20 Oct 1795. Isaac Mitchell Senr. Recorded 2 Jan 1796.

C, 507-508: Personally appeared Isaac Mitchell Senr before Jacob R. Brown, Esquire, and made oath that on 8 Jan 1772, he this deponant purchased of a certain Israel Joseph, merchant in Charleston, a tract of 300 acres on two small branches of Mudlick Creek, one now called Persimmon lick granch, which said land was originally granted to Henry Davis for which he received titles from said Joseph but the titles were destroyed and burned with and in his house by the Torys in 1781, dated 20 Oct 1795. Recorded 2 Jan 1796.

Also Thomas Eastland came and made oath that he did see Israel Joseph perfect the above mentioned titles and that he proved the same titles before John Caldwell, Esquire, in his lifetime, dated 20 Oct 1795. Recorded 2 Jan 1795.

C, 509: Personally appeared Isaac Mitchell Senr before Jacob Roberts Brown, Esquire, and made oath that at the time his houses burnt he was in the possession of a lease and release from James Williamson to John Newton for 300 acres on the south side of Little River on a branch called Plumb Branch, originally granted to said Williamson, dated 20 Oct 1795. Recorded 2 Jan 1796.

Also George Goggans made oath that some time in the year 1777 drew a lease and release from James Williamson to John Newton, 20 Oct 1795. George Goggans. Recorded 2 Jan 1796.

C, 510: South Carolina, Newberry County. Personally appeared Daniel Clary Esquire and made oath that some time in 1774 he was called upon to witness a set of titles from Edward Thomas to Timothy Thomas for 250 acres on branch of Bush River called Youngs fork, granted to Edward Thomas 15 May 1772 and which said titles he believes were destroyed in the time of war and that he saw Jeremiah Ham and Peter Hawkins subscribe their names thereto as witnesses, 20 Oct 1795 before J. R. Brown, J.N.C. Recorded 2 Jan 1796.

C, 511-512: South Carolina, Newberry County. Ann Floyd, widow, for love and affection to her grand-daughter Frances Floyd (eldest daughter of Catherine Satterwhite, wife to Bartlett), one negro girl called Silvia, 1 Oct 1795. Ann Floyd (mark (Seal), Wit: J. R. Brown, J.N.C. Recorded 4 Jan 1796.

C, 512-513: South Carolina, Newberry County. Ann Floyd, widow, for love and affection to her grand-daughter Rebecca Floyd, daughter of John Floyd, son of Ann Floyd aforesaid), one negro child called Cate, 1 Oct 1795. Ann Floyd (mark (Seal), Wit: J. R. Brown, J.N.C. Recorded 4 Jan 1796.

C, 513-514: South Carolina, Newberry County. Ann Floyd, widow, for love and affection to son John Floyd, one negro woman called Jinny and one negro girl called Winney and one sorrel mare called Jinny, 1 Oct 1795. Ann Floyd (mark (Seal), Wit: J. R. Brown, J.N.C. Recorded 4 Jan 1796.

C, 514-515: South Carolina, Newberry County. Ann Floyd, widow, to her daughter Catherine Satterwhite, wife of Bartlett Satterwhite, one small chesnut gelding, one negro woman called Hannah, 1 Oct 1795. Ann Floyd (mark (Seal), Wit: J. R. Brown, J.N.C. Recorded 4 Jan 1796.

C, 515-516: 13 Feb 1794, John Wheatingman Senr to John Wheatingman Junr, both of Newberry County, for divers considerations, 100 acres on waters of Cannons Creek adj. John Kinard, Thomas Gains, Joseph Caldwell, Mairpool. John Weddingman (Seal), Wit: John Kinard, Peter Leaner. Proved 22 Oct 1795 by the oath of John Kinard before William Houseal, J.P. Recorded 4 Jan 1796.

C, 517-518: 1 Aug 1795, David Lake of Newberry County to Thomas Lake of same, for £50 sterling, two feather beds and furniture, five pewter plates, one dish and one bason, two potts, one sorrel mare, 14 head of hogs. David Lake (Seal), Wit: Robert Mabin, Benjamin Mabin, Barber Hencock. Proved by the oath of Robert Mabin 3 Aug 1759 before Reuben Sims, J.P. Recorded 4 Jan 1796.

C, 519-520: 1 April 1795, John Weadinman to John H. Ruff, both of newberry County, for £70 sterling, 100 acres on a small branch of Cannons Creek, granted to Arthur McQuanling, recorded in Book EEE, page 164. John Weadinman (Seal), Wit: David Ruff, J.P., Philip Comer, Peter Wedinman (X). Recorded 4 Jan 1796.

C, 521-522: 15 July 1795, Uriah Wicker to John H. Ruff, both of Newberry County, for £60 sterling, on negro girl named Rachael. Uriah Wicker (Seal), Wit: Jacob Leitzey (IL), George Ridlehover, Adam Mits (mark). Proved 24 Sept 1794 by the oath of George Ridlehover before David Ruff, J.P. Recorded 4 Jan 1796.

C, 522-527: Lease and release. 20 Nov 1788, John Calegham of the settlement of Tiger River in Ninety Six District to William Davis Junr, planter, of Newberry County, for £100 sterling, 198 acres on waters of Indian Creek on a branch called Headleys Creek, adj. land of Peter Brasilman, John Lindsey, Thomas Johnson, William Davis Senr, granted to said John Calegham 2 Oct 1786, recorded in Book MMMM, page 578. John Calegham (Seal), Wit: William Speakman Junr, John Lindsey Junr, James Lindsey. Proved 22 Nov 1788 by the oath of James Lindsey before John Lindsey, J.P. Recorded 4 Jan 1796.

C, 528-533: Lease and release. 5 & 6 Nov 1795, Abraham Beach Winchester of Newberry County to Robert Floyd of same, for £75 sterling, 125 acres adj. William Moziek, Clement Davis, Andrew Felps, Thomas Reeder, part of 250 acres granted to William Winchester decd 20 Aug 1767 and conveyed to Joseph Winchester decd and by the death of said Joseph to his brother Daniel Winchester, being the heir at law, and said Daniel Winchester conveyed said 125 acres to Abraham Beach Winchester 20 & 21 Sept 1790. Abraham Beach

Winchester (Seal), Wit: B. Satterwhite Junr, John Leavell, Providence Williams. Proved 11 Nov 1795 by the oath of Bartlett Satterwhite Junr before Charles Griffin, J.P. Recorded 4 Jan 1796.

C, 534-538: Lease and release. 4 & 5 Nov 1795, Willoughby Winchester of Newberry County to William Floyd of same, for £5 SC money, 125 acres, part of 250 acres granted to William Winchester decd 20 Aug 1767 and fell unto Daniel Winchester by heirship, and said Daniel Winchester conveyed said 125 acres to Willoughby Winchester 31 March 1789. Willoughby Winchester (Seal), Mary Winchester (X) (Seal), Wit: B. Satterwhite Junr, John Leavell, Providence Williams. Proved 11 Nov 1795 by the oath of Bartlett Satterwhite Junr before Charles Griffin, J.P. Recorded 4 Jan 1796.

C, 539-541: 4 May 1795, John Coate and Susannah Coate his wife of Newberry County to Frederick Nance of same, for £5 sterling, one lot of one acre near the Court house of said county adj. and tot he south of the gaol, number 22. J. Coate (Seal), Susanah Coate (Seal), Wit: James Campbell, Samuel Lindsey, Stephen Elmore (X). Proved by the oath of Saml Lindsey 22 Oct 1795 before John Speak, J.P. Recorded 4 Jan 1796.

C, 542: 4 Jan 1796, John Wendel of Newberry County to Joseph Chapman of same, for £2 SC money, 12 acres adj. Joseph Chapman, Nathl Nichols' line. John Wendel (Seal), Wit: James Johnston, Thomas Butler. Recorded 5 Jan 1796.

C, 543-548: Lease and release. 31 Aug & 1 Sept 1792, William Chapman, planter, of Newberry County to James McNiel Senr and James McNiel Junr of same, for £35 SC money, 100 acres on south fork of Cannons Creek adj. Samuel Chapman, Abraham Thompson, Charles Burton, Robert Hannah, granted 2 Feb 1773 to Doroty Neice (which Bollus Neice) the proper heir conveyed to William Chapman. Wm Chapman (Seal), Wit: William Tweed, Moses Smith, John Livingston. Proved by the oath of William Tweed 13 Nov 1795 before Fred Nance, J.P. Recorded 6 Jan 1796.

C, 549-552: Lease and release. 13 Nov 1795, James McNiel Senr of Newberry County to James McNiel Junr of same, for £50 sterling, 100 acres on south fork of Cannons Creek adj. Samuel Chapman, Abraham Thompson, Charles Burton, Robert Hannah, granted 2 Feb 1773 to Torody Neice and by him conveyed to William Chapman, then to James McNiel Senr. James McNeil (Seal), Wit: William Tweed, David Tweed, Fred Nance. Recorded 6 Jan 1796.

C, 553-555: 7 Jan 1795, Richard Brooks of Newberry County to William Brooks of same, for £5, 200 acres, excepting a small part of said tract made over to Asa Garret, on south side Indian Creek, ranted to said Richard Brooks 13 Feb 1768, recorded in Auditor's Office, Book H. No. 8, page 418. Richard Brooks (X) (Seal), Wit: John Johnston, Thomas Speakman. Proved 13 March 1795 by the oath of Thomas Speakman before Providence Williams, J.P. Recorded 7 Jan 1796.

C, 556-557: 22 Jan 1795, John Johnston of Newberry County to Sarah Brooks of same, for £14 SC money, 100 acres on Indian Creek, part of tract granted to Thomas Lehre 4 Dec 1788, recorded in Book PPPP, page 285, adj. Uriah Conner, William Simpson, Stamock's land. John Johnston (Seal), Wit: Thomas Speakman, William Brooks (X). Proved 10 March 1795 by the oath of Thomas Speakman before Providence Williams, J.P. Recorded 7 Jan 1796.

C, 558-559: 12 March 1795, Henry Gaines and Richard George Gains of Newberry County to Jesse Owens of same for £30 sterling, 75 acres in the fork between Broad and Saluda Rivers on Second Creek adj. Caldwell, part of tract sold by William Dawkins to said Gains. Henry Gains (Seal), Richard George Gains (Seal), Wit: Thomas Owen, Thomas Riley, George Montgomery. Proved by the oath of Thomas Owens 25 Dec 1795 before Edward Finch, J.P. Recorded 8 Jan 1796.

C, 559-566: Lease and release. 24 & 25 March 1786, John Turner and his wife Francis Turner of Ninety Six District, to Zachariah Smith Brooks of same, for £500 SC money, 200 acres on Little River between Broad and Saluda Rivers adj. William Huggens, granted to John Turner 2 June 1769. John Turner (Seal), Francis Turner (X) (Seal), Wit: James Cook, Dudley Brooks, Elisha Brooks. Proved 25 Dec 1793 by the oath of Elisha Brooks before Robert Gillam, J.P. Recorded 8 Jan 1796.

C, 566-568: 1 Nov 1795, Thomas Johnston, farmer, of Newberry County, to John Moore, farmer, of same, for £12 sterling, 50 acres on waters of Indian Creek on a branch called Headley Creek, part of a tract granted to Richard Brooks then conveyed to James Wilson then to Thomas Johnston. Thomas Johnston (Seal), Mary Johnston (mark) (Seal), Wit: James Buchanan, James Johnston, Robert Johnston. Proved by the oath of James Buchanan 11 Dec 1795 before John Speak, J.P. Recorded 8 Jan 1796.

C, 568-572: Lease and release. 4 & 5 Sept 1795, Thomas Johnston Senr of Newberry County, to Thomas Johnston Junr of same, for £100 sterling, 280 acres on Enoree River, adj. land of George Awberry. Thomas Johnston (Seal), Wit: John Moore, Patrick Buchanan, James Lindsey. Proved by the oath of John Moore 15 Dec 1795 before John Speak, J.P. Recorded 8 Jan 1796.

C, 573-578: Lease and release. 4 & 5 Sept 1795, Thomas Johnston Senr of Newberry County, to James Johnston Junr of same, for £110 sterling, 100 acres, part of 200 acres granted 12 Dec 1768 to James Wilson 27 Aug 1785 and to Thomas johnston 4 Nov 1786, recorded in Book I. No. 9, page 271. Thomas Johnston (Seal), Wit: John Moore, Patrick Buchanan, James Lindsey. Proved by the oath of John Moore 15 Dec 1795 before John Speak, J.P. Recorded 8 Jan 1796.

C, 579-582: 29 Oct 1794, Robert Gilliam Senr of Newberry County to Harris Gilliam of same, for £50 sterling, 112 acres on waters of Mudlick Creek adj. McCool, Younghusband, Elizabeth Williams, John More, John Neely. Robert

Gillam (Seal), Wit: Daniel Williams Junr, B. Satterwhite, Robert Gillam Jun. Proved by the oath of Bartlett Satterwhite 8 Nov 1794 before Robert Gilliam, J.P. Recorded 8 Jan 1796.

C, 583: South Carolina, Newberry County. Ann Floyd, widow, for love and affection to her grandson Charles Gillam (son of harris Gilliam and my daughter Rebekah deceased), one negro girl called Lidda and one bay gelding called Dick, 1 Oct 1795. Ann Floyd (mark (Seal), Wit: J. R. Brown, J.N.C. Recorded 21 Jan 1796.

C, 584-589: Lease and release. 1 & 2 Oct 1795, James Wilson of Logan County, Kentucky, to William Blackburn of Ninety Six District, Newberry County, SC, for £200 sterling, 300 acres on a small branch of Indian Creek called the Long branch, adj. William Largent, Asa Garrett, Jesse Gary, James Bonds, originally granted to James Wilson deceased 12 Dec 1768 and "ascended" to William Wilson decd, being his eldest son and heir at law, & thence fell to the said James Wilson his next brother and heir at law. James Wilson (Seal), Wit: John Blackburn, James Johnston (mark), George Roberts (X). Proved by the oath of John Blackburn 28 Nov 1795 before Providence Williams, J.P. Recorded 25 Jan 1796.

C, 590-591: 1 Oct 1795, Susanah Scudder, late widow of James Wilson decd, to William Blackburn of Newberry County, relinquishment of dower to 300 acres on a small branch of Indian Creek called the Long branch, adj. William Largent, Asa Garrett, Jesse Gary, James Bonds, originally granted to James Wilson deceased 12 Dec 1768. Susanah Scudder (S) (Seal), Wit: John Blackburn, James Johnston (mark), George Roberts (X). Proved by the oath of John Blackburn 28 Nov 1795 before Providence Williams, J.P. Recorded 25 Jan 1796.

C, 592-597: Lease and release. 1 Jan 1796, Philimon Waters Senr of Newberry County to William Cole of same, for £125 SC money, 200 acres on a branch of Indian Creek, known by the name of Long branch, which tract was granted to Barbara Farbarn alias Farlarn 31 Jan 1761 and descended by Henry Metzcur by heirship being the grandson of Barbara Farbarn and son of Margaret Metzcur eldest daughter of said Barbara Farbarn. P. Waters (Seal), Wit: Stephen Williams, James Cole Junr, John Cole. Proved by the oath of James Cole 4 Jan 1796 before Prov. Williams, J.P. Recorded 26 Jan 1796.

C, 598-603: Lease and release. 27 & 28 Jan 1772, Alexander McGrigor of Berkley County, SC, to James Garner, planter, of same, for £150 SC money, 200 acres granted to said Alexander McGrigor 6 Feb 1773 [sic] on a branch of Bush River in Berkley County called Wms Beaverdams adj. James Williams, William Belton, Elijah Teague, Providence Williams, James Jones. Alex'r McGregor (Seal), Wit: John Thomas, Thomas Green, Samuel Compton (X). Proved 19 Jan 1774 in Ninety Six District by the oath of John Thomas before John Caldwell, J.P.

C, 603-607: Lease and release. 23 & 24 Jan 1786, Thomas Black of Ninety Six District, to Charles Parkins of same, for £10 sterling, 150 acres on the ridge between Bush and Beaver Dam Creeks, adj. Charles Parkins, William Turner, formerly granted to Peter Black 3 April 1775. Thomas Black (Seal), Wit: Daniel Parkins, David Parkins, James Patty. Proved in Newberry County by the oath of Daniel Parkins 6 Sep 1794 before Peter Julin, J.P. Recorded 28 Jan 1796.

C, 608-612: Lease and release. 4 & 5 April 1785, David Parkins of Ninety Six District, to Charles Parkins of same, for £10 sterling, 200 acres on waters of Saluda and a branch thereof called Beaver Dam Creek, adj. Peter Black, David Parkins, part of tract granted to Charles Parkins deceased and fell to said David Parkins by heirship, granted 13 Feb 1768. David Parkins (Seal), Ruth Parkins (R) (Seal), Wit: Daniel Parkins, Thomas Black, Joseph McDonald. Proved in Ninety Six District by the oath of Daniel Parkins 19 Sept 1785 before P. Waters, J.Q. Recorded 28 Jan 1796.

C, 613: 26 Nov 1795, Francis Davinport and Isaac Davinport of Newberry County to James Davinport of same, for £60 sterling, one negro woman named Penney. Francis Davinport (seal), isaac Davinport (seal), Wit: Francis Davinport Jun'r, Caleb Gilbert. Proved 26 Nov 1795 by the oath of Francis Davinport Jun'r before Charles Griffin. Recorded 2 Feb 1796.

C, 614-615: George Gibson and George Bridges of Newberry County for £23 s10 sterling to Michael Baites of same, mortgage 150 acres on the Reedy Branch of Buffalow Creek, granted to Andrew Keller, for payment on or before 20 March 1796, dated 20 March 1795. George Gibson (mark) (Seal), George Bridges (Seal), Wit: Moses Jacobs, George Baits. Recorded 2 Feb 1796.

C, 615-619: Lease and release. 9 & 10 April 1793, George Gray Senr, planter, of Newberry County, to Peter Gray, planter, of same, for £100 sterling, 220 acres on waters of Cannons Creek, granted to Casper Gray 21 Dec 1752 and devolved unto said George Gray, he being the lawful heir. George Gray (Seal), Wit: David Ruff, J.P., Heinrich[?] Buser[?] [German signature], Casper Piester. Recorded 2 Feb 1796.

C, 620-621: ___ April 1793, George Gray Senr, planter, of Newberry County, to Peter Gray, planter, of same, for £100 sterling, 140 acres on waters of Cannons Creek, granted to George Gray. George Gray (Seal), Wit: David Ruff, J.P., Heinrich[?] Buser[?] [German signature], Casper Piester. Recorded 2 Feb 1796.

C, 622-623: Frederick Gray, Capt. of Militia, to Peter Gray planter, both of Newberry County, for £17 s14 d8 sterling, 37 acres on waters of Cannons Creek adj. Frederick Gray, Peter Gray, Robert Moore, part of grant to George Gray and part to Frederick Gray. Frederick Gray (Seal), Wit: Casper Piester, John Piester. Recorded 2 Feb 1796.

C, 624-627: 27 Dec 1770, Leonard Bough of Berkley County, SC, planter, and Eva Susanah his wife, to Adam Summers of same place, weaver, by grant dated 16 Jan 1761 to Eva Susanah Wayman, now the lawful wife of Leonard Bought, in the fork between Broad and Saluda Rivers, recorded in Book VV, now conveyed for £50 SC money. Leonard Bough (LB) (Seal), Eva Susanah Bough (X) (Seal), Wit: George Barnard Shrum, Jesse Daniell. Proved by the oath of George Barnard Shrum 27 Dec 1770 before Moses Kirkland, J.P. Recorded 4 Feb 1796.

C, 628-633: Lease and release. 7 & 8 Jan 1796, George Summers of Orangeburgh District, SC, planter, to Daniel Davault, planter, of same, for £105 sterling, 200 acres in the fork between Broad and Saluda Rivers, recorded in Book CCC, page 247, originally granted to Susanah Wayman 16 Jan 1761, transferred to George Summers, also 200 acres in the fork between Broad and Saluda Rivers adj. land of Hagabook, Wayman, granted 19 Aug 1768 to Adam Summers, being properly transferred to George Summers. George Adam Somers (Seal), Susana Somers (X) (Seal), Wit: J. A. Houseal, Benedict Mayer, George Summers. Proved by the oath of Benedict Mayer 19 Jan 1796 before John Adam Summers, J.P. Recorded 4 Feb 1796.

C, 634-635: 29 Jan 1772, Adam Summers of Craven County, SC, planter, to George Summers his son, 200 acres on waters of Cannons Creek, adj. land of Susannah Wayman, Hagabook. Adam Somer (mark) (Seal), Susana Somers (X) (Seal), Wit: John Fulmer, John Swightenburg, William Saur. Proved by the oath of John Swightenbergh 21 Jan 1796 before John Adam Summers, J.P. Recorded 6 Feb 1796.

C, 635-636: 14 Oct 1794, Thomas Lindsey of Newberry County to Samuel Lindsey of same, for £425 SC money, Newow, Toney, Sambrit, Sambow, Andrew, all men slaves; Debro and Dinah, negro women; George a male child about 9 years old and Pat a girl child about 5 years old, Molly a girl child about 10 years old. Thomas Lindsey (Seal), Wit: J. R. Brown, J.N.C. Recorded 6 Feb 1796.

C, 636-637: 8 Jan 1796, Daniel Williams to Samuel Williams, his son, both of Laurence County, SC, for £40 sterling, one negro boy called Jacob. Daniel Williams (Seal), Wit: Elizabeth Williams and Nettey Williams authorized Daniel Williams Senr to sell said negro Jacob to our brother Samuel Williams. Recorded 6 Feb 1796.

C, 637-642: Lease and release. 4 & 5 Feb 1782, John Green, planter, of Ninety Six District, to Daniel Gorie, planter, of same, for £500 SC money, 300 acres on Kelleys Creek and Enoree River, part of 550 acres granted 10 Jan 1771 to said John Green adj. Awberry Noland, Richard Kelly, Allin, recorded in Book GGG, page 167. John Green (X), Wit: James Kelly, William Gorie, John Owen Gorie (X). Proved by the oath of John Owen Gorie 30 Sept 1789 before William Wadlington, J.P. Recorded 14 April 1796.

C, 643: 1 Feb 1791, John Lindsey, Esquire, of Newberry County, to John Anderson of same, for £600 sterling, six negroes: Pompey, Priscilla, Cain, Cato, Mack & Summer. John Lindsey (Seal), Wit: Wm Tate, Caleb Lindsey. Proved by the oath of Caleb Lindsey 28 Sept 1795 before Frederick Nance, J.P. Recorded 10 April 1790.

C, 644-645: 28 Sept 1795, John Anderson of Saluda Old Town, Newberry County, to John Lindsey, for £300 sterling, four negroes: pompey aged about 30, African born; Priscilla aged about 28, country born; Cain about 23 years, country born; Catoe about 23, all four negro slaves. John Anderson (Seal), Wit: William Elliot, James Lindsey. Proved by the oath of William Elliott 6 Oct 1795 before Robert Gilliam, J.P. Recorded 10 April 1796.

C, 645-646: 7 March 1796, John Tolleson of Newberry County to Mullican Norwood Senr of same, for d3½, all the goods, household stuff and implements, two cows and calves. John Tolleson (T) (Seal), Wit: Richard Tear, Mary Norrod (mark). Proved by the oath of Richard Tear 7 March 1796 before Edward Finch, J.P. Recorded 16 April 1795.

C, 647-648: 21 March 1796, John Windle of Newberry County, to Rachael Nave of same, for £20 sterling, 88 acres, part of survey (laid out on the Bounty) on waters of Cannons Creek, plat dated 17 March 1772 adj. Joseph Chapman Neel, Cappleman Nicholas, and Voluntine. John Windel (Seal), Wit: John B. Mitchell, Joseph Chapman, Caty Chapman. Proved 24 March 1796 by the oath of Joseph Chapman before Fred Nance, J.P. Recorded 29 Apr 1796.

C, 648-652: Lease and release. 17 March 1791, Clement Gore of Newberry County, settlement of Guilders Creek, to Isabella Morgan of same, for £30 sterling, 100 acres granted to Clement Gore in 1787 on Kings Creek. Clem't Gore (Seal), Charity Gore (X) (Seal), Wit: John Goodwin (mark), Joseph Brown, Ruth Goodwin. Proved 19 Jan 1792 by the oath of Joseph Brown before Edward Finch, J.P. Recorded 29 Apr 1796.

C, 653-654: 20 March 1795, George Gibson & George Bridges of Newberry County, to Michael Baits of Ninety Six District, same county, mortgage of 150 acres on the Reedy branch of Buffalo Creek, granted to Andrew Keller, for £23 s10 sterling due 20 March 1796. George Gibson (mark) (Seal), George Bridges (Seal), Wit: Moses Jacobs, George Baits. Proved 19 March 1796 by the oath of George Baits before Fred Nance, J.P. Recorded 2 March 1796.

C, 655-659: Lease and release. 1 & 2 Aug 1794, Hugh Reid of Newberry County, cooper, to Elizabeth McDonald of same, for £150 sterling, 100 acres granted to Elizabeth Kilpatrick 6 Feb 1774 on waters of Indian Creek adj. Jean Kilpatrick, William Kilpatrick, Ann Kilpatrick, recorded in Book FFF, page 158. Hugh Reid, Elisabeth Reid, Wit: Joseph Caldwell, William McGlamery. Proved by the oath of Joseph Caldwell (mark) before Providence Williams, J.P. Recorded 2 May 1796.

C, 660: David Glen of Newberry County, sadler, bound to Peter Brasilman of same, merchant in the sum of £300 sterling, 29 June 1795, to make title to his claim as heir at law to a tract on Enoree River known by the name of Glenns Mill containing 250 acres with the mill seat, stones &c. David Glen (Seal), wit: John Rogers, Robert Powell. Recorded 3 May 1796.

C, 661: 9 Jan 1796, Joseph Dawkins, planter, to Newberry County, appoints Alexander Bookter, merchant, attorney. Joseph Dawkins (Seal), Druscilla Dawkins (X) (Seal), Wit: Robert Powell, John Mink. Recorded 3 May 1796.

C, 662-664: 2 Jan 1795, John Adam Summers and Anne Maria his wife of Lexington County, SC, to Bartholomew Long of Newberry County, for £12 sterling, 60 acres in Ninety Six District on waters of Stephens Creek, a branch of Saluda River, part of 661 acres granted to John Adams Summers adj. Jacob Long, Andrew Craps, George Lever, Michael Kinard, and the residue of the above tract now Joseph Cullens' land. John A Summer (Seal), Mary Summer (MS) (Seal), Wit: Fred Joseph Wallern, Bartholomew Minick (BM). Proved by the oath of Bartholomew Minick 25 Feb 1796 before William Houseal, J.P. Recorded 3 May 1796.

C, 665-666: 30 Jan 1796, Bernard Sims, Mathew Sims, Reuben Sims, Obediah Hendricks & Patience his wife, Jesse Johnson & Lucy his wife of Cumberland County, Virginia, appoint Reuben Sims of Cumberland County, our attorney, to receive from the estate of Mathew Sims deceased, all such negro slaves and other interests. Bernard Sims (Seal), Matthew Sims (Seal), Reuben Sims (Seal), Elizabeth Sims (X) (Seal), Obediah Hendrick (Seal), Jese Johns (Seal), Wit: Benjamin B. Cheshier, Charles Cheshieur, William Ligon, Benjamin Partier. Cumberland County, Virginia, 4 Feb 1796, acknowledged before John Holman, J. P. Recorded 4 May 1796.

C, 667-668: 24 Nov 1795, Elizabeth Spence, widow of James Spence deceased, to my step daughter Mary Glasgow, wife of Archibald Glasgow, all my dower in the estate of James Spence deceased, 200 acres of land and negroes. Elizabeth Spence (O) (Seal), Wit: James Lindsey, Robert Spence. Proved by the oath of Robert Spence 25 March 1796 before Edward Finch, J.P. Recorded 4 May 1796.

C, 668-669: 2 Feb 1796, James Griffin Senr of Newberry County, planter, to John Simpson of Laurance County, for £20 sterling, three feather beds, two cows and yearlings marked under keel in the right ear, hole and crop in the left ear, one bay horse about 13 hands high, about 8 years old, household furniture, pewter, spoons, pots, plow irons, one black horse. James Griffin (X) (Seal), Wit: Daniel Griffin, James Waldrop. Proved 4 Feb 1796 by the oath of Daniel Griffin before John Hunter. Recorded 4 May 1796.

C, 670-675: Lease and release. 10 & 11 May 1773, Daniel Williams of Craven County, SC, to Samuel Cannon of same, for £200 SC money, 200 acres, part of 300 acres granted 12 July 1771 to aid Daniel Williams on a branch of Bush

River called Williams Beaver Dam Branch, adj. John Williams, recorded in Book III, page 149. Daniel Williams (Seal), Cassandra Williams (Seal), Wit: Elenor Davis, Lewis Linvil (L), Jno Dalrymple. Proved 17 May 1773 by the oath of John Dalrymple before John Caldwell, J.P. in Ninety Six District. Recorded 4 May 1796.

C, 676-680: Lease and release. 25 & 26 Jan 1787, Samuel Cannon of settlement of Guilders Creek, Newberry County, to Isaac Cannon, his son of same, for £100 SC money, 200 acres, part of 300 acres granted 12 July 1771 to aid Daniel Williams and conveyed to Samuel Cannon 10 & 11 May 1773, grant recorded in Book III, page 149. Saml Cannon (Seal), Lydia Cannon (Seal), Wit: John Cannon, William Cannon (L), John Williams. Proved 18 March 1796 by the oath of John Williams before John Speak, J.P. Recorded 4 May 1796.

C, 681-683: 29 Dec 1785, Philimon Bozeman & Susannah his wife of Edgefield County, SC, to George Elliott of Newberry County, for £5 sterling, 10 acres, part of 500 acres granted to John Samsam 3 Nov 1770 and by him conveyed to John Bozeman 10 & 11 Feb 1779, afterwards became Philimon Bosemans by "decent" he being Eldest son and heir at Law to John Boseman decd, adj. Isaac Mitchell, William Largent, Berry Harris, and land of the original tract divided to David Bozeman. Philimon Boseman (Seal), Susana Boseman (mark) (Seal), Wit: William Elliott, Lewis Boseman, Thomas Runnels (X). Proved in Newberry County by the oath of William Elliott 18 Jan 1796 before Robert Gillam, J.P. Recorded 5 May 1796.

C, 683-685: 9 Jan 1796, Adam Glazier of Newberry County, School Master, for £45 sterling, to James Caldwell, planter, 100 acres on Williams Creek, originally granted to Jane Wilson 6 Feb 1773. Adam Glazier (Seal), Margaret Glazier (X) (Seal), Wit: James Hall, John Hogg, Nancey Pearson (X). Proved by the oath of John Hogg 2 Feb 1796 before Edward Finch, J.P. Recorded 5 May 1796.

C, 686: 28 April 1795, Thomas Gains, planter, of Newberry County, to John Cannon of same, for £17 sterling, one negro boy named Reuben. Thos Gains, Wit: Danl Caldwell, James Caldwell. Proved by the oath of Dan Caldwell 25 April 1796 before David Ruff, J.P. Recorded 5 May 1796.

C, 687-689: 6 Feb 1795, Levi Johnson of Newberry County to John Hogg of same, for £51 s5 d8 sterling, 105 acres on branches of Kings Creek, waters of Enoree River, part of tract granted to Daniel Johnson Senr decd surveyed of and platted by George Harbirt. Levi Johnson (Seal), Salley Johnson (X) (Seal), Wit: James Caldwell, Samuel Cannon, John Cannon. Proved by the oath of James Caldwell 27 Feb 1796 before Edward Finch, J.P. Recorded 6 May 1796.

C, 690-692: 27 Feb 1795, Daniel Williams & Cassandra his wife of Newberry County, to James Teague of same, for £100 sterling, 100 acres, part of tract of 300 acres granted to said Daniel Williams 12 July 1771 on a small draught of the Beaver dam called Williams Beaver dam, adj. John Williams, Major John Caldwell, Clement Davis, Wm Beg, James Williams. Daniel Williams (Seal), Cassander Williams (Seal), Wit: Thomas Gary, Robert Madam, Wm Belton. Proved 19 March 1795 by the oath of Wm Belton before Providence Williams, J.P. Recorded 6 May 1796.

C, 692-693: South Carolina, Newberry County. Personally appeared James McCrackin Senr and sayeth that some time in the year 1770 received a lease and release from Henry Hendrix decd and Jean his wife for 26 acres laid off by Enoch Pearson, a Deputy Surveyor, and plat returned and certified and this deponant saith that the titles was either lost or mislaid as they cannot be had and they was not proved nor ever admitted to record, 8 June 1793. James McCrackin, before John Speak, J.P. Personally appeared Anthony Park, Thomas McCrackin, and Arthur McCrackin and saith that they was present and saw Henry Hendrix decd and Jane his wife both sign a title of lease and release and they also saw the rec't that was indorsed on said titles for 26 acres, 8 June 1793. Anthony Park, Thomas McCrackin, Arthur McCrackin, before John Speak, J.P. Recorded 6 May 1796.

C, 694-696: 21 March 1795, Edward Finch of Newberry County to Jonathan Jackson of same for ten shillings sterling, al that lately erected house called Bethel School with 30 acres of land including half of a spring, part of tract granted to John Lindsey for 200 acres, provided that said Jonathan Jackson, President of the Mount Bethel School, do permit such members and preachers as are under the direction of the General Conference held in Baltimore to preach and shall permit teachers as shall have a recommendation from the Bishop to teach English and other languages or sciences. Edward Finch (Seal), Wit: Samuel Dogan, Harbirt Tucker, Geo Harbirt. Proved by the oath of Samuel Dogan 30 Dec 1795 before L. Casey, J.N.C. Recorded 9 May 1796.

C, 697-698: 3 Feb 1796, John Turner of Newberry County for love and affection to John Turner Jun'r and William Turner, my two beloved sons, one negro boy named Frank to John Turner Junr and one negro boy Charles to William Turner. John Turner (Seal), Wit: John Thomas S. M., William Cox. Proved by the oath of William Cox 16 March 1796 before Danl Clary, J.P. Recorded 9 May 1796.

C, 698-699: 26 Feb 1796, John Turner of Newberry County for natural love and affection to David Turner my son and Polly Turner my daughter, one negro boy named Isaac and one negroe girl named Charlotte to David Turner Junr and one negro girl named Suck to Polly Turner. John Turner (Seal), Wit: Orsamus Spragins, John Thomas S. M. Proved by the oath of Orsamus Spragins 27 Feb 1796 before Danl Clary, J.P. Recorded 9 May 1796.

C, 700-701: 26 Feb 1796, Elizabeth Turner, widow of William Turner deceased, of Newberry County for natural love and affection to Elizabeth Turner, daughter to my son John Turner, one negro girl named Jude.

Elizabeth Turner (Seal), Wit: Orsamus Spragins, John Thomas S. M. Proved by the oath of Orsamus Spragins 27 Feb 1796 before Danl Clary, J.P. Recorded 9 May 1796.

C, 702-706: Lease and release. 19 & 20 June 1795, Samuel Lindsey of Newberry County, gent., & Elizabeth his wife, to George Lathem of same, merchant, for £23 sterling, 100 acres in the fork between Broad and Saluda Rivers on a small branch of Kings Creek adj. Gabriel Anderson, granted 6 April 1768. Saml Lindsey (Seal), Wit: Wm. Satterwhite, Saml Kelly Sen., Thomas Brooks. Recorded 9 May 1796.

C, 707-709: 9 March 1796, Thomas Pearson of Newberry County to Samuel Miles and Samuel Teague, members of Rockey Spring Meeting, Quakers, for natural love and affection, 2½ acres on a small branch of Bush River bounded on all sides by land of Thomas Pearson, part of 176 acres granted to said Thomas Pearson 7 April 1788. Thomas Pearson (Seal), Wit: Josiah Pemberton, John Furnas, William Miles. Proved 21 April 1796 by the affirmation of John Furnas before Elisha Ford, J.P. Recorded 9 May 1796.

C, 709-713: South Carolina, Ninety Six District. 28 Aug 1777, Amos Duncan and Elizabeth his wife, planter, of Ninety Six District, for £187 s10 SC money, to Abner Ellermon of same, planter, 250 acres on waters of Bush River, part of 400 acres granted to Samuel Duncan 14 Sept 1769. Amos Dunkin (Seal), Elisabeth Dunkin (Seal), Wit: Enos Elleman, Stephen Elmore, John Elleman. Proved by the affirmation of John Elleman 20 Feb 1796 before Elisha Ford, J.P. Recorded 10 May 1796.

C, 713-716: 13 June 1769, Stephen Elmore of Berkley County, SC, blacksmith, and Sarah his wife, to John Elleman Junr of same, planter, for £200 SC money, 200 acres in Berkley County on a small branch of Saluda River called Bush Creek adj. Mathias Elmore, Joseph Wright, Thomas Shaw. Stephen Elmore (Seal), Sarah Elmore (Seal), William Elmore (X) (Seal), Charity Elmore (mark) (Seal), Wit: James H. Case, Robert Bull, Jacob Hoge. Proved in Newberry County [sic] by the oath of James H. Casey 14 July 1769 before Jonathan Gilbert, J.P. Recorded 10 May 1796.

C, 717-721: Lease and release. 1 & 2 Nov 1790, Jacob Chandler, taylor, and Ann his wife, of Newberry County to Israel Chandler, son of Jacob, of same, for £48 sterling, 196 acres on south side of Bush River, part of 400 acres granted to Abraham Caradine 13 Aug 1762 on both sides Bush River, recorded in Book WW, page 86, conveyed by said Abraham Caradine to Israel Fulson 7 Feb 1764 and by said Fulson to Jacob Chandler 14 July 1767; the remaining 204 acres is conveyed to Jonathan Chandler 14 Oct 1790, whereon said Jacob Chandler now resides. Jacob Chandler (Seal), Ann Chandler (Seal), Wit: John Thomas S. M., David Miles, Isaac Case. Proved in Newberry County by the oath of John Thomas S. M. 14 Feb 1792 before Mercer Babb, J.P. Recorded 10 May 1796.

C, 722-723: 15 May 1796, Elizabeth McDaniel of Newberry County for natural love to son Hambleton McDaniel & grandson James Wallace, son of William Wallace, 100 acres of land on waters of Indian Creek, which said land I give to my son Hambleton McDaniel, he at the time my grandson James Wallace arrives to the age of 21, shall pay to said grandson the value of half of the aforesaid 100 acres; also to my son Hambleton McDaniel, one bay mare 4 years old; to my grandson James Wallice, one dark bay mare. Elizabeth McDaniel (mark) (Seal), Wit: Fred Nance, J.P., William Craig. Recorded 15 May 1796.

C, 723-727: Lease and release. 1 & 2 Nov 1790, Jacob Chandler, taylor, and Ann his wife, of Newberry County to Israel Chandler, son of Jacob, of same, for £25 sterling, 50 acres on waters of Bush River, part of 100 acres purchased of William Gilliland deceased 4 Aug 1774, which said tract was laid off by John Caldwell, Esqr., deceased, and joins old tract of 400 acres on the south side adj. Thomas Ryals, Gilliland. Jacob Chandler (Seal), Ann Chandler (Seal), Wit: John Thomas S. M., David Miles, Isaac Case. Proved in Newberry County by the oath of John Thomas S. M. 14 Feb 1792 before Mercer Babb, J.P. Recorded 16 May 1796.

C, 728-733: Lease and release. 1 & 2 Nov 1790, Jacob Chandler, taylor, and Ann his wife, of Newberry County to Jonathan Chandler, son of Jacob, of same, for £102 sterling, 204 acres on north side of Bush River, by plat laid off by David Pugh 14 Oct 1790 at the request of Jacob Chandler, adj Samuel Coates, the other part of said tract is conveyed to Israel Chandler, part of 300 acres granted 13 Aug 1762 to Abraham Caradine and conveyed to Israel Fulson 7 Jan 1764 and then to Jacob Chandler 14 July 1767. Jacob Chandler (Seal), Ann Chandler (Seal), Wit: John Thomas S. M., David Miles, Isaac Case. Proved in Newberry County by the oath of John Thomas S. M. 14 Feb 1792 before Mercer Babb, J.P. Recorded 16 May 1796.

C, 734-735: Elizabeth Spence, widow of James Spence deceased, of Newberry County, bound to Archibald Glasgow and Mary his wife, surviving heirs of the deceased of same, 24 April 1795, to abide by the division of all the estate of said James Spence both real and personal, the division to be made by Hugh Boyd, Joseph Spence, and William Taylor. Elizabeth Spence (Seal), Wit: Robert Spence, James Lindsey. Proved by the oath of Robert Spence 23 May 1796 before Edward Finch, J.P. Recorded 2 June 1796.

C, 735: 2 Nov 1795, Mary Daugherty, widow of the late James Daugherty Senr decd, to James Daugherty Junr, for £30, tract of land whereon said James Daugherty lately lived. Mary Daugherty (mark) (Seal), Wit: David Cannon, John Tygart, John Boyd (X). Proved by the oath of David Cannon 2 June 1796 before Fredk Nance, J.P. Recorded 2 June 1796.

C, 736-737: 7 Jan 1796, Egenia Virden of Warren County, Georgia, to Thomas Patten of Ninety Six District, SC, for £85 sterling, 150 acres in the fork between Broad and Saluda Rivers on SW side Enoree River, granted to said

Egenia Virden. Egenia Virden (Seal), Wit: Leroy Buford, Jno Voluntine. Proved by the oath of John Voluntine 1 March 1796 before Levi Casey, J.N.C. Recorded 2 June 1796.

C, 738-739: 6 Dec 1796, Zachariah Smith Brooks and Elizabeth his wife of Ninety Six District to James Spearman of same, for £200 sterling, 200 acres on waters of Little River adj. Wm Hugins, granted in 1769. Zachariah S. Brooks (Seal), Elizabeth Brooks (Seal), Wit: Daniel Goggans, John Adkison, Edmd Spearman. Proved in Newberry County by the oath of Edmond Spearman 16 May 1796 before Fred Nance, J.P. Recorded 9 June 1796.

C, 740-741: 4 Nov 1795, James Daugherty of Orangeburgh District to John Livingston of Ninety Six District for £10 sterling, 150 acres on waters of Second Creek adj. Joseph Caldwell, John Taylor, part of 500 acres granted to said Daugherty 7 May 1787, recorded in Book TTTT, page 122. James Daugherty (Seal), Wit: Peter Richardson (mark), James McCart (mark), Franky Richardson (mark). Proved in Newberry County by the oath of Peter Richardson 25 Jan 1796 before Thomas W. Waters, J.P. Recorded 9 June 1796.

C, 742-743: 18 Feb 1796, John Michael Kromer of Newberry County to George Henry Suber of same, for £20, 112½ acres, part of two tracts: the SW part of tract of 250 acres granted to John Michael Kromer 9 Jan 1755 recorded in Book PP, page 285 on Campen Creek, waters of Saluda River; the SW part of 200 acres granted to said John Michael Kromer 25 May 1774, recorded in Book FFF, page 392 on waters of Campen Creek. John Michael Kromer (Seal), Wit: Abraham Chapman (AC), George Swigart, George Harbirt. Proved in Orangeburgh District by the oath of Abraham Chapman 2 May 1796 before John Hampton, J.Q. Recorded 9 June 1796.

C, 743-746: 19 March 1796, Lewis Hogg and Clary his wife of Newberry County to William Gilliam of same, for £150 sterling, 100 acres on a branch of Broad River called Enoree granted to John Clarke 1 Dec 1769. Lewis Hogg (Seal), Clary Hogg (X) (Seal), Wit: John Henderson, W. Wadlington, Charles Littleton. Proved by the oath of William Wadlington 14 May 1796 before Edward Finch, J.P. Recorded 10 June 1796.

C, 746-749: 19 March 1796, Lewis Hogg and Clary his wife of Newberry County to William Gilliam of same, for £150 sterling, 250 acres on a branch of Broad River called Enoree granted to Benjamin Hampton 17 June 1774. Lewis Hogg (Seal), Clary Hogg (X) (Seal), Wit: John Henderson, W. Wadlington, Charles Littleton. Proved by the oath of William Wadlington 14 May 1796 before Edward Finch, J.P. Recorded 10 June 1796.

C, 750-752: 17 Feb 1796, Thomas Hogg and Martha his wife of Newberry County to William Gilliam of same, for £100 sterling, 100 acres on a branch of Broad River called Enoree granted to John Hogg Senr by will, it being left to his son Thomas Hogg, half of 200 acre tract granted 22 Nov 1771. Thomas

Hogg (Seal), Martha Hogg (X) (Seal), Wit: Joseph Jones, W. Wadlington, John Shaw (X). Proved by the oath of William Wadlington 14 May 1796 before Edward Finch, J.P. Recorded 10 June 1796.

C, 753-755: 14 May 1796, Thomas Gordon & Elizabeth his wife of Newberry County, planter, to John Stewart, planter, of same for £100 sterling, 150 ares on Sims' corner, Stewart's line. Thomas Gordon (Seal), Elizabeth Gordon (X) (Seal), Wit: Reuben Sims, William Neely, Robert Wilson. Proved 16 May 1796 by the oath of Reuben Sims before Fred Nance, J.P. Recorded 13 June 1796.

C, 756-757: Archibald Glasgow and Mary of Newberry County his wife bound to Elizabeth Spence of same, widow of James Spence, in the sum of £200 sterling, 15 Nov 1795, to stand by the division of the estate of James Spence to be made by Hugh Boyd, Joseph Spence, and William Taylor. Archabald Glasgow (Seal), Mary Glasgow (Seal), Wit: Andrew McDaniel, Robert Spence (R). Proved by the oath of Robert Spence 23 May 1796 before Edward Finch, J.P. Recorded 13 June 1796.

C, 757-758: 30th day of fifth Monday 1794, Edward Benbo of Newberry County having in my possession a negro man David, 36 years of age, and believing that liberty is the natural right of all mankind, set him free. Edward Benbo (Seal), Wit: Isaac Jenkins, David Jenkins, Martha Jenkins. Proved by the affirmation of David Jenkins 16 May 1796 before Peter Julin, J.,P. Recorded 14 June 1796.

C, 758-760: 12 March 1795, George Womelsdorf and Elizabeth his wife of Newberry County to James Coate of same, for £53 sterling, 150 acres on waters of Bush River adj. John Williams, Widow Winchester, Leavell, James Williams, William Belton, granted to Stephen Elmore 1 August 1774 and conveyed by Mathias Elmore to Rebekah Norris and by said Rebekah Norris to Thomas Reed and by him to George Womelsdorf. George Womelsdorff (Seal), Elisabeth Womelsdorff (X) (Seal), Wit: Thomas Coate (T), Sarah Ann Coate (X), Wm. Belton. Proved by the statement of Wm Belton 18 May 1796 before Fred Nance, J.P. Recorded 14 June 1796.

C, 761-763: 2 May 1796, Henry Butler of Newberry County to Benjamin Butler his son, for natural love, good will & affection, 50 acres, part of 350 acres granted to John Sims 27 Sept 1769, adj. Daniel Butler, on south side Sandy Run. Henry Butler (X) (Seal), Hannah Butler (mark) (Seal), Wit: Michael Sanders, George Goggans, Daniel Butler. Proved by the oath of George Goggans 27 May 1776 before Fred Nance, J.P. Recorded 15 June 1796.

C, 764-768: Lease and release. 21 & 22 March 1791, James Barret of Ninety Six District, Newberry County, to James Barret, blacksmith, for £20 sterling, 135½ acres granted to James Barret 1 Dec 1788 on waters of Saluda River adj. Isaac Bozier, recorded in Book YYYY, page 179. James Barret (Seal), Wit: Joshua Inman, Mercer Babb. Proved 26 Nov 1791 by the oath of Joshua Inman before Mercer Babb, J.P. Recorded 14 June 1796.

C, 769-771: 21 March 1796, Thomas Brooks of Ninety Six District, Newberry County, and Susannah his wife, to Benjamin Evans of same, for £113 s5, 188 3/4 acres adj. land of the late Benjamin Pearson, Samuel Gaunt, Nebo Gaunt, James Wadlington, Henry Stidman, William Pearson Senr, part of two tracts of land contiguous, there was granted 19 Sept 1758 to Jacob Brooks Senr 550 acres and said Jacob Brooks and wife Mary conveyed 9 Nov 1785 200 acres of said tract to Thomas Brooks (recorded in Book A, page 972-3), and there was granted 5 June 1786 to John Reagan 137 acres and said John Reagan and Elizabeth his wife conveyed to Thomas Brooks 7 Dec 1789 (recorded in Book A, page 913). Thomas Brooks (Seal), Susannah Brooks (Seal), Wit: Isaac Kirk, Nathan Galbreath, Joseph Thompson. Proved by the affirmation of Isaac Kirk 25 April 1796 before Elisha Ford, J.P. Recorded 14 June 1796.

C, 772-773: Daniel Reagan of Newberry County for £10 sterling to Joshua Stewart of same, one waggon, three pair of gears, two horses (marks given), three feather beds and furniture, dishes, plates, etc., 3 Feb 1796. Daniel Reagan (Seal), Wit: Robert Speer, Thomas Reagan, Daniel Stewart. Proved by the oath of Robert Speer 29 Feb 1796 before Peter Julin, J.P. Recorded 14 June 1796.

C, 773-776: Lease and release. 9 & 10 Jan 1795, Edward Rutledge of State of SC, Esquire, to Stephen Sparks Ninety Six District, for £60 sterling, 345 acres, part of 2000 acres granted to Henry Middleton Esqr, deceased, by plat made by John hunter, Esquire, 15 March 1791. Edw'd Rutledge (seal), Wit: Thomas Davis (X(), Keat'g Lewis Simons. Proved 16 May 1796 in Newberry County by the oath of Thomas Davis before Providence Williams, J.P. Recorded 16 June 1796.

C, 777-782: Lease and release. 5 & 6 March 1771, Col. William Thompson of Berkley County, SC, to John Abernathy, planter, of same, for £70 SC money, 200 acres in Berkley County on a branch of Saluda River called Bush Creek, granted 2 May 1770 to John Swetman [Leviston?], recorded in Book EEE, page 317. William Thompson (Seal), Wit: Lewis Thompson, Robert Leviston, Eli. Hunt (X). Proved 8 March 1771 by the oath of Elizabeth Hunt before Thomas Turner, J.P. Recorded 2 July 1796.

C, 783-788: Lease and release. 14 & 15 Sept 1772, Isaac Williams, planter, of Berkley County, and Sarah his wife, to Simeon Ellis, Millwright, for £150 SC money, 100 acres of land granted to said Isaac Williams 19 Sept 170 on a branch of saluda River called Bush River, Recorded in Auditor's Office in Book K. No. 12, page 263. Isaac Williams (Seal), Sarah Williams (Seal), Wit: John Hudgens, Mary Hudgens, John Entrekin. Proved in Craven County by the oath of John Hudgens 17 Sept 1772 before Thomas Wadlington, J.P. Recorded 2 July 1796.

C, 789-793: Lease and release. 28 & 29 Oct 1795, Jacob Chandler & Ann his wife, Jonathan Chandler and Rehemah is wife, and Israel Chandler & Lydia his wife, to John Leavell and John Abernathy of Newberry County, for £150

SC money, 100 acres on a branch of Saluda river called Bush River granted to Isaac Williams 19 Sept 1770 and conveyed by Isaac Williams and Sarah his wife to Simeon Ellis 14 & 15 Sept 1772 [see preceding deed]. Jacob Chandler (Seal), Ann Chandler (Seal), Jonathan Chandler (Seal), Rehemah Chandler (Seal), Israel Chandler (Seal), Lydia Chandler (Seal), Wit: Thomas Coate (T), Joseph Jones, James Leavel. Proved in Newberry County by the oath of Thomas Coate 13 May 1796 before Prov. Williams, J.P. Recorded 4 July 1796.

C, 794-795: Ebenezer Potter, attorney for the Estate of the late Dr. Benjamin Farrow, formerly of this State, for £45 sterling, of John Abernathy and John Leavel of same, 150 acres in the fork between Broad and Saluda Rivers on a branch of Saluda River called Bush River or Creek, adj. Isaac Williams, Robert Level, granted to Henry Demonge 4 Nov 1772, and conveyed by him to Simeon Ellis 8 Sept 1774 and by him to Benjamin Farrow 17 June 1777. Eben'r Potter (Seal), Wit: Saml Kelly Senr, Saml Kelly Junr, Richard Leavell. Proved in Newberry County by the oath of Richard Leavell 13 May 1796 before Prov. Williams, J.P. Recorded 4 July 1796.

C, 796-797: 28 July 1795, Philimon Waters, Esquire, of Newberry County to Henry Baits of same, for £35 sterling, 150 acres on a small branch of Saluda River called Hawlick Creek adj. Patrick Quatermas, Passinger, David Waters, granted to James Morehead 24 Jan 1768. P. Waters (Seal), Wit Dennis Lark, John Lark. Proved by the oath of Jno Lark 6 May 1796 before Peter Julin, J.P. Recorded 5 July 1796.

C, 798-799: 21 June 1796, Henry Baits of Newberry County to George Baldree of same, for $20, 8 acres, part of tract of land I live on. Henry Baits (X) (Seal), Wit: Zachariah Baits (X), Benjamin Lindsey, Rebekah Baits (X). Proved by the oath of Benjamin Lindsey 2 July 1796 before Peter Julin, J.P. Recorded 5 July 1796.

C, 799-800: 22 June 1796, Ursula Eigleberger of Newberry County, spinster, for love, good will and affection to son Martin Koone, of same, 100 acres on waters of Saluda River adj. Michael Leitner, granted to Elisabeth Vitlook[?] 25 May 1774, recorded in Book M. No. 13, page 56, and transferred by her unto George Eigleberger 1 & 2 Feb 1775 and to said Ursula Eigleberger 1 Dec 1785. Ursula Eigleberger (X) (Seal), George Souter (GS), Mary Houseal (X). Proved 11 July 1796 by the oath of George Souter before Wm Houseal, J.P. Recorded 23 July 1796.

C, 801-802: 18 July 1796, Daniel Beem, planter, of Newberry County, to Jacob Beem, planter, of same, for £50, 100 acres on Mill Creek adj. Alexr Davidson, granted to Ezekiel Beem 28 Nov 1771. Danl Beem (X) (Seal), Wit: David Ruff, J.P. George Neely, Nancy Taggart (X). Recorded 27 July 1796.

C, 803-805: 7 Dec 1792, John Dunkin of Newberry County to Benjamin Herndon of Wilks County, North Carolina, for £300 sterling, 100 acres on both sides Dunkins Creek, adj. the land James Campbell purchased of Col.

Brandon, James Robt Wilson, including the grist and saw mill said Herndon is now in possession of and purchased of James Campbell. John Dunkin (mark) (Seal), Wit: Rob Wilson, Amos Prather, James Campbell. Proved in Newberry County by the oath of James Campbell 30 July 1793 before Edward Finch, J.P. Recorded 8 Aug 1796.

C, 806-808: 11 March 1796, James Campbell of Newberry County to Benjamin Herndon of same, for £100 sterling, 65 acres adj. land of John Speake, Robert Wilson, Obediah Edwards, Richard Fowler, including the waggon road called the Ninety Six Road and on Dunkins Creek, part of 250 acres granted to William Hendrix and conveyed to James Campbell by Thomas Brandon as attorney for said William Hendrix, 1 May 1786, recorded in Clerks Office in Book A, page 548. Jas Campbell (Seal), Wit: Stephen Herndon, Joseph Herndon. Proved by the oath of Jos Herndon 19 July 1796 before R. Brown, J.N.C. Recorded 8 Aug 1796.

C, 809-810: South Carolina, Newberry County, Kings Creek. Samuel Ragland of county and district aforesaid bound to John Tolleson of same, in the sum of £50 sterling, to make right to John Tolleson to a tract of land on Kings Creek formerly granted to Clem. Gore adj. lands of James Wilson, Samuel Yeargan, 12 Nov 1794. Samuel Ragland (Seal), Wit: Samuel Yeargan, Simon Reeder. John Tolleson (T) assigns his right to James Spence 25 July 1796, Test: Samuel Yeargan. Proved by the oath of Samuel Yeargan 25 July 1796 before Fred Nance, J.P. Recorded 17 July 1796.

C, 811: 12 Dec 1795, John Wyld atty for John Wickley, to John Dunkin of Ninety Six District, 112 acres on waters of Duncans Creek. John Wyld atty for John Wickley (Seal), Wit: Lucy Smith Wyld, March Dunkin (mark). Proved in Newberry County by the oath of March Dunkin 26 July 1796 before John Speak, J.P. Recorded 17 Aug 1796.

C, 812-813: John Lindsey, Esqr., of Newberry County, bound to Jacob Frost of Frederick County, Virginia, in the sum of £1000 VA money, 15 Dec 1789, to make title to tract adj. Saml Lindsey, William Wilson, Duckett, said John Lindsey, it being a tract laid out to Clowney. John Lindsey (LS), Wit: James Lindsey, Thos Williams. Proved in Newberry County by the oath of James Lindsey Senr 19 Aug 1796 before Elisha Ford, J.P. Recorded 20 Aug 1796.

C, 814-816: 6 April 1795, Herman Davis Senr of Newberry County, planter, to George Sparks of same, for £50 sterling, 200 acres granted to said Hermon Davis in the fork between Enoree and Saluda Rivers 26 April 1766, entered in the Auditors Office in Book H. No. 8, page 147, in the Secretaries Office Book AAAA, page 253, near William Dunlap's branch, John Boyd. Hermon Davis (Seal), Wit: William Tinney, Andrew Spence, Josiah Elliott. Proved 28 July 1796 by the oath of William Tinney before Fred Nance, J.P. Recorded 23 Aug 1796.

C, 817-818: 6 Nov 1795, Jeremiah Williams of Newberry County to William Hall of same, for £40 sterling, 118 acres granted to Mathew Tulley in the fork between Broad and Saluda Rivers on the waters of Kings Creek adj. Thomas Cross, Henry Thompson, Thomas Cross Senr, recorded in Book SSS, page 474, in the Auditors Office in Book M. No. 13, page 253, 24 Feb 1775, the said land was sold to Gilbert Gilder and from him to Jeremiah Williams. Jeremiah Williams (Seal), Wit: John Baggs, George Harris, John Caldwell (JC). Proved by the oath of John Baggs 29 Feb 1796 before David Ruff, J.P. Recorded 23 Aug 1796.

C, 819-821: 29 July 1796, James Young and Mary his wife of Newberry County to Patrick Carmichael of same, for £50 sterling, 304 acres, part of tract of 456 acres granted to said Young 5 Nov 1792. James Young (Seal), Mary Young (mark) (Seal), Wit: B. H. Saxon, John Roberson. Mary Young, wife of James Young, relinquished dower 29 July 1796 before Jacob Roberts Brown, J.N.C. Proved by the oath of John Robertson 29 July 1796 before Jacob Roberts Brown, J.N.C. Recorded 3 Aug 1796.

C, 822-824: 5 Oct 1794, William Hubbard of Newberry County for £40 sterling to William Chambers, 52 acres granted to William Hubbard 1 Dec 1788, recorded in Book YYY, page 243, on waters of Broad River on Kings Creek adj. Robert Brown, Isaac Parmer, Simon Reeder, Mulican Norrod. William Hubbard (Seal), Jane Hubbard (X) (Seal), Wit: Alexander Blair (mark), John Speak, J.P. Recorded 24 Aug 1796.

C, 825-828: 27 Jan 1795, John Sparks and wife Margaret of Newberry County to Lewis Hogg of same, for £75 sterling, 197 acres on a branch of Enoree called Hoggs branch, 32 acres granted to Daniel Johnson, 100 acres granted to Abraham Anderson and 765 acres John Hampton. John Sparks (Seal), Margaret Sparks (Seal), Wit: George Johnston, W. Malone Jun'r, Richard Darby (R). Proved 28 July 1796 by the oath of George Johnston before John Speak, J.P. Recorded 24 Aug 1796.

C, 829-831: 1 Aug 1788, Simon Reeder Junr of Newberry County to William Hubbard for £10 sterling, 20 acres, part of grant to Simon Reeder on Kings Creek. Simon Reeder (Seal), Wit: Mullican Norwood (mark), Thos Rutherford. Proved 5 Aug 1788 by the oath of Mullican Norwood before John Lindsey, J.P. Recorded 21 Aug 1796.

C, 832-834: 14 April 1796, Thomas Hogg and Martha his wife and Sarah Chandler of Newberry County to John Clark, for £60 sterling, 300 acres on north side Enoree River, part of tract surveyed for John Clarke Senr, the same being a tract bought of John Clarke senr by Samuel Chandler father to Martha Hogg and Sarah Chandler, part of tract granted to John Clarke 5 March 1770. Thomas Hogg (Seal), Martha Hogg (X) (Seal), Sarah Chandler (Seal), Wit: Lewis Hogg, William Gilliam, Ann Gilliam (X). Proved by the oathof William Gilliam 14 May 1796 before Edward Finch, J.P. Recorded 30 Aug 1796.

C, 835-836: 28 Dec 1795, Frederick Booser of Newberry County to Daniel Davault of same, for £5 sterling, 17½ acres on waters of Eleasers Creek, a branch of Cannons Creek adj. said Daniel Davault and now Daniel Davaults son, Frederick Booser, part of tract granted to Elisabeth Hare. Frederick Booser (Seal), Wit: John Eigleberger, Philip Sligh (LS), Peter Quaddlebaum. Proved by the oath of John Eigleberger 31 May 1796 before William Houseal, J.P. Recorded 30 Aug 1796.

C, 836-837: 10 Oct 1795, Elizabeth Jennings of Newberry County binds her son Miles Jennings, an infant of the age of 10 years the seventh of this instant, an apprentice to William Teer of same, till said Miles arrives at the age of 21 years, to learn the art and mistery of a farmer. Elizabeth Jennings (Seal), William Teer (Seal), Wit: Peter Julin, J.P. Recorded 30 Aug 1796.

C, 839-843: Lease and release. 29 & 13 Dec 1794, Martha Chester and Fanny his wife of Newberry County to Cloidas Longshore of same, for £50 sterling, 80 acres, part of 300 acres granted to John Abney 3 Dec 1787 and conveyed to John Newton and by John Newton to Martin Chester 12 May 1794 on Beaver Dam Creek, waters of Saluda River, adj. Steddom, Bartlett, Polley Taylor. Martin Chester (Seal), Fanny Chester (X) (Seal), Wit: Henry Steddom, Isaiah Burton, Abel Chester (A). Proved by the oath of Henry Steddom 1 Oct 1795 before Elisha Ford, J.P. Recorded 31 Aug 1796.

C, 844-849: Lease and release. 7 & 8 Aug 1795, John Caldwell Senr of Newberry County to James Creswell and Co. of same, for £3 s5 SC money, 6½ acres, part of tract of 200 acres granted to said John Caldwell Senr 16 Sept 1774 on a small creek of the waters of Saluda River adj. land transferred by said John Caldwell to his son William Caldwell. John Caldwell Sr (Seal), Wit: Elihu Creswell, Robert Mayson, Rich'd Watts. Proved by the oath of Richard Watts Esqr 30 July 1796 before Fred Nance, J.P. Recorded 31 Aug 1796.

C, 849-854: Lease and release. 5 Nov 1770, Michael Hunt of Berkley County, SC, planter, to John Crumley, planter, of same, for £100 SC money, 125 acres, part of 250 acres granted to William Thompson 19 Aug 1768 and transferred by said Thompson to Michael Hunt on a branch of Bush River. Michael Hunt (M). Elizabeth Hunt (+) (Seal), Wit: William Gilliland, David Rees. Proved 29 July 1796 by the evidence of Nathaniel Hayworth and Elenor Large (mark) who testified to the handwriting of William Gilliland before Charles Griffin, J.P. Recorded 31 Aug 1796.

C, 855-856: 10 May 1796, Heniary Smith of Orangeburgh District, hatter, for love and good will and affection to my wife's two children Elizabeth and John Ellis, two cows and calves and two feather beds & furniture, which I got with my wife. Heniary Smith (X) (Seal), Wit: John Brit (X), Elizabeth Cask (E). Proved in Orangeburgh District by the oath of John Brit 10 May 1796 before William Calk, J.P. Recorded 8 Sept 1796.

C, 857-858: Elizabeth Dominick of Newberry County, widow, for love, good will and affection to my son Jacob Dominick of same, 100 acres, part of tract of land originally granted to John Dominick on Bounty of 150 acres, adj. Peter Wilhelm, Conasad[?] Roads, and George Stoudmires, if said Jacob should die before the age of 21 without a lawful will then to be equally divided between Margaretha and Christiana Dominick his sisters or their heirs, 1 Feb 1796. Elizabeth Dominick (X) (Seal), Wit: John Eigleberger, Thomas Rikard (X). Proved by the oath of John Eigleberger 12 Sept 1796 before William Houseal, J.P. Recorded 7 Oct 1796.

C, 858-862: Lease and release. 24 & 25 Sept 1795, John Coats of Newberry County, yeoman, and Rachael his wife, to Wright Coats, son of said John Coates, yeoman, for £30, 70 acres on waters of Beaver dam, adj. land of John Coate, Richard Thompson, part of two tracts of land: 100 acres granted to John Wright 17 Sept 1769 and conveyed by John Wright to John Coats 26 Jan 1778 on north side of Saluda River on waters of Beaver dam & 123 acres granted to John Coats 5 June 1786. John Coates (I) (Seal), Rachael Coates (X) (Seal), Wit: Richard Thompson, James Copeland. Proved by the oath of James Copeland 27 Sept 1796 before Elisha Ford, J.P. Recorded 8 Oct 1796.

C, 863-864: 25 July 1796, John Livingston to Samuel Livingston, both of Newberry County, for £15, 100 acres I have sold and 100 acres I give him without fee, total 200 acres granted to Thomas Hollinshead 6 Jan 1794 for 299 acres and conveyed to John Livingston by deed recorded in Book C, page 59. John Livingston (seal), Wit: Peter Richardson (mark), Job Richardson. Proved by the oath of Peter Richardson 30 Sept 1796 before William Houseal, J.P. Recorded 8 Oct 1796.

C, 865-866: South Carolina, Newberry County. Whereas on 20 Feb 1795, I, John C. Royston, of county aforesaid, purchased of George Hart and Delilah his wife of Rutherford County, North Carolina, for £150 sterling, all their right, title and interest, in the real and personal estate of Solomon Nichols deceased, whose grand daughter the said Delilah was reputed to be and have a release and general warrantee for the same, and whereas Elizabeth Nichols, widow of said Solomon Nichols deceased, and executrix of his will, hath purchased the same from me, now I, John Cary Royston, for £150 sterling paid by said Elizabeth Nichols, have sold all my right, title and interest in said estate, dated 5 July 1796. John C. Royston (Seal), Wit: William Wilson, John Renwick. Proved by the oath of John Renwick 14 Sept 1796 before Edward Finch, J.P. Recorded 11 Oct 1796.

C, 867-868: 8 Feb 1794, Hugh Creighton of Newberry County, to Samuel McGlamery of same, for £5 SC money, 2 acres, two rods and 15 poles or perches, part of tract granted to said Hugh Creighton. Hugh Creighton (Seal), Wit: Richard Wright, James Daugherty. Proved by the oath of Richard Wright 28 Sept 1796 before W. Craig, J.P. Recorded 13 Oct 1796.

C, 869-874: Lease and mortgage. 19 July 1796, Samuel Lindsey and James Campbell of Newberry County to George Latham of same, for £40 s5 d1½ sterling, six lots in Newberry Village, each one ¼ acre adj. land of John Criek, Peter Buffington, known by the names of Cobbs two lots and the other four numbers 28, 27, 29, 30, bounded by Market and Union Streets, by bonds dated 1 Nov 1794, 12 Jan 1795, 16 Sept 1795. Saml Lindsey (Seal), Wit: Wm Satterwhite, Frederick Nance, J.P. Recorded 14 Oct 1796.

C, 875-876: 27 Dec 1793, John Hill of Newberry County, for $30 sterling, 50 acres on waters of Peters Creek between Tyger ad Enoree Rivers, part of tract belonging to Thomas Hill, adj. land that formerly belonged to John Robinson Senr, John Hunter, Hardy, to Thomas Hill's spring branch. John Hill (mark) (Seal), Susanah Hill (X) (Seal), Wit: Andrew Hunter, James Waters, John Shaw. Proved 16 July 1794 by the oath of Andrew Hunter before Reuben Sims, J.P. Recorded 14 Oct 1796.

C, 877-878: 12 Nov 1789, Mary Morris of Newberry County to William Davis Senr of Laurence County, for £10, 30 acres, part of 200 acres on waters of Indian Creek on a small branch of Headley Creek, originally granted to William Davis 22 Sept 1769 and conveyed by said William Davis to Mary Morris on the main wagon road, 27 Sept 1787. Mary Morris (Seal), Wit: William Gray, James Lindsey. Proved 16 June 1796 by the oath of John Lindsey Senr before John Speak, J.P. Recorded 14 Oct 1796.

C, 879-882: Lease and release. 22 & 23 Dec 1793, David Edwards of Newberry County to Peter Julin of same, for £50 sterling, 190 acres on a small branch of Bush River called Hals branch, granted to Samuel Edwards 6 June 1785 and conveyed by him 2 Oct 1791 to David Edwards. David Edwards, Mary Edwards (mark). Wit: William Spencer, William Conwill. Proved by the oath of William Spencer 10 Oct 1796 before Elisha Ford, J.P. Recorded 22 Oct 1796.

C, 882-883: 23 Aug 1796, John Satterwhite Senr of Newberry County to John Satterwhite Junr of same, for £100 sterling, 200 acres on Mudlick Creek adj. Bartlett Satterwhite Senr, David Davenport, Danl McKie, Bartlett Satterwhite Junr, part of two tracts, one granted to William Thompson 2 Aug 1768 and conveyed 7 May 1769 and the other granted 2 April 1773 for 500 acres to said Satterwhite. John Satterwhite Senr (Seal), Wit: Jacob R. Brown, Drury Satterwhite. Mary Satterwhite (X), wife of John Satterwhite Senr, relinquished dower 23 Aug 1796 before J. R. Brown, J.N.C. Recorded 24 Oct 1796.

C, 884-885: 23 Aug 1796, John Satterwhite Senr of Newberry County to John Satterwhite Junr of same, for £129 sterling, 258 acres on lick branch and Pages Creek whereon said John Satterwhite now lives, part of 600 acres granted to William Thompson 14 Aug 1772 and 2 August 1768 and conveyed 7 May 1796, reserving to myself the free use and benefit of the water of said Pages Creek and benefit of the road from my house by the said John Satterwhite Junr fence into the public road near Wadsworth and Turpins Crossroad Store. John

Satterwhite Senr (Seal), Wit: Jacob R. Brown, Drury Satterwhite. Mary Satterwhite (X), wife of John Satterwhite Senr, relinquished dower 23 Aug 1796 before J. R. Brown, J.N.C. Recorded 24 Oct 1796.

C, 886-887: 1 June 1794, Stephen Norris and Rebekah White, his mother, of Edgefield County, SC, to Dudley Brooks of Newberry County, for £200 sterling, 167 acres adj. Joseph Towles, William Stripling, part of 400 acres on Little River adj. John Spiller, William Turner, John Edwards, granted to Coleman Brown 15 Feb 1769. Ste'n Norris (Seal), Rebekah White (Seal), Wit: Thomas Eastland, S. Butler, L. Smith. Proved in Newberry County by the oath of Thomas Eastland 17 Oct 1796 before Fred Nance, J.P. Recorded 26 Oct 1796.

C, 888-890: 2 June 1794, Stephen Norris and Rebekah White, his mother, of Edgefield County, SC, to Thomas Eastland of Newberry County, for £100 sterling, 100 acres, part of 400 acres granted to Coleman Brown 15 Feb 1769, and conveyed to Thomas Norris decd, and Stephen Norris being his eldest son and heir at law and Rebekah being his lawful widow and mother of said Stephen Norris. Ste'n Norris (Seal), Rebekah White (Seal), Wit: Dudley Brooks, S. Butler, L. Smith. Proved in Newberry County by the oath of Dudley Brooks 17 Oct 1796 before Fred Nance, J.P. Recorded 26 Oct 1796.

C, 891-894: 25 Oct 1785, David Humphrey and Jane his wife of Spartanburg County, SC, to Elisha Ford of the settlement of Bush River, for £60 sterling, 200 acres on waters of Bush River, adj. Stephen Elmore, Mathias Elmore, granted to Henry LittleJohn 7 Nov 1770 and conveyed by said Henry LittleJohn 2 & 3 Oct 1772 to said David Humphrey. David Humphrey (Seal), Jane Humphrey (X) (Seal), Wit: William Ford, Elizabeth Thompson (X), Mary Humphrey. Proved in Newberry County 20 Sept 1793 by the oath of Wm Ford before Mercer Babb, J. P. Recorded 7 Nov 1796.

C, 894-896: 18 July 1791, Samuel Fickling of the Parish of Saint Pauls, Colleton County, planter, to James Boulware of Edgefield County, Ninety Six District, for 10 shillings sterling, 100 acres of bounty land in Newberry County on a small branch of Cannons Creek adj. Arthur McQueenling, Saml McQueenling, Gray, Agnes Wilson, originally granted to John Stevenson. Saml Fickling (Seal), Wit: Russel Wilson Senr, Jonah Rivers, Sarah Rivers. Proved in Newberry County 19 Nov 1791 by the oath of Russel Wilson Senr 19 Nov 1791 before Jas Mayson, J.N.C. Recorded 7 Nov 1796.

C, 897-898: 7 Oct 1796, John Coate of Newberry County for £10 sterling to Rosanah Russell of same, 200 acres, part of 300 acres granted to Giles Chapman and conveyed by Chapman to John Jones. John Coate (seal), Wit: Fred Nance J.P., J. R. Brown, J. N. C. Susanah Coate, wife of John Coate, relinquished dower 7 Oct 1796 before J. R. Brown, J. N. C. Recorded 7 Nov 1796.

C, 899-900: 20 April 1796, John Edwards of Newberry County, planter, to George Latham and John Kelley Senr, both of same, a moiety of a tract of 500 acres granted to Enoch Anderson adj. lands of Benjamin Long, Joseph Towles, Thomas Spearman, and on Saluda River. John Edwards (mark), Wit: Samuel Kelly Senr, James Daugherty, Robert McClure. Proved in Newberry County by the oath of Samuel Kelley Senr 18 Oct 1796 before Fred Nance, J.P. Recorded 9 Nov 1796.

C, 901-902: 14 Sept 1796, Reuben Sims of Newberry County for £120 sterling to John Sanders of Union County and Nally Henderson of Newberry County, 200 acres on Tyger River and Broad River, adj. land of said Reuben Sims, David Sims, it being the land whereon the late Mathew Sims lived and purchased by said Reuben Sims for his said father but not released by reason of his the said Mathew's sudden death. Reuben Sims (Seal), Wit: John Stewart, Charles Sims, Nancy H. Brummit. Acknowledged in open court 18 Oct 1796. Recorded 9 Nov 1796.

C, 902-903: 4 Dec 1783, Mathew Hall of Ninety Six District, to son James Hall, tract of 10 acres adj. land of Mathew Hall, James Crawson, William Wadlington, Henry Anderson, being land which Mathew Hall purchased of Henry Anderson. Mathew Hall (X) (Seal), Wit: William Caldwell, Ant'y Elton. Proved in Newberry County by the oath of William Caldwell 25 Oct 1796 before David Ruff, J.P. Recorded 9 Nov 1796.

C, 904-905: 19 July 1796, John Perry of Newberry County for £24 to Moses Coates of same, 150 acres on waters of Indian Creek adj. John Goodwin, Richard Butts, Kincaid, David Boyd. John Perry (mark) (Seal), Elizabeth Perry (mark) (Seal), Wit: Marmiduke Coate, Saml Teage, Sarah Smith (X). Proved by the oath of Samuel Teague and affirmation of Marmaduke Coate and Sarah Smith 3 Nov 1796 before Fred Nance, J.P. Recorded 9 Nov 1796.

C, 905-906: Philimon Waters of Newberry County, planter, bound to Frederick Passinger of same, in the sum of £100, 25 Feb 1795, to make title to tract of land adj. Andrew Lee, Henry Bates, David Lindsey, Levi Manning, Passinger by the last day of May next. P. Waters (Seal), Wit: Philm Waters, Levi Manning. Proved by the oath of Philimon Waters 10 Nov 1796 before D. Clary, J.P. Recorded 1 Nov 1796.

C, 907-908: John Coate of Newberry County for s40 to Jacob Roberts Brown, esquire, of same, lot of one acre in the village of Newberry adj. Frederick Nance's lot, numbers 83, 84, 58, and 86. Jno Coate (Seal), Wit: Fred Nance, J.P., Levi Casey, J.N.C. Susanah Coate, wife of John Coate, relinquished dower 19 Oct 1796 before Levi Casey, J.N.C. Recorded 11 Nov 1796.

C, 909-910: Samuel Lindsey of Newberry County, for £65 to Michael McKie of Edgefield County, one half or moiety of several lotts, houses, barns, gardens, etc., numbers 27, 28, 29, and 30 occupied by said Lindsey and James Campbell, also one half of two lotts called Cobbs Lots, 24 Oct 1796. Saml

Lindsey (Seal), Wit: Wm Satterwhite, Thomas Chappel, William Mackie. Elizabeth Lindsey, wife of Samuel Lindsey, relinquished dower 25 Oct 1796 before Levi Casey, J.N.C. Proved by the oath of Wm Satterwhite 28 Oct 1796 before Fred Nance, J.P. Recorded 12 Nov 1796.

C, 911: James Shearer of Newberry County for £25 SC money to William Craig, merchant, my eldest negro girl about 10 years of age named Nan, 22 July 1796. James Sherer (Seal), Wit: Saml Lindsey, James Campbell. Proved by the oath of James Campbell 4 Nov 1796 before Fred Nance, J.P. Recorded 14 Nov 1796.

C, 912: Samuel Lindsey of Newberry County for £30 s4 SC money to William Craig, Esquire, 150 acres on Kings Creek, part of tract granted to Abel Anderson 29 April 1768, dated 21 July 1796. Saml Lindsey (Seal), Wit: Fred Nance, James Campbell. Recorded 14 Nov 1796.

C, 913-917: Lease and release. 30 Dec 1793 & 1 Jan 1794, John Tolleson of the settlement of Kings Creek, Newberry County, to Andrew Spence of same, for £60 sterling, 150 acres granted to Clement Gore 7 May 1787, recorded in Book SSSS, page 363, on Kings Creek between Broad and Saluda Rivers, part of 361 acre tract adj. John Goodwin, Thomas Morgan. John Tolleson (Seal), Wit: Richard Sloan, William Spence, Andrew Spence. Proved by the oath of Richard Sloan 29 July 1796 before Wm Craig, J.P. Recorded 14 Nov 1796.

C, 917: George Kromers Mark (viz) a Crop in Each Ear with a round hole in each Ear. Geo: Kromer. Recorded 28 Feb 1797.

C, 918: 15 Oct 1796, Eva Margarette Gray of Newberry County, widow, to Peter Gray, her son, for love and affection, 200 silver dollars, also all my stock of cattle and all of what I have of house furniture. Eva Marg. Gray (X) (Seal), Wit: Casper Piester, Wm. Houseal, G. Adam Piester (X). Proved 15 Oct 1796 by the oath of Casper Piester before Wm Houseal, J.P. Recorded 21 Nov 1796.

C, 919: 15 Oct 1796, Eva Margarette Gray of Newberry County, widow, to Casper Piester, her son, for love and affection, a negro girl named Molley, going or about 16 years of age. Eva Marg. Gray (X) (Seal), Wit: Peter Gray, Wm. Houseal, G. Adam Piester (X). Proved 15 Oct 1796 by the oath of Peter Gray before Wm Houseal, J.P. Recorded 21 Nov 1796.

C, 920-922: John Barrot of Newberry County, carpenter, for £80 to Moses Evans of same, planter, 100 acres conveyed from Peter Buffington to John Barrett 24 & 25 Feb 1793, recorded in Book B, page 386, part of tract granted to John Brooks 19 Sept 1758 adj. land of Benjamin Pearson, Kelly, Rosanah Russell. John Barrett (Seal), Rhoda Barrett (Seal), Wit: Moses Kelly, Samuel Miles, Joseph Evans. Proved by the oath of Joseph Evans 29 July 1796 before J. R. Brown, J.N.C. Rhoda Barrett, wife of John Barrett, relinquished dower 29 July 1796 before J. R. Brown, J.N.C. Recorded 21 Nov 1796.

C, 922-924: 14 Nov 1795, William Satterwhite, Esqr., Sheriff of Newberry County, to Daniel Clary, Esquire, whereas Philimon Waters, Esqr., was seized of 530 acres on waters of Bush River and whereas Joacim Bulow at a court held for Newberry County in the District of Ninety Six at February Term 1795, judgment was obtained in the sum of £13 s13 s1 to levy on the goods and chattles of said Waters, now sheriff sells tract of 537 acres adj. Philimon Waters, Jonathan Waits, Gen Huger, Reuben Morgan, for £21 sterling. Wm Satterwhite Shff (Seal), Wit: John Summers, Daniel Richardson, David Jay. Proved by the oath of Daniel Richardson 28 May 1796 before Fred Nance, J.P. Recorded 26 Nov 1796.

C, 925-927: 14 Nov 1795, William Satterwhite, Esqr., Sheriff of Newberry County, to Daniel Clary, Esquire, whereas Charles Goodwin indorsee of Mary Turner obtained judgment against Philimon Waters Senr in the sum of £20 d8 3/4 and by writ of fieri facias 12 March, sheriff sells two tracts of land, one in Edgefield County on waters of Big Saluda of 730 acres adj. lands of Richard Merchant, Elisha Boatner, John Hubs, and 450 acres on waters of Bush River adj. Joseph King, originally granted 16 July 1765 to William Turner deceased and descended by heirship to William Turner Senr who conveyed 30 Aug 1788, now sells for £23 to Daniel Clary. Wm Satterwhite Shff (Seal), Wit: Thomas Starks, Philimon B. Waters, Robt Royston. Proved by the oath of Philimon B. Waters 28 May 1796 before Fred Nance, J.P. Recorded 26 Nov 1796.

C, 928-929: 9 Nov 1796, George Latham of Newberry County to Thomas Brooks of same, for £200 sterling, 215 acres on Scotts Creek, waters of Saluda adj. Kelly, Rosanah Russell, John Coats, Benjamin Pearson, John Barrett, part of tract granted 19 Sept 1758 to John Brooks and conveyed by him to Peter Buffington, and them to said George Latham. George Latham (Seal), Wit: Wm. Satterwhite, Clements Horner. Proved 29 Nov 1796 by the oath of Wm Satterwhite before Fred Nance, J.P. Recorded 29 Nov 1796.

C, 930-931: 29 Nov 1796, George Latham of Newberry County, merchant, to Samuel Lindsey of same, for £23 sterling, 100 acres on a small branch of Kings Creek, part of land of Gabl Anderson. George Latham (Seal), Wit: Wm. Satterwhite, Geo Wells. Proved 30 Nov 1796 by the oath of Wm Satterwhite before Fred Nance, J.P. Recorded 30 Nov 1796.

C, 932-935: Lease and release. 1 & 2 Nov 1793, Henry Summer of Lexington County, SC, planter, to Martin Kinard of Newberry County, planter, for £25 sterling, 50 acres, part of 200 acres granted to Francis Huet 14 June 1753 and conveyed to said Henry Summer 1 & 2 June 1785 on a branch of Crims Creek. Henry Summer (Seal), Wit: John Wurts, G. Adam Hiett, Fred Jos Wallern. Proved in Newberry County by the oath of Revd. Fred Jos Wallern 3 June 1796 before Wm Houseal, J.P. Recorded 30 Nov 1796.

C, 936-937: 15 Feb 1794, Michael Lohner of Fairfield County, planter, to Martin Kinard of Newberry County, for £40 sterling, tract of 100 acres between Broad and Saluda Rivers adj. Conrad Shirer, Casper Bierley, Francis Hewett, John and Martin Kinard, by platt to said Michael Lohner 30 May 1763, recorded in Book XX, page 118. Michael Lohner (M) (Seal), Wit: Fred Jos Wallern, Wm. Houseal. Proved in Newberry County by the oath of Revd. Fred Jos Wallern 3 June 1796 before Wm Houseal, J.P. Recorded 30 Nov 1796.

C, 938-939: 10 Nov 1796, Isaac Davenport of Newberry County for $300 to James Davinport of state of SC, one negro man named Cago. Isaac Davinport (Seal), Wit: Joseph Davinport, William Plunkit. Proved 3 Dec 1796 by the oath of Jos Davinport before Wm Craig, J.P. Recorded 3 Dec 1796.

C, 940: 4 Nov 1796, Francis Davinport and Isaac Davinport of Newberry County for £50 to Joseph Davinport of state of SC, one negro boy named Mingo. Francis Davinport (Seal), Isaac Davinport (Seal), Wit: James Davinport, David Davinport. Proved 3 Dec 1796 by the oath of James Davinport before Wm Craig, J.P. Recorded 3 Dec 1796.

C, 941-943: 10 Oct 1788, William Murray Junr of Newberry County to William Wilson of same, for £10 sterling, 190 acres on Kings Creek, granted to William Murray, 3 April 1786, recorded in Book KKKK, page 202, adj. Joseph Hampton, John Johnston, Gabriel Anderson, William Wilson. W. Murray (Seal), Wit: Robt Powell, John Anderson, James Murray. Proved 10 Oct 1788 by the oath of Robt Powell before John Lindsey, J.P. Recorded 12 Dec 1796.

C, 944-945: 24 Sept 1796, William Langford of Newberry County for £45 sterling, 100 acres, part of 400 acres granted 2 Jan 1754 to Jacob Kelly on waters of Saluda and Buffelow Creek, adj. Shadrack Carter. Wm. Langford (Seal), Wit: James Calk, Asa Langford, Elias Banks. Proved by the oath of James Calk 15 Dec 1796 before Peter Julin, J.P. Recorded 17 Dec 1796.

C, 945-947: 22 Nov 1796, James Grainger, Chair maker, of Charleston, for £50 sterling, to William Craig, Esqr., of Newberry County, 300 acres on east side Saluda River, formerly in Berkley County, adj. land surveyed for Philimon Waters, originally surveyed for Ellenor Grainger 2 Feb 1773, and afterwards granted to William Nisbett 10 Feb 1775, conveyed to said James Grainger by Jane Nesbitt, widow and sole executor of William Nesbitt, 12 Nov 1783. James Grainger (Seal), Wit: B. T. Sloops, Joseph Johnson. Proved in Charleston District by the oath of Joseph Johnson 22 Nov 1796 before W. Cunnington, J.P. Recorded 17 Dec 1796.

C, 947-948: 14 Oct 1791, John Goodwin of Newberry County to Simon Reeder Junr of same, for £60 sterling, 200 acres on waters of Guilders Creek, adj. Elender Rilly, Clement Gore, Jacob Buzzard. John Goodwin (mark) (Seal), Wit: Abraham Goodwin (A), Richd Tear. Proved by the oath of Richard Tear 13 Feb 1795 before Edward Finch, J.P. Recorded 23 Dec 1796.

C, 949-950: 19 Feb 1795, Simon Reeder Junr of Newberry County to James Spence of same, for £50 sterling, 100 acres on waters of Guilders Creek adj. William Kilpatrick, Joseph Caldwell, Andrew Spencer. Simon Reeder, Lucynda Reeder (X), Wit: William Spence, Andrew Spence. Proved by the oath of Andrew Spence 23 Dec 1796 before Fred Nance, J.P. Recorded 23 Dec 1797 [sic].

C, 951-956: Lease and release. 16 Nov 1774, John Reid and Nancy his wife of Craven County, Ninety Six District, SC, taylor, to James Finlay of said province, for £50 currency, 50 acres, part of 200 acres granted to John Reid 1 Sept 1768 on south fork of Indian Creek, adj. Jacob Guilder, William Cannon, Mathew Guilder. John Reid (Seal), Nancy Reid (mark) (Seal), Wit: James Glassgow, William Tamrey, James Cannon. Proved by the oath of William Tinney 18 Aug 1784 before John Lindsey, J.P. Recorded 27 Dec 1796.

C, 957-961: Lease and release. 16 Dec 1776, Patrick Riley of Craven County, Ninety Six District, to John Steel of same place, for £200 SC money, 200 acres in the fork of Broad and Saluda Rivers adj. Tarrance Riley, granted to said Patrick Riley 31 Aug 1775. Patrick Riley (mark), Alese Riley (X) (Seal), Wit: Abel Anderson, John Caldwell, Robert Teer. Proved by the oath of John Caldwell [date not included] before John Lindsey, J.P. Recorded 31 Dec 1796.

C, 961-962: 9 Dec 1796, Richard Wrainek and Alexander Clarkson, merchants in the city of Charleston, executors of H. Philip Wisener deceased, to Peter Richardson, of Newberry County, for £52 s10, 150 acres by plat certified 28 June 1757, granted 22 Jan 1759, recorded in Book TT, page 175. Alex'r Clarkson (Seal), Richard Wrainek (Seal), Wit: George Smith, William Beard (X). Proved in Newberry County by the oath of George Smith 24 Dec 1796 before Fred Nance, J.P. Recorded 31 Dec 1796.

C, 963-964: 12 Feb 1796, Martin Livingston to Peter Richardson, both of Newberry County, for £15 sterling, 50 acres, part of 100 acres conveyed from John Livingston to Martin Livingston on waters of Cannons Creek, granted to Martin Timberman[?] 12 Feb 1755, recorded in Book PP, page 366. Martin Livingston (Seal), Wit: Jno B. Mitchell, Barnet Livingston. John May (X). Proved 24 Dec 17896 by the oath of Jno B. Mitchell before Fred Nance, J.P. Recorded 31 Dec 1796.

C, 965-969: Lease and release. 3 & 4 June 1784, John Valentine Lattiner of Ninety Six District, to David Boyd of same, planter, for £28 s11 d5 sterling, 200 acres on a branch of Guilders Creek adj. Jacob Hoofman, granted 2 Jan 1773 to said John Valentine Lattiner. John Valentine Lattiner (IL) (Seal), Mary Lattener (M) (Seal), Wit: William Hutchison, David Ruff, Barbara Ruff (B). Proved in Ninety Six District by the oath of William Hutchinson 4 June 1784 before George Ruff, J.P. Recorded 5 Jan 1797.

C, 970-972: 13 Oct 1796, James Lindsey Senr to George Powell, sadler, both of Newberry County, for £60 sterling, 580 acres on waters of Kings Creek, waters of Enoree, and also on waters of Bush River near John Coates' Road, John Wilson, Martin Halleback, Philimon Waters decd, Clement Davis decd, Widow Morris, granted to James Lindsey, recorded in Book O No 5, page 148. James Lindsey (Seal), Wit: Mary Pemberton (O), James Dobbins. Ruth Lindsey, wife of James Lindsey, relinquished dower 18 Oct 1796 before J. R. Brown, J.N.C. Proved by the oath of James Dobbins 4 Jan 1797 before Fred Nance, J.P. Recorded 30 Jan 1797.

C, 973-974: 5 Jan 1797, Alexander Bell and Robert Lithgow, exrs. of the will of Mathias Libecap deceased, for £50 sterling, 100 acres on Little River, a branch of Saluda adj. John Turner, and one Cozens. Alexr Bell (Seal), R. Lithgow (Seal), Wit: R. Evans Junr, Edm'd Spearman. Proved by the oath of Edmond Spearmon 6 Jan 1797 before Fred Nance, C.N.C. Recorded 30 Jan 1797.

C, 974-975: 10 Jan 1797, Barbara Weddinman of Newberry County, widow, for love, good will & affection to my son John Adam Stockman of same, planter, 50 acres, part of 100 acres on waters of Broad River granted to Henry Summer 2 Oct 1786 and transferred unto John Wheadinman decd 12 May 1795, recorded in Book C, page 331, then lawfully signed over 1 Jan 1797 to Barbara Wheadinman by John Kinard, admrs. for John Wheatinman decd. Barbara Wedinman (mark (Seal), Wit: Adam Lagrone (AL), Wm Houseal, Mary Lagrone (X). Proved 10 Jan 1797 by the oath of Adam Lagrone before Wm Houseal, J.P. Recorded 30 Jan 1797.

C, 976-977: 10 Jan 1797, Barbara Weddinman of Newberry County, widow, for love, good will & affection to my son John George Stockman of same, planter, 50 acres, part of 100 acres on waters of Broad River granted to Henry Summer 2 Oct 1786 and transferred unto John Wheadman decd 12 May 1795, recorded in Book C, page 331, then lawfully signed over 1 Jan 1797 to Barbara Wheadinman by John Kinard, admrs. for John Wheatinman decd. Barbara Wedinman (mark (Seal), Wit: Adam Lagrone (AL), Wm Houseal, Mary Lagrone (X). Proved 10 Jan 1797 by the oath of Adam Lagrone before Wm Houseal, J.P. Recorded 30 Jan 1797.

C, 978-982: Lease and release. 17 & 18 Dec 1792, Peter Willhelm of Newberry County to Charles Bridges of same, for £45 sterling, 72 acres on waters of Bush River granted 14 Oct 1774, recorded in Book GGG, page 74; 28 acres joining said tract; 100 acres adj. said two tracts, granted 25 May 1774. Peter Willhelm (X) (Seal), Charlotta Willhelm (X) (Seal), Wit: William Mills, John Dobbins, Alex'r Mills. Proved by the oath of Alex'r Mills 13 April 1793 before Elisha Ford, J.P. Recorded 31 Jan 1797.

C, 983-986: Lease and release. 1 May 1790, John Burney, planter, of Ninety Six District, planter, to David Glenn of same, for £90 sterling, 150 acres, part of 250 ares granted to John Burney 22 June 1767 on waters of Second Creek, adj. Fight Resinger, David Dunn. John Burney (Seal), Wit: Andrew Dunn,

Andrew Maxwell. Proved in Newberry County by the oath of Andrew Dunn before David Ruff, J.P., 5 Jan 1796. Recorded 4 Feb 1797.

C, 987: Mary Ann Smith, widow, of Newberry County, for good will and affection to my daughter Susanna Smith of same, a bed and furniture, one womans saddle, one spinning wheel and one loom, 25 Aug 1796. Mary Ann Smith (X), Wit: David Ruff, J.P., John Wiseman. Recorded 6 Feb 1797.

C, 988-989: 10 Dec 1789, John Tolbert of Ninety Six District to Robert Tolbert of same, for £5 sterling, 100 acres, part of 200 acres granted to Lydia Matox 8 March 1768, recorded in Book CCC, page 379, and said 100 acres was transferred unto William Richardson by Lydia Mattocks 28 March 1770, and then to John Tolbert 5 & 6 April 1774. John Torbet (Seal), Wit: James Penny, John Riley. Proved 15 Aug 1791 by the oath of James Penny before Geo Ruff, J.N.C. Recorded 6 Feb 1797.

C, 990-991: 22 Aug 1796, John Smith of Newberry County, planter, to Robert Smith of same, planter, for £100 sterling, 70 acres on a branch of Second Creek adj. Jno Smith, John Wair, George Neeley, Widow McLin[?], part of 150 acres granted to George Smith. John Smith (LS), Wit: David Ruff, J.P., John Wiseman, Nancy Taggart (X). Recorded 6 Feb 1797.

C, 992: South Carolina, Newberry County. David Watts of county aforesaid appoint my friend John Harmon of same lawful attorney, 28 Nov 1795. David Watts (Seal), Test: James Johnson. Proved by the oath of James Johnson 28 Nov 1795 before Thos W. Waters, J.P. Recorded 10 Feb 1797.

C, 993-995: 11 Sept 1792, William Jay Senr, planter, of Newberry County, to James Jay, planter, of same, for £23 SC money, 30 acres on north side Saluda River on Beaverdam, part of tract granted to William Jay and conveyed from him to William Morow and from him to David Pugh then to first mentioned Jay. William Jay (Seal), Wit: William Wright, Nathan Wright, Layton Jay. Proved by the oath of Layton Jay 16 Jan 1797 before Elisha Ford, J.P. Recorded 10 Feb 1797.

C, 996-997: 28 Oct 1796, Margaret Callegham of Laurens County to William Davis of Newberry County for £10 sterling, 198 acres in Newberry County on waters of Indian Creek, granted to William Davis 2 Oct 1786, recorded in Book MMMM, page 578, adj. William Davis Senr, Peter Brasilman, John Lindsey, Thomas Johnson. Margaret Callegham (mark) (Seal), Wit: Moses Lindsey, Sibbeller Lindsey, Jacob Frost. Proved 1 Feb 1797 by the oath of Moses Lindsey before P. Williams, J.P. Recorded 27 Feb 1797.

C, 998-999: 18 July 1795, Thomas Wadsworth and William Turpin, merchants, to Francis Higgins, planter, of Newberry County, for £15 s15 SC money, 50 acres on Saluda River granted to George Cox and relapsed by Wadsworth & Turpin granted to them __ Jan 1787. Thos Wadsworth (LS), William Turpin

(LS), Wit: Saml Word, James Boyes. Proved in Newberry County 25 July 1795 by the oath of Saml Word before Charles Griffin, J.P. Recorded 27 Feb 1797.

C, 999-1000: 4 April 1793, Robert Spence of Newberry County to Francis Higgins of same, for £50 sterling, 100 acres on north side of Big Saluda River adj. lands of James Cox, Thomas Wadsworth, Francis Higgins, granted 13 May 1763 to said Robert Spence as his Bounty. Robt Spence (R), Wit: Thos W. Waters, Jas. Strother. Recorded 27 Feb 1797.

C, 1001-1008: Lease and release. 1 Dec 1789, Henry Metzker to Francis Higgins for £130 sterling, three tracts of land in Ninety Six District on both sides Saluda River, one tract granted to Henry Metzker 16 Dec 1766; another of 100 acres on north side of said river adj. Henry Metzker, granted to John Gotleb Baltz 1 Sept 1768, the other of 50 acres on north side Saluda River. Henry Metzker (Seal), Wit: Thos W. Waters, John Adam Sumer. Proved 10 June 1790 by the oath of John Adam Sumer before George Ruff, J.P. Recorded 27 Feb 1797.

C, 1009-1010: Godfrey Adams and Frances Adams of Newberry County appoint our friend John Henderson of same, our lawful attorney to receive from William Waddleton Esqr and William Malone, exrs., of Edward Waddleton, late of said county, deceased, £100 sterling, 12 Jan 1797. Godfrey Adams (Seal), Frances Adams (X-her mark) (Seal), Wit: Wm. Calmes, Betsy Calmes, David Henderson. Proved 23 Feb 1797 by the oath of David Henderson before Fredk Nance, J.P. Recorded 28 Feb 1797.

C, 1011-1013: 2 Jan 1797, John Swettenburgh of Lexington County, yeoman, to William Hutchison of Newberry County, for £25 sterling, 100 acres in the fork between Broad and Saluda Rivers on a branch of Second Creek in Craven County now Newberry County adj. land surveyed for William Tyger, William Dochody, Michael Lightner, Christian Keeler, granted to Margaret Godfrey wife of John Godfrey 2 Feb 1773, recorded in Book NNN, page 538, conveyed by John Godfrey and Margaret his wife to John Swettenburgh. John Swittenburgh, Wit: John High, George Setzler, John Hutchison. Proved in Orangeburg District 4 Jan 1797 by the oath of George Setzler before John Adam Sumer, J.P. Recorded 28 Feb 1797.

C, 1013-1016: 13 Dec 1790, Aron Cates of Newberry County to William Finch of same, for £25, 37 acres on north side Second Creek, part of tract granted to Samuel Wilson 3 Aug 1762 and conveyed from Wilson to John Hampton and from said Hampton to Aron Cates. Aron Cates (Seal), Wit: John Hampton, John Malone, Thomas Bauskett. Acknowledged by Aron Cates 17 June 1793 before David Ruff, J.P. Recorded 28 Feb 1797.

C, 1016-1017: 1 April 1795, John Henry Ruff to Peter Weddenman, both of Newberry County, for s20, 5½ acres on Cannon Creek. John Henry Ruff (LS), Wit: David Ruff, J.P. Philip Cromer, Johannes Wideman [German signature]. Recorded 28 Feb 1797.

C, 1018-1019: 1 April 1794, John Adam Summer of Lexington County to Petre Wedenman of Newberry County, planter, for £54 sterling, 100 acres on waters of Cannons Creek, waters of Broad River, one half of 200 acres granted to George Gray 26 Sept 1772 on the north east part of the old Mill Tract, adj. George Gallman, Frederick Gray, John Buzzard, James Shepherd. John Adam Summer (Seal), Wit: Daniel Devault, Dav'd Ruff, J.P., John H. Ruff. Recorded 28 Feb 1797.

C, 1020-1021: Bartlett Brooks of Ninety Six District for £75 sterling to William Turpin, merchant of Charleston, tract on both sides of Mudlick Creek, a branch of Little River, waters of Saluda, 235½ acres, being three original surveys: one granted to Henry Duke recorded in Book CCC, page 288, 190 May 1768; tract granted to Henry Duke, 2 May 1771, recorded in Book EEE, page 300; tract of 35½ acres granted 7 Dec 1795, recorded in Book P. No. 5, page 510, _____ 1797. Bartlett Brooks (X) (Seal), Wit: James Young, James Boyd. Proved by the oath of James Young 25 Feb 1797 before William Neil, J.P. Recorded 28 Feb 1797.

C, 1022-1024: John Steel of Newberry County bound in the sum of £100 sterling, 27 Feb 1797, to John Riley of same, to abide by the verdict of Frederick Gray, Ephraim Cannon, James Beard, Micajah Harris, George Gray & Michael Dickert Senr, to be determined between the first Monday and Saturday in next March at David Ruff's. John Steel (Seal), Wit: David Ruff, Nathan Rice (A). Proved by the oath of Nathan Rice 17 March 1797 before Fred Nance, J.P.

We the arbitrators determine that John Steel shall hold the land agreeable to the lines, corners, and stations of his platt bought of Patrick Riley, calling for 200 acres and that John Steel shall have no further claim on said John Riley, 6 March 1797. Fred'k Gray, Ephraim Cannon, James Baird, Micajah Harris, George Gray, Ephraim Liles Senr. Recorded 27 March 1797.

C, 1025-1026: 1 Nov 1796, James Mayson of Glasgow in South Carolina, planter, to George Adams, planter, of state aforesaid, for £76 sterling, 300 acres known by the name of goodwood bottom adj. lands of said Adams, Maxfield's Neck in Newberry County. Jas Mayson (Seal), Wit: W. Mayson, Rich'd M. Owen. Proved 1 Nov 1796 by the oath of William Mayson before William Anderson, J.P. for Edgefield County. Recorded 17 March 1797.

C, 1026-1027: 25 July 1789, John Fletchall of Newberry County bound to William Garey of same, int he sum of £115 sterling, to make title by 25 July 1792 to tract where said Fletchall now lives on waters of Bush River. John Fletchall (Seal), Wit: Thomas Gary (mark, John Gary. Proved 3 May 1797 by the oath of Thomas Gary before John Speak, J. P. Recorded 27 March 1797.

C, 1028-1029: James Vardiman of Newberry County to Jonathan Pratt, mortgage of a sorrel horse, a waggon and hind gears first built by William Dawkins and sold to Christian Morgan,. for payment of $60, also two cows and calves, three good feather beds, etc., 13 Jan 1796. James Vardeman (Seal), Wit: Levi Johnson, Gideon Nelson. Proved by the oath of Gideon Nelson 8 Nov 1796 before Edward Finch, J. P. Recorded 17 March 1797.

C, 1029-1030: 30 May 1796, James Vardiman and Jean his wife of Newberry County to Jonathan Pratt of same, for £20 43 acres on waters of Heller Creek adj. Widow Collins, Thomas Resinger, Daniel Johnson. James Vardeman (Seal), Jean Vardeman (X) (Seal), Wit: Gideon Nelson, Zachariah Hogg. Proved by the oaths of both witnesses 8 Nov 1796 before Edward Finch, J. P. Recorded 17 March 1797.

C, 1031-1032: 9 Jan 1796, William Richards of Newberry County to Jonathan Pratt for £40, tracts adj. Bartholomew Johnson (now heirs of William Collins deceased), 35 acres, and on a line made between William Malone and his son William Malone Junr. William Richards (Seal), Wit: Gideon Nelson, William Satterfield, Wm Richards (mark). Proved by the oath of Gideon Nelson 24 Jan 1797 before Edward Finch, J. P. Recorded 17 March 1797.

C, 1033-1034: 20 Oct 1796, Nathaniel Davis of Union County for £40 to Elijah Lake, 100 acres in Newberry County adj. John Caldwell, John Maxedun, David Fargusson, Andrew Hunter, Nathaniel Davis. Nathaniel Davis (Seal), Elizabeth Davis (Seal), Wit: James Townsend, Robert Williams (X), John Lake (X). Proved 20 Dec 1796 in Newberry County by the oath of John Lake before Reuben Sims, J.P. Recorded 17 March 1797.

C, 1034-1037: Lease and release. 24 & 25 March 1795, Tobias Myers to Gassiway Rogers of Newberry County, for £100 sterling, 350 acres on Saluda River, granted to David McLearn 21 June 1765, recorded in Book C No. 7, page 398 conveyed by David McLearen to Tobias Myers, recorded in Book Z No. 5, page 44. Tobias Myers (Seal), Wit: Charles Wm Bulow, John J. Bulow, Lewis Grassman. Proved by the oath of Charles Wm Bulow 26 March 1795 before John Johnson, J.P. Recorded 18 March 1797.

C, 1037-1038: Edward Rutledge of Charleston, Esqr., for £30 to Jacob Gary of Ninety Six, 263 acres adj. Benjamin Neel, John and Thomas Gary, Leopard, dated 1 Dec 1796. E. Rutledge (Seal), Wit: John Hunter, John Dunlap. Proved in Newberry County by the oath of John Dunlap before Providence Williams, J.P. Recorded 18 March 1797.

C, 1038-1039: Edward Rutledge of Charleston, Esqr., for £63 s3 d6 to Thomas Davis, 226 acres adj. Davis, William Blackburn, Jesse Gary and Ann Gary, dated 2 Feb 1797. Ed. Rutledge (Seal), Wit: Benj. Smith, Dudley Bonds (mark). Proved 25 Feb 1797 in Newberry County by the oath of Dudley Bonds before Providence Williams, J.P. Recorded 18 March 1797.

C, 1040-1041: 30 Jan 1797, George Godfrey of Fairfield County, planter, for s20 to Sandford Cockriel of Newberry County, 200 acres granted to Benjamin Shullinor[?] in the fork of Broad and Saluda Rivers adj. Mathias Wicker, John

Heller, Mike Suber, Jacob Felker. George Godfrey (Seal), Wit: Samuel Wood, John Glymph. Proved in Newberry County by the oath of John Glymph 28 Feb 1797 before Fred Nance, J.P. Recorded 18 March 1797.

C, 1041-1042: Peggy Gains of Newberry County for £60 sterling to Joseph Caldwell of same, one negro wench named Mary, 30 years old, 9 May 1796. Peggy Gains (Seal), Wit: Samuel Cannon, Levi Johnson. Proved by the oath of Saml Cannon 27 Feb 1797 before David Ruff, J.P. Recorded 18 March 1797.

C, 1043: 21 Jan 1797, Joseph Davinport of Newberry County to Isaac Davinport of same, for £65 sterling, one negro boy named Mingo, 21 Jan 1797. Joseph Davenport (Seal), Wit: James Davinport, Benjamin Johnson. Proved by the oath of James Davinport 1 March 1797 before Danl Clary, J.P. Recorded 18 March 1797.

C, 1044-1045: 22 Feb 1797, William Day of Laurens County to Nathan Road of Newberry County for £30 sterling, 72½ acres on waters of Mudlick and Mill Creeks, part of tract granted to John Red 300 acres and conveyed to Richard Griffin and by Richard Griffin to William Day. Wm Day (Seal), Wit: Isaac Grant, John Day. Proved by the oath of Isaac Grant Sr. 2 Feb 1797 before J. R. Brown, J.N.C. Mary Day (X), wife of William Day, relinquished dower 22 Feb 1797 before J. R. Brown, J.N.C. Recorded 19 March 1797.

C, 1046-1047: 1 Aug 1794, George Eigleberger of Newberry County to Christian Eigleberger, planter, of same for £20 sterling, 100 acres in Berkley County on a small branch of Cannons Creek called Coiners branch, adj. land of Frederick Aman, granted to Francis Duford 9 Feb 1770 on Bounty transferred to said George Eigleberger 1 & 2 April 1770, recorded in Book EEE, page 336. George Eigleberger (Seal), Maria Ursula Eigleberger (X) (Seal), Wit: Wm Houseal, J.P., John Eigleberger, Jacob Counts. Recorded 17 April 1797.

C, 1048: South Carolina, Ninety Six District. William Tennant, Sheriff of District aforesaid by virtue of writ of fieri facias from the court of common pleas at the suit of Abraham Markley against Alexander Bookter, sheriff sells at Cambridge to Benedict Myer for £285, six negroes: Sam and his wife Henny, and their four children Anny, Darby, Abruster & Frank, 31 Oct 1796. Wm Tennant Shff 96 Ds. (Seal), Wit: William Burton, John Eigleberger. Recorded 17 April 1797.

C, 1049-1051: 1 Aug 1794, George Eigleberger of Newberry County to Christian Eigleberger, planter, of same for £25 sterling, 100 acres in Craven County on waters of Cannons Creek, adj. land of Christopher Lee, Samuel Cannon, granted to said Christian Eigleberger alias Catharine Sheely which was lawful wife to the above George Eigleberger 14 June 1773. George Eigleberger (Seal), Ursula Eigleberger (X) (Seal), Wit: John Eigleberger,

Adam Lagrone (AL), Wm Houseal, J.P. Proved by the oath of John Eigleberger 6 Feb 1797 before William Houseal, J.P. Recorded 17 April 1797.

C, 1051-1052: South Carolina, Ninety Six District. William Tennant, Sheriff of District aforesaid by virtue of writ of fieri facias from the court of common pleas at the suit of Abraham Markley against Alexander Bookter, sheriff sells at Cambridge to John Eigleberger for £167, three negroes: Champ and his wife Sally, and Chatty, 31 Oct 1796. Wm Tennant Shff 96 Ds. (Seal), Wit: William Burton Senr, Benedick Mayer. Proved in Newberry County by the oath of Benedick Mayer 1 Nov 1796 before William Houseal, J.P. Recorded 18 April 1797.

C, 1053-1055: 19 March 1796, Thomas Harlock of St. Bartholomews Parish, Charleston District, carpenter, for £70 sterling to John Lowe of Lexington County, planter, tract in Newberry County on Second Creek, waters of Broad River, granted to Maria Briggette Hardlockin who was my grandmother on the 8 march 1755 to whom I am now heir at law at the several affidavits of Jacob Zahler of Beaufort District and Daniel Strobels of Charleston, 250 acres bounded on land granted to Christian Collar and land granted to Adam George Keller, Michael Kromer. Thomas Harlock (Seal), Wit: Jacob Zahler Junr, Barkley Fergusson. Margaret Harlock, wife of Thomas Harlock, relinquished dower in Prince Williams Parish, Beaufort District, 19 March 1796 before John Lightwood. Proved in Beaufort District by the oath of Jacob Zahler Junr before John Lightwood. Recorded 18 April 1797.

C, 1055-1056: South Carolina, District of Beaufort. Affidavit of Jacob Zahler the eldest before John Lightwood, Justice of the Quorum, that Brigetta Hardlocken (widow) came into the said state with whom he was acquainted among the Pallentines and took up on a bounty warrant 250 acres on Second Creek and she died and left a son Jasper who changed his name of Harlocken to Harlock and by which name his descendants now go, and the said Jasper Harlock was married to Mary Epp by whom he has two sons now alive, Thomas the eldest and Daniel, that Jasper Harlock died in 1785 and left his widow Mary and her two sons Thomas and Daniel, 12 Oct 1795. Jacob Zahler.

State of South Carolina. Affidavit of Captain Daniel Strobel, 15 March 1796, before John Sanford Dart, Justice of the Quorum, that he was well acquainted with Brigetta Hardlocken, she having been a passenger with him in a ship from Germany to this State, that some time after her arrival here her husband died and left her a widow with a son named Jasper Harlocken alias Harlock who is since deceased and left a son named Thomas whose father Jasper was an overseer to the Deponant in the year 1779, that Bridgitta Harlocken after the decease of her husband did obtain from the Government and Council a Grant for her bounty lands. Daniel Strawbell. Recorded 18 April 1797.

C, 1057: Elisabeth Turner of Newberry County, widow, for love, good will and affection to my granddaughter Mika Abney, of Edgefield County, one negro girl named Luce, of a yellow complexion or mullatto colour, 15 Feb 1797.

Elisabeth Turner (Seal), Wit: Ben: Long, Francis Higgins. Proved in Newberry County by the oath of Benjamin Long 28 Feb 1797 before Danl Clary, J.P. Recorded 18 April 1797.

C, 1058-1059: Jacob Gary and Sarah his wife of Newberry County, 96 District, for £5 sterling, to William Cole of same, 39 acres on waters of indian Creek on Long Branch, part of 200 acres granted to Henry Middleton and covneyed by Edw'd Rutledge to Jacob Gary, adj. John Leopard, William Cole, Benjamin Neal, dated 7 Feb 1797. Jacob Gary (Seal), Sarah Gary (X) (Seal), Wit: Isaac Taylor, Wm James Wilson. Proved by the oath of Isaac Taylor before Prov. Williams, J.P. Recorded 19 April 1797.

C, 1060-1061: 3 Oct 1796, William Tennant, Sheriff of Ninety Six District by virtue of writ of fieri facias from the court of common pleas at the suit of James McNees and John Boyd against the estate of James Williams deceased, sheriff sells at Cambridge to Washington Williams for £6, 100 acres on waters of Little River called Carson Creek, adj. William Caldwell, William Johnson, James Griffin, James Liffant. Wm Tennant Shff 96 Ds. (Seal), Wit: Daniel Mitchell, Thomas Burnside. Proved in Laurens County by the oath of Thos Burnside 11 Feb 1797 before Charles Saxon, J.P. Recorded 24 April 1797.

C, 1062-1063: 14 March 1797, John Coate of Newberry County, planter, to William Turpin, merchant of Charleston, for five shillings, two lotts each being ¼ acre, at the court houseof said county adj. lotts of WIlliam Satterwhite Esqr., and the publick ground, numbers 31 and 32. J. Coate (Seal), Suanna Coate (Seal), Wit: Wm. Satterwhite, Henry Coate. Proved in Newberry County 16 March 1797 by the oath of Wm Satterwhite before Fred Nance. Recorded 24 April 1797.

C, 1064: South Carolina, Ninety Six District. Gibeon Jones of district aforesaid sells to William Burton of same place, one negro girl named Milley about seven years old. Gibeon Jones (C) (Seal), Wit: George Goggans, Ben Wod (X). Proved in Newberry County by the oath of George Goggans 15 March 1797 before Fred Nance, J.P. Recorded 24 April 1797.

C, 1065-1067: 3 Aug 1796, Jonathan Reeder & Rebekah his wife of Neberry County to Daniel Williams Senr of same, for £50 sterling, 100 acres on a branch of Bush River called the Beaverdam, adj. land of Wlliam Mosaih, Winchester, recorded in Grant book LL, pgae 268, in the Auditor office in Book L, page 268, 17 Aug 1773, granted to William Simpson. Jonathan Reeder (seal), Rebekah Reeder (Seal), Wit: Daniel Williams Junr, William Belton. Proved 10 Aug 1796 by the oath of Daniel Williams before PRov. Williams, J. P. Recorded 24 April 1797.

C, 1067-1069: 29 March 1796, Margaret Clarondon formerly Margaret Mick, now of the City of Savannah, Georgia, widow, to Peter Stuckman, for £15 sterling, 100 acres run for said Margaret Clarendon 12 Dec 1752 on the head of a small branch of Crims Creek. Marget C (Seal), Wit: Huyler, John Long,

Peter Dickert. Proved in Newberry County by the oath of Peter Dickert 16 April 1796 before David Ruff, J.P. Recorded 24 April 1797.

C, 1069-1074: Lease and release. 2 & 3 Nov 1792, Abrahart Sweetenburgh and Anna Catharine his wife of Orangeburgh District, Lexington County, SC, to Peter Stuckman of Newberry County, Ninety Six District, for £30 sterling, 86 acres on Crims Creek adj. land of Stockman and Folk, granted 5 June 1786 to Abrahart Sweetenburgh, recorded in Book KKKK, page 77. Abrahart Sweetenburg (Seal), Anne Catharine Sweetenburgh (X) (Seal), Wit: Thomas Lane, John Folk, Jacob Folk. Proved in Lexington County by the oath of Thos Lane 3 Nov 1792 before John Adam Summer, J.P. Recorded 25 April 1797.

C, 1074-1077: 6 Oct 1796, Samuel Saxon, Sheriff of 96 District, to John Satterwhite of Newberry County, for £21 sterling, 150 acres on Beaverdam Creek, late the property of William Turner deceased, said William Turner was indebted to John Satterwhite in the sum of £75 sterling by bond, and at the court of common pleas at Cambridge against the estate of said William Turner recovered judgment, 8 April 1794. S. Saxon, Shff 96 Ds. (Seal), Wit: Jas Wardlaw, John Trotter. South Carolina, Ninety Six District: Mary Davenport, late widow of William Turner, relinquished dower 3 Feb 1797 before R. Brown, J. H. C. Mary Davenport (mark), Francis Davinport. Recorded 4 May 1797.

C, 1078-1079: Delilah Chapman of Pendleton County, appoints J. W. Grissam of same, lawful attorney to recover or receive of from and in the county of Newberry anything due me, 14 Jan 1797. Delilah Chapman (mark), Wit: John Duglass, Lydia Duglass (X). Proved in Pendleton County by the oaths of both witnesses 14 Jan 1797 before William Millwee, J.P. Recorded 4 May 1797.

C, 1079-1081: 21 Jan 1797, John W. Grissam and Mary his wife, John Douglass and Lydia his wife, attorney for Delila Chapman, all heirs at law and sole Representatives of the estate of William Chapman deceased of Pendleton County, to Joshua Griffin of Newberry County, 100 acres on waters of Cannons Creek, granted to Wm Chapman deceased, adj. land of Stone. Jno W. Grissam (Seal), Mary Grissam (O) (Seal), John Doughlass (seal), Lydia Douglas (Seal), Delilah Chapman (Seal), Wit: Joshua Teague, James Teague. Proved in Newberry County by the oath of Joshua Teague before Providence Williams, J.P. Recorded 4 May 1797.

C, 1081: 12 Sept 1796, James Campbell of Newberry County for 20 guineas to Frederick Nance of same place, one negro man named Joe about 26 years of age. Jas Campbell (Seal), Wit: Wm Craig, J.P. Recorded 4 May 1797.

C, 1082: Daniel Reagan of Newberry County for £14 s1 sterling, to Thomas W. Furnass of same, two horses, three cows and calves, five sheep, three feather beds and furniture, 6 Sept 1796. Danl Reagan (Seal), Wit: Benjamin Pearson, Samuel Pearson, Joseph Reagan. Proved by the affirmation of

Benjamin Pearson 27 March 1797 before Fred Nance, J.P. Recorded 4 May 1797.

C, 1083-1084: 26 Dec 1795, John Smyley and Margarett his wife of Orangeburgh District to Isaac Luster of Newberry County, for £10 sterling, tract on Big Creek of Saluda River, 100 acres granted to Caldwell, adj. Caldwell. John Smyley (Seal), Margaret Smyley (Seal), Wit: Nathan Tate, John Kinard, Ephraim Cannon. Proved in Newberry County by the oath of John Kinard 23 April 1796 before David Ruff, J.P. Recorded 4 May 1797.

C, 1085-1087: 11 Aug 1796, William Ellemon of Newberry County to Joseph Evans, farmer, of same, for £88 SC money, 148 acres, part of two tracts, one granted to Thomas Dodd of 150 acres 13 July 1770, the other granted to Enos Elleman 31 Aug 1775, 131½ acres, bequeathed by the will of said Enos Ellemon to his children and by partition of said tracts, 148 to the said William Elleman. William Ellemon (Seal), Jean Ellemon (X) (Seal), Wit: Benjamin Pearson, Moses Kelly, Benjamin Weeks (X). Jean Ellemon, wife of William Elleman, relinquished dower 2 March 1797 before J. R. Brown, J.N.C. Proved by the oath of Moses Kelly before Providence Williams, J.P. Recorded 5 May 1797.

C, 1088: William Hunter of Laurens County for £40 sterling to Joseph Caldwell of Newberry County, one negro woman slave named Jude about 33 years of age, yellow complexion with one of her forefingers cut off, 4 May 1797. William Hunter (Seal), Wit: Moses Lindsey, John McMorris. Proved by the oath of Jno McMorris 5 May 1797 before Jno Speak, J.P. Recorded 6 May 1797.

C, 1089-1090: South Carolina, Abbeville County. James Cummins of county aforesaid for £70 sterling to Thomas Cummins of Laurens County, one gray mare about 3 years old, one horse, one cow and calf, 100 bushels of corn, two feather beds and all household furniture, 27 March 1797. James Cummins (Seal), Wit: Matt. Wilson, John Cummins. Proved in Newberry County by the oath of John Cummins 1 April 1797 before J. R. Brown, J.N.C. Recorded 6 May 1797.

C, 1090-1091: 2 Nov 1796, Elizabeth Lofton, wife of John Lofton, of the settlement of Indian Creek in Newberry County to Thomas Barlow, her grandson, son of Thomas Barlow and Rachel his wife, one feather bed and furniture, six delf plates, one small pot and hooks, one large pine chest, two chairs and six pewter spoons, one large water pail, to be left in the care of Rachael his mother. Elizabeth Lofton (mark) (Seal), Wit: James Lindsey Senr, Moses Lindsey. Proved 24 Dec 1796 by the oath of Jas Lindsey before John Speak, J.P. Recorded 8 May 1797.

C, 1092-1093: 16 May 1797, William Hall, eldest son of William and Hannah Hall late of Frederick County, Virginia, for natural love and affection to William Hall, my eldest son, lawfully begotten on the body of my then wife

Elizabeth Hall deceased, said William Hall now resident of Berkley County, Virginia, all my right and title to the estate and plantation lately occupied by my brother Joseph Hall deceased in Berkley County, Virginia, on a creek formerly called Howards Mouth, waters of Shannando River. William Hall Senr (Seal), Wit: Wm Satterwhite, Henry Coate, John Edwards. Proved in Newberry County 16 May 1797 by the oath of John Edwards before J. R. Brown, J.N.C. Recorded 18 May 1797.

C, 1094-1095: South Carolina, Newberry County, William Hall of state and county aforesaid, late of Frederick County, Virginia, eldest son of William Hall deceased, appoint my beloved son William Hall of Berkley County, Virginia, my attorney, to transact business on the estate of my brother Joseph Hall deceased. 16 May 1797. William Hall Senr (Seal), Wit: Wm Satterwhite, Henry Coate, John Edwards. Proved in Newberry County 16 May 1797 by the oath of John Edwards before J. R. Brown, J.N.C. Recorded 18 May 1797.

C, 1096-1099: South Carolina, Laurens County. 1 Oct 1792, Samuel Saxon, Sheriff of Ninety Six District, to Henry Wilson of aforesaid place, for £41 sterling, for £98 s d10, 200 acres and 150 acres in Newberry County, by writ of fieri facias from the court of common pleas, suit of Joachim Bulow against Richard Strawther, tract whereon said Strawther now lives including his spring, plantation, dwelling house and other out houses on Broad River, adj. Mr. Kaller, Ulrigh Eaney, Jacob Oxner, granted to Jacob Felker Junr and from him conveyed to Richard Strawther. S. Saxon, Shff 96 Ds. (Seal), Wit: Mathew Ramsay, Jno Trotter. Proved in Abbeville County by the oath of Mathew Ramsey 3 Aug 1795 before Jno Trotter, J.P. "I do hereby assign over all my right title claim or interest of the within mention tracts of land unto the representatives of Richard Strawther deceased" 24 April 1797. H. Wilson. Wit: G. Glover, Thomas Butler. Proved in Abbeville County by the oath of Benjamin Glover 24 April 1797 before Wm Kinley, J. P. Recorded 24 May 1797.

C, 1099-1100: Benjamin Atkins of Newberry County for £150 to Isaac Jenkins of same, 190 acres on waters of Bush River called Scotts branch, granted to said Benjamin Atkins 20 Aug 1767, 8 Feb 1797. Benj'a Atkins (mark) (Seal), Wit: Fred Nance, J.P., Joseph Chapman. Sarah Atkins renounced her dower in Newberry County, February Term 1797 before James Mayson, J. N. C. Recorded 26 May 1797.

[There is no page numbered 1101.]

C, 1102-1103: Isaac Jenkins of Newberry County for £30 sterling to David Jenkins of same, 74 acres on waters of Palmeter branch and Bush River, adj. Martha Coppock, part of tract granted to Samuel Dunkin 31 Aug 1774, dated 15 May 1797. Isaac Jenkins (Seal), Wit: Edw'd Benbow, Thomas Atkins, Fred Nance, J.P. Rebecca Jenkins (mark), wife of Isaac Jenkins, relinquished dower 15 May 1797 before J. R. Brown, J.N.C. Recorded 26 May 1797.

C, 1104: Elizabeth Turner of Newberry County for love to my granddaughter Polly Long, one negro girl named Henrietta about three years old, 25 March 1797. Elizabeth Turner (Seal), Wit: Thomas W. Waters, Francis Higgins. Proved by the oath of Francis higgins 15 May 1797 before J. R. Brown, J.N.C. Recorded 26 May 1797.

C, 1105-1106: Enoch Pearson of Newberry County to Samuel Pearson of same, for £40 sterling, 100 acres, half of 200 acres on waters of Bush River, Scotch Creek, granted to Benjamin Pearson 13 Aug 1771, adj. land of Hugh Creighton, Robert Bull, John Brooks, dated 18 Feb 1797. Enoch Pearson (Seal), Wit: Samuel Russell, Jno Pearson. Hannah Pearson (mark), wife of Enoch Pearson, relinquished dower 16 May 1797 before J. R. Brown, J.N.C. Proved by the oath of Samuel Russell 16 May 1797 before Fred Nance, J.P. Recorded 29 May 1797.

C, 1107-1108: Samuel Pearson of Newberry County to Abel Pearson of same, for £30 sterling, 100 acres, half of 200 acres granted to Thomas Brooks and from him conveyed to Enoch and Margaret Pearson, exrs. of Benjamin Pearson deceased, on Beaver dam, adj. Caleb Gilbert, James Johnson, dated 18 Feb 1797. Samuel Pearson (Seal), Wit: Samuel Russell, John Pearson. Joseph Pearson. Abbigal Pearson (mark), wife of Samuel Pearson, relinquished dower 16 May 1797 before J. R. Brown, J.N.C. Proved by the oath of Samuel Russell 16 May 1797 before Fred Nance, J.P. Recorded 29 May 1797.

C, 1109-1111: 24 Aug 1796, John Satterwhite Junr of Newberry County to Daniel McKie of same, for £25 sterling, 200 acres on waters of Mudlick Creek adj. Bartlett Satterwhite, David Davenport, Daniel McKie and Bartlett Satterwhite Junr, and is part of two tracts, one of 600 acres granted to William Thompson 2 Aug 1768 and conveyed to John Satterwhite Senr 7 May 1769, the other of 500 acres granted to John Satterwhite Senr. John Satterwhite Junr (Seal), Wit: Drury Satterwhite, J. R. Brown, J.N.C. Susannah Satterwhite, wife of John Satterwhite Junr, relinquished dower 24 Aug 1796 before Jacob Roberts Brown, J.N.C. Plat included certified 3 Feb 1795 by Wm Caldwell, D. S. Recorded 29 May 1797.

C, 1111-1114: 25 Feb 1793, James White of Laurens County, planter, to John Gary of Newberry County, for £38 sterling, 185 acres on south side Enoree granted to James Wilson decd 1 Sept 1768, recorded in Book DDD, page 467. James White (Seal), Jane White (O) (Seal), Wit: Thomas Gary, Benjamin Ozburnd. Proved in Newberry County by the oath of Thomas Gary 14 May 1797 before Providence Williams, J.P. Recorded 29 May 1797.

C, 1115-1116: South Carolina, Newberry County. Thomas Butler mortgages to Thomas W. Waters, a negro boy named Jack 14 years of age, in consideration of his being my security to Capt. Frederick Gray for a debt pass security for with James johnston to the estate of Strawther to Gerrard Gerald exor or admr for £36 and costs of suit. Thomas Butler (Seal), Wit: William Julien.

Proved by the oath of William Julien 9 June 1797 before Fred Nance, J.P. Recorded 9 June 1797.

C, 1117-1119: William Pearson of Newberry County for £38 s10, 116 acres adj. William Hilburn, part of 350 acres granted to Michael Dormer and from him conveyed to Philimon Waters then to James Donnavan and them to Samuel Pearson then by deed of gift to his son William Pearson, dated 20 April 1797. Wm Pearson (seal), Wit: P. W. Waters, William Hilburn, Jno Summers. Anna Pearson (mark), wife of William Pearson, relinquished dower 17 May 1797 before J. R. Brown, J.N.C. Proved by the oath of William Hilburn 9 May 1797 before Fred Nance, J.P. Recorded 9 June 1797.

C, 1120-1122: William Pearson of Newberry County for £35 sterling, 142 acres adj. William Hilburn, Peter Hawkins, part of 350 acres granted to Michael Dormer and from him conveyed to Philimon Waters then to James Donnavan and them to Samuel Pearson then by deed of gift to his son William Pearson, dated 20 April 1797. Wm Pearson (seal), Wit: P. W. Waters, William Hilburn, Jno Summers. Anna Pearson (mark), wife of William Pearson, relinquished dower 17 May 1797 before J. R. Brown, J.N.C. Proved by the oath of William Hilburn 9 May 1797 before Fred Nance, J.P. Recorded 9 June 1797.

C, 1122-1124: 19 April 1797, Lewis Blalock Senr of Newberry County for £60 sterling, planter, to John McMorris of same, one negro man slave named Lond about 40 years of age, one woman named Leah about 33 years of age, one negro boy named Harry about 2½ years of age, also a sorrel horse not branded. Lewis Blalock (Seal), Wit: Saml Park, Donald McDonald. Proved 5 May 1797 by the oath of Saml Park before John Speak, J.P. Recorded 9 June 1797.

C, 1124-1126: 16 March 1797, Charles Crow of Newberry County to Richard Leavell of same, for £8 s5 sterling, 16½ acres, part of tract of 150 acres granted to said Charles Crow on waters of Bush River. Charles Crow (mark) (Seal), Wit: Mary Leavell (X), W. Belton. Proved by the oath of William Belton 16 March 1797 before Providence Williams, J.P. Recorded 9 June 1797.

C, 1127-1130: 1 Nov 1796, William McMorries of Fairfield County, Camden District, to John Leavell and John Abernathy both of Ninety Six District, Newberry County, for £80 sterling, 250 acres on north side of Bush River, part of tract granted to Hugh Marshall 15 Oct 1784, conveyed by Hugh Marshall and wife Mary to William McMorries 16 & 17 May 1787. Wm McMorris (Seal), Wit: James Lindsey Senr, Alexander Turner, Charles Crow. Proved in Newberry County by the oath of Alexander Turner 1 March 1797 before Charles Griffin, J.P. Recorded 10 June 1797.

C, 1030-1034: Lease and release. 17 Aug 1790, George Arnold of Newberry County to Nathan Wright of same, for £10 sterling, 70 acres on waters of Saluda, on the north said,e part of 400 acres granted to William Stuart 12 Jan 1769 and conveyed to George Arnold 20 Sept 1777. George Arnold (Seal),

Wit: Charles Patty, Joseph Reagan. Proved 22 May 1797 by the oath of Joseph Reagan before Elisha Ford, J.P. Recorded 20 June 1797.

C, 1035-1039: Lease and release. 17 & 18 Sept 1792, Charles Patty, planter, of Newberry County to Nathan Wright of same, for £10 SC money, 88 acres on waters of Saluda River on the north side, part of tract granted to James O'Harror 2 May 1785. Chas Patty (Seal), Mary Patty (Seal), Wit: Wm. Wright, John Abernathy, Robert Kelly. Proved by the oath of Robert Kelly 26 Nov 1795 before Danl Clary, J.P. Recorded 10 June 1797.

C, 1140-1141: 7 Jan 1797, Thomas Gains of Newberry County for £70 sterling, two negroes: one woman named Nann and her son Pompey. Thos Gains (Seal), Wit; Saml Cannon, Sarah Cannon. Proved by the oath of Saml Cannon 17 April 1797 before David Ruff, J.P.

C, 1141-1142: 10 Nov 1796, Robert Rutherford to James Kelly, both of Newberry County, for £8 sterling, 166 acres on Foster Creek, a branch of Enoree, adj. John Means, Benjamin Hampton, Thomas Leher, James Blayer, James Vardeman. Robt Rutherford (Seal), Wit: Stephen Kelly, Young John Harrington, Rich'd Darby (R). Proved by the oath of Stephen Kelly 10 Feb 17[97] before Edwd Finch, J.P. Recorded 12 June 1797.

C, 1142-1143: For £8 sterling paid by Richard Darby to John Kelly, 500 acres on Dry Creek a branch of Enoree River adj. Charles Littleton, Joel Chandler, Mary Maband[?], 13 Feb 1797. John Kelly (X) (Seal), Wit: Stephen Kelly, James Kelly, Elizabeth Smith (X). Proved by the oath of Stephen Kelly 8 June 1797 before Edw'd Finch, J.P. Recorded 12 June 1797.

C, 1144-1146: Martha and David Martin, exrs. of the will of David Martin deceased, to William Summers, for £65 s5 sterling, 150 acres, half part of 300 acres granted to Henry Bradshaw 9 Jan 1755 and conveyed by James Bradshaw to David Martin deceased, on north side Saluda River, recorded in Book ___, page 276. Martha Martin (X) (Seal), David Martin (X) (Seal), Wit: Elijah Worthington, John Black, Isaac Toland (X). Proved by the oath of Elijah Worthington 28 Jan 1797 before Danl Clary, J.P. Recorded 12 June 1797.

END OF BOOK C

D2, 1-3: Francis Higgins of Newberry County stands indebted for $214.25 to Mercer Babb of same place, by note, payable 20 Dec 1797, with interest at 7%, mortgage of 100 acres on north side Saluda River adj. Henry Metzgon [sic, for Metzger], granted to John G. Baltz 1 Sept 1768, and another tract whereon the said Francis Higgins now lives, also called the Ferry Tract, and the original debt between the said Francis Higgins and said Mercer Babb arose by virtue of an indorsement on a note of hand given from James D. Cole and William Malone of the State of Georgia made payable to the said Francis Higgins for $214, for which note the said Higgins has given this present mortgage, 3 June 1797. Francis Higgins (Seal), Wit: Fred Nance, Wm Irby. Proved in Newberry County by the oath of William Irby 3 June 1797 before Fred Nance, J.P. Recorded 12 June 1797.

D2, 4-5: 12 Jan 1796, Joseph Nichols of Newberry County to John Dennis of same, for £50, 100 acres on a small branch of Big Creek, part of 200 acres granted to Reason Reagan 31 Aug 1794, part of this 200 acres was sold by Joseph Nichols to Ellis Pugh, and part to Robert Yeldon. Joseph Nichols (mark) (Seal), Wit: William Spencer, William Dennis. Proved by the oath of Wm Dennis (X) 16 June 1797 before Fred Nance, J.P. Recorded 16 June 1797.

D2, 5-11: Lease and release. 8 Jan 1773, Thomas Shaw and wife Sarah of Craven County, SC, to George McKinny of same, for £250 SC money, 150 acres in Craven County adj. William Hilburn, Nelson Dunkin, part of tract granted to said Thomas Shaw 10 Sept 1765, 100 acres of which is laid off to said Nelson Dunkin. Thomas Shaw (Seal), Sarah Shaw (Seal), Wit: Wm Mills (M), Wm. Hilbirn, Richard Holeman. Proved in Ninety Six District by the oath of William Hilburn 28 Aug 1773 before Michael Dickert, J.P. Recorded 16 June 1797.

D2, 12-17: Lease and release. 21 & 22 Jan 1779, William Hilburn and wife Jane of Ninety Six District, farmer, to George McKinney of same, for £200 SC money, 100 acres on waters of Bush River adj. Mathias Elmore, Thomas Shaw, granted 3 Sept 1774 to said William Hilburn. William Hilburn (mark) (Seal), Jane Hilburn (mark) (Seal), Wit: William Hilburn, John Ellemon, Abner Ellemon. Proved in Newberry County by the statement of John Elleman 30 May 1797 before Fred Nance, J.P. Recorded 16 June 1797.

D2, 17-22: Lease and release. 30 & 31 Oct 1786, Mercer Babb and Benjamin Heaton, both of Ninety Six District, lawful executors of the will of William Weeks deceased) to Jonathan Gilbert of same, for ten shillings, 150 acres on waters of Bush Creek, part of tract of 350 acres granted to Joseph Ruchman 18 May 1771 adj. James Cheek, Joshua Gilbert, one Dunkin, conveyed by said Joseph Ruchman to William Weeks 17 & 18 June 1771. Mercer Babb (Seal), Benj'a Heaton (Seal), Wit: Abner Ellemon, Timothy Thomas, Catharine Ellemon (C). Proved 24 March 1792 by the statement of Timothy Thomas before Elisha Ford, J.P. Recorded 17 June 1797.

D2, 23-24: Benjamin King, one of the legatees of Benjamin King decd, formerly of Cambridge, SC, but now of Charleston, bound to Elizabeth Swift and James Robert Mayson, as admrs. of William Swift decd, in the sum of £500 sterling, to abide by the final decision of William Anderson, Oswell Eve, James Caldwell and Julius Nichols Junr, or any three of them, concerning cause of actions, reckoning sums of money, etc., 29 May 1797. Benjamin King (LS), Wit: James Forrest Proved in Newberry County by the oath of James Forrest 28 June 1797 before James Mayson, J.N.C. Recorded 30 June 1797.

D2, 25-26: William Anderson, Oswell Eve, James Caldwell and Julius Nichols Junr-- whereas Benjamin King by his last will appointed William Moore and William Swift exors and guardian to his two sons Benjamin King and John King, and said William Moore and William Swift are since deceased and the said Benjamin King come of age and desirous of receiving his portion of the state, the arbiters fin a balance of £59 sterling in favor of the estate of Benjamin King which we do award to be paid by Elizabeth Swift and James R. Mayson on or before 1 January next, and do deliver up all the estate of said Benjamin King deceased and papers, etc., dated 1 June 1797. W. Anderson (Seal), Oswell Eve (Seal), James Caldwell (Seal), Julius Nichols (Seal). Proved by the oath of James Robt Mayson 28 June 1797 before James Mayson, J.N.C. Recorded 30 June 1797.

D2, 27-31: Lease and release. 30 & 31 Oct 1786, Enos Ellemon and wife Catharine of Ninety Six District to Jonathan Gilbert of same, for ten shillings sterling, 32½ acres on waters of Beaverdam Creek, waters of Saluda River adj. Hannah Cook, Benjamin Inman, William Weeks, Enos Ellemon, part of 131½ acres granted to said Enos Ellemon 30 Aug 1774. Enos Ellemon (Seal), Catharine Ellemon (mark) (Seal), Wit: Mercer Babb, Benjamin Heaton, Abner Elleman. Proved in Newberry County by the affirmation of Mercer Babb 6 March 1797 before Elisha Ford, J.P. Recorded 30 June 1797.

D2, 32-36: Lease and release. 16 & 17 Feb 1792, Jonathan Taylor of Newberry County to John Barritt of same, for five shillings sterling, 40 acres, part of 200 acres granted to Philip Phagan 19 Aug 1768, recorded in Book CCC, page 377, conveyed by said Phagan to Jonathan Taylor 23 & 24 Jan 1769. Jonathan Taylor (Seal), Wit: Alex'r Stuart, Thos Brown. Proved 19 March 1792 by the oath of Alexander Stuart before Mercer Babb, J.P. Recorded 1 July 1797.

D2, 37-39: 28 Sept 1796, Ann Finley, late widow of James Finley deceased of Ninety Six District and Newberry County, to Hugh Boyd of the settlement of Gilders Creek, county aforesaid, for £30 sterling, 50 acres on south side Indian Creek, part of tract granted to John Reed 1 Sept 1768 adj. Jacob Guilder, William Cannon, and conveyed by John Reed and Nancy his wife to said James Finley, 50 acres at the corner of Mathew Gillespie's division, 16 Nov 1774. Ann Finlay (mark) (Seal), Wit: John Glasgow, Wilson Glasgow, James Lindsey Sen. Proved 10 May 1797 by the oath of James Lindsey Junr before John Speak, J.P. Recorded 1 July 1797.

D2, 40-41: 17 June 1797, John Elleman and William Elliman, admrs. of the estate of Abner Elliman decd, to John Harrison, all of Newberry County, said Abner Elleman gave a bond to John Harrison to make a title to 199 acres for which said Harrison was to pay £130 sterling, £45 of which purchase money was paid to said Abner Elleman and the remainder being paid to us as admrs., now we do confirm to said John Harrison said tract of 199 acres, part of 400 acres formerly granted to Saml Duncan and by his decease became the property of Amos Duncan his oldest son & heir and 250 acres of which was conveyed by said Amos Dunkin to Abner Elleman. John Elleman (Seal), William Elleman (Seal), Wit: Ridgeway Elmore, Joseph Elmore, Thomas Elmore. Proved by the oath of Joseph Elmore 21 June 1797 before Fred Nance, J.P. Recorded 1 July 1797.

D2, 42-44: 17 June 1797, John Elleman of Newberry County, planter, and William Elleman of same, admrs. of Abner Elleman decd, to Daniel Smith of same county, planter, whereas a certain Amos Duncan and Elizabeth his wife on 28 Aug 1777 conveyed to Abner Elleman 250 acres on waters of Bush Creek, a branch of Saluda, recorded in Newberry County Book C, page 709, and said Abner Elleman for £12 sterling did sell but did not actually convey to said Daniel Smith, tract adj. Danl Smith, land late William Elmore's, and said Abner Elleman, 51 acres, said Abner Elleman by bond dated 31 Oct 1791 to make title. John Elleman (Seal), William Elleman (Seal), Wit: Ridgeway Elmore, Joseph Elmore, Thomas Elmore. Proved by the oath of Thomas Elmore 23 June 1797 before Fred Nance, J.P. Recorded 3 July 1797.

D2, 45-49: Lease and release. 1 & 2 Dec 1795, George Stowdmyer and Anna Margaret his wife, planter, of Newberry County, to Jacob Bear of same, planter, for £75 SC money, tract granted to John Stowdmyer for 150 acres 9 Jan 1755 adj .land of Margaret Brukten, Conrad Rotes, George Michael Stearley, Geo: Michael Gadsinger, Tobias Lagrone. George Stoudmyer (X) (Seal), Anne Margaret Stoudmyer (X) (seal), Wit: John McDaniel, Mathias Yan (X), Peter Willhelm (X). Proved by the oath of Mathias Yans 14 Nov 1795 before Wm Houseal, J.P. Recorded 3 July 1797.

D2, 50-53: Lease and release. 2 & 3 Jan 1788, Harmon Davis Junr of Newberry County, and wife Phebe, to James Daugherty of same, for £14 s7 d2 SC money, 30 acres on Scotts Creek, waters of Bush River, granted 24 Sept 1784. Harman Davis (Seal), Phebe Davis (X) (Seal), Wit: Samuel Kelly Senr, Mary Davis (X). Proved by the oath of Samuel Kelly Senr 24 June 1797 before Fred Nance, J.P. Recorded 3 July 1797.

D2, 54-55: 1 Dec 1791, John Wilkinson Senr of Newberry County, yeoman, to James Daugherty of same, farmer, for £2 SC money, 2 acres, part of 200 acres granted to said John Wilkinson on NW side Scotts Creek, a branch of Bush River, adj. Rosanah Russell, James Daugherty. John Wilkinson (Seal), Wit: Samuel Kelly Senr, Enoch Pearson. Proved by the oath of Samuel Kelly Senr 24 June 1797 before Fred Nance, J.P. Recorded 5 July 1797.

D2, 56-57: Whereas on 27 Feb 1795, John Barlow of Newberry County did by bill of sale convey to Andrew Smith, all his estate both real and personal, a tract of 400 acres and negro slaves Wigson, Tom, Major, Jacob, Bobb, Thomas, Mary, Ann, Susanna, Fortune, St. Croix, Hariott, and Ireland, with stills, horses, cattle, hoggs, etc., for £1500 sterling, recorded in Book C, page 147, and said Andrew Smith has not paid any part of the said consideration, and whereas the whole of the said property except the land and four negroes Bobb, Fortune, St. Croix and Harriott was conveyed to me in trust for the said John Barlow aforesaid, and said Barlow is desirous to have his property returned to him again, for consideration of the four negroes excepted, do exonerate and release said John Barlow from all mortgages, deeds, etc., 26 Jan 1797. Andrew Smyth (Seal), Wit: Thomas Coffey, James McCary. Proved 27 June 1797 by the oath of James McCary before Charles Griffin, J.P. Recorded 5 July 1797.

D2, 58-59: 2 July 1797, Andrew Smyth, planter, of Newberry County to John Barlow of same, planter, for £200 sterling, three negro children Fortune, Santa Cruix, and Hariott, and a negro man named Bobb. Andrew Smyth (Seal), Wit: James Creswell, Reuben Golding. Recorded 5 July 1797.

D2, 59-60: 28 Jan 1792, Lewis Shepherd for £70 sterling to George Ruff, Esqr., a negro fellow named Edinborough. Lewis Shepherd (Seal), Wit: H'y Ruff, George Shepherd. Proved in Newberry County by the oath of John Henry Ruff 9 July 1797 before David Ruff, J.P. Recorded 16 July 1797.

D2, 60-61: David Mason of Laurens County for £160 to George Ruff, negroes Sampson, his wife Sall, and a boy Sam, 5 March 1797. David Mason (Seal), Wit: Jno H. Ruff, Sebilla Frye (S). Proved by the oath of David Ruff, J.P. Recorded 13 July 1797.

D2, 62-63: South Carolina, Newberry County. Thomas Gains for £40 to George Ruff, negro man named Daniel, 6 Feb 1795. Thos Gains (Seal), Wit: Conrod Rahm, John Weddinman. Proved 9 July 1797 by the oath of Conrod Rahm before David Ruff, J.P. Recorded 13 July 1797.

D2, 63-65: 12 Jan 1796, Stephen Pearson, planter, to George Ruff, both of Newberry County, for £50 sterling, 100 acres on a branch of Broad River called Red Creek adj George Ruff, granted in 1768, recorded in Book DDD, page 13, to Rob. Moore. Stephen Pearson (Seal), Wit: Henry Ruff, Adam Glazier, Joel Graham. Proved by the oath of John Henry Ruff 29 Oct 1796 before David Ruff, J.P. Recorded 13 July 1797.

D2, 66-67: 18 Jan 1794, Jacob Tarrer of Orangeburgh District to Frederick Tarrer of Ninety Six District, for one shilling, 125 acres in Ninety Six district, part of grant to Margaret Breshter 1 Jan 1754 adj. Lagrone, Pickley, three conveyances the 9 Feb 1765, 8 April 1773, 24 May 1773, recorded in Grant Book OO, page 325. Johan Jacob Tarrer (Seal), Wit: Jacob Lever (IL), Moses

Townsen (X). Proved by the oath of Jacob Lever 20 Jan 1794 before Thomas Rall, J.P. Recorded 22 July 1797.

D2, 68: 12 April 1797, Henry Dunn of Newberry County, to Richard Marchant and Benjamin Coppock, for £14 s5, one sorrel horses branded O. Henry Dunn (Seal), Wit: Daniel Perkins. Proved by the oath of Daniel Perkins Junr 8 Aug 1797 before Danl Perkins, J.,P. Recorded 10 Aug 1797.

D2, 69-71: Levi Johnson of Newberry County and wife Sarah for £30 sterling to John Hogg, planter, 50 acres on a branch of Gossetts Creek, waters of Enoree River, part of tract granted to Daniel Johnson Senr decd adj. Lewis Hogg, John Hogg, George Johnson, James Blair, 9 Feb 1797. Levi Johnson (Seal), Sarah Johnson (X) (Seal), Wit: Zachariah Hogg, James Blair (X), Stephen Hogg. Proved in Newberry County by the oath of Jas Blair 29 June 1797 before Edward Finch, J.P. Recorded 10 Aug 1797.

D2, 72-77: Lease and release. 4 & 5 Aug 1785, George Eigner (Egnar) of Ninety Six District, planter, to David Wheatman of same, for £50 SC money, 150 acres on a branch of Second Creek adj. Cornelius Seigler, granted to Conrad Folk 4 July 1754 and conveyed by him to Paul Townsent 14 & 15 Dec 1772, and by Paul Townsent to George Egnar 27 & 29 Aug 1773. George Egner (mark) (Seal), Rachael Egner (R) (Seal), Wit: Michael Dickert Senr, John Seigler (mark), Michael Dickert Junr. Proved in Newberry County by the oath of Michael Dickert Jr 13 April 1793 before David Ruff, J.P. Recorded 10 Aug 1797.

D2, 78-79: 14 April 1796, Thomas Turner of Newberry County to William Caldwell of same, for £100 sterling, 100 acres on a branch of Saluda called the Mill Creek in Sampsons fork, surveyed for Benjamin Burgess 25 Oct 1755 and granted to said Thomas Turner 10 May 1768. Thomas Turner (X) (Seal), Wit: Jno Glover, William Turner (X). Proved by the oath of John Glover 25 April 1797 before W. Anderson, J.E.C. Recorded 10 Aug 1797.

D2, 80-82: Lease and release. 23 & 24 Oct 1795, Philimon Waters Esqr to Philimon Waters, son of Thomas, for £75 sterling, 400 acres on waters of Buffalo Creek granted to said Philimon Waters 5 Feb 1787, recorded in Book QQQQ, page 547. P. Waters (Seal), Wit: Elizabeth Musgrove (O), David Waters. Proved by the oath of David Waters 24 Oct 1785 before Peter Julin, J.P. Recorded 10 Aug 1797.

D2, 83-85: 28 May 1797, William Andrew of Newberry County for £110 sterling to Samuel Waldrop of Laurens County, 310 acres in Newberry County on Mudlick Creek, granted to James McCool 31 Oct 1796 and conveyed to Moses Embre 29 Sept 1794 and by said Embre to Robert Gillam 29 Oct 1792 [sic], and by said gillam to William Andrew 19 July 1794. William Andrew (X) (Seal), Wit: Charles Porterfield, Christian Brown. Proved in Laurens County by the oath of Charles Porterfield 10 July 1797 before J. R. Brown, J.N.C.

Martha Andrew (X), wife of William Andrew, relinquished dower 29 June 1797 before J. R. Brown, J.N.C. Recorded 11 Aug 1797.

D2, 86-88: Richard M. Owen of Abbeville County for £50 to Josiah Gates of Newberry County, 100 acres on waters of Mudlick and Mill Creeks, part of tract granted to John Robbin and devolving to Richard Robinson by heirship and by him conveyed to said Owen, 28 March 1797. R. M. Owen (Seal), Wit: Richard Watts, James Gates. Proved in Newberry County by the oath of James Gates 27 July 1797 before J. R. Brown, J.N.C. Nancy Owen (signed as Ann Owen), wife of Richard M. Owen, relinquished dower 14 July 1797 before Jacob R. Brown, J.N.C. Recorded 11 Aug 1797.

D2, 88-90: Richard M. Owen of Abbeville County for £50 to James Gates of Newberry County, 100 acres on waters of Mudlick and Mill Creeks, part of tract granted to John Robin and devolving to Richard Robinson by heirship and by him conveyed to said Owen, 28 March 1797. R. M. Owen (Seal), Wit: Richard Watts, Josiah Gates. Proved in Newberry County by the oath of Josiah Gates 27 July 1797 before J. R. Brown, J.N.C. Nancy Owen (signed as Ann Owen), wife of Richard M. Owen, relinquished dower 14 July 1797 before Jacob R. Brown, J.N.C. Recorded 11 Aug 1797.

D2, 91-95: Lease and release. 17 & 18 June 1794, Richard Mauldin Owen of Abbeville County, House Carpenter, and wife Nancy, for £50 to John Williamson of Laurens County, 121 acres on a small branch of Mudlick Creek, adj. J. R. Brown, Robert Johnston, land in dispute between William Andrew & said Owen, and Josiah Gates, the remainder of a tract granted to John Robertson and devolving to Richard Robertson by heirship and by him conveyed to said Owen. Rich'd M. Owen (Seal), Nancy Owen (X) (Seal), Wit: Archibald Sawyers, Charles Wilson, before J. R. Brown, J.N.C. Nancy Owen (signed as Ann Owen), wife of Richard M. Owen, relinquished dower 14 July 1797 before Jacob R. Brown, J.N.C. Recorded 11 Aug 1797.

D2, 96-97: Olleman Dodgen of Edgefield County for £147 s10 to Thomas Chappel, one mullatto man slave about 27 years of age named Joel, one negro woman about 25 years of age named Fillis, and a boy child two years of age named Harry, 17 Feb 1797. Olleman Dodgen (Seal), Wit: James Chappel, Abraham Dyson. Proved in Newberry County by the oath of James Chappel 27 July 1797 before Robert Gillam, J.P. Recorded 11 Aug 1797.

D2, 97-98: William Burton of Newberry County to make over to William Burton Senr and George Goggans of same, all my crop of corn and tobacco that I have growing the year 1797, bond for condition of payment to Benjamin Long £9 principal and interest for 12 months. William Burton Junr, George Goggans, William Burton, Wit: Etheldred King, George Powell. Proved by the oath of George Powell before Providence Williams, J.P. Recorded 12 Aug 1797.

D2, 98-99: Thomas Perry of Newberry County for good will and affection to my daughter Delilah Perry of same, 113½ acres, being the tract where I now live, with half of my stock, hoggs, horses, cattle, and sheep, and household furniture, 9 Jan 1797. Thomas Perry (K) (Seal), Wit: David Glenn, Andrew Hunter. Proved by the oath of Andrew Hunter 3 July 1797 before Saml E. Kenner, J.P. Recorded 12 Aug 1797.

D2, 100-101: 1 Aug 1797, David McClelland of Newberry County to William Aspinell of same, for £10, 100 acres formerly granted to William McClelland as his bounty and fell to the said David McCleland as heir at law, adj. Wm McCleland Senr, James Fleming, land formerly granted to Elizabeth Debit. David McCleland (Seal), Wit: Wm Satterwhite, Fred Nance, J.P. Recorded 12 Aug 1797.

D2, 102-103: 1 March 1795, Abel Pearson Senr and wife Mary of Union County to Joseph Hill of Newberry County for $138.28, 125 acres granted to Abel Pearson 4 April 1785 on waters of Duncans Creek adj. Col. Benjamin Herndon, John Henderson, John Hendrix. Abel Pearson (Seal), Mary Pearson (Seal), Wit: Robert Johnston, done before Levi Casey, J.N.C. Mary Pearson, wife of Abel Pearson, relinquished dower 21 March 1796 before Levi Casey, J.N.C. Recorded 12 Aug 1797.

D2, 104-105: 29 July 1797, Joseph Caldwell of Newberry County to William Hunter of Laurens County, for £50 sterling, one negro boy named Samson about 25 years old formerly the property of Capt. Charles Littleton. Joseph Caldwell (Seal), Wit: John Wilson, Wm Wilson. Proved by the oath of William Wilson 29 July 1797 before Prov. Williams, J.P. Recorded 12 Aug 1797.

D2, 105-106: 22 July 1797, Moses Strahan of Newberry County to William Kelly of same, for £20 sterling, 50 acres, the westward of that tract George Hipp conveyed to James Strawhan & said James Strahan conveyed to Moses Strahan, granted to Robert Johnson 3 July 1786 adj. John Swinford, Richard Fowler, James Young. Moses Strahan (Seal), Wit: Robert Johnson, Levi Casey, J.N.C. Recorded 12 Aug 1797.

D2, 107-108: Thomas Perry of Newberry County for good will and affection to my daughter Sarah Hunter of same, 113½ acres, being the tract where I now live, with half of my stock, hoggs, horses, cattle, and sheep, and household furniture, 9 Jan 1797. Thomas Perry (X) (Seal), Wit: David Glenn, Andrew Hunter. Proved by the oath of Andrew Hunter 3 July 1797 before Saml E. Kenner, J.P. Recorded 12 Aug 1797.

D2, 108-110: 22 July 1797, Robert Johnson and Ann his wife of Newberry County for £28 SC money to James Strahan of same, 73½ acres on waters of Duncans Creek, part of tract granted to Robert Johnson 3 July 1786, recorded in Book LLLL, page 47, and another of 50 acres conveyed by said Johnson to William Kelly, being one moiety or half of 247 acres granted to said Robert Johnson adj. James Young, John Hipp, Robert Mars, John Swinford, by a line of partition agreed upon by William kelly and James Strahan 15th of this present month. Robert Johnston (Seal), Ann Johnston (X) (Seal), Wit: William Kelly, Levi Casey, J.N.C. Recorded 14 Aug 1797.

D2, 111-116: Lease and release. 27 & 28 Nov 1789, Jeremiah Williams of Newberry County, planter, to James Caldwell of same, for £20 sterling, 100 acres, half of 200 acres in Craven county on Broad River adj. Thomas Hamilton, granted to John Cargil Senr 28 Nov 1771 and conveyed by him to Jeremiah Williams 18 Nov 1771. Jeremiah Williams (Seal), Joshua Edwards, Dan Tolbirt, Henry Anderson. Proved by the oath of Daniel Tolbirt 29 July 1797 before Saml E. Kenner, J.P. Recorded 14 Aug 1797.

D2, 117-118: 21 July 1797, James Hutchinson and Susannah Hutchinson of Newberry County for £15 sterling, 55 acres, part of tract granted 2 March 1773 to Daniel horsey for 147 acres on Second Creek. James Hutchinson (Seal), Susanah Hutchinson (X) (Seal), Wit: Edwd Finch, J.P. Patrick Martin, William McCraw. Susanah Hutchinson, wife of James Hutchinson, relinquished dower 21 July 1797 before Edward Finch, J.P. Proved by the oath of Patrick Martin (X) 21 July 1797 before Edward Finch, J.P. Recorded 14 Aug 1797.

D2, 119-123: Lease and release. 17 June 1794, Richard Robinson of Newberry County, hatter, to Richard M. Owen of Abbeville County, carpenter, for £200 sterling, 200 acres on two small branches of Mudlick and Mill Creeks, granted to John Robertson but through mistake was called John Robin and devolving to Richard by heirship. Richard Robertson (Seal), Wit: Andrew Smyth Jr., John Motes, John Wilson. Proved in Newberry County by the oath of Andrew Smith 29 July 1797 before J. R. Brown, J.N.C. Recorded 14 Aug 1797.

D2, 123-124: 25 May 1797, Simon Reeder Senr of Newberry County to David and Daniel Reeder of same, for five shillings, 150 acres on waters of Kings Creek a branch of Enoree River, granted to Simon Reeder. Simon Reeder (X) (Seal), Wit: Richard Tear, Mullican Norred. Proved by the oath of Richard Tear before Providence Williams, J. P. Recorded 14 Aug 1797.

D2, 125-127: 22 July 1797, Robert Johnson and Ann his wife of Newberry County for $65 to William Kelly of same, 50 acres on waters or branches of Duncans Creek, granted to said Robert Johnson 3 July 1786, recorded in Book LLLL, page 47, on the NE side of Mire branch dj. Richard Fowler, near the path leading from James Strahans to the place where Moses Strahan formerly resided, James Young, John Walter. Robert Johnston (Seal), Ann Johnston (mark) (Seal), Wit: John Hipp, Levi Casey, J.N.C. Recorded 15 Aug 1797.

D2, 128-130: Daniel Hertel of Newberry County for £9 s1 d9 3/4 sterling to George Bower of same, 75 acres where said George Hartle now lives, part of 200 acres granted to Francis Hewit 4 Sept 1763 and transferred by heirs of said Francis Hewit to said George Hertel, 16 Jan 1797. George Hartel (Seal), Wit: Jer. McDaniel, Jacob Bower (X). Proved by the oath of Jacob Bower 9 Aug 1797 before William Houseal, J.P. Recorded 15 Aug 1797.

D2, 131-132: Elizabeth McCinsey of Newberry County to Robert Montgomery, son of George Montgomery, for natural love and affection to said Robert Montgomery, 10 acres of land that was my bounty and my thirds of the fifty that was bought, 21 Nov 1796. Elizabeth McKinzey (X) (Seal), Wit: Alexander Johnson, John Davidson. Proved by the oath of Alexander Johnson 13 May 1797 before Edw'd Finch, J.P. Recorded 18 Aug 1797.

D2, 132-137: Lease and release. 4 & 5 Nov 1784, William Brooks and Ann his wife of Ninety Six District, SC, to John Adkison of same, for £1000 SC money, 300 acres on north side Saluda River in Berkley County, granted to William Hudgens 20 Aug 1767, recorded in Book BBB, page 141. William Brooks (Seal), Ann Brooks (X), Wit: William Carson, Sterling Dickson. Proved in Ninety Six District by the oath of Sterling Dickson 15 Oct 1784 before Bartlett Satterwhite, J.P. Recorded 18 Aug 1797.

D2, 138-140: 21 Aug 1797, John Harrison of Newberry County, tanner, to Isaac Elmore, taylor of same, for £32 s10, 50 acres on waters of Bush Creek, a branch of Saluda adj. land late William Gilliland now in tenure of John Large, adj.said john Harrison, part of 199 ares which John Elleman and William Elleman 17 June 1797 conveyed to John Harrison, recorded in Book D, page 40. John Harrison (Seal), Wit: Reason Reagan, Ridgeway Elmore, William Gilleland. Proved by the oath of William Gilleland 21 Aug 1797 before Fred Nance, J.P. Recorded 21 Aug 1797.

D2, 141-142: 26 July 1797, Alexander Turner of Newberry County, planter, for £50 sterling, to John McMorries of same, merchant, 100 acres, part of tract granted to John Johnson on Rockey Branch, waters of Kings Creek, 350 acres, tract of 100 acres from Johnson to Robert Turner. Alexander Turner (Seal), Wit: Wm Wilson, Robert Anderson. Proved by the oath of Wm Wilson 22 Aug 1797 before John Speak, J.P. Recorded 8 Sept 1797.

D2, 143-144: 26 July 1797, Alexander Turner of Newberry County for $150 to John McMorries of same, one roan horse, one iron gray colt, seven head of cattle, two sows and piggs, 11 shoats, 2 feather beds and furniture, six chairs, one iron pot and iron Dutch oven, four pewter plats, one dish and two basons, two shovel plows, and two pair iron traces and hames. Alexander Turner (Seal), Wit: Wm Wilson, Robert Anderson. Proved by the oath of Wm Wilson 22 Aug 1797 before John Speak, J.P. Recorded 8 Sept 1797.

D2, 145-147: 5 Nov 1792, Henry Butler of Newberry County to Daniel Butler of same, for love, good will, and affection to Daniel Butler, 100 acres, part of tract granted to John Sims of 350 acres, of which part hath been conveyed to said Henry Butler on a branch of Little River of Saluda called Sandy Run. Henry Butler (H) (Seal), Wit: Benjamin Butler, William Butler, Nimrod Goggans. Proved by the oath of Benjamin butler 6 Sept 1797 before Fred Nance. Recorded 8 Sept 1797.

D2, 148-150: 27 Feb 1797, William Knox of Newberry County to James Campbell of same, for £19 s13 d4 sterling, tract of 175 acres on waters of Indian Creek called Hendrixes branch adj. John Smith, land formerly granted to Samuel Lindsey, with one brown cow and pided calf, one red heifer, one mans saddle, one womans saddle, two plows, one walnut table, one feather bed Y& furniture, one chest, mattock & hoe, one beehive, two pewter dishes, 7 plates and one bason, four chairs, one bay mare, two sows and piggs, one pot and one flax wheel. William Knox (Seal), Wit: John McMorries, John Toland, Richard Bennett. Proved by the oath of John McMorries 7 Sept 1797 before John Speak, J.P. Recorded 8 Sept 1797.

D2, 151-153: 17 Oct 1797, William Hall, the elder of Newberry County, SC, eldest son and heir at law of William Hall deceased, late of Frederick County, Virginia, to William Hall, eldest son of the first named William Hall, of Berkley County, Virginia, tract of land and undivided moiety thereof in Berkley County, Virginia, on a creek formerly called Howards Marsh, which empties into the Shennandoah River, it being the same tract which was devised by William Hall, father to the first named William Hall, by his will dated 21 Oct 1764 to his sons Thomas Hall and Joseph Hall, by the name of the testators new dwelling plantation and the mill thereon. William Hall Senr (Seal), Wit: M. W. Moon, Wm Satterwhite, John Satterwhite. Susannah Hall, wife of William Hall, relinquished dower 17 Oct 1797 before J. R. Brown, J.N.C. Acknowledged in court held for Newberry County 17 Oct 1797 by the William Hall. Recorded 17 Oct 1797.

D2, 154-156: 7 Sept 1792, Joseph Austill of Spartanburgh County, Pinckney District, SC, eldest son of William Austill, late of SC, deceased, to William Gilliland, eldest son of William Gilliland, late of Newberry County, Ninety Six District, decd., 150 acres on waters of Bush Creek, a branch of Saluda, adj. land of Jeremiah Riley, Daniel Smith, John Harrison, Levi Hilburn, recorded in Book L. No. 11, page 95, in the Auditors office, granted to Samuel Duncan and conveyed 16 May 1770 to William Austill and aid Austill to William Gilliland deceased, by bond dated 30 Sept 1778. Joseph Austill (seal), Wit: Isaac Chapman, Amos Austill, Samuel Large. Proved in Newberry County by the oath of Samuel Large 14 Sept 1797 before Fred Nance, J.P. Recorded 17 Oct 1797.

D2, 156-157: 27 July 1797, Joseph Caldwell of Newberry County to Hugh Boyd of same, for $10, amount to £2 s6 d8 sterling, 14 head of hoggs. Joseph Caldwell (Seal), Wit: John Turner, James Lindsey. Recorded 17 Oct 1797.

D2, 158-159: 1 Jan 1797, David Reed of Newberry County, for £75 sterling to John Kippleman of same, tract on which said David Reed now lives, 200 acres on a branch of Broad River, by instrument dated 16 July 1793 from John Elmore, Stephen Elmore and Rachael Elmore to said David Reed, recorded in Bok B, page 783, 17 June 1794. David Reed (Seal), Wit: James Daugherty, William Craig. Proved by the oath of William Craig 23 Sept 1797 before Fred Nance, J.P. Recorded 18 Oct 1797.

D2, 160-161: 18 Jan 1797, George Gibson of Newberry County for £100 sterling to Joseph Jacobs of same, 60 acres on waters of Buffalow Creek, a branch of Saluda River, part of tract granted to Andrew Keller, then conveyed to John Harmon who conveyed to George Gibson. George Gibson (mark) (Seal), Wit: David Walls, George Bridges, Zilpah Walls (X). Proved 26 July 1797 by the oath of George Bridges before John Livingston, J.P. Recorded 18 Oct 1797.

D2, 162-166: Lease and release. 1 & 2 Nov 1790, Jacob Chandler, taylor, and Ann his wife of Newberry County to David Miles of same, planter, for £25 sterling, 50 acres on Bush Creek, the other moiety of 100 acres conveyed to Israel Chandler, part of tract of 250 acres granted to Jeremiah Lewis 27 Nov 1770, the said 100 acres conveyed by William Gilliland to said Jacob Chandler, 1 & 2 Aug 1774, plat laid off by John Caldwell, Esqr., decd, 3 Aug 1774. Jacob Chandler (Seal), Ann Chandler (Seal), Wit: John Thomas S. M., Israel Chandler, Isaac Cox. Proved 20 Feb 1792 by the oath of John Thomas S. M. before Mercer Babb, J.P. Recorded 28 Oct 1797.

D2, 167-171: Lease and release. 1 & 2 Nov 1790, Jacob Chandler, taylor, and Ann his wife of Newberry County to David Miles of same, planter, for £25 sterling, 93 acres on waters of Bush River, granted to Jacob Chandler Lewis 5 June 1786, recorded in Book LLLL, page 404. Jacob Chandler (Seal), Ann Chandler (Seal), Wit: John Thomas S. M., Israel Chandler, Isaac Case [sic]. Proved 20 Feb 1792 by the oath of John Thomas S. M. before Mercer Babb, J.P. Recorded 28 Oct 1797.

D2, 172-174: 2 Oct 1797, William Tennent, Sheriff of Ninety Six District, to William Cooper, by virtue of a writ of fieri facias issued from the court of common pleas at the suit of Benjamin Evans against the estate of William Gillam decd, sold at Cambridge for £130 to William Cooper, tract adj. Saml Brown, David miles, John Duncan, Benjamin Evans, James Carmack, 200 acres. Wm Tennent Shff 96 Dist. (Seal), Wit: Wm Nibbs, Robert McCombs, Samuel Pearson. Proved in Newberry County by the oath of Saml Pearson 10 Oct 1797 before Fred Nance. J.P. Recorded 28 Oct 1797.

D2, 175-177: 4 Nov 1797, William Wadlington of Newberry County and William Malone of Oglethorpe County, Georgia, executors of Edward Wadlington deceased, for £261 s3 d4 to Aron Cates of Newberry County, 400 acres, it being in different tracts and part of a tract of land granted to Adam Stephens and from him conveyed to Thomas Wadlington Senr 17 Aug 1773 and by the will of Thomas Wadlington to his son Edward Wadlington, also one tract granted to William Johnson 4 June 1787 and conveyed to William Johnson 4 June 1787 and conveyed to Edward Wadlington; another tract granted to Charles Lyttleton and conveyed to Edward Wadlington, all in Newberry County by a resurvey on the bank of the Enoree River. W Wadlington (Seal), W. Malone Senr exors (Seal), Wit: William Malone Junr, James Hatton, David Hatton (X). Proved 10 Nov 1797 by the oath of William Malone Junr before Fred Nance, J.P. Recorded 11 Nov 1797.

D2, 178: George Bridges of Newberry County to Isaac Mills of same, one set of black smiths tools, one bellows, one anvill, one vice, 3 hammers, 3 June 1797. George Bridges, Test: Daniel Kinard (X). Proved by the oath of Daniel Kinard 2 Dec 1797 before Daniel Perkins, J.P. Recorded 1 Jan 1798.

D2, 179: Recd 29 Dec 1797 of George Hertel the sum of £9 s1 d9 3/4 for a mortgage given by said Hertel 16 Jan 1797, dated 2 Jan 1798. George Bower (X), Wit: William Houseal, J.P. Recorded 3 Jan 1798.

D2, 179-180: George Johnson of Newberry County to Jonathan Pratt, all that part of my lands on the other side of a certain branch beginning where my line on the Widow Collins' line crosses the branch above, for five shillings per acre, 30 March 1796. George Johnson, Wit: Gideon Nelson, Sarah Collins (mark). Proved by the oath of Gideon Nelson 28 July 1797 before John Livingston, J.P. Recorded 2 Jan 1798.

D2, 180-187: Lease and release. 30 & 31 Jan 1789, Christopher Weddiman of Newberry County, planter, to Christian Weddingman of same, planter, for 150 sterling, 125 acres, a tract of 50 acres granted to Terrance Riley in Berkley County, plat dated 3 June 1769, recorded in Book K No. 10, page 155, which said 50 acres devolved into the possession of Terrel Riley, he being the son and heir at law of said Terrance Riley and 75 acres, part of 200 acres granted to Terrance Riley in 1755, recorded in Book PP, page 329, on waters of Cannons Creek, conveyed 7 & 8 Sept 1785 to Christopher Wheaddinman. Christopher Wheaddingman (W) (Seal), Wit: David Wheaddingman (D), Michael Dickert Senr, Christopher Dickert. Proved by the oath of David Wheaddingman 16 Oct 1797 before Fred Nance, J.P. Recorded 3 Jan 1798.

D2, 187-188: Jacob King of Newberry County mortgages for £60 sterling, to William Gary of same, one negro man named Peter, woman Gin and her two children Minny and Sam, 16 March 1797. Jacob King (Seal), Wit: John B. Bennett, Barber Hancock, Abner Teague. Proved by the oath of Thomas Gary 16 Oct 1797 before Fred Nance, J.P. Recorded 3 Jan 1798.

D2, 189-191: 10 Aug 1797, George Bridges, blacksmith, of Newberry County, to Robert Drennon, farmer, for £31 sterling, 150 acres, part of 350 acres granted to Andrew Healter 12 Sept 1768 and after several conveyances became the property of George Bridges, on SW side main waggon road that comes by Lees ferry to Charleston. George Bridges (Seal), Ann Bridges (X) (Seal), Wit: Charles Thompson, Moses Jacobs, Saml McQuerns. Proved by the oath of Charles Thompson 2 Sept 1797 before John Livingston, J.P. Recorded 3 Jan 1798.

D2, 191-192: 16 March 1796, James Barret of Newberry County to William Shaw of same, for £5 sterling, 35 acres on waters of Beaverdam. James Barrett (Seal), Elizabeth Barrett (mark) (Seal), Wit: Abel Pearson, Voluntine Braswell.

D2, 192-193: 26 March 1796, David Downs of Newberry County to William Shaw of same, for £5 sterling, 30 acres on waters of Beaver dam Creek. David Downs (S) (Seal), Sarah Downs (X) (Seal), Wit: Abel Pearson, Voluntine Braswell. Proved by the affirmation of Abel Pearson 3 Dec 1796 before Elisha Ford, J.P. Recorded 4 Jan 1798.

D2, 194-195: William Craig and Robert Powell, arbitrators, and John McMorries, umpire, all of Newberry County, mutually chosen by Captain Saml Lindsey and James Campbell to settle and finally determine all matters of controversy, 18 Sept 1797, now after seriously perusing the books, notes & other papers, to determine First that Samuel Lindsey is indebted to James Campbell the sum of £9 s18 d6 sterling; secondly that all debts, dues, and demands against the late firm of Samuel Lindsey and James Campbell after said shall be equally paid by the said parties; thirdly, that all bonds, notes and book accompts now due to the said firm shall be collected and be equally shared, dated 22 Sept 1797. W. Craig (Seal), Robt Powell (Seal), John McMorries (Seal). Recorded 4 Jan 1798.

D2, 196-198: 4 March 1794, Martin Cook of Newberry County to Jacob Cook of same, for £50 sterling, 125 acres on branches of Cannons Creek, waters of Broad River, part of two tracts (via) 78 acres part of tract granted to Jacob Cook Senr decd for 150 acres; 57 acres is part of tract granted to Postun Cook Senr decd for 100 acres. The 150 acres was recorded in Book CCC, page 309 grant dated 2 Aug 1768, and the 100 acres was recorded in Book FFF, page 310, grant dated 25 May 1774. Martin Cook (X) (Seal), Wit: Michael Kinard, Jacob Frey, Peter Rikard (X). Proved by the oath of Capt. Michael Kinard 28 May 1796 before Wm Houseal, J.P. Recorded 4 Jan 1798.

D2, 199-202: 14 Jan 1791, Elizabeth Hunt, widow, of Ninety Six District, to Robert McCiterick, weaver, of same, for £50 sterling, 250 acres on waters of Bush River adj. John Gray, Charles Crow, granted 2 April 1773 to Thomas Coate, conveyed by Thomas Cole [sic, for Cote?] and Sarah his wife 4 & 5 July 1785. Elizabeth Hunt (X) (Seal), Wit: William Dunlap, Nathl Haworth, James Lindsey. Proved 8 July 1791 by the oath of James Lindsey before Providence Williams, J.P. Recorded 4 Jan 1798.

D2, 203-204: Samuel Lindsie of Newberry County for £50 sterling to William Ragland of same, tract on Kings Creek granted to Samuel Clowney 6 April 1768, part of tract of 100 acres, 29 Nov 1796. Saml Lindsey (Seal), Wit: Wm Satterwhite, George Wells. Proved by the oath of Geo Wells 28 July 1797 before Edw'd Finch, J.P. Elizabeth Lindsey (X) relinquished dower 18 Aug 1797 before L. Casey, J.N.C. Recorded 4 Jan 1798.

D2, 205-207: 14 Sept 1797, Benjamin Hollinhead of Newberry County to Deason Enlow of same, for £14 sterling, 50 acres on both sides Camping Creek, waters of Saluda, granted to Victor Harris 15 Sept 1797. Benjn Holinshead (X) (Seal), Jenney Hollinshead (X) (Seal), Wit: Henry Long, John

Enlow. Proved by the oath of John Enlow 28 Dec 17897 before John Livingston, J.P. Recorded 4 Jan 1798.

D2, 208-210: 12 Jan 1796, David Glynn & Elizabeth his wife of Newberry County to David Owen of same, for £51 s7 d6 sterling, 137 acres on waters of Second Creek, a small branch of Broad River, part of tract granted to John McBurney of 250 acres which said McBurney conveyed to said Glynn 1 May 1790. David Glen (Seal), Elizabeth Glen (Seal), Wit: Edmund Gaines, Stephen McCraw. Proved 10 Dec 1797 by the oath of Stephen McCraw before P. Williams, J.P. Recorded 5 Jan 1798.

D2, 210-212: 15 Dec 1794, Thomas Lindsey & Lydda his wife of Newberry County to Stephen Johnson of same, for £100 sterling, 200 acres on waters of Enoree River, No. Kings Creek, adj. land surveyed for John Woodall, Simon Reader, Capt. Charles King, William Malone Senr, surveyed for Thomas Lindsay 17 Dec 1771 by Enoch Pearson, Deputy Surveyor, in Berkley County. Thomas Lindsey (Seal), Lyda Lindsey (Seal), Wit: W Malone Senr, Jacob Lindsey, Kizia King (X). Proved 4 Jan 1798 by the oath of Jacob Lindsey before Fred Nance, J.P. Recorded 5 Jan 1798.

D2, 213-214: Isaac Cook of the town of Charlotte, Mecklinburg County, North Carolina, for $80 to Seth Hatcher of Ninety Six District, SC, 100 acres on waters of Kings Creek on south side Enoree River adj. James Wilson, Misibeth Brown, William Dial, John McColah, 27 Aug 1797. Isaac Cook (Seal), Wit: James Abernathy, Saml Kelley Senr. Proved 16 Dec 1797 by the oath of James Abernathy before Elisha Ford, J.P. Recorded 5 Jan 1798.

D2, 215-220: Lease and release. 2 Jan 1797, William Jackson of Newberry County to Charles Bridges of same, for £30 sterling, 100 acres on waters of Cannons Creek, part of 200 acres surveyed for Thomas Shaw 9 Sept 1772 and granted to Wm Aspanell 21 Jan 1785, conveyed by William Aspanell to said William Jackson 2 & 3 Jan 1787. William Jackson (mark) (Seal), Rebecah Jackson (X) (Seal), Wit: Peter Connor, Moses Smith. Proved by the oath of Moses Smith 30 Dec 1797 before Fred Nance, J.P. Recorded 5 Jan 1798.

D2, 221-222: 5 Jan 1798. William Johnson, eldest son of heir of Richard Johnson deceased, eldest son & heir of Sarah Johnson decd, for £20 sterling, to Daniel Pits Junr, both of Newberry County, tract on a spring branch of Carsons Creek adj. land whereon said Daniel Pitts Junr now lives, granted to William Gilliland for 40 acres and by said Gilliland sold to Sarah Johnson deceased, and devolving to me, said William Johnson, by heirship. William Johnson (Seal), Wit: William Pitts, Charles Porterfield. Proved by the oath of William Pitts 8 Jan 1798 before Robert Brown, J.N.C. Recorded 13 Jan 1798.

D2, 223-228: Lease and release. 26 & 27 Dec 1773, William Gilliland and Elenor his wife of Craven County, SC, to Sarah Johnson of same, for £50 SC money, 40 acres on waters of Little River in Craven County adj. Samuel Ford, James Johnson, James Daniel, Charles Pitts, granted 19 Nov 1772. William

Gilliland (Seal), Elenor Gilliland (Seal), Wit: John Thomas, David Cantey, Luke Waldrop Junr. Proved by the oath of Luke Waldrop 4 May 1774 before John Caldwell, J.P. Recorded 13 Jan 1798.

D2, 229-231: 30 March 1793, William Chandler Senr of Newberry County to Menoah Bonds, planter, for £125 sterling, tract on north side Enoree River, granted to John Welch 11 Feb 1750, entered in Book QQ, 150 acres, and conveyed by him to Tobias Puteet and from Putteet to said William Chandler. William Chandler (Seal), Wit: Jonathan Hunt, Claudes Gorre (X), John Gorre. Proved 13 Nov 1793 by the oath of Claudis Gorre before Reubin Sims, J.P. Recorded 13 Jan 1798.

D2, 231-233: 13 Jan 1798, James Douglass and Mary his wife of Fairfield County to Jacob Crosswhite, for $1000, 200 acres granted to John Wright 5 May 1773, recorded in Bok O, page ccc, memorial entered in Book M. No. 12, page 403, 25 Aug 1773 and on 26 & 27 March conveyed by John Wright and wife to James Douglass. James Douglass (Seal), Mary Douglass (mark) (Seal), Wit: Henry Ederington, John Eastland, Thomas Eastland. Proved by the oath of Thomas Eastland 13 Jan 1798 before Fred Nance, J.P. Recorded 13 Jan 1798.

D2, 233-235: 13 Jan 1797, William Malone, late inhabiter of Newberry County, SC, but now inhabitant of the state of Georgia, to Jonathan Pratt of Newberry County, for £50 sterling, tract on a branch of Enoree River called Gossets Creek, by the mouth of Wm Richards' spring branch, Wm. Finch's line, corner made to William Malone Junr, where the said William Malone lived in 1792, granted to Daniel Johnson 10 Aug 1774 and conveyed to William Malone Junr 30 & 31 Dec 1779. W. Malone (Seal), Wit: John Murphy Jnr, Robt Rutherford, Rhoda Harrington. Proved 15 Jan 1798 by the oath of Robert Rutherford before Fred Nance, J.P. Recorded 15 Jan 1798.

D2, 236-240: Lease and release. 19 & 20 Feb 1787, John Lewis of Newberry County, settlement of Bush River, planter, to Hugh Gragg of same, weaver, and settlement of Saluda River, for £50, 100 acres on north side Saluda River adj. Richard Lewis, Matthew Young, James O'Harron, granted to said John Lewis 3 April 1786, recorded in Book IIII, page 89. John Lewis (Seal), Wit: James Lindsey, Isaac Bosser. Proved 29 July 1791 by the oath of James Lindsey before P. Williams, J.P. Recorded 16 Jan 1798.

D2, 240-242: South Carolina, Newberry County. 14 Sept 1792, Thomas Willoughby Waters to Hugh Gragg, for £60 sterling, 125 acres on Lewis Branch adj. John Turner, binds on land of said Waters sold to Henry Dunn, binds on 25 acres said Gragg bought of John Boyd, John Arnold, part of tract granted to Stephen Elmore. Thos. W. Waters (Seal), Wit: John Worthington, Jesse Davis (X). Proved by the oath of John Worthington 2 Dec 1797 before D. Clary, J.P. Recorded 16 Jan 1798.

D2, 243-247: Lease and release. 19 & 20 Feb 1787, John Boyd of Newberry County, to Hugh Gragg of same county, settlement of Saluda, weaver, for £20 SC money, 25 acres, part of 250 acres granted to Stephen Elmore 8 March 1773 and fell to his eldest son Mathias Elmore, conveyed by said Mathias Elmore to John Boyd adj. land on the bounty and John Turner. John Boyd (mark) (Seal), Wit: John Arnold, John Arnold Junr, James Lindsey. Proved 10 Sept 1791 by the oath of James Lindsey before P. Williams, J.P. Recorded 16 Jan 1798.

D2, 248-249: South Carolina, Newberry County. John Grout of Oringburg District for £23 s6 d8 sterling to Daniel Dewalt of same state, 200 acres on Canons Creek adj. Jacob Keppleman, William Elmore, 25 March 1797. John Grout (Seal), Elizabeth Grout (X) (Seal), Wit: Frederick Gray, Jacob Bossart, Frederick Booser. Proved in Newberry County by the oath of Frederick Booser 25 March 1797 before John Livingston, J.P. Recorded 22 Jan 1798.

D2, 249-254: Lease and release. 10 & 11 Nov 1788, James Matthews, planter, to Robert Plunkett, planter, both of Newberry County, 96 District, for £ 20 sterling, 119 acres on waters of Beaver Dam, adj. John Crumly, Matthew Brooks spring branch, Robert Plunkett, surveyed for Stephen Lewis 28 May 1785, granted 4 Dec 1786 to said James Matthews. James Mathews (mark) (Seal), Wit: Onslow Barrett, Robt Russel. Proved by the oath of Onslow Barrett 24 Jan 1798 before J. R. Brown, J.N.C. Recorded 24 Jan 1798.

D2, 254-259: Lease and release. 17 & 18 Oct 1790, John Crumly, planter, to Robert Plunkett, planter, both of Newberry County, 96 District, for s10 sterling, 40 granted to John Crumly, on waters of Beaver Dam adj. Nathaniel Howard, James Mathews, John Crumly, recorded in Book B. No. 5, page 154. John Crumly (Seal), Wit: Onslow Barrett, Samuel Hughens (mark) (Seal). Proved by the oath of Onslow Barrett 24 Jan 1798 before J. R. Brown, J.N.C. Hanah Crumly, wife of John Crumly, relinquished dower, 24 Jan 1798 before J. R. Brown, J.N.C. Recorded 24 Jan 1798.

D2, 260-262: 2 May 1797, Thomas Wadsworth, merchant of State of SC for the same value in land conveyed to me by William Turpin, have conveyed to said William Turpin, all my right to tract having fallen to him on a division of certain tracts of land which were held jointly by Thomas Wadsworth and William Turpin, 500 acres on waters of Crims Creek, north of Saluda River, surveyed by James Daugherty on 19 June 1786 for George Stoudmire and granted to Thomas Wadsworth 2 June 1788; 247 acres on Mudlick Creek resurveyed by William Caldwell, adj. Thomas Turner, Thomas Burden, John Satterwhite, Thomas Davidson, William Pettitpool, also two lotts at Newberry Court House, ¼ acre each, adj. lotts of William Satterwhite, esqr., and the publick ground, numbers 31 and 32; 35½ acres on Mudlick granted to B. Brooks 7 Dec 1795. Thos Wadsworth (Seal), James Boyce, William Turpin Junr. Proved by the oath of William Turpin Junr 25 Jan 1798 at Charleston before P. Boneatheau, J.Q. Jane Wadsworth, wife of Thomas Wadsworth, relinquished dower 6 June 1797 before William Mitchell, one of the Judges of Laurens County. Recorded 29 Jan 1798.

D2, 263-264: 14 Nov 1795, Michael Witt and Catharine his wife of Newberry County to John Mowrer of same, for £10 sterling, 47½ acres, part of tract granted to Jacob Mowrer deceased in 1771 and recorded in Book EEE, page 461, and from said Jacob to his daughter Elizabeth Rachel Mowrer and from said Rachel Mowrer to the said Michael Witt by heirship. Michael Witt (mark), Catharine Witt (mark) (Seal), Wit: Thomas Hughs, John McDaniel, Adrian Witt (mark). Proved by the oath of Adrian Witt 23 Dec 1797 before John Livingston, J.P. Recorded 1 Feb 1798.

D2, 265-266: 22 Jan 1798, Daniel Williams Junr of Laurens County to Joseph Williams of Rockingham County, North Carolina, for $600, a negro man slave called Moses about 6 feet high, about 22 years old. Danl Williams Junr (Seal), Test: Reubin Griffin, Eliz'a Williams. Proved in Newberry County by the oath of Reuben Griffin 31 Jan 1798 before J. R. Brown, J.N.C. Recorded 1 Feb 1798.

D2, 266-267: 22 Jan 1798, Daniel Williams Junr of Laurens County to Joseph Williams of Rockingham County, North Carolina, for $300, a negro boy called George about six years old. Danl Williams Junr (Seal), Test: Reubin Griffin, Eliz'a Williams. Proved in Newberry County by the oath of Reuben Griffin 31 Jan 1798 before J. R. Brown, J.N.C. Recorded 1 Feb 1798.

D2, 267-268: 22 Jan 1798, William Lofton Senr of Newberry County to John Cannon of same, for £50 sterling, 82 acres on NW side Indian Creek on south side George's branch, part of 250 acres on Indian Creek granted to William Lofton. William Lofton (Seal), Wit: James Lindsey Senr, Dudley Bonds (mark). Proved by the oath of James Lindsey 22 Jan 1798 before P. Williams, J.P. Recorded 1 Feb 1798.

D2, 268-269: 22 Jan 1798, Samuel Beaks of Edgefield County to John Cannon for £25 sterling, 80 acres, part of tract granted to Daniel Blackburn and conveyed to Samuel Beaks on waters of Indian Creek. Saml Beaks (Seal), Wit: James Lindsey Senr, Dudley Bonds (mark), William Lofton. Proved by the oath of James Lindsey 22 Jan 1798 before P. Williams, J.P. Recorded 1 Feb 1798.

D2, 269-271: 27 Feb 1797, Joseph Davenport & Margaret his wife of Newberry County to David Waldrope of same, for £70 sterling, 125 acres granted to Frederick Glover and from him conveyed to said Joseph Davenport. Joseph Davenport (seal), Margaret Davenport (mark) (Seal), Wit: Jariot Campbell, Ezekiah Waldrop (mark), Jesse Kirby, James Davenport. Proved 20 Nov 1797 by the oath of Ezekiah Waldrop before Charles Griffin, J.P. Recorded 1 Feb 1798.

D2, 271-272: 16 Jan 1798, Edward Rutledge for £5 to John Cannon, 208 acres in Newberry County, part of 200 acres granted to Henry Midleton, Esqr., formally late acted for by Saml Beaks who surrendered his contract to said John Cannon. Edward Rutledge (Seal), Wit: Ezekial Lofton, Thomas Neel. Proved in Newberry County 21 Jan 1798 by the oath of Ezekiah Lofton before P. Williams, J. P. Recorded 1 Feb 1798.

D2, 273: 16 Jan 1798, Edward Rutledge for £13 s1 to John Cannon, 127 acres in Newberry County, part of 200 acres granted to Henry Midleton, Esqr., on Indian Creek, adj. land of John Lindsey, John Cannon formerly Beaks, John Boyd. Edward Rutledge (Seal), Wit: Ezekial Lofton, Thomas Neel. Proved in Newberry County 21 Jan 1798 by the oath of Ezekiah Lofton before P. Williams, J. P. Recorded 1 Feb 1798.

D2, 274-275: 22 Jan 1798, John Cannon of Ninety Six District, and Elenor his wife, to Garret Gray, late of Fauquier County, Virginia, but now of South Carolina, planter, tract in Newberry County on waters of Indian Creek conveyed by Edward Rutledge 16 Jan 1798 for 208 acres and tract conveyed by Samuel Beaks for 80 acres, being the plantation whereon the said Garrett Gray now lives, adj. William Lofton. John Cannon (Seal), Elenor Cannon (X) (Seal), Wit: James Lindsey Senr, Dudley Bounds (mark), Saml Beaks. Proved in Newberry County 22 Jan 1798 by the oath of James Lindsey before P. Williams, J.P. Recorded 1 Feb 1798.

D2, 276-277: John Cannon of Newberry County, for love, good will and affection to my eldest daughter Sarah Cannon at present under the age of 18 years, one molatoe girl named Patt born 26 Aug 1796, the issue of the body of Beck, the just claim of said John Cannon, dated 19 Sept 1796. John Cannon (Seal), Wit: Wm Lofton, Abigail Lofton (mark), James Lindsey. Proved 20 Sept 1796 by the oath of James Lindsey before John Speak, J.P. Recorded 1 Feb 1798.

D2, 277-279: 10 Jan 1798, Stephen Johnson and wife Mary, of Newberry County to William Chambers of same, for £100, 200 acres on Kings Creek, waters of Little River adj. John Woodall, Simon Redd, Charles King. Stephen Johnston (Seal), Mary Johnston (Seal), Wit: Sims Brown, Obed Parrish, David Chambers. Proved by the oath of David Chambers 20 Jan 1798 before John Speak, J.P. Recorded 12 Feb 1798.

D2, 279-281: 20 June 1797, James Daugherty of Newberry County to Moses Evans of same, for £50 sterling, 32 acres on waters of Bush River called Scotts Creek, granted to Harmon Davis and by him conveyed to James Daugherty 24 Sept 1781 and 2 acres on east side of said 30 acres, part of 200 acres granted to John Wilkinson, adj. Rosannah Glenn, Enoch Pearson. James Daugherty (Seal), Jane Daugherty (mark) (Seal), Wit: Saml Kelly Senr, John Kelly Senr, Jos Evans. Jane Daugherty, wife of James Daugherty, relinquished dower 28 July 1797 before J. R. Brown, J.N.C. Proved by the affirmation of James Evans 28 July 1797 before Elisha Ford, J.P. Recorded 19 Feb 1798.

D2, 282-284: 17 Jan 1798, Andrew Yeargain of Greenville County, SC, to Samuel Yeargain of Newberry County, 129 acres in the fork of Kings Creek, a branch of Enoree River, part of tract granted to James Cato Senr 23 June 1774, and recorded in Book QQQ, page 518, adj. Andrew Yeargain. Andrew Yeargain (Seal), Wit: Bartlett Yeargain, Harmon Davis, James Hays. Proved by the oath of Bartlett Yeargain 28 Feb 1798 before Edward Finch, J.P. Recorded 19 Feb 1798.

D2, 285-288: 4 Jan 1790, Peter Brasilman, merchant, of Newberry County, to John David Brasilman, manufacturer, of the City of Elberfeld in the Electorat of Palatine, and Brethern Braselmann, manufacturer of the same city, for £600 sterling, three tracts of land on Kings Creek, 343 acres, adj. land of Edward Finch, William Glenn, Baley Chandler with two negro men Derry and Thom, and two bay mares, a colt, one cow, four heifers, calves, 30 hogs, and 5000 acres on Congaree Creek. Peter Braselmann (Seal), Wit: Robt Powell, Danl Henning. Proved in Newberry County by the oath of Robert Powell 20 Feb 1798 before Fred Nance, J.P. Recorded 20 Feb 1798.

D2, 288-293: Lease and release. Ninety Six District. 15 May 1784, John Valentine Lutringer, of Ninety Six District, planter, to Jacob Buzzard of same, for £28 s11 d4 sterling, 200 acres in the fork between Broad and Saluda Rivers on the road of Guilders Creek, a small branch of Broad River, adj. Herman Davis, recorded in Book OOO, page 65. John Valentine Lutringer (mark) (Seal), Wit: Barbara Ruff (mark), And'w Glazier, David Ruff. Proved 22 May 1784 by the oath of Adam Glazier before George Ruff. Recorded 26 Feb 1798.

D2, 294-295: 8 Oct 1796, Thomas Waters of Newberry County for £17 sterling to John Inman of same, 76 acres on a branch of Little River, waters of Saluda, adj. Robert Stewart, Joshua Stewart, Richard Lewis, John Duglas, Caleb Gilbert. Thomas Waters (X) (Seal), Wit: Joshua Inman, James Price (P), David Downs (mark). Lydia Waters, wife of Thomas Waters, relinquished dower 2 March 1797 before Jas Mayson, J.N.C. Proved by the oath of David Downs before P. Williams, J.P. Recorded 26 Feb 1798.

D2, 296-297: South Carolina, Newberry County. William Craige for £20 sterling to David Cannon, all my claim of a Fishery on Broad River known by the name of Craige Fishery, 16 Oct 1797. William Craige (Seal), Wit: Saml Cannon, Ephraim Cannon, Saml Martin. Proved by the oath of Ephraim Cannon 7 March 1798 before David Ruff, J.P. Recorded 7 March 1798.

D2, 297-299: 5 Dec 1796, William Tennent, Sheriff of Ninety Six District, to David Shelton, by writ of fieri facias from the court of common pleas at the suit of David Shelton against Thomas Johnston, William Tennent sells for £27 s6 d8 sterling, tract on Enoree River and Indian Creek, 287 acres, by plat dated 7 Nov 1795. Wm Tennent (Seal), Wit: W. McMillan, John Heard. Proved by the oath of John Heard 27 Oct 1797 before Julius Nichols, J.P. Recorded 28 Feb 1795.

D2, 299-300: 22 July 1797, James Mayson, Esqr., of Newberry County, for £20 to Allen Cox, planter, in the state aforesaid, 9¼ acres out of a tract known by the name of Butchers tract adjoining Peach Hill land and land formerly held by Joshua Gillam. Jas Mayson (Seal), Wit: Joshua Gillam, Joseph White. Proved by the oath of Joseph White 1 March 1798 Robert Gillam, J.P. Recorded 1 March 1798.

D2, 300-302: 3 Aug 1797, Joshua Gillam of Newberry County, planter, to Allen Cox of same, for £35 sterling, 142¼ acres, by plat certified by Wm Swift and gave to Joshua Gillam by his father Robert Gillam Senr, Esqr., by will 22 Jan 1796, said will recorded in Newberry County. Joshua Gillam (Seal), Wit: Robt Gillam, Joseph White, Archey G. Mayson. Proved 4 Aug 1797 by the oath of Robert Gillam before Jas Mayson, J.N.C. Recorded 2 March 1798.

D2, 302-303: 3 Jan 1798, James Kelly and Sarah his wife of Newberry County, to Ann Kelly, widow of same, for £7 sterling, 83 acres granted to Robert Rutherford Senr and from said Rutherford to said James Kelly, being land laid off by George Harbirt, part of 166 acres granted to said Robert Rutherford. James Kelly (Seal), Sarah Kelly (Seal), Wit: Lewis Hogg, Stephen Kelly, Thomas Kelly. Proved by the oath of Stephen Kelly 23 Feb 1798 before Edw'd Finch, J.P. Recorded 2 March 1798.

D2, 304-305: 10 Nov 1797, William Devinport and wife Sarah of Newberry County for £13 s6 sterling to James Spearman of same, tract on south side of Little River, a branch of Saluda, adj. Edmond Spearman, James Spearman. William Devinport (X) (Seal), Sarah Devinport (X) (Seal), Wit: John Adkinson, David Waldrop, Jesse Stripling (X). Proved by the oath of John Atkinson 28 Feb 1798 before Fred Nance, J.P. Recorded 2 March 1798.

D2, 305-310: Lease and release. 9 & 10 Nov 1789, Jonathan Gilbert of Ninety Six District, Newberry County, to Alexander Cathern [Cothran] for £10 sterling, 150 acres on waters of the Beaver Dam of Saluda River, part of 350 acres granted 18 May 1771 to Joseph Ruckman bounded at time of survey by land of James Cheek, conveyed by said Joseph Ruckman to Wm Weeks 17 & 18 June 1771 and conveyed by Benjamin Heaton and Mercer Babb, exrs. of Wm Weeks 30 & 31 Oct 1786. Jonathan Gilbert (Seal), Hannameil Gilbert (Seal), Wit: James Wadlington, Cary Gilbert, Hephzibah Gilbert (X). Proved by the oath of Cary Gilbert 2 March 1798 before Elisha Ford, J.P. Recorded 14 March 1798.

D2, 311-313: Mary Kelly, widow of Edmond Kelly deceased, of Newberry County by bond dated 3 Oct 1797 to Edmond kelly in the penal sum of £40 sterling, for the payment of £20 sterling with lawful interest, mortgage of negro wench named Beck 30 years old, 4 Oct 1797. Mary Kelly (X) (Seal), Wit: John Goree, John Wells. Proved by the oath of John Goree 28 Feb 1798 before Fred Nance, J.P. Recorded 14 March 1798.

D2, 313: South Carolina, Newberry County. Francis Devinport Senr to Isaac Devinport of same, one negro girl named Rachel, 10 Feb 1798. Francis Devinport (Seal), Wit: James Goggans, George Goggans. Proved by the oath of George Goggans 28 Feb 1798 before Fred Nance, J.P. Recorded 14 March 1798.

D2, 314-315: 18 Dec 1792, James Johnston & Sarah his wife of Newberry County to James Lewis of same, for £28 s11 d5 sterling, 80½ acres on waters of Sandy Run, adj. James Goggans, Danl Johnson, William Pitts, Jonathan Neale. James Johnston (Seal), Sarah Johnston (Seal), Wit: Stephen Waldrop, John Pitts, Richard henderson Waldrop, George Goggans. Proved by the oath of George Goggans 28 Feb 1798 before Fred Nance, J.P. Recorded 14 March 1798.

D2, 315-316: 29 May 1795, George Bridges of Newberry County and wife Nancy to William Lester of same, for five shillings, 30 acres. George Bridges (Seal), Ann Bridges (A) (Seal), Wit: James Johnston, Wright Coats, Sarah Champneys. Recorded 14 March 1798. [see deed on D2, 321-323, apparently the release portion of the deed]

D2, 317-319: 17 March 1795, Elisha Brooks, heir to Elisha deceased, & Nancy his wife of Newberry County, for two shillings sterling, to William Allen of same, 150 acres on north side Saluda River adj. John Norris but now by the heirs of Allen Cox decd, James Maxwell, granted to John Finlay 20 Oct 1770 and conveyed from him to Elisha Brooks now deceased 7 Feb 1780. Elisha Brooks (Seal), Nancy Brooks (Seal), Wit: George Slaughter, James Caldwell, Deliah Mabray (mark). Proved in Newberry County by the oath of Delila Mabery 24 Feb 1798 before Robt Gillam. Recorded 14 March 1798. [see deed on D2, 323-326, apparently the release portion of the deed]

D2, 319-320: 3 Nov 1797, Charles Burton and wife Grizel of Newberry County to John Levingston, Esquire, for £10 sterling, 100 acres, part of 200 acres on waters of Cannons Creek, adj. Abrm Thompson, John Lewis, James McNeil, Kirkland. Charles Burton (Seal), Grizel Burton (mark) (Seal), Wit: John B. Mitchell, Peter Richardson (mark), Saml Levingston (X). Proved by the oath of Peter Richardson 31 Jan 1798 before David Ruff, J.P. Recorded 14 March 1798.

D2, 321-323: 30 May 1795, George Bridges and wife Nancy to William Lester of same, for £30 sterling, 30 acres on the waggon road that leads to Lees bridge, part of tract granted to Andrew Keller 23 Sept 1768. George Bridges (Seal), Ann Bridges (A) (Seal), Wit: James Johnston, Wright Coats, Sarah Champneys. Proved by the oath of Jas Johnston before Thos W. Waters 30 May 1795. Recorded 14 March 1798. [see deed on D2, 315-316, apparently the lease portion of the deed]

D2, 323-326: 17 March 1795, Elisha Brooks, heir to Elisha deceased, & Nancy his wife of Newberry County, for two shillings sterling, to William Allen of same, 150 acres on north side Saluda River adj. John Norris but now by the heirs of Allen Cox decd, James Maxwell, granted to John Finlay 20 Oct 1770 and conveyed from him to Elisha Brooks now deceased 7 Feb 1780. Elisha Brooks (Seal), Nancy Brooks (Seal), Wit: George Slaughter, James Caldwell, Deliah Mabray (mark). Proved in Newberry County by the oath of Delila Mabery 24 Feb 1798 before Robt Gillam. Recorded 14 March 1798. [see deed on D2, 317-319, apparently the lease portion of the deed]

D2, 327-328: 9 Dec 1797, Joseph Caldwell of Newberry County, planter, to John Caldwell of same, planter, for £30 sterling, 74 3/4 acres on waters of Builders Creek adj. Rachel Dunkin, James Caldwell, Hugh Reid. Joseph Caldwell (Seal), Wit: Hugh Reid, James Caldwell (X), Wm. Alexander. Proved by the oath of Hugh Reid 27 Jan 1798 before John Speak, J.P. Recorded 14 March 1798.

D2, 328-329: Joseph Caldwell acknowledges himself indebted to Joab Mayson in for £12 s10 sterling, mortgage of 130 acres on waters of Kings Creek known by the name of John Caldwells old place now rented this year to Widow Bone, 2 March 1798. Joseph Caldwell (Seal), Wit: David Speirs, David Mason, George Pemberton Junr. Proved by the oath of David Mason 2 March 1798 before John Levingston, J.P. Recorded 14 March 1798.

D2, 330-335: Lease and release. 7 & 8 Feb 1780, John Fendley of Ninety Six District, to Elisha Brooks of same, for £1000 SC money, 150 acres on north side Saluda River adj. John Norris, James Maxwell, granted to said John Fendley 12 Oct 1770. John Fendley (Seal), Wit: Francis Sinquefield, John Low, Charles Findley. Proved in Edgefield County by the oath of John Low 3 Aug 1789 before William Anderson, J.P. Recorded 14 March 1798.

D2, 335-336: Giles Chapman & wife Mary to John Levingston, Esqr., for £50 sterling, 100 acres, tract granted to Giles Chapman 19 June 1772, dated 13 Feb 1798. Giles Chapman (Seal), Mary Chapman (Seal), Wit: John Stewart, Charles Burton, Joseph Chapman. Proved by the oath of Charles Burton 1 March 1798 before Elisha Ford, J.P. Recorded 14 March 1798.

D2, 337-340: Lease and release. 23 & 24 Oct 1795, Philimon Waters, Colonel, of Newberry County, to Peter Lester of same, for £200 sterling, 223 acres, part of 500 acres granted to Wm Mazyck 14 Sept 1771 and conveyed to Philiman Waters. Philiman Waters (Seal), Wit: Smith Musgrove, David Pugh. Proved by the oath of Smith Musgrove before Thomas W. Waters, J.P. Recorded 14 March 1798.

D2, 341-343: 6 Jan 1797, John Thomas of Newberry County, for £24 SC money to Moses Kelly of same, tract on waters of Indian Creek, 50 acres, granted to Jonathan Taylor for 200 acres, bequeathed by the will of Jonathan Taylor to John Thomas. John Thomas (Seal), Martha Thomas (X) (Seal), Wit: William Burton Junr, Valintine Braswell, Abel Pearson. Martha Thomas (X), wife of John Thomas, relinquished dower 14 Jan 1797 before J. R. Brown, J.N.C.

Proved 14 July 1797 by the affirmation of Valintine Braswell before Elisha Ford, J.P. Recorded 15 March 1798.

D2, 343-346: 20 Feb 1797, David Boyd of Ninety Six district, farmer, and Ellinor his wife, to James Caldwell of same, for £30 sterling, 100 acres, part of 200 acres in Newberry County on waters of guilders Creek granted to Valintine Luttner in 1773 and by him conveyed to David Boyd in 1784. David Boyd (Seal), Eleanor Boyd (Seal), Wit: John Slan, Robt Dickson (mark), John Caldwell (mark). Proved by the oath of John Caldwell 27 Jan 1798 before John Speak, J.P. Recorded 15 March 1798.

D2, 346: Daniel Clary of Newberry County bound to Philiman Berry Waters in the sum of £500 sterling, 7 Nov 1795, to make title to land bought at sheriffs sale date first mentioned. Daniel Clary (Seal), Wit: Wm Satterwhite. Recorded 15 May 1798.

D2, 347-348: John Waits of Newberry County for £50 to John King of same, 60 acres granted in said John Waits' name adj. Henry Crick, Henry Tate, Allen Roberson, being the plantation whereon the said Waits formerly lived, 27 Feb 1798. John Waits (Seal), Wit: William Langford, Etheldred King. Proved by the oath of Etheldred King 28 Feb 1798 before Daniel Clary, J.P. Recorded 15 March 1798.

D2, 348-343: Lease and release. 9 & 10 Nov 1789, Jonathan Gilbert of Ninety Six District, to Alexander Cotheran of same, for £10 sterling, 32½ acres on waters of the Beaver Dam of Saluda River, adj. Hannah Cook, Benjamin Inman, Wm Weeks, Enos Elleman, part of 131½ acres granted to Enos Elleman 31 Aug 1774. Jonathan Gilbert (Seal), Hanameil Gilbert (Seal), Wit: James Wadlington, Cary Gilbert, Hephzebah Gilbert (X). Proved by the oath of Cary Gilbert 2 March 1798 before Elisha Ford, J.P. Recorded 15 March 1798.

[N. B. An error in pagination occurred in the original deed book: the page following 351 is numbered 342.]

D2, 344: 10 Feb 1798, Isaac Devinport of Newberry County to Francis Devinport Senr of same, one negro woman named Rachel &* one negro man named Peter & one negroe man named Bay, also all household furniture & stock of cattle, hogs, horses & sheep. Isaac Devinport (Seal), Wit: James Goggans, George Goggans. Proved by the oath of James Goggans 2 March 1798 before Daniel Perkins, J.P. Recorded 15 March 1798.

D2, 345-347: 26 Jan 1792, John Harman of Newberry County and wife Mary to George Bridges of same, for £100 sterling, 150 acres on Bigg Creek, part of 3450 acres granted to Andrew Keller 12 Sept 1768 and after several conveyances became the property of John Harman on the SW side of the main waggon roade that runs by Lees ferry to Charleston. John Harman (seal), Mary Harman (mark) (Seal), Wit: James Johnston, George Gibson.

Proved by the oath of James Johnson 16 March 1798 before Thos W. Waters, J.P. Recorded 16 March 1798.

D2, 347-349: State of North Carolina, Pitts [sic for Pitt] County. 8 Jan 1798, James Samson Clark, Holland Johnson, Elizabeth Clark, Mary Clark, Elizabeth Quarturmos, and Sarah Quarturmos, of county aforesaid to Etheldred King of Newberry County, SC, for £150 currency, all our right, title in a tract in Newberry County on north side Saluda River, 343 acres, formerly belonging to Patrick Quarturmos deceased. James S. Clark (Seal), H. D. Johnson (Seal), Elizabeth Clark (Seal), Mary Nolath (Seal), Elizabeth Quarturmos (Seal), Sarah Quarturmos (Seal), Wit: Zelots Collins, Thomas Jones, John King. Proved in Newberry County by the oath of John King 28 Feb 1798 before D. Clary. Recorded 16 March 1798.

D2, 349-351: 7 April 1796, Francis Devinport Senr of Newberry County to Daniel McKie Junr of same, for £25 sterling, 50 acres on a branch of Little River called Rocky Creek adj. David Devinport, Francis Devinport, part of tract granted to Joseph Devinport 6 April 1773 and conveyed to Francis Devinport 10 May 1775. Francis Devinport (Seal), Mary Devinport (X) (Seal), Wit: Stephen Waldrop, Saml Harris. Mary Devinport, wife of Francis Devinport, relinquished dower 8 Aug 1796 before J. R. Brown, J.N.C. Proved by the oath of Stephen Waldrop 8 Sept 1797 before Charles Griffin, J.P. Recorded 16 March 1798.

D2, 351-352: John More of Ninety Six District for £40 paid by John Buchannan deceased, late of Penalton [sic, for Pendleton] County, SC, conveys to his heirs Alex M. Buchannan, Jane Buchannan, & Martha Buchannan & Rody Buchannan, tract of 225 acres, each to have equal part when comes of lawful age, said land in Penelton County on Cherokee Creek, a branch of Heancoop. [not dated]. John Moores (Seal), Wit: John Johnson, Katrin Buckhanning (X), Thos Johnston. Proved in Newberry County by the oath of John Johnston 19 Feb 1798 before John Speak, J.P. Recorded 16 March 1798.

D2, 353-354: Robert Gillam, exr. of Robert Gillam deceased, of Newberry County for £100 sterling, 200 acres on Pages Creek by plat made by William Caldwell 9 May 1796, 29 July 1797. Robert Gillam (Seal), Wit: Fredr. Gray, Philip Proctor, Saml E. Kenner. Proved 29 July 1797 by the oath of Philip Proctor before Saml E. Kenner, J.P. Recorded 16 March 1798.

D2, 354-355: I do certify that I saw the full sum of $80 paid to Samuel Waldrope by James Devinport, the full consideration money for the within note. Charles Griffin, 15 Feb 1798.

Newberry County. Personally came Saml Waldrop and stated that a certain note of hand signed by James Devinport and payable to him the said Saml Waldrop for $80 dated 16 Nov 1796 was delivered by him to said Devinport and said note is mislaid and lost, 28 Dec 1797. Saml Waldrop, before Charles Griffin, J.P. Recorded 16 March 1798.

D2, 355-357: 27 Feb 1792, Wm Irby to Arthur Barret for £10 sterling, 25 acres, part of 435 acres granted 15 Oct 1784, recorded in Book FFFF, page 269. William Irby (Seal), Henritter Irby (X) (Seal), Wit: Joseph Towles, Edward Thweatt, Michael Abney. Proved 17 March 1798 in Newberry County by the oath of Michael Abney stating that he saw Capt. William Irby sign, before Daniel Clary, J.P. Recorded 23 March 1798.

D2, 357-358: 14 March 1798, John Coate of Newberry County for £100 sterling to Peter Julien of same, two lots in Newberry village, each ¼ acre, number 34 and 36, bounded by Church Street, Benjamin Cobb's lotts. Jno Coate (Seal), Wit: William Davis, James Johnson. Proved by the oath of James Johnson 14 March 1798 before Fred Nance, J.P. Recorded 23 March 1798.

D2, 359-360: Isaiah Shirer of Newberry County laberer, appoints friend Robert Neely of same, lawful attorney to receive from the estate of Richard Strawther deceased, or perviso should any deficiency arise in the rights of a tract of 161 acres which I bought of said Richard Strother & Delila his wife, dated 8 Feb 1796. Isaiah Shirer (Seal), Wit: David Ruff, J.P. Elizabeth Ruff (mark), George Cromer Junr (mark). Recorded 23 March 1798.

D2, 360: To the Clerk of the County Court of Newberry. Sir, in consequence of my having recd full satisfaction on a mortgage given by Capt. Benja Long to me, which has been recorded, I request that you may enter full satisfaction for the same, 3 April 1798. George Latham. Recorded 3 April 1798.

D2, 361-365: Lease and release. 6 & 7 Dec 1797, Daniel OHara and Peter Bounetheau, both of Charleston, admrs. of the estate of William Downs, late of Charleston, gentleman, deceased, to Wright Coats of Newberry County, SC, for $155, 150 acres in Craven county, Ninety Six District, on east side Saluda River on Beaver Dam, adj. Peter Scot, one Murphy, John Wright. Daniel OHara (Seal), Peter Bouneatheau (Seal), Wit: Charles OHara, Henry OHara. Proved 7 Dec 1797 by the oath of Henry OHara before Adam Gilchrist, City warden. Recorded 3 April 1798.

D2, 366-368: 25 Oct 1797, John Caldwell, and Mary his wife of Newberry County, to William Hutchinson Junr, for £55 sterling, tract in Newberry County on a small branch called Collins Branch, waters of Enoree River, 120 acres adj. Widow Davis, part of tract granted to John Caldwell Senr deceased. John Caldwell (Seal), Mary Caldwell (Seal), Wit: Joseph Caldwell, William Scott, Enoch Lake (X). Proved by the oath of Enoch Lake 17 Feb 1798 before Saml E. Kenner, J.P. Recorded 7 April 1798.

D2, 369-371: William Pearson, Henry Steddom, and Benjamin Pearson, of Newberry County, exrs. of Samuel Pearson, decd., for £200 sterling, to Rhoda Babb and Samuel Miles, exrs. of Mercer Babb, decd., 98 acres, part of tract granted to Conrad Immunuk 28 Jan 1773 and conveyed to John Embree then to Moses Embree then to Joachim Beaulow and Peter Karr in company or fellowship but by agreement said Karr became possessed of the whole, but said Joachim Beaulow having obtained a judgment against said Peter Karr in the court of common pleas at Ninety Six in consequence of which the said land was conveyed to the said Joachim Beaulow by Robert Rutherford, then high sheriff of Ninety Six District, 11 Dec 1785, and by said Joachim Beaulow [Bulow] to Mercer Babb and Saml Pearson, and 2½ acres, part of a tract granted to Stephen Elmore 2 April 1762 and conveyed by Stephen Elmore to John Embree and by said John Embree to Mercer Babb and Saml Pearson in partnership, with a grist and saw mill thereon, dated 21 March 1798. William Pearson (Seal), Henry Steddom (Seal), Benjamin Pearson (Seal), Wit: Geo Bowie, Mathew Fox, R. McCoombs. Proved in Abbeville County by the oath of George Bowie, Esqr., 21 March 1798 before Julius Nichols, J.P. Recorded 12 April 1798.

D2, 372-373: 23 Jan 1798, Lewis Blalock Senr, planter, of Newberry County to Samuel Law Senr of same, for $60, one negro girl slave named Beck. Lewis blalock (Seal), Wit: J. McMorris, Edmond Lindsey. Proved by the oath of John McMorris 3 Feb 1798 before John Speak, J.P. Recorded 12 April 1798.

D2, 373-376: Martin Souter of Newberry County, planter, for £50 sterling to Andrew Russel of same, 100 acres granted to John Souter Ju'r 5 May 1754, recorded in Book P. page 337, and whereas the said John Souter died intestate the 100 acres devolved into the possession of his oldest son the said Martin Souter, on Second Creek adj. John Souter Senr, Hans George Ellenwyers, dated 28 March 1798. Martin Souter (S) (Seal), Wit: Andrew Swan, Emmanuel Glymph, George Crumer. Proved by the oath of Andrew Swan 28 March 1798 before David Ruff, J.P. Recorded 18 April 1798.

D2, 376: July 8th day 1797. Then rec'd of Mildred Griffin, wife and executor of the estate of John Griffin her deceased husband, £55 sterling, my part of the estate. John Mansil (X), Wit: Jacob Croswhite, Henry Edderington. Recorded 23 April 1798.

D2, 377-378: Edward Rutledge of South Carolina for £4 s10 to Providence Williams, 30 acres in Newberry County on waters of Indian Creek, part of 2000 acres granted to Henry Middleton, Esquire, dated 17 Aug 1796. Ed: Rutledge (Seal), Wit: Keating Simons, Wm Clements. Proved by the oath of Keating Simons at the City of Charleston 29 Oct 1796 before Wm Blamyer, J. Q. Recorded 21 April 1798.

D2, 378-379: Andrew Montgomery of York County and Wm Montgomery of Newberry County for £35 sterling to William Craig, 100 acres on Scots Creek adj. Nathaniel Nicholes, Jas Brown, Jonathan Reid, part of two tracts granted to Wm McGlamery Senr in 1768 and 1773, land on which the said Andrew Montgomery formerly lived, dated 3 Jan 1798. Adr Montgomery (Seal), William Montgomery (Seal), Wit: Fred Nance, J.P. Saml Montgomery. Recorded 27 April 1798.

D2, 379-380: 8 Sept 1797, Patty or Martha Gary of Newberry County to Providence Williams, esqr., said Martha Gary for and in consideration of an article in my father's will, leaving to me the following property or sum of money arising from the sale thereof, which sale took place since my fathers death by my consent, £200 sterling, in compliance with my said father Thomas Gary's will, and in consideration of a bond given by the said Providence Williams, to find me in good house room victualing and clothing such as he finds for his own family during my life. Martha Gary (X) (Seal), Wit: Thomas Gary, Jacob Taylor, William Cote. Recorded 27 April 1798. [See bond below, D2, 383.]

D2, 381-383: 18 April 1798, Reuben Griffin and wife Jane of Newberry County to Daniel Griffin of same, for £54 s7 d4 sterling, tract on SW side of the Quaker branch, 74 acres and 36 perches, part of tract of 350 acres granted to James Griffin, elder, deceased, 12 Dec 1768 and then fell to Charles Griffin by virtue of being heir at law to his father James Griffin deceased, and conveyed to Charles Griffin 21 Feb 1794. Reuben Griffin (Seal), Jane Griffin (Seal), Wit: James Galligly, John Golding. Proved by the oath of John Galligly 18 April 1798 before Charles Griffin, J.P. Recorded 16 May 1798.

D2, 383: South Carolina, Ninety Six District, Newberry County. Providence Williams of Newberry County bound to said Martha Gary for £400, 8 Sept 1797, whereas said Martha Gary has made choice to live in my family during her life and hath signed her part of her father's legacy to me, for which I bind myself to find her a good house room, victualing, & clothing. P. Williams (Seal), Wit: Thomas Gary, Jacob Taylor, William Cote. Recorded 16 May 1798. [See item above, D2, 379-380.]

D2, 384: 14 May 1798, Samuel Lindsey of Newberry County, captain, for £470 sterling to Thomas Lindsey of same, Nerow, Toney, Lambert, Sambo, Andrew, all men slaves, Debio and Diner, wenches, George a boy about 13 years old, Pat a girl about 9 years old, Molly a girl child about 6 years old, and a girl child about one year and a half old. Saml Lindsey (Seal), Wit: Thomas Stark, John McMorries. Proved by the oath of Capt. Thos Stark 14 May 1798 before John Speak, J.P. Recorded 16 May 1798.

D2, 385-386: South Carolina, Newberry County. Jno Worthington, Elizabeth Worthington, Elijah Worthington & Milly Worthington, Joseph Jones & Nancy Jones, Jno Abernathy & Rhoda Abernathy, Thomas W. Waters & Fany Waters & Chesley Davis, Saml Davis, Thomas Davis, & Jesse Davis and Molly Davis, all joint heirs & legatees of Mary Davis decd, to enfranchise a certain negro wench named Pat about 40 years old, yellow complexion, which is our just right and property, 4 Aug 1797. Thos W. Waters (Seal), Fanny Waters (Seal), John Worthington (Seal), Elizabeth Worthington (mark (Seal), Eli'h Worthington (Seal), Milly Worthington (X) (Seal), Chesley Davis (Seal), Saml Davis (Seal), Tho's Davis (Seal), Jesse Davis (X) (Seal) and Molly Davis (Seal), Joseph Jones (Seal), Nancy Jones (X) (Seal), John Abernathy (Seal), Rhoda Abernathy (X) (Seal), Wit: Thos Berry, Jacob Berry. Proved by the oath of Jacob Berry 21 April 1798 before D. Clary, J.P. Recorded 17 May 1798.

D2, 386: Jacob Cromer's mark to be Recorded both ears crop't and a round hole in each ear, and the right Ear in under keel. May 17, 1798. John Cromer. Recorded 21 May 1798.

D2, 387-388: Thos W. Waters of Newberry County for $20 to Saml Waites of same, 150 acres on waters of Buffalo, part of 1000 acres granted to said Thomas W. Waters, adj. Cruse, Dominick, Counts, Igleberger, 14 Feb 1798. Thos W. Waters (Seal), Wit: Daniel Brooks, Jas Johnson. Proved by the oath of Jas Johnson 10 March 1798 before Daniel Parkins, J.P. Recorded 21 May 1798.

D2, 388-389: Saml Waites of Newberry County for $130 to John Stewart of same, 150 acres on waters of Buffalo, part of 1000 acres granted to said Thomas W. Waters, adj. Cruse, Dominick, Counts, Igleberger, 8 March 1798. Saml Waites (mark) (Seal), Wit: Jas Johnson, William Seigler, Henry Counts (H). Proved by the oath of Jas Johnson 10 March 1798 before Daniel Parkins, J.P. Recorded 21 May 1798.

D2, 390-393: 7 Jan 1774, William Rhodus of Ninety Six District to Isaac Davinport of same, for £200 SC money, 200 acres on waters of Saluda, granted to William Rhodus 3 July 1772. William Rhodus (W) (Seal), Wit: Francis Davinport, James Davinport. Mary Rhodes (X), wife of William Rhodes, relinquished dower 21 March 1798 before L. E. Casey, J.N.C. Proved by the oath of Francis Davinport 1 Feb 1774 before Jno Caldwell, J.P. Recorded 21 May 1798. [The lease portion of this deed, dated 6 Jan 1774, is recorded on pages 395-396.]

D2, 393-395: South Carolina, Ninety Six District. Joseph Furnas of Newberry County for £75 sterling to Rhoda Babb & Samuel Miles, exrs. of the will of Mercer Babb decd, 100 acres on Bush River, part of two larger tracts granted 100 acres to Stephen Elmore 2 April 1762 and 300 acres granted to Conrad Imunick 28 Jan 1771, adj. Elisha Ford, 9 acres conveyed by John Embree to said Mercer Babb and Saml Pearson decd, one third of that part of the original grant conveyed to Joseph Furnas by John Embree and conveyed to said John Embree by Stephen Elmore and Conrad Imunick 21 & 22 Nov 1771 and the other 15 & 16 Nov 1771, dated 16 May 1798. Joseph Furnas (Seal), Wit: Elisha Ford, William Wright, Benjamin Inman. Sarah Furnas, wife of Joseph Furnas, relinquished dower 22 May 1798 before J. R. Brown, J.N.C. Proved by the affirmation of Benjamin Inman 16 May 1798 before Elisha Ford, J.P.

D2, 395-396: Lease portion of deed recorded on D2, 390-393 above.

D2, 397-398: 18 March 1796, George Nealy and wife Mary of Newberry County to Robert McKee of same, for £20 sterling, 100 acres granted to Mary

Proctor 1 Sept 1768 on a small branch of Indian Creek called Aseys branch adj. said Robert McKee, Arthur McCracken, William Knox, James Munford. George Nealy (Seal), Mary Nealy (Seal), Wit: Edward Gore, Jesse Graham. Mary Nealy, wife of George Nealy, relinquished dower 21 Oct 1796 before L. E. Casey, J.N.C. Proved by the oath of Edward Gore 28 May 1798 before John Speake, J.P. Recorded 28 May 1798.

D2, 399-402: Lease and release. 21 & 22 May 1798, John Kinnard of Ninety Six District, son and heir of John Kinnard deceased, for £80, to William Jackson of same, 175 acres on waters of Cannons Creek, part of 350 acres granted to John Kinnard deceased 12 Aug 1768, recorded in Book DDD, page 421, and in the Aud'rs Office in Book I No 9, page 176., adj. John Perry, Israel Gaunt, Samuel Kelly, an undivided moiety of the original survey. John Kinnard (Seal), Wit: Robert Rutherford, George Pemberton, James Baird. Margaret Kinnard (X), wife of John Kinnard, relinquished dower 22 May 1798 before L. E. Casey, J.N.C. Acknowledged in open court May term 1798. Recorded 28 May 1798.

D2, 402-404: 29 June 1797, John Hogg and wife Ann Elizabeth of Newberry County to James Hutchinson of same, for £40 sterling, 123 acres on the N side Second Creek, part of tract granted to Daniel Horsey for 147 acres surveyed 2 March 1773, conveyed from Sarah Horsey to said John Hogg. John Hogg (Seal), Anne Elizabeth Hogg (X) (Seal), Wit: Gabriel Anderson, Lewis Hogg, James Blare (X). Proved by the oath of James Blare 29 June 1799 before Edward Finch, J.P. Recorded 28 May 1798.

D2, 404-405: 27 Dec 1797, David Jenkins Senr of Newberry County to David Jenkins Junr, for five shillings sterling, 200 acres on waters of Bush River adj. David Jenkins, surveyed for Cornelius Cothran 10 March 1767 and granted to James Ballinger 10 April 1771. David Jenkins (Seal), Wit: Edward Benbow, John Coate. Proved by the oath of Ed'wd Benbow 21 May 1798 before Fred Nance, J.P. Recorded 28 May 1798.

D2, 406: Thomas Gary of Laurence County for $425 to Stephen Sparks of Newberry County, two negroes: one girl named Gill about 8 years and one boy named Will about 7 years old, 28 April 1798. Thomas Gary, Wit: John Cannon. Proved in Newberry County by the oath of John Cannon 21 May 1798 before Fred Nance, J.P. Recorded 28 May 1798.

D2, 407-408: William Pearson & Benjamin Pearson of Newberry County, exrs. of Samuel Pearson decd, bound to Mercer Babb of same, in the sum of £100 sterling, 16 April 1792, to make title to 104 acres on both sides Bush River with a grist and saw mill thereon, by lease and release made to said Samuel Pearson & Mercer Babb in company or partnership by John Embree and Joacham Bulow adj. land of Mathias Elmore, William Elmore, Walter Harbert. William Pearson (Seal), Benjamin Pearson (Seal), Wit: Thomas Haskit, Saml Kelly. Proved by the oath of Thos Haskit 24 May 1798 before Elisha Ford, J.P. Recorded 28 May 1798.

D2, 408-409: 21 April 1798, William Craig of Newberry County to Samuel Lindsey of same, for £34 sterling, 150 acres on Kings Creek, part of tract granted to Abel Anderson 9 April 1768. W. Craig (Seal), Wit: John McMorris, David Reed, Major T. Hall. Proved by the oath of John McMorris 16 May 1798 before John Speak, J.P. Recorded 5 June 1798.

D2, 410-411: 18 Jan 1797, Daniel Johnson and wife Mary of Newberry County to Stephen Shell for £70 sterling, 200 acres, part of tract granted to Daniel Johnson Senr, surveyed 19 April 1771, on the drafts of Second Creek and Gossets Creek, recorded in Book NNN, page 398, 200 acres, part of the land conveyed by Daniel Johnson Senr to his grandson Daniel Johnson, son of Thomas Johnson, by will. Daniel Johnson (Seal), Mary Johnson (X) (Seal), Wit: Jonathan Pratt, Levi Johnson, George Shell. Proved by the oath of Jonathan Pratt 25 Jan 1797 before Edward Finch, J.P. Recorded 28 May 1798.

D2, 412-413: 4 Oct 1796, William Finch and wife Elizabeth of Newberry County to Stephen Shell of same, for £150 sterling, 294 acres, part of two tracts of land, 37 acres thereof being part of grant to Samuel Wilson 3 Aug 1762 on Second Creek and 257 acres, part of grant 2 May 1774 to Robert Moore for 150 acres. William Finch (Seal), Elizabeth Finch (X) (Seal), Wit: Jonathan Pratt, Zacheriah Hogg, John Finch, Edwd Finch, J.P. 9 Jan 1797 Elizabeth Finch acknowledged deed before Edward Finch, J.P. Recorded 28 May 1798.

D2, 413-416: Lease and release. 18 & 19 Oct 1794, James Vardiman, planter, of Ninety Six District, to Samuel Murray of same, for £60 sterling, 100 acres on a branch of Indian Creek by the name of Hunting fork. James Vardiman (Seal), Jean Vardiman (Seal), Bridget Vardiman (mark) (Seal), Wit: William Murray, William Beard, James Murray. Recorded 2 June 1798.

D2, 417-420: Lease and release. 12 & 13 Dec 1766, Samuel Awberry of Craven County, SC, merchant, to William Vardiman, merchant, for £50 sterling, 150 acres on south side Enoree River on Indian Creek. Samuel Awbrey (Seal), Wit: Charles D. Bradford, Thos Gordon, George Strawn. Proved by the oath of Capt. Thomas Gordon 15 Dec 1766 who swore that Capt. Saml Awbery did sign the deed, before Edward Musgrove, J.P. Recorded 2 June 1798.

D2, 420-423: 11 January [1776], William Hays of the Province of north Carolina to Saml Murray of South Carolina, for £50 SC money, 100 acres adj. land of Wm Vardiman. William Hays (Seal), Wit: James Caldwell, Charles McClure, Sarah Johnston. Frederick Nance certifies that the balance of the original lease and release was so old & worn out that it was not "elegible" & could not be made out & recorded, 2 June 1798.

D2, 424: 1 May 1798, William Finch of Newberry County to Aaron Cates of same, for 325 silver dollars, one negro woman named Clary. William Finch (Seal), Wit: John Morrow, John Finch. Proved by the oath of John Finch 8 June 1798 before David Ruff, J.P. Recorded 8 June 1798.

D2, 425-426: 1 Dec 1794, John Eigleberger and Barbara his wife of Newberry County to Jacob Long of same, for £50 sterling, 100 acres on the branches of Cannons Creek, waters of Broad River, part of a tract granted to Herman Noulfer for 300 acres, recorded in Book PP, page 288. John Eigleberger (Seal), Barbara Eigleberger (X) (Seal), Wit: Wm Houseal, George Long (GL), Joseph Whyett (W). Proved by the oath of Joseph Whyett (X) 18 March 1795 before William Houseal, J.P. Recorded 25 June 1798.

D2, 427: 15 Dec 1797, Anne Langford of Newberry County for £6 to Jacob Bare of same, 2 acres, part of tract granted 5 Feb 1787 to John Langford, on waters of Buffalow Creek. Anne Langford (Seal), Wit: Jacob Langford, Adrine Witt (mark), Jer. McDanal. Proved 23 Dec 1797 by the oath of Adrine Witt before John Livingston, J.P. Recorded 26 June 1798.

D2, 428-429: 15 Dec 1797, Thomas Monk of Orangeburgh District, SC, planter, to Jacob Bare of Newberry County, for £26 sterling, 100 acres on north side Saluda River on NE side Buffalow Creek. Thomas Monk (Seal), Wit: Jer: McDanal, Michael White, Adrin Witt (mark). Proved 23 Dec 1797 by the oath of Adrine Witt before John Livingston, J.P. Recorded 26 June 1798.

D2, 430: State of Georgia. Mary Sibel Folk, the abandoned wife of John Folk, late of Effingham County, state aforesaid, acknowledge receipt of £10 and other considerations delivered unto Michael Dickart, Esqr., Citizen of Newberry County, for all parts of the estate of said John Folk, real and personal, in which I may be interested, 16 May 1798. Mary Sible Folk (X), Wit: Peter Rab, Jacob Frederick (mark). Proved in Newberry County by the oath of Peter Rub 30 June 1798 before David Ruff, J.P. Recorded 28 July 1798.

D2, 431: 3 July 1798, Margaret Hendricks, widow of William Hendricks, decd, and Isaac Hendricks, son of said deceased, and Charity Sarvarris and Rebeccah Hendricks, daughters of the same, appoint my two trusty sons and brothers John and Thomas Hendricks our lawful attorneys, to recover land and chattles in South Carolina of said William Hendricks. Margaret Hendrick (X) (Seal), Isaac Hendricks (Seal), Charity Sarvarris (X) (Seal), Rebekah Hendricks (X) (Seal), Wit: Nathaniel Hall, J.P., Mary Kelly (X). Recorded 30 July 1798.

D2, 432-435: Lease and release. 10 & 11 Feb 1794, William Gillam of Ninety Six District, to John Duncan of same, for £14 s10, 25 acres on waters of Bush River adj. land of John Justices, William Gillam, estate of Wm Taylor deceased, part of 500 acres granted to said William Gillam deceased, 15 Feb 1769. William Gillam (Seal), Wit: William McDowell, Saml Peatchey (X), Joseph Furnas. Proved in Newberry County by the oath of Joseph Furnas 5 Oct 1795 before Elisha Ford, J.P. Recorded 30 July 1798.

D2, 435-436: 14 Oct 1797, James Griffin Senr of Newberry County to John Simpson, merchant, of Laurens County, for £75 sterling, 412 acres on Cason Creek, waters of Little River, part of two tracts, one of 100 acres laid off to Levi Pitts and conveyed to Saml Ford & by said Ford conveyed to James Griffin Senr & 200 acres laid out to Saml Ford and conveyed to James Griffin Senr. James Griffin (+) (Seal), Wit: John Golding, Charles Griffin. Proved by the oath of Charles Griffin 31 July 1798 before P. Williams, J.P. Recorded 30 July 1798.

D2, 437-439: Lease and release. 8 & 9 May 1794, Jesse Pugh of Newberry County to John Daily of same, for £30 sterling, tract of land belonging to him by his former marriage with Elizabeth Debit granted to Ann & Elizabeth Debit 9 Sept 1774 and recorded in Book LLL, page 639, for 200 acres, but by a resurvey found to be 175 acres. Jesse Pugh (Seal), Wit: James Pugh (X), Jacob Brooks, David Pugh. Proved by the oath of James Pugh 30 July 1798 before John Levingston, J.P. Recorded 30 July 1798.

D2, 439-442: Lease and release. 8 & 9 April 1798, Reason Reagan of Newberry County to William Aspinell of same, for £50 sterling, 100 acres on waters of Bush Creek, being a tract surveyed for Jacob Barret 9 March 1773 and granted to Reason Reagan 21 Jan 1785. Reason Ragan (Seal), Wit: Giles Chapman, Hezekiah Riley, Thos W. Waters. Proved 9 April 1798 by the oath of Thos W Waters, J.P. Recorded 30 July 1798.

D2, 442-444: 5 March 1798, Abraham Larrowe of Fairfield County, Camden District, for £80 sterling to John Mink of Newberry County, 136 acres granted to William Nobles and conveyed to John Anderson and from Anderson to Solomon Hancock and from him willed to Elijah Parrott from Parrot to Abraham Larrowe, land adj. Henry Mills, Williamson Liles decd, Alex'r Bookter's land on Enoree River. Abraham Larrowe (Seal), Wit: Jacob Minks, William Liles (X), James May. Sarah Larrour (X), wife of Abraham Larrowe, relinquished dower 5 March 1798 before Arramanos [Liles], J.P. in Fairfield County. Proved in Fairfield County by the oath of Jacob Minks 5 March 1798 before Arramanos Liles, J.P.

D2, 444-445: 16 April 1798, David Davenport of Newberry County to Francis Davenport of same, for £30 sterling, 50 acres, part of 250 acres granted to Joseph Davenport Senr. David Davenport (Seal), James Davenport, Lucrecy Davenport (X), George Goggans. Proved by the oath of James Davenport 30 July 1798 before Robt Gillam, J.P. Recorded 30 July 1798.

D2, 446-447: 30 July 1798, John Gordon of Pinckney District, Union County, for £100 sterling, to Posey Gordon of same, 150 acres near the house wherein Phillip Awbery now lives, adj. John Gordon's old line, part of tract granted to John Gordon 10 Nov 1756, recorded in Book 2, page 175, in Union County on both sides of the road from Anderson Ford on Enoree to Hills ford on Tyger River. John Gordon (Seal), Wit: Geo B. Wadlington, Thomas

Wadlington, David Glenn. Proved by the oath of Geo B. Wadlington 30 July 1798 before Samuel E. Kenner, J.P. Recorded 30 Aug 1798.

D2, 447-448: 9 June 1798, John Dickey of Fairfield County, planter, for $100 to Joseph Etcherson of Newberry County, 100 acres on south side of Broad River on the south fork of Dunkins Creek, at the time of survey in Berkeley County but now in Newberry County, adj. Nathan Brown, Reubin Flanigan, granted to John Dickey 8 Dec 1774. John Dickey (Seal), John Boys, Alexr Dickey, James Dickey. Jane Dickey (X), wife of John Dickey, relinquished dower in Fairfield County before John Turner, J. F. C. Proved in Newberry County by the oath of John Boys (Buoys) 30 July 1798 before John Speak, J.P. Recorded 4 Aug 1798.

D2, 447-448: 25 Jan 1798, John Chandler of Greenville County, planter, and Ritter his wife, to David Henderson of Newberry County, for £60 sterling, 100 acres on north side of Enoree River on a branch called Collins Creek in Newberry County, granted to Francis Wafer 5 Sept 1765, memorial entered in Book FFFF, page 15, being the upper part of said tract of 100 acres. John Chandler (X) (Seal), Wit: John Clark, Joseph Caldwell, William Lavender. Proved in Newberry County by the oath of Jos. Caldwell 21 May 1798 before Edward Finch, J.P. Recorded 4 Aug 1798.

END OF DEED BOOK D-2

D, 1: John Sanders & Massa his wife of Union County for £60 sterling to David Sims of Newberry County, 100 acres on Broad River and Tyger Rivers lately conveyed by Reuben Sims to said Sanders & Nathaniel Henderson, 28 May 1798. John Sanders (Seal), Massy Sanders (X) (Seal), Wit: John S. Sims, Reuben Sims, Nancey Sims. Proved in Newberry County by the oath of Reuben Sims 30 July 1798 before Fred Nance, J.P. Recorded 30 July 1798.

D, 2-3: 30 Dec 1789, Dowdle Murphey of Newberry County to Rebekah Murphey of same, for £6 sterling, 200 acres on north side Enoree River adj. Littleton, granted 6 Nov 1786. Dowdle Murphy (Seal), Wit: John Murphey, Zachariah Chandler (X), Sarah Murphey (X). Proved by the oath of John Murphey 28 July 1798 before John Livingston, J.P. Recorded 4 Aug 1798.

D, 3-4: James McMaster of South Carolina for ten shillings to Owen Daly of same, planter, remainder of tract of 100 acres granted to James McMaster 17 March 1775 adj. George Fouser, Michael Kibler, Mathias Kinard, Frederick Shaver, 21 Nov 1797. James McMaster (Seal), Wit: Daniel Dewalt, James McMeen (mark), James Clary (mark). Proved in Newberry County by the oath of Daniel Dewalt 21 Nov 1797 before John Levingston, J.P. Margaret McMaster (X), wife of James McMaster, relinquished dower 30 July 1798 before J. R. Brown, J.N.C. Recorded 4 Aug 1798.

D, 5: 6 July 1798, Henry D. Adkinson of Claremont County, SC, to Daniel Dyson of Newberry County, for $650, two negroes one boy about 16 years of age named Joe, the other a girl about 15 named Susanah. Henry D. Adkinson (Seal), Wit: James E. Harwin, James Dyson. Proved by the oath of James Dyson 30 July 1798 before Fred Nance, J.P. Recorded 4 Aug 1798.

D, 6-7: 26 March 1798, John McDaniel and Elender his wife of Edgefield County, SC, to Beverly Borroum, for £30 sterling, tract on north side Bigg Saluda in Newberry county, 100 acres adj. land of Christopher Cains, John King, John Royal, part of tract granted to Patrick McDugal deceased 12 Sept 1768. John McDaniel (Seal), Elendar McDaniel (Seal), Wit: Mark Matthews, Higdon Borroum, Peterson Borroum. Elenor McDaniel, wife of John **McDonold**, relinquished dower in Edgefield County 5 April 1798 before W. Anderson, J. C. E. Proved in Edgefield County by the oath of Mark Matthews 6 April 1798 before W. Anderson, J. C. E. Recorded 4 Aug 1798.

D, 7-8: 16 Jan 1794, John Chandler Senr and wife Caty of Newberry County to John Henderson of same, for £75 sterling, 100 acres in the fork between Broad & Saluda Rivers on north side Enoree River on the Cool spring branch adj. Clark, Samuel Chandler, John Chandler Junr, Caldwell, part of tract formerly granted to John Clark. John Chandler Sr (Seal), Caty Chandler (Seal), Wit: Edward Finch, J.P., Godfrey Adams, Alex'r Glenn. Recorded 4 Aug 1798.

D, 8-9: South Carolina, Pinckney District, Union County. John Gordon of county aforesaid, planter, for £100 sterling, to David Glenn of newberry

County, sadler, 123 acres adj. Nathaniel Davis, John Gordon, Thomas Gordon, John Caldwell, part of tract granted to John Gordon 10 Nov 1756 by Mathew Rowan, Esqr. [Governor of North Carolina], recorded in Grant Book Q, page 175, in the counties of Union and Newberry on both sides of the road leading from Anderson ford on Enoree to Hills ford on Tiger. John Gordon (Seal), Wit: George B. Wadlington, Posey Gordon, Thomas Wadlington. Proved in Newberry County by the oath of George B. Wadlington 30 July 1798 before Saml E. Kenner, J.P. Recorded 4 Aug 1798.

D, 9: Frederick Foster of Newberry county, carpenter, for $275 to Thos Clark of same, a negroe boy named Kitt about 12 or 13 years old of black complexion, 16 Jan 1798. Frederick Foster (Seal), Wit: Robert McKiterick (mark), Priscilla Clark. Proved by the oath of Robert McKiterick 31 July 1798 before Charles Griffin, J.P. Recorded 4 Aug 1798.

D, 10: Samuel Lindsey of Newberry County for £150 sterling to Nathan Anderson of same, 150 acres on waters of Kings Creek granted to Jacob Anderson, 13 Aug 1798. Samuel Lindsey (Seal), Wit: Wm. Satterwhite, Fred Nance, J.P. Recorded 13 Aug 1798.

D, 11: William Day of Laurens County, tavern keeper, for £35 sterling, to Rutherford Bowler of Newberry County, 88 acres part in Laurens and part in Newberry County, whereon Larkin Brown now lives, 3 Feb 1796. William Day (mark) (Seal), Mary Day (X) (Seal), Wit: J. R. Brown, J.N.C., Joseph Davis. Mary Day, wife of William Day, relinquished dower 7 July 1796 before J. R. Brown, J.N.C. Recorded 13 Aug 1798.

D, 12: 4 May 1798, John Murphy and Rebekah Murphy for £50 sterling to Lewis Hogg, 330 acres on north side Enoree River on Dry Creek adj. Charles Littleton, granted to Thos Gordon 6 Nov 1786. John Murphy (Seal), Rebekah Murphy (mark) (Seal), Wit: Thos Wadlington, William Richards, Ephraim Liles Senr. Proved by the oath of Ephraim Liles Senr 21 July 1798 before Samuel E. Kenner, J.P. Recorded 13 Aug 1798.

D, 13: 7 Nov 1797, Robert Johnson and wife Sarah of Newberry County to William Plunkit of same, for £100, 33 acres on head of Daveses Beaverdam, part of tract of 400 acres granted to James Johnson 14 Aug 1770. Robert Johnson (+) (Seal), Sarah Johnson (+) (Seal), Wit: John Plunket, Jesse Johnson, George Goggans. Proved by the oath of George Goggans 28 July 1798 before Fred Nance, J.P. Recorded 13 Aug 1798.

D, 14: 26 May 1798, Richard Darby and wife Elizabeth to Lewis Hogg of Newberry County for £50 sterling, 500 acres on north side Enoree River on Dry Creek adj. John Clark, Joel Chandler, Chas Littleton. Richard Darby (R) (Seal), Elizabeth Darby (X) (Seal), Wit: Jesse Chandler (X), John hogg, William Darby (mark). Proved by the oath of Jesse Chandler before Samuel E. Kenner, J.P. Recorded 13 Aug 1798.

D, 15: Samuel Waites of Newberry County for £30 sterling to William Seigler of same, 80 acres on waters of Buffalow Creek, part of 158 acres granted to Samuel Waites 6 March 1786 adj. John Harman, William Holeman, dated 8 March 1798. Samuel Waites (X) (Seal), Wit: Jas Johnson, William Harrel (X), Thos Donnon. Proved by the oath of James Johnson 31 March 1798 before Daniel Parkins, J.P. Recorded 13 Aug 1798.

D, 16: 20 July 1797, James Caldwell of Newberry County for £15 sterling to Patrick Martin of same, 30 acres, part of tract granted 8 Dec 1774 to Jane Dickey for 100 acres on the drains of Second Creek. James Caldwell (Seal), Wit: Edward Finch J. P., James Hutchinson, William McCraw. Proved by the oath of James Hutchinson 21 July 1797 before Edward Finch, J.P. Recorded 13 Aug 1798.

D, 17: 8 July 1798, David Reeder of Laurance County to Daniel Reeder of Newberry County, for $43, 75 acres, part of tract granted to said David and Daniel Reeder by Simon Reeder on waters of Kings Creek, a branch of Enoree in Newberry County. David Reeder (+) (Seal), Wit: Stephen Tear (X), Richard Tear. Anne Reeder, wife of David Reeder, relinquished dower 30 July 1798 before J. R. Brown, J.N.C. Proved by the oath of Stephen Tear 28 July 1798 before John Levingston, J.P. Recorded 14 Aug 1798.

D, 18: 3 May 1798, Elijah Lake of Newberry County to John Maxedon Junr of same, for £40 sterling, 100 acres adj. John Maxedon, David Ferguson, Andrew Hunter, Nathaniel Davis, Caldwell. Elijah Lake (Seal), Jane Lake (X) (Seal), Wit: William Wadlington, Martha Mexedon, John Bottoms (X). Proved by the oath of John Bottoms 29 June 1798 before Samuel E. Kenner, J.P. Recorded 14 Aug 1798.

D, 19: South Carolina, Newberry County. Certify that Thomas Clark and Charity Campbell was married together on 4 September 1797, by Providence Williams, J.P. Recorded 14 Aug 1798.

D, 19-22: Lease and release. 24 & 25 Aug 1772, Isaac Horsey and wife Mary of Second Creek in Berkley County, to Samuel Lonam of same place, wheelwright, for £300 SC money, 150 acres on Second Creek in Berkley County adj. land of Philip Hale, originally granted to Margaretta Bomgardenner, at that time the widow of Muller deceased, since when she has entermarried with the said Clement Bomgardenner, grant dated 4 June 1759. Isaac Horsey (X) (Seal), Mary Horsey (mark) (Seal), Wit: John Lindsey Junr, William Hillburn (mark), Samuel Duncan. Proved 24 Aug 1772 by the oath of John Lindsey Junr before Samuel Cannon, J.P. Recorded 14 Aug 1798.

D, 22-26: Lease and release. 2 & 3 Sept 1765, Clement Bomgardenner and Margaretta his wife, of Second Creek in Berkley County to Isaac Horsey of same place, planter, for £50 SC money, 150 acres on Second Creek in Berkley County adj. land of Philip Hale, originally granted to Margaretta Bomgardenner, at that time the widow of _____ Muller deceased, since when she has entermarried with the said Clement Bomgardenner, grant dated 14 June 1759. Clement Bomgardiner (CB) (Seal), Margaretta Bomgardiner (Seal), Wit: John Moncrieff, George Wood. Receipt witnessed by Chas Woodmason. Proved 4 Sept 1765 by the oath of George Wood before Chas Woodmason. Recorded 11 Sept 1798.

D, 27: South Carolina, Ninety Six District, Newberry County. Jacob Brown of county aforesaid, late Lieut. in the first Virginia Regiment on Continental establishment, for $1200 to Abijah Oneal of same, several tracts of land obtained or to be obtained by my Military warrant No. 630, says 3110 2/3 acres, also the several warrants numbered 3347, 3350, 3351, 3352, 3352 & 3349, 8 Sept 1798. Jacob R. Brown (Seal), Wit: Squire Lonam, Samuel Kelly Junr. Proved by the affirmation of Samuel Kelly 10 Sept 1798 before Fred Nance, J.P. Recorded 13 Sept 1798.

D, 28: 3 Sept 1798, Squire Lonam of newberry County for $300 to William Rutherford of same, 150 acres on Second Creek, waters of Broad River, adj. lands of Philip Hoyle, granted to Margaretta Muller 4 June 1759 and conveyed from said Margaretta Muller to Isaac Horsey decd and from the said Isaac Horsey to the father of said Squire Lonam, heir at law &c. Squire Lonam (Seal), Wit: Fred Nance J.P., J. R. Brown, J.N.C. Recorded 11 Sept 1798.

D, 29: 6 Sept 1798, Joseph Caldwell of Newberry County to Marmaduke Coate of same, part of tract of land known by the name of Tea Table Rock plantation adj. lands of Goodwin. Joseph Caldwell (Seal), Wit: Jno B. Mitchell, Moses Coate, Elizabeth Coate. Proved by the oath of John B. Mitchell 8 Sept 1798 before Fred Nance, J.P. Recorded 11 Sept 1798.

D, 30-33: Lease and release. 27 & 28 July 1795, Azariah Pugh of Newberry County to William Pugh of same, for £60 sterling, 143 acres, part of tract on waters of Bush River granted to Enoch Smith 4 Dec 1786, recorded in Book PPPP, page 251, transfered unto Azariah Pugh 13 & 14 Oct 1794, recorded in Book C, Newberry County. Azariah Pugh (Seal), Wit: Samuel McQuerns, Reason Reagan, Richard Clegg. Proved by the oath of Richard Clegg 30 July 1795 before Peter Julien, J.P. Recorded 29 Sept 1798.

D, 33-37: Lease and release. 7 July 1792, Christian Leitner of Lexington County, yeoman, to Charles Bundrick of Newberry County, planter, for £100 sterling, two tracts together 224 acres, 288 acres granted to Christopher Leitner 20 Oct 1752 and the residue of 36 acres being part of a tract granted to Christopher Leitner originally granted to Michael Leitner decd, the above 24 acres transferred into the possession of Michael Leitner decd and said Michael Leitner died intestate, the above 224 acres devolved into the possession of Christian Leitner, he being true heir at law to his fathers estate. Christian Leitner (Seal), Wit: Michael Dickert Senr, George Setsler, Jacob Fulmer. Proved in Lexington County by the oath of Michael Dickert Senr 7 July 1792 before John Adam Summer, J.P. Recorded 4 Oct 1798.

D, 37-38: John Adam Setzler of Newberry County, planter or Gun Smith, for love, good will and affection to my son George Adam Setzler of same, blacksmith, 100 acres granted to Catherinah Setzler and properly transferred into my possession by said Catherina Setzler 27 Oct 1788 in Berkley County in the fork between Broad and Saluda Rivers on a small branch of Cowpen Creek, waters of Broad River, adj. George Risner, Jacob Son, Charles Seigler, 20 Aug 1787. John Adam Setzler (Seal), Wit: Jacob Folmer Senr, Jacob Folmer Junr, Wm Fulmer. Proved 17 April 1797 by the oath of Wm Fullmer before John Adam Summer, J.P. Recorded 9 Oct 1798.

D, 39: South Carolina, Newberry County. Personally appeared Michael Dickert Senr before David Ruff and sayeth on his oath that he made or drawed a certain lease and release between John Kountz and Chatharen Countz and John Adams Setzler for 100 acres in 1770 and that the said titles were proved before him, dated 8 Jan 1796. Michl Dickert Senr before David Ruff, J.P. Recorded 9 Oct 1798.

Also came Adam Keller who sayeth on his oath to the best of his knowledged that he was present & did see John Countz and Catharine his wife signed the lease and release to John Adam Setzler in 1770, 8 Jan 1796 before David Ruff, J.P. Adam Keller (mark). Recorded 9 Oct 1798.

D, 40: 12 March 1798, Charles Clack of Newberry for £40 sterling to David Bozman of same, one negro girl slave about 9 years of age named Chat. Charles Clack (X) (Seal), Wit: James Hill, John Hill. Proved by the oath of John Hill 28 Sept 1798 before Robert Gillam, J.P. Recorded 9 Oct 1798.

D, 41: Simon Reeder of Pendleton County, SC, for $214.28 to Marmeduke Coate of Newberry County, tract of 100 acres on waters of Guilders Creek, part of tract granted to John Goodwin, adj. James Spence, Moses Coate, Joseph Caldwell, Jacob Buzzard, David Boyd, 28 Aug 1798. Simon Reeder (Seal), Lucynda Reeder (X) (Seal), Wit: Robert McLees, John Woodall. Proved in Newberry County by the oath of Robert McLees 8 Oct 1798 before Fred Nance, J.P. Recorded 9 Oct 1798.

D, 42-43: 18 Aug 1798, Robert Johnson of Newberry County to Charles Scott of same, for 200, 50 acres on a branch of Little River called Davises beaverdam, granted to James Johnson 15 Aug 1770. Robert Johnson (Seal), Wit: John Mangum, Jesse Johnson, Daniel Goggans. Sarah Johnson (X), wife of Robert Johnson, relinquished dower 15 Oct 1798 before J. R. Brown, J.N.C. Recorded 15 Oct 1798.

D, 43-46: 4 May 1784, Mary Keller, Ann King, Elizabeth Keller, Dorothy Keller and Mary Keller Junr, of the District of Orangeburgh, to Richard Strother of Ninety Six District, SC, for £10 sterling, 450 acres granted to Johannes Keller 19 Oct 1759 on Hans Creek. Mary Keller (X) (Seal), Ann King (X) (Seal), Elizabeth Keller (X) (Seal), Dorothy Keller (X) (Seal), Mary Keller (Seal), Wit: David Crum, Michael Bradley, John Ad. Beater. Proved in

Orangeburgh District by the oath of David Crum 7 July 1798 before James Carmichael J. P. Recorded 15 Oct 1798.

D, 47-51: Lease and release. 5 June 1789, Richard Strother and Delila his wife of Newberry County to Isaiah Shirer of same, planter, for £225 sterling, 161 acres, part of 450 acres granted 27 Aug 1751 to Johannes Keller on Hans's Creek recorded in Book NN, page 143, and said Johannes Keller died intestate and said land devolved on Mary Keller, Ann King, Elizabeth Keller, Dorothy Keller and Mary Keller Junr, who conveyed to Richard Strother 3 & 4 May 1784, said land adj. Joseph Lloyd, estate of Michael Leitner Esqr., decd., John Sweetenburgh, James Daugheries. Rich'd Strother (Seal), D. Strother (Seal), Wit: John Buchanan Senr, Jonathan Pratt, Peter Dickert. Proved by the oath of Peter Dickert 8 Feb 1796 before David Ruff, J.P. Recorded 20 Oct 1798.

D, 52-53: Richard Watts of Newberry County, Sheriff, to William Craig, that this is the second title made to a tract of 157 acres, the first tiles bearing date the first Saturday in June 1795, being in the house of said Craig was consumed by fire some time in the month of November 1796, by writ of fieri facias from the court of Newberry County at the suit of William Malone, Treasurer of said county, against Philemon B. Waters, to sell said tract, dated 7 Nov 1798. Richard Watts, Shff (Seal), Wit: Nimrod Chiles, Robert A. Cunningham. This deed was executed in my presence, Jas. Mayson, J. N. C. Affidavit of William Craig that the first title was burned, 7 Nov 1798. Recorded 12 Nov 1798.

D, 54: 13 Oct 1798, William Satterwhite, sheriff of Newberry County, to William Craig of same, for $200, one negro fellow named Daniel, which said negro was taken up and sold agreeable to an act of the General Assembly of this state made & provided for Runaway negroes. W. Satterwhite Shff N. C. (Seal), Wit: Fred Nance J.P, James Spearmon. Recorded 12 Nov 1798.

D, 55-57: Isaiah Shirer of Newberry County for £50 SC money to Robert Neely, 161 acres, part of 450 acres granted 27 Aug 1751 to Johannes Kuller (alias Keller) on Hans's Creek recorded in Book NN, page 143, and said Johannes Keller died intestate and said land devolved on Mary Keller, Ann King, Elizabeth Keller, Dorothy Keller and Mary Keller Junr, who conveyed to Richard Strother 3 & 4 May 1784, and said Richard Strother and wife Delila conveyed to Isaiah Shirer 5 June 1789, said land adj. Joseph Lloyd, estate of Michael Leitner Esqr., decd., John Sweetenburgh, James Daughter-ies. Isaiah Shirer (Seal), Elizabeth Shirer (mark) (Seal), Wit: Jesse Buchanan, James Neely, John Stegall. Proved by the oath of James Neely 5 Oct 1798 before David Ruff, J.P. Recorded 12 Nov 1798.

D, 58-59: Isaac Cook of Union County for £60 sterling to James Insco of Newberry County, tract in Newberry County on Scotch Creek, 116 acres adj. lands at the original survey of Stephen Elmore, Phebe Coppock, Benjamin Pearson, Jacob Brooks, said tract originally granted to Robert Milhouse 31 Oct 1769 and devolved to Sarah Milhouse (now Cook), she being heir of the said Robert Milhouse decd, dated 19 March 1798. Isaac Cook (mark) (Seal), Wit: Fred Nance J. P., Robert Malone. Sarah Cook, wife of Isaac Cook, relinquished dower 5 July 1798 before Levi Casey, J.N.C. Recorded 12 Nov 1798.

D, 59-60: 29 March 1798, Roderick McDaniel, carpenter, of Newberry County, to John McMorries, merchant, of same, for 26 specie dollars, one black and white cow and black yearling calf, one black year old calf and one sorrel mare, two heifers and one black no horned cow and spotted year old calf. Roderick McDonald (Seal), Wit: Hezekiah Speak, Ann Aytheson (mark). Proved by the oath of Hezekiah Speak 8 July 1798 before John Speak, J.P. Recorded 12 Nov 1798.

D, 61: 15 Dec 1795, James Hathorn to Levi Fowler, both of Newberry County, for £60 sterling, tract surveyed for David Hathorn 5 May 1772 and granted to said David Hathorn 30 Oct 1772 on Pattersons Creek, a branch of Broad River. James Hathorn (Seal), Wit: Thos Duckett, Andrew Hamilton. Proved by the oath of Thomas Duckett 29 Sept 1798 before John Speak, J.P. Recorded 12 Nov 1798.

D, 62-64: Lease and release. 18 & 19 Oct 1793, John Simpson, merchant of Laurance County, SC, to Joseph Hays of Newberry County, for £78 s10 sterling, 350 acres but by resurvey 278 acres on west side Bush River granted to James Wright 15 Sept 1775 and by said James Wright and wife Rebekah conveyed to William Downs 20 & 21 Sept 1775 and conveyed to John Simpson 8 & 9 Nov 1792 by Daniel OHara and Peter Bounetheau admrs. of William Downs. Jno Simpson (Seal), Wit: Robert Hayes, Charles Jones, James Hayes. Proved in Newberry County by the oath of Robert hayes 15 Oct 1798 before Charles Griffin, J.P. Recorded 12 Nov 1798.

D, 64-65: Owen Flinn of the Town of Suffolk, State of Virginia, for $550 to Isaac Davenport of Newberry County, negro woman slave named Milly & two children Selay and Jack, 19 Sept 1798. O. Flynn (Seal), Wit: Caleb Lindsey, Sarey Waldrop. Proved by the oath of David Waldrop 17 Oct 1798 before Providence Williams, J.P. Recorded 12 Nov 1798.

D, 65-66: 26 Jan 1797, George Stoudemayer and wife Margaret of Orangeburgh District to William Zeagler of same, for £40 sterling, 72 acres, part of tract granted to Samuel Waits 6 March 1786 for 188 acres, recorded in Book HHHH, page 230. George Stoudenmyer (X) (Seal), Margaret Stoudenmyer (X) (Seal), Wit: J. A. Houseal, John Fulmer, William Houseal, J.P. Recorded 14 Nov 1798.

D, 67-71: Lease and release. 7 & 8 Dec 1794, Samuel Waits, planter, of Newberry County, to George Stoudemire of same, for £50 sterling, 72 acres, part of 188 granted to Samuel Waits 6 March 1786, recorded in Book HHHH, page 230, on waters of Saluda River on Buffelow Creek adj. Col. Waters. Sam'l Waits (mark) (Seal), (Seal), Wit: Meck White, William Holman (X).

Proved in Newberry County by the oath of Mick White 14 March 1795 before William Houseal, J.P. Recorded 14 Nov 1798.

D, 71-75: Lease and release. 3 & 4 Feb 1794, Gasper Byerly Senr of Newberry County, planter, and wife Mary, to Sybard Byerly of same, planter, for £100 sterling, 50 acres, the NW part of 100 acres, part of 250 ares granted to Conrod Shirer 17 Aug 1751, recorded in Book NN, page 130 and conveyed 27 & 28 Feb 1767 to Gasper Byerly Senr. Gausper Byerly (B) (Seal), Mary Byerly (mark) (Seal), Wit: George Oster (mark), Adam Byerly, Martin Byerly (M). Proved 17 Jan 1795 by the oath of Martin Byerly before John Hampton, J.Q. Recorded 14 Dec 1798.

D, 76: 26 Oct 1798, Mary Byerly of Newberry County to John Siport Byerly of same, one negro boy named Peter. Mary Byerly (X) (Seal), Wit: Peter Dickert, George Oster (X). Proved 17 Jan 1795 by the oath of Peter Dickert 6 Dec 1798 before Wm. Houseal, J.P. Recorded 14 Dec 1798.

D, 77-78: _____ 1798, Jonathan Taylor Senr of Newberry County for £100 to George Abernathy of same, farmer, 160 acres, part of tract of 200 acres granted to Philip Feagan in the fork of Broad and Saluda Rivers surveyed 19 Aug 1768. Jonathan Taylor (Seal), Wit: John Abernathy, Thomas Coppock, Abraham Large (A). Rhoda Taylor, wife of Jonathan Taylor, relinquished dower 15 Oct 1798 before L. E. Casey, J.N.C. Acknowledged in open court October Term 1798. Recorded 14 Dec 1798.

D, 78-79: James Campbell of Newberry County sold to Charity Patterson of same, for £60, negro girl named Sal, 12 years old, 10 Oct 1798. Jas Campbell (Seal), Wit: John B. Bennett, Jacob King. Proved by the oath of Jacob King 5 Nov 1798 before John Speak, J.P. Recorded 14 Dec 1798.

D, 79-80: William Craig of Newberry County for $150 to Capt. John Wilson and Samuel McQuerns, both of Newberry County, 100 acres near Newberry Court House purchased from Andrew and William McGlamery by deed 3 Jan 1798 recorded in Book D, page 378; also tract of 150 acres on Halls branch purchased at Sheriffs sale by deed from Richard Watts, recorded in Book E, page 52, 7 Nov 1798... 14 Nov 1798. W. Craig (Seal), Wit: Arthur Carmichael, Christian Hope. Proved by the oath of Christian Hopt 5 Dec 1798 before John Levingston, J.P. Recorded 14 Dec 1798.

D, 80-81: Jacob King of Newberry County, planter, for £30 specie, to John Phillips of same, planter, 105 acres, part of tract granted to Jacob King, recorded in Book F No. 5, page 247, 115 acres but now made less by ten acres, granted to Levi Fowler on south side Pattersons Creek, dated 12 Nov 1798. Jacob King (Seal), Wit: F. Foster, Lewis Bennett. Proved by the oath of Lewis Bennett 12 Nov 1798 before John Speak, J.P. Recorded 19 Dec 1798.

D, 81-82: Jacob King of Newberry County, planter, for £10 specie, to Levi Fowler, 10 acres, part of tract granted to Jacob King, recorded in Book F No.

5, page 247, 115 acres, dated 12 Nov 1798. Jacob King (Seal), Wit: Lewis Bennett, John B. Bennett. Proved by the oath of Lewis Bennett 12 Nov 1798 before John Speak, J.P. Recorded 19 Dec 1798.

D, 82-83: 25 June 1798, William Lindsey of Newberry County to Edmund Lindsey of same, for £10 sterling, 50 acres, part of 203 acres granted to James Campbell adj. James Kincaid. William Lindsey (Seal), Wit: Jacob Lindsey (X), Partrick Hallad, George Hagood, George Hews (A). Proved 18 Dec 1798 by the oath of Jacob Lindsey before John Speak, J.P. Recorded 19 Dec 1798.

D, 84-85: 30 June 1798, Richard Johnson and wife Mary of Ninety Six District to William Pitts of same, for £30 sterling, 50 acres on waters of Sandy Run, part of 100 acres granted to John Pitts 14 Aug 1772 and conveyed by said John Pitts to William Johnson 13 & 14 May 1775, and said Richard Johnson became seized by virtue of being heir at law to his father William Johnson decd. Richard Johnson (Seal), Mary Johnson (X) (Seal), Wit: Jacob Croswhite, Stephen Johnson, William Johnson. Proved by the oath of Jacob Croswhite 30 June 1798 before Charles Griffin, J.P. Recorded 21 Dec 1798.

D, 86-87: 29 Oct 1798, George Elliott and wife Sarah to William Johnson, all of Ninety Six District, for £50 sterling, 100 acres in Newberry County on waters of Little River adj. Charles Pitts, granted to Jacob Jones by a precept 3 April 1770. George Elliott (X) (Seal), Salley Elliott (X) (Seal), Wit: William Pitts, Wm. Elliott, Mary Elliott. Proved by the oath of William Pitts 21 Dec 1798 before Charles Griffin, J.P. Recorded 21 Dec 1798.

D, 87: William Hall's Ear mark is as follows a smoothe crop and a slit in the right ear & a slit in the left. Recorded 24 Dec 1798.

Thomas Hall's Ear mark is as follows two slits & the middle piece cut out half way down in the right ear and an under keel in the left. Recorded 24 Dec 1798.

D, 88: South Carolina, Orangeburgh District, Winton County, 20th day of the 12th Month 1791. This is to certify to all people that I have set a mullatter woman named Juno Wilson free with all her children. Isaiah Pemberton, Wit: Sarah Pemberton, John Pemberton. Proved in Newberry County by the affirmation of Sarah Pemberton 13 Dec 1796. Recorded 26 Dec 1798.

D, 89-94: Lease and release. 3 & 4 Feb 1794, Gasper Byerly Senr of Newberry County, planter, and wife Mary, to Martin Byerly of same, planter, for £100 sterling, 100 acres, part of 200 ares granted to 25 Aug 1751 to Jacob Hofner, in the fork of Broad and Saluda Rivers opposite to Saxegotha township, on one of the branches of Broad River, recorded in Book NNNN, page 137 and conveyed 15 & 16 March 1751, recorded in the Auditor Genls Office in Book Co. No. 7, page 46, dj. George Riser, John Hipp, Ulrick Coone. Gasper Byerly (B) (Seal), Mary Byerly (mark) (Seal), Wit: George Oster (mark), Adam

Byerly, Sybard Byerly (X). Proved 17 Jan 1795 by the oath of Sybard Byerly before John Hampton, J.Q. Recorded 8 Jan 1799.

D, 94-95: Mary Edwards (widow of John Edwards dec'd) of Newberry County appoint my friend William Smith of Warren County, Kentucky, my lawful attorney to receive of Robert Moses in the state of Kentucky and County of Christian, one negro wench named Hannah and her increase, which said negro Hannah, her mother and their increase was bequeathed to me by my father William Turner decd, 15 Jan 1799. Mary Edwards (M) (Seal), Wit: Gabriel H. Davis, James Davis, Elisha Brooks. Acknowledged by Mary Edwards 15 Jan 1799 before J. R. Brown, J.N. C. Recorded 17 Jan 1799.

D, 96: 28 Dec 1798, James Golding and William Golding of Laurens County, Ninety Six District, SC, grandsons and heirs of James McGill dec'd, for £100 Virginia currency to Gabriel H. Davis of Frederick County, Virginia, 207 acres in Frederick County, Virginia, on Hoggs Creek whereon David Davis formerly lived, adj. land of Adam Hart, Gasper Renker, Sarah Darlington, John Fainton, being one moiety of tract granted to said McGill, the other moiety was sold to Adam Hart. James Golding (Seal), William Golding (Seal), Wit: J. R. Brown, Edward Edwards, James Davis. Recorded 17 Jan 1799.

D, 97-100: Lease and release. 1 & 2 Sept 1778, Thomas Wiley (Wyley) of Ninety Six District, SC, to George Pemberton of same, for £200 SC money, 100 acres in Craven County near Bush River adj. Henry Wiley, John Brooks. Thomas Wyley (Seal), Wit: Henry Wyley, Wm Hanvey. Proved 18 Sept 1798 by the oath of William Hanvey before James Patterson. Recorded 17 Jan 1799.

D, 101-102: 5 Jan 1799, Thomas Pemberton of Orangeburgh District for $500 to George Pemberton of Newberry County, half of a tract on waters of Broad River, 125 acres, which was wiled to me the said Thomas Pemberton by the will of my father Isaiah Pemberton dec'd, said tract granted to James Walker Moore 24 Aug 1770, memorial entered in Auditor's Office, in Book K. No. 10, page 230, 17 Sept 1770 adj. Robert Evans, John Brooks. Thomas Pemberton (Seal), Wit: Jesse Reeder, Thomas Weeks (X). Proved 5 Jan 1799 by the oath of Jesse Reeder before Wittenhall Warner, J. P. for Orangeburgh District. Easter Pemberton, wife of Thomas Pemberton, relinquished dower 5 Jan 1799 before Wittenhall Warner, J. P. for Orangeburgh District. Recorded 20 Jan 1799.

D, 103-107: Lease and release. 19 & 20 Sept 1791, John Ruth of Edgefield County, to Henry Werts of Newberry County, planter, for £20 sterling, 450 acres granted to John Ruth, recorded in Book B. no. 5, page 243, on waters of Big Creek, a branch of Saluda, in Edgefield County, adj. Benjamin Obannion, heirs of John Higdon, Sherwood Corley, Mr. Hall. John Ruth (Seal), Wit: Thomas Hughes, Adrine Witt (A). Proved in Newberry County by the oath of Adrine Witt 1 Jan 1799 before Wm. Houseal, J.P. Recorded 20 Feb 1799.

D, 107-110: Lease and release. 1 & 2 Nov 1787, Laurence Rikert of Newberry County, to Henry Werts of same, planter, for £20 SC money, 100 acres adj. Andrew Myers, John Fellers, Andrew Bowers, Laurence Rikert, recorded in Book OOO, page 37. Laurence Rikart (LR) (Seal), Wit: Wm Houseal, Adam Houseal. Proved in Lexington County by the oath of Wm Houseal 25 April 1791 before John Hampton, J. P. Quo. Recorded 20 Feb 1799.

D, 110-112: 23 Sept 1794, Jacob Singley and wife Isabella of Newberry County to Henry Werts for £50 sterling, 45 acres in the fork of Broad & Saluda Rivers, part of tract granted to Hermon Noulfer 9 Jan 1755 for 300 acres, recorded in Book PP, page 288. Jacob Singley (X) (Seal), Isabella Singley (X) (Seal), Wit: Michael Kinard, Jacob Long (X), Martin Cook (X). Proved by the oath of Jacob Long (IL) 1 Jan 1799 before Wm Houseal, J.P. Recorded 20 Feb 1799.

D, 112-113: Henry Gissendence [Gissendanner], planter, for £60 to John Miller of Charleston, merchant, a negro slave named Isaac about 13 years of age, 27 Nov 1798. Henry Gissendence (Seal), Wit: Jas Hueston, Jeremiah Brown. Charleston, Decem'r 6th 1798: I will warrant the within Bill of sale to be god and sufficient to Daniel Davault of my right and claims of within negro named Isaac. for my Papa John Miller, E. Miller. Wit: Robert Cameron, Jeremiah Brown. Recorded 20 Feb 1799.

D, 113-114: 20 May 1788, Peter Strozer of State of Georgia, Wilks County, to John Williams Junr of Laurens County, SC, for £100 SC money, 200 acres in Newberry County in the fork between Little River & Mudlick Creek, granted to Stephen Screach 16 Dec 1766 and conveyed 25 & 26 March 1770 to said Peter Strozer. Peter Strozer (P) (Seal), Wit: B. Smith, Wm Hammett J. P. Proved in Wilks County, GA, by the oath of Benajah Smith 3 Feb 1798 before John Sims, J.P. Recorded 20 Feb 1799.

D, 114-118: Lease and release. 24 & 25 June 1791, Alexander Cothran of Newberry County to Samuel Brown of same, for £10 sterling, 357 acres granted to said Alexander Cothran 5 Sept 1785, adj. John Jay, Joseph Reagan, Enos Elleman. Alex'r Cothran (Seal), Wit: Richard Thompson, Elizabeth Ellemon (mark). Proved by the oath of Richard Thompson 7 Feb 1799 before Fred Nance, J.P. Recorded 20 Feb 1799.

D, 118-121: 17 & 18 Dec 1794, William McDowell of Newberry County and wife Susanna to Samuel Brown of same, for £100 sterling, 125 acres on a small branch of Bush River adj. William Murdock, Samuel Dunkin, William Gillam, Zimri Gaunt, Walter Harbirt, part of tract of 250 acres granted to Peter Ruble 22 March 1769 and conveyed to William McDowell. William McDowall (Seal), Susanna McDowall (X) (Seal), Wit: Jehu Inman, Rich'd Thompson, Peter Lester (P). Proved by the oath of Richard Thompson 7 Feb 1799 before Fred Nance, J.P. Recorded 20 Feb 1799.

D, 122-123: Thomas Campbell Senr of Newberry County, planter, bound to William Hare in the sum of $500, 10 Jan 1798, to make title to tract whereon Thomas Campbell now lives, 100 acres, part of 200 acres granted to John Evans and conveyed to Abraham Wright, and then Abraham Wright conveyed 100 acres to said Thomas Campbell Senr, and then to William Hare (son of eyre Hare), so that at the decease of said Thomas Campbell the said William Hare shall be lawfully possessed of said land. Thomas Campbell (seal), wit: John McMorries, James Marshall. Proved by the oath of John McMorris 12 Nov 1798 before John Speak, J.P. Eyre Hare in consideration of the within bond to my son William Hare, said Thomas Campbell Senr has agreed that Eyre Hare do cultivate and attend the said plantation during the life of said Thomas Campbell, Eyre Hare will give for the rent of said land 40 bushells of corn, 200 weight of flour, 200 weight of good pork, and fodder for two cows and a horse, 10 Jan 1798. Eyre Hare, Wit: John McMorries, James Marshall. Recorded 21 Feb 1799.

D, 123-126: Lease and release. 21 & 22 Dec 1773, John Caldwell, Esqr., of Ninety Six District, to James McCool of same, for £500 SC money, 200 acres in Berkley County on Beaverdam granted to John Caldwell 15 Feb 1770. Jno Caldwell (Seal), Jean Caldwell (Seal), Wit: Richard Golding, John Ritchey, Margret Ritchey. Proved 22 Sept 1775 by the oath of Richard Golding before Robt Cunningham, J.P. Recorded 26 Feb 1799.

D, 126-129: Lease and release. 15 Feb 1777, James McCool of Ninety Six District, planter, to John Douglass of same, for £250 SC money, 200 acres in Berkley County on Beaverdam granted to John Caldwell 15 Feb 1770 and conveyed to James McCool 22 Dec 1773. James McCool (Seal), Wit: Joseph Jay, Thomas Pugh, Robt Speer. Proved in Newberry County 26 Feb 1799 by the oath of Robt Speer before Fred Nance, J.P. Recorded 26 Feb 1799.

D, 130-131: 1 Feb 1799, Clement Gore of Chester county, SC, to Sarah Ragland of Pendleton County, for $120, part of 461 acres on Kings Creek, 200 acres on NE side or lower part of said tract adj. lands of Procklus Thomas Morgan, John Goodin. Clem't Gore (Seal), Wit: Thos Lindsey, Saml Lindsey. Proved in Newberry County by the oath of Thomas Lindsey 4 Feb 1799 before Fred Nance, J.P. Recorded 26 Feb 1799.

D, 131-133: Lease and release. 12 Jan 1796, Philip Phagins of Pendleton County, SC, to David Brooks of Newberry County, for £50 sterling, 150 acres granted to Samuel Powel 12 April 1771 and conveyed 12 April 1773 to George Goggins and then 25 Oct 1784 to Philip Phagins. Philip Phagins (Seal), Ann Phagins (A) (Seal), Wit: Daniel Goggans, John Atchison, Abraham Crews. Proved in Newberry County by the oath of Daniel Goggans 10 Oct 1796 before Peter Julien, J.P. Recorded 28 Feb 1799.

D, 133: State of South Carolina, County of Newberry. Personally appeared Ellenor Large, now the wife of John Large but formerly the wife of William Gilliland decd, made oath that William Gilliland Junr is her son that he was born in wedlock of her body during the life time of her late husband William Gilliland decd, that the said William Gilliland Junr her said son is the eldest son of them, and that her said husband died first day of next March will be Eighteen years ago, dated 25 Feb 1799. Ellenor Large (O), before Frederick Nance, J.P. Recorded 28 Feb 1799.'

D, 134: State of South Carolina, Newberry County. Know all men by these presents that I Andrew Loretz, Minister of the Dutch Presbiterin Congregation in Newberry County and other places, do hereby certify that I have this day Joined Eve Margaret Dickert in holy matrimony unto John Folk according to our rule and profession. Certifyed by me this 23d day of October 1798. Andrew Loretz, V. D. M. Wit: Peter Dickert, Michl Dickert Senr. Recorded 28 Feb 1799.

D, 134: Joseph Herndon of Wilks County, North Carolina, appoint my trust friend Charles Crenshaw of Newberry County, SC, my attorney to sell and convey all my lands in South Carolina on Enoree River and both sides of Duncans Creek in Newberry County, 29 Aug 1797. Jo's Herndon (Seal), Wit: Obed Parrish, Archibald Crenshaw. Proved by the oath of Obed Parrish 28 Feb 1799 before Fred Nance, C.N.C. Recorded 28 Feb 1797.

D, 135-136: 16 April 1789, David Dickson of Green County, Georgia, to Joseph Herndon of Wilks County, North Carolina, for £40 sterling, 100 acres in Newberry County, SC, in the fork of Broad and Saluda Rivers, granted to William Dickson 25 Aug 1769, recorded in the Auditor Generals Office in Book I No. 9, page 396 on 12 Oct 1769, recorded in Book DDD, page 364. David Dickson (Seal), Wit: Charles Crenshaw, Edward Finch, Eunice Crenshaw. Proved in Newberry County by the oath of Charles Crenshaw 28 Feb 1799 before Fred Nance, J.P. Recorded 28 Feb 1799.

D, 136-140: Lease and release. 5 & 7 May 1787, George Lever of Newberry County to Ludwick Ritter of same, for £21 s10 sterling, 142 acres granted to said George Lever on waters of Camping Creek, adj. Jacob Jumpet [sic, for Schumpert], granted 7 Aug 1786. Jorg Ludwig Lever [German signature] (Seal), Wit: George Long (GL), Michael Lang, Michael Kromer. Proved by the oath of Michael Cromer/Kromer of Newberry County 9 Feb 1797 before John Hampton, J.Q. Recorded 28 Feb 1799.

D, 140-141: John Miller of City of Charleston, merchant, appoints friends Lewis Ritter and Mary Ritter my attorneys to receive from the heirs, administrators, etc. of Jacob Replagel deceased, any money, etc., due, 13 Jan 1796. John Miller (Seal), Wit: Adam Setzler [German signature], Michael Kromer [German signature]. Proved 9 Feb 1797 by the oath of Michael Cromer/Kromer of Newberry County before John Hampton, J.P. Recorded 28 Feb 1799.

D, 141-143: David Owen of Newberry County for £25 sterling to Thomas Owen of same, 50 acres, part of tract on which said David Owen now lives, 27

Feb 1799. David Owen (Seal), Wit: Stephen Shell, Edward McCraw, G. Harbirt. Proved in by the oath of George Harbirt 27 Feb 1799 before Edwd Finch, J.P. Plat included by G. Harbirt, D.S., 27 Dec 1798 "part of tract said David Owen now lives on which he purchased of George Montgomery in Newberry County on a branch of Second Creek" showing adjacent land owners: Edmond Gaines, David Glenn, David Owen, Robert Rutherford. Recorded 28 Feb 1799.

D, 143-144: 13 Oct 1798, Jacob Arehart and wife Elizabeth, Henry, john, and Catharina Oxner, of Orangeburgh District, to Samuel Wood of Ninety Six District, for £20 sterling, 150 acres in Newberry County on south side Broad River adj. Jacob Falker, certified 5 Oct 1771, granted to Henry Oxner (now deceased) 16 June 1772. Jacob Airhurt (mark) (Seal), Elizabeth Airhurt (mark) (Seal), Henry Oxner (Seal), John Oxner (X) (Seal), Catharina Oxner (X) (Seal), Wit: Jacob Oxner (mark), Jacob Oxner Jun'r (mark), Samuel Brown (mark). Proved in Newberry County by the oath of Jacob Oxner Junr 23 Oct 1798 before David Ruff, J.P. Recorded 28 Feb 1799.

D, 145-146: 17 Feb 1795, William Moor of Ninety Six District to William Shepherd of same, for £23 d8 sterling, 50 acres, part of 250 acres granted to William Moore, father of Robert Moore, in March 1768, recorded in Book CCC, adj. James Penney. William Moor (mark) (Seal), Wit: Thomas Shepherd, James Shepherd, David Lessly. Proved in Newberry County by the oath of Thomas Shepherd 9 March 1796 before David Ruff, J.P. Recorded 28 Feb 1799.

D, 146-149: Lease and release. 9 & 10 Nov 1786, Baltes Neise in Maclingburgh County, North Carolina, planter, to Thomas Hughes in Newberry County, SC, for £20 sterling, 150 acres, part of 250 acres granted unto Conrad Neise by George II and recorded in Book PP, on a branch of Saluda called Camping Creek, adj. Christopher Kriser. Baltzer Neis [German signature] (Seal), Wit: Humphrey Williamson, John Domminick (X). Proved 25 April 1791 by the oath of John Domannick before John Hampton, J. Qu. Recorded 28 Feb 1799.

D, 150-152: 8 Feb 1799, John Douglass of Newberry County for $600 to Robert McClure, 200 acres on waters of Saluda River granted to John Caldwell Esqr. 15 Feb 1770, conveyed by Caldwell to James McCool 22 Dec 1773 and from McCool to said John Douglass 15 Feb 1777. John Douglass (Seal), Wit: John Tinsley, John Griffin (X). Mary Douglas (mark), wife of John Douglass, relinquished dower 5 March 1799 before J. R. Brown, J.N.C. Proved by the oath of John Griffin 28 Feb 1799 before Fred Nance, J.P. Recorded 28 Feb 1799.

D, 152-153: Jacob King and wife Elizabeth, John B. Bennett, Richard Bennett, Lewis Bennett, Micajah Bennett, Mary Bennett, Charity Bennett, and Sary Bennett, legatees of the late Micajah Bennett deceased, all of Newberry County, bound to Elender Bennett widow of the late Micajah Bennett deceased, in the sum of $250, 20 Nov 1798, whereas a compromise hath taken place between the above named Ellender Bennett widow of Micajah Bennett deceased, and the above bound legatees, and have delivered unto said Ellender Bennett such a part of the property of the said Micajah Bennett to be her full right of dower, and whereas the said late Micajah Bennett deceased during his life time and in wedlock had a child by the said Ellender Bennett which is named Johnston Bennett, and said legatees will deliver the amount of Johnston Bennett's legacy, 76 acres on waters of Headleys Creek, part of tract formerly purchased by Micajah Bennett deceased of Joseph Cooper. Jacob King (Seal), Elizabeth King (Seal), John B. Bennett (Seal), Richard Bennett (Seal), Lewis Bennett (Seal), Micajah Bennett (Seal), Mary Bennett (mark (Seal), Charity Bennett (Seal), Sarah Bennett (Seal), Wit: John McMorries, Levi Fowler. Proved by the oath of John McMorries 12 nov 1798 before John Speak, J.P. Recorded 28 Feb 1799.

D, 154-155: 1 March 1799, Aron Cates of Newberry County to Ezra Cates of same, for £80 sterling, 100 acres, part of two tracts of land granted to Samuel Wilson and from Wilson to John Hampton and from Hampton to said Cates, the other part granted to Robert Moore and from said Moore to Fight Risinger and from Risinger to George Dawkins and by Joseph Dawkins to Richard Speak, and from Speak to William Finch, and from Finch to said Cates, on Second Creek. A. Cates (Seal), Wit: Nathl Henderson, George Johnson. Proved by the oath of Nathaniel Henderson 1 March 1799 before Fred Nance, J.P. Recorded 1 March 1799.

D, 155-156: 1 March 1799, Aron Cates of Newberry County to Isaah Cates of same, for £80 sterling, 100 acres, part of two tracts of land granted to Edward Connerly and conveyed from said Connerly to John Malone Junr and from Malone to Andrew Russell and from Russell to said Cates, the other part granted to Samuel Wilson and from said Wilson to John Hampton and from Hampton to said Cates, on Second Creek. A. Cates (Seal), Wit: Nathl Henderson, George Johnson. Proved by the oath of Nathaniel Henderson 1 March 1799 before Fred Nance, J.P. Recorded 1 March 1799.

D, 156-158: Whereas Col. Joseph Kershaw, late of the Town of Camden, in his life time, on or about 25 Feb 1790 being seized of a tract of 200 acres in the fork between Broad and Saluda Rivers on a branch of Enoree called Indian Creek adj. John Evans, William Cannon, and by deeds made between said Joseph Kershaw and William Ancrum, Edward Darrel, James Fisher, Robert Henry, and James Kershaw, five of the creditors and trustees of said Joseph Kershaw, after reciting that the said Joseph Kershaw was justly indebted to the said trustees and sundry other creditors to a large amount which he was then unable to pay off, now by their letter of attorney 20 Feb 1794, recorded in the office of the clerk of Kershaw county 15 April in Book A, pages 135-139, attested by Francis Boykin, Esquire, clerk of said county, now for $270 paid by Jacob Rhodes of Newberry County, sell said tract, 26 July 1798. John Kershaw (Seal), Wit: Thos W. Waters, J. D. Duraux. Proved in Newberry County by the oath of Thos W. Waters 1 March 1799 before Fred Nance, J.P. Recorded 1 March 1799.

D, 159: George Ruff of Newberry County for good will and affection to my son John Pester and my daughter Sally his wife, a negro woman Hannah, a boy named John, a bay mare, 18 Jan 1799. George Ruff (Seal), Wit: Henry Ruff, Peter Gray. Proved by the oath of Peter Gray 1 March 1799 before Fred Nance, J.P. Recorded 1 March 1799.

D, 159-160: South Carolina, Newberry County. These are to certify that Henry Gallman discharges a certain negro man named Bob for him to be free, 5 Nov 1798. Henry Gallman, Wit: David Ruff, Elizabeth Ruff (mark). Proved by the oath of Elizabeth Ruff 1 March 1799 before Fred Nance, J.P. Recorded 1 March 1799.

D, 160: 30 Nov 1798, Gasper Bierly for £40 sterling to Mathew Smith, one negro boy Peter aged 8 years. Gasper Biely (B) (Seal), Wit: Frederick Pasinger (mark), George Lever. Proved in Newberry County by the oath of Frederick Pasinger 1 March 1799 before Fred Nance, J.P. Recorded 1 March 1799.

D, 161-162: 24 May 1796, Isabella Morgan of Abbeville County, planter, to Joseph Caldwell of Newberry County, for £20, 100 acres granted to Clement Gore 7 ____ 1787, adj. Land of William Caldwell, widow Morgan, Andrew Spence, David Boyd, on waters of Guilders Creek in Newberry County. Asbell Morgan (O), Wit: William Chambers, Reason Davis. Proved in Newberry County 4 March 1799 by the oath of William Chambers before Fred Nance, J.P. Recorded 4 March 1799.

D, 162: South Carolina, Newberry County. Whereas Jesse Pugh has become my security to the executors of Levi Manning decd for the sum of £205 p'r our notes given 16th of this month, also £25 sterling given by said Pugh and Thomas W. Waters due this winter with interest, now mortgage two negroes Moses about 8 years old and Rose about 7 years old, 17 Nov 1798. Thos. W. Waters. Test: John Harrisson. Recorded 4 March 1799.

D, 162-164: Cosper Peister of Newberry County, miller, for $300 to John Peister, 150 acres granted to Casper Peister 19 June 1772, recorded in Book LLLL, page 351, adj. Robert Wiseman, Hugh Wiseman. Caspar Pister [German signature] (Seal), Wit: Dav'd Ruff J.P., John Zuber Sr. (mark), Henry Gallman. Recorded 4 March 1799.

D, 164-165: 14 Dec 1798, Richard Johnston and wife Mary of Ninety Six District for £40 sterling to William Burton, 50 acres on Carsons Creek on south side of a small branch thereof, part of 100 acres granted to Samuel Ford 22 Aug 1771 and conveyed by him to James Griffin 15 & 16 March 1773 and by him to Thomas Pitts 9 & 10 March 1784 and then by Thomas Pitts to Elizabeth Toland 28 & 29 Feb 1791 and then to Wm Pitts 26 Nov 17-- and then to Richard Johnston 7 Jan 1796 adj. Charles Pitts, Reuben Golding. Richard Johnson (Seal), Mary Johnston (X) (Seal), Wit: William Pitts, Stephen Johnston, Winnefred Johnston (mark).Proved in Newberry County by the oath of William Pitts 14 Dec 1798 before Charles Griffin, J.P. Recorded 4 March 1799.

D, 166-167: 16 Dec 1798, Mathias Hare and wife Fanne of Newberry County, planter, to Jeremiah McDaniel of same, for $200, 100 acres in Craven County when granted but now called Newberry County on south side Broad River adj. Michael Dukeras, Jacob Mason, granted to Peter Hare Senr 13 March 1772, 200 acres, recorded in Book L No. 11, page 37, the above 100 acres was left to the said Michael Hare by his father's will 25 Sept 1774. Mathias hare (H) (Seal), Fanne Hare (+) (Seal), Wit: John William Stone, John McDanel, William Stone. Proved by the oath of John McDaniel 4 March 1799 before Fred Nance, J.P. Recorded 4 March 1799.

D, 168: Olive Lonam and Squire Lonam of SC for $150 to Frederick Nance, Esqr., 100 acres in Newberry County on the main Road leading from Andersons ford to Charleston joining land of Robert Rutherford Esquire, granted to George Hattale and by said Hattale conveyed to Samuel Lonam (now deceased) and by the said Lonam devised to us by his will, 28 Sept 1798. Olive Lonam (Seal), Squire Lonam (Seal), Wit: Patrick Carmichael, Henry Coate, Peter Julien, Daniel Richardson. Proved in Newberry County by the oath of Patrick Carmichael 4 March 1799 before Edwd Finch, J.P. Recorded 4 March 1799.

D, 169-170: William Davenport of Newberry District for £40 sterling to Manasah Man and John Jarrah of Laurens County, 100 acres on Little River, being tract laid out to Morgan Dollars on Little River in Newberry County adj. William Turner, James Spereman, William Davenport, John Griffen, 12 Feb 1798. William Davenport (X) (Seal), Wit: Alexander Fillson, John Man (mark), Robt Oliphant. Sarah Davenport (mark), wife of William Davenport, relinquished dower 4 March 1799 before L. E. Casey, J.N.C. Proved by the oath of John Man 4 March 1799 before L. E. Casey, J.N.C. Recorded 4 March 1799.

D, 170-171: George Bridges of Newberry County bound to John Hillbourn of same in the sum of £50 sterling, 18 Jan 1794, to make title to tract of land granted to Godfrey Trayer on the Waggon Road, 30 acres. George Bridges (Seal), Wit: Jas Johnson, Thos Butler. Proved by the oath of James Johnson 4 March 1799 before Fred Nance, J.P. Recorded 4 March 1799.

D, 171-173: Joseph Cook of Newberry County for £40 sterling to Samuel McQuerns of same, 10 acres on a small branch of Bush River now joining on lands of Abel Thomas, James Young, Walter Harbert, William Farr, formerly granted to William Lee 6 Dec 1768 and conveyed by William Lee to John Hillhouse 17 & 18 March 1788 and conveyed by John Millhouse to Joseph Cook 11 & 12 Dec 1792. Joseph Cook (Seal), Wit: Mercer Babb, Thomas Hasket, John Arnold. Mary Cook, wife of Joseph Cook, relinquished dower 4 March 1799 before L. E. Casey, J.N.C. Proved by the oath of Thomas Hasket 5 Nov 1796 before Fred Nance, J.P. Recorded 4 March 1799.

D, 173-174: Ephraim Cannon and wife Ellender of Newberry County for £1 s16 sterling to Aaron Cates of same, 315 acres granted to John Johnson and Mary Frost and said Mary Frost her part properly transferred from her to said John Johnson esqr and from said John Johnson to David Glen and after the decease of said David Glen said land was sold by Richard Watts sheriff of said county by virtue of a judgment against the executors of said Glen decd, 2 June 1789, and conveyed by Richard Watts to me, said Ephraim Cannon, said land on the river bank, adj. Braselmans line on Enoree River, dated 3 Jan 1798. Ephraim Cannon (Seal), Elenor Cannon (C) (Seal), Wit: Robt Rutherford, Dav'd Ruff. Elenor Cannon, wife of Ephraim Cannon, relinquished dower 4 March 1799 before L. E. Casey, J.N.C. Proved by the oath of Robert Rutherford 4 March 1799 before Fred Nance, J.P. Recorded 4 March 1799.

D, 175-176: South Carolina, Ninety Six District. Joseph Caldwell of Newberry County for £25 to James Spence of same, 100 acres, part of tract granted to Clement Gore in 1787 on waters of Gilders Creek adj. William Calwell, Widow Morans, Andrew Spence, David Boyd, __ March 1799. Joseph Caldwell (Seal), Wit: William Caldwell (O), Rignal Williams. Jenney Caldwell (mark), wife of Joseph Caldwell, relinquished dower 4 March 1799 before L. E. Casey, J.N.C. Proved by the oath of William Caldwell 4 March 1799 before Fred Nance, J.P. Recorded 4 March 1799.

D, 176-178: Hugh Marshell of Newberry County for $600 to Jacob Ducket of same, 235½ acres, 108 acres of the tract granted to William Gray on a small branch of Indian Creek adj. John Lindsey, Jacob Penington, Henry Roberts, recorded in Book LLLL, page 92, conveyed by Abraham Gray to Hugh Marshell, 135½ acres part of a tract of 271 acres on a small branch of Indian Creek, it being the land where Hugh Marshell now lives, 19 Jan 1799. Hugh Marshell (Seal), Wit: Lewis Bennett, James Williams. Mary Marshell (X), wife of Hugh Marshell, relinquished dower 2 March 1799 before L. E. Casey. Wit: Lewis Bennett, Uriah Conner. Proved by the oath of Lewis Bennett 2 March 1799 before L. E. Casey, J.N.C. Recorded 4 March 1799.

D, 178-179: 19 Jan 1799, George Dawkins of Jefferson County, Georgia, to William Hayne of Newberry County, SC, for £80 sterling, 150 acres in Newberry County between Broad and Saluda Rivers on a small branch of Second Creek called Belues cabbin branch, granted to George Dawkins 13 April 1771. Geo Dawkins (Seal), Wit: Thos Gaines, James Liles (X), Mary Bookter (X). Proved in Newberry County by the oath of Thomas Gaines 4 March 1799 before Fred Nance, J.P. Recorded 4 March 1799.

D, 180-181: Robert Tate of Newberry County for £137 s3 sterling to Capt. Samuel Tate of Pendleton County, SC, said Robert Tate as admr. of the estate of James Tate Jun'r decd, have caused to be sold the following negro slaves at public auction agreeable to the order of the court of Newberry: Isaac and Prince and Charlotte and Milla and Hannah and Lusey, and also for £11 s9 sterling, three cows and calves and 25 head of small hogs and some corn and a few plantation tools, 9 June 1797. Robt Tate administrator (Seal), Wit: Wm

Irby, Thos Kay, Farley Thompson. Proved in Newberry County by the oath of Thomas Kay 5 March 1799 before Wm Nibbs, J. Q. Proved by the oath of John Anderson 7 March 1799 before Fred Nance, C.N.C. Recorded 5 March 1799.

D, 181-182: 9 June 1797, William Goggins and wife Rachel of Newberry County to James Newman of same, for £60 sterling, 285 acres on Beaverdam, waters of Little River, adj. Henry Butler, George Goggans, Gibbeon Jones, Benjamin Wood. William Goggins (Seal), Rachel Goggans (R) (Seal), Wit: Joseph Johnson, James Johnson, Keziah Johnson (mark). Rachel Goggins, wife of William Goggans, relinquished dower 6 March 1799 before J. R. Brown, J.N.C. Proved by the oath of Joseph Johnson 6 March 1799 before Elisha Ford, J.P. Recorded 5 March 1799.

D, 183-184: 7 April 1797, William Goggins and wife Rachel of Newberry County to James Newman of same, for £50 sterling, 174 acres on waters of Sandy Run, waters of Little River, adj. Philip Phagans, John Johnson, James McLang, William Goggins, Henry Butler. William Goggins (Seal), Rachel Goggans (R) (Seal), Wit: Joseph Johnson, James Johnson, Keziah Johnson (mark). Rachel Goggins, wife of William Goggins, relinquished dower 6 March 1799 before J. R. Brown, J.N.C. Proved by the oath of Joseph Johnson 6 March 1799 before Elisha Ford, J.P. Recorded 5 March 1799.

D, 184-186: 4 March 1799, John Coate of Newberry County for $300 to Henry Coate of same, 150 acres on waters of Bush River called Scotch Creek, part of plantation belonging to said John Coate, adj. John Coate, Jonathan Reed, George Latham. Jno Coate (Seal), Wit: Jno P. Bond, Wm. Sumers, James Dobbins. Plat included by P. B. Waters, D. S., dated 8 Sept 1798, showing adjacent land owners and Newberry Court House. Susanna Coate, wife of John Coate, relinquished dower 6 March 1799 before L. E. Casey, J.N.C. Proved by the oath of John P. Bond 4 March 1799 before Fred Nance, J.P. Recorded 6 March 1799.

D, 186-187: 22 Nov 1798, James Weeks of Newberry County for £23 sterling to David Boyd of same, 100 acres on the waters of Kings Creek, part of tract granted to Francis Davis for 200 acres and conveyed to John Adkin and by said Akin to Benjamin Heaton and by Heaton to James Weeks. James Weeks (Seal), Wit: Saml Pearson, Ralph Campbell, James Pearson. Acknowledged in open court and recorded 6 March 1799.

D, 187-188: James McLonan of Chester County, SC, for £60 to Jacob Croswhite of newberry County, 150 acres on waters of Little River adj. Samuel Nelson, John Caldwell, James Stewart, John Write, formerly granted to said James McLonan 8 July 1774. James McLonan (Seal), Wit: Edmond Griffin, Mathew Harbison, Nicodemus Bans. Proved in Newberry County by the oath of Edmond Griffin 26 March 1799 before Fred Nance, J.P. Recorded 26 March 1799.

D, 189-192: Lease and release. 1 & 2 June 1775, George Montz of Ninety Six District, SC, planter, to John Bushard Junr of same, for £100 sterling, 100 acres in Craven County on waters of Cannons Creek granted 25 May 1774 to George Montz adj. John Buzzard, James Shepherd, land name unknown. George Mantz (Seal), Wit: Michael Rigard (M), George Ruff. Proved in Ninety Six District by the oath of Michael Rickard 22 July 1775 before Michael Dickert, J.P. Recorded 11 April 1799.

D, 192: State of So Carolina, Ninety Six District. Personally appeared John Bushard and declared that in the year 1770 he made over 250 acres by way of a deed of gift to his son Jacob Boshard mearly for no other purpose but to keep off an unjust & unlawful debt, and this Depon't further saith that since, as he understands, through some evill disposing person or other, has persuaded his son to take and keep this land to himself, and it would shurly put him and his wife in their old age to sufference, 13 March 1778. Johannes Boshard [German signature] before Michael Dickert, J.P.   N.B. the Said Jacob Bushard never had said mentioned deed of gift in his possession a Day. Recorded 11 April 1799.

D, 193-196: Lease and release. 5 & 6 March 1778, John Posser (alias) John Bushard Senr of Ninety Six District, SC, to John Bushard Junr of same, planter, for £200 sterling, 100 acres, part of 250 acres granted 21 May 1772 to John Bushard Senr, recorded in Book LLL, page 256, on Cannons Creek. Johannes Boshard [German signature], Wit: John Sigler (mark), Martin Soulter (mark), Margaret Dickert (mark). Proved in Ninety Six District by the oath of John Sigler 13 March 1778 before Michael Dickert, J.P. Recorded 11 April 1799.

D, 197-198: 8 April 1799, John Buzzard of Newberry County to James Sheppard of same, for $140, 100 acres on waters of Cannons Creek adj. John Buzzard, James Shepherd, recorded in Book GGG, page 33. John Buzzard (Seal), Wit: John Peter Kinard, William Shephard, Jacob Bossart. Proved by the oath of William Shepherd 11 April 179 before Fred Nance, J.P. Recorded 11 April 1799.

D, 198-199: 23 Jan 1795, Frederick Gray of Newberry County to James Shepherd of same, for three guineas, 25 acres adj. land of John Buzzard, part of 71 acres granted to Frederick Gray 26 May 1794. Fred'r Gray (Seal), Wit: William Shepherd, Michal Long, Daniel Dewalt. Proved by the oath of Daniel Dewalt 11 May 1795 before David Ruff, J.P. Recorded 11 April 1799.

D, 199-200: 16 July 1792, Robert Moor of Newberry County, weaver, to James Shepherd of same, planter, for £2 sterling, 16 acres, the remainder of 100 acres of land which said More sold to George Mountz, originally granted to George Gray. Robert Moor (Seal), Dav'd Ruff, Johannes Bolland [German signature]. Proved by the oath of John Bolan 16 July 1792 before Dav'd Ruff J.P. Recorded 11 April 1799.

D, 201-202: 21 Jan 1799, John Embree of the State of Georgia for £200 Virginia money to Walter Harbour Jun'r admr. of his father Walter Harbour Senr deceased in Newberry County, SC, 200 acres on Bush River granted to Robert Bull 10 Jan 1771 and was surveyed for Daniel Campbell 12 Oct 1756 and also recorded in Book GGG, page 172, from said Bull conveyed 12 & 13 April 1771 to John Embree. John Embree Senr (Seal), Wit: Daniel Williams, William Patten, Rachel Parham. Proved in Columbia County, Georgia, by the oath of William Patten 22 Jan 1799 before Samson S. Stub, J.I.C. Proved in Newberry County by the oath of Daniel Williams 13 April 1799 before Fred Nance, J.P. Recorded 13 April 1799.

D, 203-204: 14 Jan 1795, John Park of State of SC to Thomas Herron of same, for £40 sterling, 50 acres, part of 200 acres granted to Jaret Smith, said 5-0 acres sold to Isaac Parker, adj. James Wilson, William Gray; also 50 acres, part of 150 acres granted to Elizabeth Brown and sold to Robert Brown 10 Jan 1787, adj. William Gray, Jean Wilson. John Park (Seal), Wit: John Garmany, James Park, Jeremiah Hubbard. Proved in Newberry County by the oath of John Garmany 27 July 1796 before Wm Craig, J.P.

D, 205: South Carolina, Newberry County. March 18, 1799. This may certify that I do relinquish my dower of the estate of my husband William Happer deceased both real and personal. Jan Hopper (mark), Wit: Willm Chalmers, Willm Happer. Proved in Newberry County 13 April 1799 by the oath of William Chalmers before Fred Nance, J.P. Recorded 13 April 1799.

D, 205: South Carolina, Laurens County. John Hazlet of Laurens County to Phillip Procter of Newberry County, for $400, one negroe boy about 13 years old named George, country born, 15 Feb 1799. John Hazlet (Seal), Wit: John Walls, Thos Farrow. Recorded 16 April 1799.

D, 206: 1799, April 15th. Phillip Procter's mark to be recorded (Viz) a crop and slit in the left ear and slit in the right. Recorded 15 April 1799.

D, 206: March 21st 1799. Received from Doct'r Meredith William Moon $300 for a negro man named Joe. Dn'l Dyson (Seal), Wit: Wm Irby. Proved in Newberry County by the oath of William Irby 17 April 1799 before Fred Nance, J.P. Recorded 17 April 1799.

D, 206-207: Jonathan Taylor of Newberry County for $120 to John Jay of same, 100 acres on waters of Bever Dam, a small branch of Saluda granted to Mathew Brooks 31 Aug 1774 and conveyed 1 & 2 June 1786 to said Jonathan Taylor, dated 18 April 1799. Jonathan Taylor (Seal), Wit: Joseph Furnace, Amos Dunkin. Proved in Newberry County by the oath of Amos Dunkin 9 May 1799 before Fred Nance, J.P. Recorded 9 May 1799.

D, 208-209: Andrew Boddan of Town of Columbia, Camden District, SC, for $280 to Peter Stockman of Ninety Six District, Newberry County, 200 acres adj. Christopher Seas, surveyed for James Henry 98 June 1785 and granted to

John Vanderhorst 1 May 1786, recorded in Book IIII, page 196, conveyed 13 Feb 1798 by Arnoldus Vanderhorst and Thomas Wearing Sr., Exrs. of the will of John Vanderhorst, Esqr., deceased, to Andrew Boddan, dated 8 Feb 1799. Andrew Boddan (Seal), Wit: J. A. Houseal, Michael Eigelberger, Johannes Stockman [German signature] 8 Feb 1799 before John Adam Sumers, J.P. Recorded 11 May 1799.

D, 209-210: Frederick Williams of Newberry County appoint my friend Mr. Van Davis of same, my true and lawful attorney to receive from Mr. William OByon, citizen of the state of Georgia, the approved and lawful executor of the estate of Joshua Morgan (deceased), all that quota that was bequeathed unto Susannah Capers as appears in the will of said Joshua Morgan, 16 May 1799. Fredk Williams (Seal), Wit: Joshua Teague, Samuel Teague. Proved by the oath of Joshua Teague 28 May 1799 before Charles Griffin, J.P. Acknowledged in open court 20 May 1799. Recorded 120 May 1799.

D, 210-211: Cary Gilbert of Newberry County for £70 sterling to Samuel Pearson, 150 acres, part of tract of 200 acres granted to John Clark of North Carolina 28 March 1754 but since the late resurvey of the boundary line was granted to Jonathan Gilbert in Charleston 22 June 1774 on Beverdam Creek, dated 26 Jan 1799. Cary Gilbert (Seal), Wit: Joseph Furnas, Amos Dunkin. Proved by the oath of Josh Furnas 20 May 1799 before Fred Nance, J.,P. Recorded 20 May 1799.

D, 212-215: Lease and release. 3 & 4 Feb 1772, Michael Schover of the Fork in Craven County, Sc, planter, to Conrad Suber of same, for £100, 150 acres being part of 200 acres granted to Michael Schover 22 Sept 1769 in Berkley County in the fork of Broad and Saluda Rivers on a small branch of Broad River called Buck Sheal Creek, adj. John Hillerd. Michael Scober (mark) (Seal), Wit: James Daugharty, James Daugharty Junr (X), Nicless Bunderick [German signature]. Proved by the oath of James Daugharty 28 Feb 1772 before Michl Dickert, J.P. Recorded 20 May 1799.

D, 216-220: Lease and release. 7 July 1792, Christian Leitner of Lexington County, SC, yeoman, to Conrad Zuber of Newberry County, planter, for £100 sterling, all that parcel or separated tracts 224 acres and 50 acres (originally granted to John Michael Wagner 2 Oct 1752) 50 acres granted to John George Wagner 19 Oct 1752 and 50 acres granted to John Andrew Hicker 12 Feb 1755 and the residue of 24 acres being part of a tract of 250 acres granted to Christopher Leitner 20 Oct 1752 being property transferred into the possession of Michael Leitner deceased, and said Michael Leitner died intestate the above tracts devolved in the possession of his son Christopher Leitner, he being heir at law. Christian Leitner (Seal), Wit: Michael Dickert Senr, George Setzler, Jacob Folmer. Proved in Lexington County by the oath of Michael Dickert before John Adam Summers, J.P., 7 July 1792. Plat included showing adjacent land owners Neeley, Grimes or Graham, dated 4 June 1792, by Geo. Harbirt, D.S. Recorded 20 May 1799.

D, 221-225: Lease and release. 9 & 10 Oct 1795, James Wadlington of Newberry County, planter, and wife Margaret, to David Miles of same, planter, for £150 SC money, 160 acres in the fork between Broad and Saluda Rivers on a branch of Bush River, part of two tracts of land, the first 150 acres formerly granted to Benjamin Busby 20 April 1768 and conveyed by said Benjamin Busby to Moses Embree 15 & 16 May 1769 and conveyed by said Moses Embree to James Wadlington 25 & 26 Oct 1785, recorded in Newberry County 22 June 1786 in Book A, page 49; the second part of tract granted to William Gilam, said 10 acres conveyed by William Gilam to James Wadlington 1 & 2 March 1786, recorded in Newberry County in Book A, page 63, 27 June 1786. James Wadlington (Seal), Margret Wadlington (mark) (Seal), Wit: Mercer Babb, Samuel Miles, Thomas Hasket. Proved by the oath of Thomas Haskit 20 May 1799 before John Speake, J.P. Recorded 20 May 1799.

D, 225-228: Lease and release. 14 & 15 Feb 1769, David Spence of Berkley County, SC, planter, and wife Martha, to Samuel Lonam of same, carpenter, 200 acres on waters of Saluda adj. David Reese, Samuel Lonam, James Hogan. granted 12 Aug 1768 to said David Spence. David Spence (D) (Seal), Wit: George Barnard Shrum, Joseph Spence (S), George Drafts (H). Proved in Craven County by the oath of George Drafts 1 Jan 1771 before Jno Caldwell, J.P. Recorded 20 May 1799.

D, 229-232: Lease and release. 24 & 25 May 1772, George Hattell and Sharlot his wife of Craven County, SC, planter, to Samuel Lonam of same, carpenter, for £150 CS money, 100 acres in Craven County in the fork between Broad and Saluda Rivers, adj. Daniel Horsey, Bounty land, granted to George Hattel 15 March 1771, recorded in Book FFF, page 1. Georg ____ [German signature] (Seal), Saraha Hattel (+) (Seal), Wit: Wm Hausihl, James Cannon, John Armstrong. Proved in Craven County by the oath of Wm Hausihl 25 May 1772 before Saml Cannon, J.P. Recorded 20 May 1799.

D, 232-235: Lease and release. 23 & 24 Oct 1778, William Gilliland, planter, and wife Elenor, to Robert Plonket, planter, both of Ninety Six District, for £900 SC money, 200 acres granted to Henry Morgan 9 Sept 1774 and conveyed by Henry Morgan and wife Deborah 19 Dec 1777 to William Gilliland on north side Saluda River on a small branch of Beaver dam Creek, waters of Saludy, adj. Benjamin Pearson. William Gilliland (Seal), Elinor Gilliland (Seal), Wit: Robert Speer, James Plonket, Charles Plonket. Proved in Newberry County by the oath of James Plunket 21 May 1799 before J. R. Brown, J.N. C. Recorded 21 May 1799.

D, 236: John Embree of Columbia County, Georgia, for £200 sterling to Joseph Furnas of Newberry County, SC, 300 acres on Bush River adj. Elisha Ford, Amos Dunkin, William Murdock, John Embree, Mercer Babb, part of two other tracts granted to Stephen Elmore and Conrad Immuniac, one of 300 acres and the other of 100 acres, conveyed by John Embree the one tract 21 & 22 Nov 1771 and the other 15 & 16 Nov 1771... dated 3 Feb 1798. John Embree Senr (Seal), Wit: Samuel Teague, Jonathan Embree. Proved by the affirmation of Samuel Teague 20 July 1798 before Elisha Ford, J.P. Recorded 20 May 1799.

D, 237-239: Lease and release. 3 & 4 Jan 1776, Joseph Yeatman of Berkley County, SC, to James Plunket of same, for £150 SC money, 150 acres granted to Simeon Ellis 4 Nov 1772 in Berkley County on a branch of Beaver dam Creek adj. John Coate, surveyed for Simeon Ellis 2 July 1770. Joseph Yeatman (X) (Seal), Wit: Charles Plonket, Robert Cleland, George Goggans. Proved in Newberry County by the oath of Robert Cleland 21 May 1799 before J. R. Brown, J.N.C. Recorded 21 May 1799.

D, 240: 2 March 1799, John Justis Senr of Newberry County to granddaughters Mary Justice and Epsey Justis, daughters of Jesse Justis, for natural love, good will and affection, to Mary Justis one cow and feather bed and furniture and bedstead, one pewter dish and five plates, one table and one pot and one wheel; to Epsey Justis, one feather bed and furniture and one black walnut chest and one big iron pot and one frying pan, one griddle and two chairs and two basons and one pair of cards. John Justis (Seal), Wit: John Rees, Jacob Lewis. Proved by the oath of Jacob Lewis 20 May 1799 before J. R. Brown, J.N.C. Recorded 20 May 1799.

D, 241-243: Lease and release. 5 & 6 Jan 1795, Thomas and Charles Scott with Ann Morrow, their mother, to Samuel Hughen of Newberry County, for £50 sterling, 250 acres on waters of Ready River adj. Jacob Gray, James McGill, Thomas Carter, granted to said Thomas Scott 4 May 1775, recorded in Book XXX, page 410. Thomas & Margret Scott (Seal), Charles & Elisabeth Scott (Seal), Ann Morrow (X) (Seal), Wit: Samuel Freeman, John Hughn. Proved in Newberry County by the oath of John Hughen 21 May 1799 before J. R. Brown, J.N.C.

D, 243-244: 20 March 1787, William Tate of South Carolina to James Tate Senr of same, for "valuable consideration," 398 acres on north side Saluda River in Ninety Six District adj. William Anderson. Wm Tate (Seal), Wit: John Lindsey, Angus Campbell. Proved 4 Feb 1799 by the oath of Angus Campbell before Charles Griffin, J.P. Recorded 21 May 1799.

D, 244-245: 14 May 1799, John Belton of Newberry County to Joshua Teague of same, for $250, 100 acres on a small branch of Bush Creek called Mire branch, adj. Thomas Pearson, Marmaduke Coate, Joshua Teague, part of 250 acres granted to Elijah Teague 22 Feb 1771, descended by hereditary succession to Joshua Teague son of said Elijah Teague, and conveyed 1 April 1791 to John Belton. John Belton (Seal), Wit: Ben Long, Henry Coate. Charity Belton, wife of John Belton, relinquished dower 22 May 1799 before J. R. Brown, J.N.C. Proved by the oath of Henry Coate 21 May 1799 before J. R. Brown, J.N.C. Recorded 22 May 1799.

D, 246-247: Plat included. Saml Crumly of Newberry County for $50 to Samuel Hughen of same, for $50, 27½ acres of land, part of tract granted to John

Crumly and devolving to said Samuel Crumly by heirship, dated 21 May 1799. Samuel Crumly (Seal), Wit: Jacob Lewis, John Hughon. Ann Crumbly (X), wife of Saml Crumly, relinquished dower 21 May 1799 before J. R. Brown, J.N.C. Proved by the oath of John Hughon 21 May 1799 before J. R. Brown, J.N.C. Recorded 21 May 1799.

D, 247-248: 14 March 1798, John Coate of Newberry County to Joseph Evans of same, for £1 sterling, two lots in Newberry Village each of them ¼ acre, numbers 87 and 89 adj. Henry Coate, Second Street, Union Street. Jno Coate (Seal), Wit: Wm Satterwhite, Henry Coate. Proved by the oath of Wm Satterwhite 21 May 1799 before John Speake, J.P. Recorded 21 May 1799.

D, 248: Frederick Nance of Newberry County for $220 to John Belton of same, one negro girl named Minerva about 7 or 8 years old, 21 May 1799. Fred Nance (Seal), Wit: Ben Long, Francis Higgins. Acknowledged 21 May 1799 before J. R. Brown, J.N.C. Recorded 21 May 1799.

D, 249: Squire Lonam of Newberry County for $460 to Robert Plunket, 230 acres granted to David Spence for 200 acres and conveyed to Samuel Lonam 14 & 15 Feb 1769 in Newberry County on waters of Beverdam Creek & Bush River adj. Samuel Lonam, whereon William Morrow now lives, and devolving to me by heirship. Squire Lonam (Seal), Wit: J. R. Brown, J.N.C., Timothy Goodman. Recorded 21 May 1799.

D, 249-250: William Turner and Susannah Turner his wife of Edgefield County, SC, for £125 to Thomas Spearman of Newberry County, planter, all the tract of land that old William Turner willed to his grandson William Turner on north side Saluda River, 180 acres in Newberry County adj. Joseph Goodman & Brown and Saluda River. William Turner (X) (Seal), Susannah Turner (Seal), Wit: James Spearman, Joseph Trotter (mark), William Powers. Proved in Newberry County by the oath of James Spearman 20 May 1799 before Fred Nance, J.P. Recorded 21 May 1799.

D, 250-251: 11 Dec 1798, Thomas Wadsworth and William Turpin, merchants, for £15 to William Clary of Newberry County, 480 acres on the north side Saluda River surveyed by John Abney 22 Dec 1785 for William Clary and granted to Thomas Wadsworth 6 Nov 1786, adj. Daniel Clary, Mary Davis, Daniel Harps, James Galloway, John Reagan, Mathew Young, and Boyd. Wm Turpin, Thomas Wadsworth. Wit: Ben Long, William Thomerson (W). Jane Wadsworth, wife of Thomas Wadsworth, relinquished dower before William Turpin, J. Q. for Charleston District. Proved by the oath of Capt. Ben Long 21 May 1799 before J. R. Brown, J.N.C. Recorded 21 May 1799.

D, 252: State of South Carolina, Newberry County. The legatees of the estate of John Johnston, decd., namely Michael Johnston, John Johnston, James Johnston also Elinore Bennett, Hugh Marshell and Mary his wife, Uriah Conner and Margret his wife, John Ray and Catharine his wife, do acknowledge that we have received full satisfaction of Charles Johnston, executor of the late John Johnston decd., 1 April 1799. Michael Johnston (Seal), John Johnston (Seal), James Johnston (Seal), Hugh Marshell (Seal), Mary Marshall (mark) (Seal), Uriah Conner (Seal), Margret Connor (X) (Seal), John Ray (Seal), Catharine Ray (X) (Seal), Elionor Bennett (mark) (Seal), Wit: Alexander Turner, George Marshall, William Sparks. Proved in Newberry County by the oath of Alex'r Turner 20 May 1799 before John Speak, J.P. Recorded 21 May 1799.

D, 253-254: Plat of 26 acres included. South Carolina, Newberry County. 24 March 1794, James Williams of Newberry County, settlement of Beaverdam, heir at law to James Williams deceased, to Job Colvin of same, for £10 sterling, 26 acres, part of tract of 300 acres recorded in Book III, page 278, and memorial entered in Book L. No. 11, page 86 on 24 Oct 1771. James Williams (Seal), Wit: James Lindsey, John Clark. Proved 8 June 1796 by the oath of James Lindsey Senr before P. Williams, J.P. Recorded 6 June 1799.

D, 254-255: 8 Sept 1795, Job Colvin of Newberry County to Robert Coldwell of same, for £50 sterling, tract on waters of Bush River and Gilders Creek, waters of Indian Creek, 126 acres, granted to said Job Colvin and part granted to James Williams deceased, recorded in Book III, page 278, and memorial entered in Book L. No. 11, page 86 on 24 Oct 1771 [see preceding deed]. Job Colvin (Seal), Wit: James Lindsey, John Sloan, Andrew Spence. Proved 8 June 1796 by the oath of James Lindsey Senr before P. Williams, J.P. Recorded 6 June 1799.

D, 256-258: Lease and release. 19 & 20 April 1786, William Dickson of settlement of Gilders Creek, Newberry County, and wife Hannah, to Robert Caldwell of same, for £100, 100 acres, part of 400 acres granted to Nicholas Dickson and thence given to said William Dickson, he being heir at law of said Nicholas Dickson, on the head draughts of Gilders Creek. William Dickson (Seal), Hannah Dickson (mark) (Seal), Wit: Robert McAdam, James Lindsey, Robert Dickson (mark). Proved 3 June 1789 by the oath of James Lindsey before John Lindsey, J.P. Recorded 6 June 1799.

D, 259: 16 Aug 1794, James Campbell of Newberry County, to William Lindsey of same, for £20 sterling, 100 acres on a small draught of Patterson Creek of Indian Creek, part of tract granted to James Campbell 2 Jan 1792, recorded in Book E No. 5, page 170. Jas Campbell (Seal), Wit: Lewis Blalock, Edmond Lindsey, John Campbell. Proved 30 Jan 1799 by the oath of Edmond Lindsey before John Speak, J.P. Recorded 8 June 1799.

D, 260: 23 Oct 1798, William Lindsey of Newberry County to Robert Rogers of same, for £30 "specia", 100 acres on a small draught of Patterson Creek of Indian Creek, part of tract granted to James Campbell 2 Jan 1792, recorded in Book E No. 5, page 170. William Lindsey (Seal), Ellinner Lindsey (X) (Seal), Wit: Jno B. Bennett, John McCracken. Proved 22 May 1799 by the oath of John B. Bennett before John Speak, J.P. Recorded 8 June 1799.

D, 261-263: Lease and release. 18 & 19 Oct 1774, David Mote of Ninety Six District, SC, to Isaac Cook of same, for £50 SC money, 200 acres on north side Saluda on the Beaverdam granted to said David Mote 24 Aug 1770 and 50 acres, part of tract granted to said David Mote from Henry Haford 23 Aug 1774 which said Haford had by lease and release from Stephen Holson 10 June 1759. David Mote (Seal), Dorkas Mote (+) (Seal), Wit: William Wright, James McCool, Benjamin Morrow (M). Proved in Newberry County ___ 1791 by the oath of William Wright before Elisha Ford, J.P. Recorded 10 June 1799.

D, 264-265: Samuel Murray of Buncombe County, North Carolina, for £100 sterling to Lemon Shell of Newberry County, SC, 319 acres, part of 200 acres purchased by Samuel Murray from Robert Mars, by plat certified 30 Aug 1775 and part of tract of 150 acres certified for Pearce Noland 2 March 1762, dated 4 Feb 1799. Samuel Murray (Seal), Wit: Stephen Shell, James Kelly, Thomas Murray. Proved in Newberry County by the oath of Stephen Shell 15 June 1799 before Edward Finch, J.P. Plat included "pursuant to the request of Lemon & Harmon Shell," part of the land purchased by them of Samuel Murray, divided by consent, on a branch called Hunting fork, a branch of Indian Creek, waters of Enoree River, 21 Dec 1798. G. Harbirt, D. S. Shows adj. land owners David Chambers, John Mares[?], Charles Crenshaw, Levi Anderson, Harmon Shell, Luellen. Recorded 25 June 1799.

D, 266-267: Samuel Murray of Buncombe County, North Carolina, for £100 sterling to Harmon Shell of Newberry County, SC, 306 acres, part of 200 acres purchased by Samuel Murray from Robert Mars, by plat certified 30 Aug 1775 and part of tract of 150 acres certified by Pearce Noland 2 March 1762, dated 4 Feb 1799. Samuel Murray (Seal), Wit: Stephen Shell, James Kelly, Thomas Murray. Proved in Newberry County by the oath of Stephen Shell 15 June 1799 before Edward Finch, J.P. Plat included "pursuant to the request of Lemon & Harmon Shell," part of the land purchased by them of Samuel Murray, divided by consent, on a branch called Hunting fork, a branch of Indian Creek, waters of Enoree River, 21 Dec 1798. G. Harbirt, D. S. Shows adj. land owners McCrackin, James Murrow, William Beard, Benjamin Herndon, Smiten[?], Lemon Shell. Recorded 25 June 1799.

D, 268: Jeremiah McDanal of Newberry County, bachelor, for love, good will and affection to my cousin and name sake Jeremiah McDanal Junr of same, one negro boy named Peter, 20 Aug 1798. Jer. McDanal (Seal), Wit: Peter Hawkins, John Mowrer, Michael Witt (mark). Proved in Newberry County by the oath of Michael Witt 8 June 1799 before Daniel Parkins, J.P. Recorded 5 July 1799.

D, 268-269: Jeremiah McDanal of Newberry County, bachelor, for $50 and for my maintenance during my natural life for which John McDanal gives me full assurance, eleven head of neat cattle, marked in each ear with a crop & slit, also between 30 and 40 head of hogs marked as aforesaid, all my household and plantation furniture, one sorrel gelding, 17 May 1799. Jer. McDanal

(Seal), Wit: Mich'l Dickert Senr, Adrian Witt (A), Michael Witt (mark). Proved in Newberry County by the oath of Michael Witt 8 June 1799 before Daniel Parkins, J.P. Recorded 5 July 1799.

D, 269-270: 7 May 1799, Jeremiah McDanal of Newberry County, planter, for _____ to John McDanal, 200 acres granted to Peter Hare Senr 13 March 1772, recorded in Book "LIVII," page 377 and left by the will of said Peter Hare to his son John Hare and the other 100 devolved by the said will to his son Mathias Hare and said John Hare did convey 100 acres to Jacob Counts and Jacob Counts did convey to Jeremiah McDanal. Jer. McDanal (Seal), Wit: Mich'l Dickert Senr, Adrian Witt (A), Michael Witt (mark). Proved in Newberry County by the oath of Michael Witt 8 June 1799 before Daniel Parkins, J.P. Recorded 5 July 1799.

D, 271-273: Lease and release. 1 & 2 Aug 1774, Robert Yeldal of Ninety Six District, to Joseph Summers of settlement of Bush River, for £500 SC money, 300 acres on a branch of Bush River called Palmeto Branch, in two separate tracts: 150 acres granted to George Adde 2 Jan 1759 and conveyed to Mathias Elmore 11 & 12 July 1759 and by said Matthias Elmore to Robert Yeldall 4 Oct 1765; the other tract of 150 acres granted to said Robert Yeldall 8 Feb 1772. Robert Yeldall, Phebe Yeldell (X), Wit: William Summers, Robert Yeldell Jun'r. Proved by the oath of William Summers 6 April 1775 before Jno Caldwell, J.P. Recorded 6 July 1799.

D, 274-276: Lease and release. 2 & 3 Oct 1772, Henry Littlejohn of Berkley County, SC, planter, and wife Rachel to David Humphrey of same, blacksmith, for £100 sterling, 200 acres in Berkley County on waters of Bush River adj. Stephen Elmore, Mathias Elmore. Henry LittleJohn (H) (Seal), Rachel LittelJohn (Seal), Wit: Moses Embree, Enos Ellemon, James Moore. Proved in Ninety Six District by the oath of Enos Ellemon 31 Aug 1773 before Jno Caldwell, J.P. Recorded 6 July 1799.

D, 277: Joseph White of Newberry County bond to Cason Hill of same, in the sum of £80 s1 d8 sterling, 5 Feb 1798, for payment of £409 s10 sterling by 4 Feb 1803. Joseph White (Seal), Wit: Larkin Cason, Daniel Goodman. Proved in Edgefield County by the oath of Lar'k Cason 18 June 1799 before William Anderson, J.E.C. Recorded 26 July 1799.

D, 278: Joseph White of Newberry County bond to Cason Hill of same, in the sum of £80 s1 d8 sterling, 5 Feb 1798, for payment of £409 s10 sterling by 4 Feb 1803, mortgage of negro Pompey 12 years of age. Joseph White (Seal), Wit: Larkin Cason, Daniel Goodman. Proved in Edgefield County by the oath of Lar'k Cason 18 June 1799 before William Anderson, J.E.C. Recorded 26 July 1799.

D, 279: Spencer Morgan of Orangeburg District for love, good will and affection to my daughter Nancy McMorries, wife of Capt. John McMorries, of Newberry County, negroes: Randol a man slave about 21 years of age,

Betty a black girl slave about 15 years of age, Peter a boy slave about 9 years of age. Spencer Morgan (Seal), Wit: John Nuckolls, Thos Murray. Acknowledged in open court 29 July 1799. Recorded 28 July 1799.

D, 280: Spencer Morgan of Orangeburg District for love, good will and affection to my daughter Fanny Morgan of Newberry County, negroes: Pompey a man slave, a negro woman slave Dinah and her three children Littye, Newman, and Mary. Spencer Morgan (Seal), Wit: John Nuckolls, Thos Murray. Acknowledged in open court July term 1799. Recorded 28 July 1799.

D, 281-285: South Carolina, Ninety Six District. 5 March 1799, Elizabeth Swift of Newberry County, widow and relict of William Swift, late of same county, merchant, deceased, to Elihu Creswell and Archey Mayson, merchants, of same, whereas the said William Swift died intestate but long previous to his death had determined how he would disposed of his possessions: that the real and personal property should be divided into three shares and one lot should be to the said Elizabeth Swift and the other two shares should be the property of his two sons Jonathan and William Swift, that very shortly before his death said William Swift applied to council to write his will to that effect but being advised that the law of this state commonly called the primogeniture law would answer all the objects and wishes of his mind in case of intestacy, he declined the execution of a will; administration was granted to Elizabeth Swift his widow and James Robert Mayson her brother; said Elizabeth Swift was the sole purchaser of the real and principal purchaser of the personal estate... she has determined to divest herself of the estate to Elihu Creswell and Archey Mayson as trustees to comply with the intentions of the late William Swift until Jonathan and William Swift arrived at the age of 21 years. Elizabeth Swift (Seal), Elihu Creswell (Seal), Archey Mayson (Seal), Wit: John Finley, Henrietta Mayson, Kitty Creswell. Proved by the oath of John Finley 29 June 1799 before Jas Mayson, J.N.C. Recorded 29 July 1797.

D, 286: 25 July 1798, Lewis Boatner of Edgefield County to Thomas Chappell of Newberry County for £10 sterling, 50 acres on Saluda River, adj. David Anderson, William Anderson, Inman. Ludwig Bottner [German signature] (Seal), Wit: Olley Man Dodgin, James Chappell. Proved in Newberry County by the oath of James Chappell 11 May 1799 before Robert Gillom, J.P. Recorded 29 July 1799.

D, 287-288: South Carolina, Laurens County, Ninety Six District. William Day of said county for £100 sterling to Thomas Chappell of Newberry County, 100 acres on the main road leading from the Fish dam road on Broad River to the Island ford on Saluda adj. J. r. Brown, Anthoney Griffin, Samuel Bradshaw, Rutherford Boland, Asa Griffin, James Williamson, the remainder of a tract granted to John Ray for 300 acres whereon William Day now lives, 29 Dec 1798. Wm Day (Seal), Wit: J. R. Brown, J.N.C., Iraad Grant Sen'r. Mary Day (X), wife of William Day, relinquished dower 29 Dec 1798 before J. R. Brown, J.N.C. Recorded 29 July 1799.

D, 288-289: 23 Jan 1799, James Cox, Allen Cox, Robert Cox, Henry Hazle, George Gothard, Lewis Watson, Zebulon Savage, Daniel Cox of Ninety Six District, heirs and legatees of Allen Cox deceased, for £80 sterling to Thomas Chappell of same district, 100 acres on north side Saluda River adj. James Cox, Thomas Chappell and James Dyson, granted to Andrew Cook 21 March 1768. James Cox (Seal), Allen Cox (X) (Seal), Robert Cox (Seal) Henry Hazle (X) (Seal), George Gothard (X) (Seal), John Watson (X), Zebulon Savage (Seal), Daniel Cox (Seal), Wit: James Dyson, James Chappell, Elisha Brooks. Proved in Newberry County by the oath of James Dyson 23 April 1799 before Robert Gillam, J.P.

D, 289-290: 21 May 1798, Thomas Reed of Newberry County to James Spearman of same, for £40 sterling, 60 acres on Scotch Creek, waters of Bush River, part of tract granted to John Wilkinsons for 200 acres, adj. Enoch Pearson, Robert McClure, Edward Benbow, John Wilkinson. Tomas Reed (Seal), Wit: Henry Coate, Fred: Nance. Proved by the oath of Henry Coate 30 June 1799 before Fred Nance, J.P. Henrietta Reed (mark), wife of Thomas Reed, relinquished dower 29 July 1799 before J. R. Brown, J.N.C. Recorded 29 July 1799.

D, 290-291: Plat included for 20 acres showing adjacent land owners; Butler, John Sterling, Floyd.

John Floyd of Newberry County for $60 to Benjamin Butler of same, 20 acres between Sandy Run and a branch thereof, part of tract originally granted to John Lucas for 100 acres, dated 7 Jan 1799. John Floyd (Seal), Wit: Joseph Pitts, J. R. Brown, James Toland. Nanny Floyd (X), wife of John Floyd, relinquished dower 22 March 1799 before J. R. Brown, J.N.C. Recorded 29 July 1799.

D, 292: South Carolina, Newberry County, January 23d 1799. Then received of Elisha Brooks, guardian and representative of William Cox (deceased), $22.85 being the full amount of said William Coxes part of the estate of Allen Cox deceased: James Cox, Allen Cox (X), George Gothard (mark), Henry Hazle (X), John Watson, Lewis Watson, Robert Cox, Zebulon Savag, Daniel Cox, Wit: James Dyson, James Chappell, John Dyson. Recorded 29 July 1799.

South Carolina, Newberry County, January 23d 1799. Then received of Elisha Brooks, guardian and representative of Rebecca Cox the sum of £60 sterling being the full amount of said Daniel Coxes part of the estate of Allen Cox (deceased). Zebulon Savag, Wit: James Dyson, James Chappell, John Dyson. Recorded 29 July 1799.

South Carolina, Newberry County, January 23d 1799. Then received of Elisha Brooks, guardian and representative of Rebecca Cox the sum of £60 sterling being the full amount of said Rebecca Coxes part of the estate of Allen Cox (deceased). Daniel Cox, Wit: James Dyson, James Chappell, John Dyson. Recorded 29 July 1799.

D, 293-294: 12 Jan 1799, William Hall and wife Martha of Newberry County to Isaac Gilder of same, for $20, 18 acres, part of 118 acres granted to Matthew Tully in the fork of Broad and Saluda Rivers on waters of Kings Creek, adj. line of Isaac Gilder formerly by John Wilson, Edward Hill. William Hall (Seal), Martha Hall (X) (Seal), Wit: James Wilson, Robt Gowan, Obed Parrish. Proved by the oath of Obed Parrish 5 March 1799 before Edward Finch, J.P. Recorded 29 July 1799.

D, 294-295: 22 Jan 1799, George Johnston and wife Elizabeth to James Chandler, all of Newberry County, for £45 sterling, 100 acres on waters of Enoree adj. Jonathan Batt, John Hogg, George Johnsons spring branch, Widow Collinsworth, road to Goodman's store. George Johnson (Seal), Elizabeth Johnson (X) (Seal), Wit: Jonathan Pratt, Gideon Nelson, William Pratt. Proved by the oath of Gideon Nelson 27 July 1799 before Edward Finch, J.P. Recorded 29 July 1799.

D, 295-296: Amos Parkins of Newberry County to Daniel Parkins, Esqr., of same, for $300, 150 acres on Saluda River adj. Daniel Parkins, Col. P. Waters decd, Charles Parkins, part of 450 acres granted to Charles Parkins deceased and conveyed by him to David Parkins, deceased, who died intestate and the said Amos Parkins, being the oldest male heir. Amos Parkins (Seal), Wit: Daniel Parkins, Jacob Buller. Proved 29 July 1799 by the oath of Jacob Buller before Fred Nance, C.N.C. Recorded 29 July 1799.

D, 296-297: 25 April 1795, James Daugherty of Newberry County to Martin Souter, planter, for £15 sterling, 28 acres (originally granted to James Daugherty 3 Sept 1792, recorded in Book F No. 5, page 160), adj. Martin Souter, Jacob Sligh, Jacob Risinger, Adam Setzler. James Daugharty (X) (Seal), Wit: Michl Dickert Senr, Peter Dickert, Christopher Dickert. Proved by the oath of Peter Dickert 30 March 1796 before David Ruff, J.P. Recorded 29 July 1799.

D, 298-300: Lease and release. 20 Sept 1793, Robert Whitten of Ninety Six District, planter, to John Whitten, planter, of same, for £50 SC money, 175 acres, part of 320 acres on branches of Mulberry Run a draft of Duncan Creek, granted to said Robert Whitten 6 July 1789, recorded in Book YYYY, page 553. Robert Whitten (Seal), Wit: Charles Whitten, Robert Watkins. Proved in Newberry County by the oath of Charles Whitten 20 July 1799 before John Speak, J.P. Recorded 29 July 1799.

D, 301: 15 July 1799, John Stuart of Newberry County to David Sims of same, for £34 s 13 sterling, 66 acres in Newberry County adj. Thomas Jones, John Morris, John O'Neal, Reuben Sims, David Sims, Thomas Jones, granted to said John Stuart 31 Aug 1774. John Stuart (Seal), Wit: Reuben Sims, Charles Sims, Wm. D. Sims. Proved by the oath of William D. Sims 27 July 1799 before Saml E. Kenner, J.P. Recorded 28 July 1799.

D, 302: South Carolina, Newberry County. Moses Kelly, one of the heirs of John Kelly decd., having come into possession of two slaves left by the aforesaid John Kelly (namely) George, a yellow man about 22 years of age, and Frank, a black girl; about 8 years old, and believing the Liberty is the natural right of all mankind, have manumitted them forever, done at Bush River, 18th day of the sixth month 1795. Moses Kelly (Seal), Wit: Joseph Thompson, John Jay, Joseph Furnas. Proved by the statement of Joseph Thompson 26 March 1798 before Elisha Ford, J.P. Recorded 29 July 1799.

D, 303-304: 20 April 1799, Alexander Johnston and wife Margaret of Newberry County to Henry Wicker of same, for $200, 150 acres, granted 6 Feb 1774 to said Alexander Johnston for 100 acres and 50 acres conveyed to said Alexander Johnston by John Gant 18 March 1773, part of 200 acres granted to said John Gant 28 Aug 1773 on a small branch of Second Creek, waters of Broad River. Alexander Johnston (Seal), Margaret Johnston (X) (Seal), Wit: David Owen, G. Harbirt. Proved by the oath of David Owen 29 July 1799 before Edward Finch, J.P. Recorded 29 July 1799.

D, 304-307: Lease and release. 26 & 27 Feb 1787, Mick White and wife Jane of Newberry County to Samuel Hughins of same, for ____, 100 acres granted 21 March 1768 to James Hogan on Beaverdam Branch adj. Saml Lonam, recorded in Book CCC, page 450. Mick White (Seal), Jane White (Seal), Wit: John Crumly, James Abernathy, Burgess Stone. Proved by the oath of James Abernathy 30 July 1799 before J. R. Brown, J.N.C. Recorded 30 July 1799.

D, 308-309: William Greenwood of Charleston, merchant, for $3000 to Samuel Mays of Ninety Six District, Edgefield County, planter, 1600 acres in Newberry County on waters of Saluda River surveyed 7 June 1751, granted to James Maxwell, late of Belfast in the State of Georgia, Esqr., deceased, and afterwards descended to his eldest son John Maxwell Esqr., also deceased, and afterwards descended to John Butler Maxwell, as the only surviving son and heir at law of his father said John Maxwell deceased, on 16 Dec 1788 conveyed by John Butler Maxwell to William Greenwood, dated 14 Feb 1799. Wm Greenwood (Seal), Wit: Matt Michel, R. M. McCoombs. Proved in Ninety Six District by the oath of Robert McCombs 7 May 1799 before Wm Nibbs, J. Q. Recorded 30 July 1799.

D, 309-310: James Cox, Allen Cox, Robert Cox, Daniel Cox, Henry Hazle, Lewis Watson, John Watson, George Gothard, Zebulon Savage, all of Ninety Six District, heirs and legatees of Allen Cox deceased, for £52 sterling to John Dyson of same district, 100 acres on Goosepond Creek, waters of Saluda River adj. James Dyson deceased, John Dyson, Thomas Chappel, William Burgess and Abra'm Dyson, granted to William Sutliff 6 Feb 1773 and by him conveyed to John Wallace and from John Wallace to Allen Cox deceased, 23 Jan 1799. James Cox (Seal), Allen Cox (X) (Seal), Robert Cox (Seal) Henry Hazle (X) (Seal), George Gothard (X) (Seal), Lewis Watson (Seal), John Watson (X), Zebulon Savage (Seal), Daniel Cox (Seal), Wit: James Dyson,

James Chappell, Elisha Brooks. Proved in Newberry County by the oath of James Dyson 23 April 1799 before Robert Gillam, J.P.

D, 310-311: Allen Cox, Robert Cox, Daniel Cox, Henry Hazle, Lewis Watson, John Watson, George Gothard, Zebulon Savage, all of Ninety Six District, heirs and legatees of Allen Cox deceased, for £111 sterling to James Cox of same district, several tracts all adj. each other whereon Allen Cox Senr late deceased formerly lived, 300 acres: 100 acres granted to Allen Cox 22 Aug 1771, 100 acres granted to Allen Cox 2 Feb 1771, 50 acres granted to Thomas Turke 23 June 1774, 50 acres granted to John ___ 12 Feb 1775 and conveyed to said Allen Cox Senr, dated ___ Jan 1799. Allen Cox (X) (Seal), Robert Cox (Seal) Henry Hazle (X) (Seal), George Gothard (X) (Seal), Lewis Watson (Seal), John Watson (X), Zebulon Savage (Seal), Daniel Cox (Seal), Wit: James Dyson, James Chappell, Elisha Brooks. Proved in Newberry County by the oath of James Dyson 23 April 1799 before Robert Gillam, J.P. Recorded 30 July 1799.

D, 311-312: John Justis of Newberry County for $200 to Jacob Lewis of same, 79 acres on north side Little River on a branch of Beverdam adj. John Reece, Solomon Reece, Robert Russel, Benjamin Wood, James Jones, Widow Collins, Wm. Burton, dated 25 Feb 1799. John Justis (Seal), Wit: Robert Hilburn, Levi Hilburn (L). Anna Justis (mark), wife of John Justis, relinquished dower 4 March 1799 before L. Casey, J.N.C. Proved by the oath of Robert Hilburn 29 July 1799 before Providence Williams, J.P. Recorded 30 July 1799.

D, 312-313: James Newman of Newberry County for £100 sterling, 98 acres on waters of Beaverdam and waters of Little River, adj. George Goggans, Daniel Butler, James Newman, part of 285 acres granted to William Goggans and conveyed to James Newman 8 April 1797, plat by William Caldwell 20 Jan 1799, deed dated 30 July 1799. James Newman (Seal), Wit: George Goggans, William Pitts, Jeremiah Goggans. Elisabeth (Betty) Newman, wife of James Newman, relinquished dower 30 July 1799 before J. R. Brown, J.N.C. Proved by the oath of George Goggans 30 July 1799 before J. R. Brown, J.N.C. Recorded 30 July 1799.

D, 314: William Scott of Newberry County to John Scott of same, for $100, 100 acres on a small branch of Indian Creek called Patterson Creek, part of 450 acres granted to said William Scott, dated 13 May 1799. William Scott (O) (Seal), Wit: John Boys Senr, Joseph Scott, Robert Boys. Proved by the oath of John Boys Senr 29 July 1799 before P. Williams, J.P. Recorded 30 July 1799.

D, 315: State of South Carolina, Ninety Six District. Thomas Green of Laurens County for £25 to Robert Golding of Newberry County, 50 acres, part of 200 acres granted to said Thomas Green 22 Aug 17--, on south side Little River, dated 3 June 1799. Thomas Green (Seal), Wit: John Gallegly, Joel Foster, James Sproll. Proved by the oath of John Gallegly 22 June 1799 before Charles Griffin, J.P. Recorded 30 July 1799.

D, 316: 10 May 1799, Squire Lonam of Newberry County for $250 to William Morrow of same, 125 acres on Beverdam Creek, granted to Samuel Lonam and devolving to me by heirship whereon the said William Morrow now lives. Squire Lonam (Seal), Wit: J. R. Brown, Timothy Goodman. Proved by the oath of Jacob R. Brown 30 July 1799 before Daniel Parkins, J.P. Recorded 30 July 1799.

D, 317: 29 Sept 1798, Samuel Wood and wife Elizabeth to Emanuel Glymph, all of Newberry County, for £50 SC money, 100 acres, part of 350 acres granted to Jacob Furger (alias Falker) conveyed to Thomas wood and given from him to said Samuel Wood, plat made out by David Ruff, D. S. Samuel Wood (Seal), Elizabeth Wood (X) (Seal), Wit: John Glymph, John Wood, Benjamin Buchanan. Proved by the oath of John Glymph 30 July 1799 before Edward Finch, J.P. Recorded 30 July 1799.

D, 318-319: Michael Kinard of Newberry County for £55 sterling to William Wats and Samuel Wats Junr jointly of same, planters, 150 acres in Craven County on Buffelow Creek, waters of Saluda River, granted to John Leonard Harman 15 May 1772 and by him conveyed to said Michael Kinard 25 & 27 Oct 1789 and recorded 11 June 1794 in Newberry County Book B, page 767, dated 23 March 1799. Michael Kinard (Seal), Wit: William Righard (W), Adam Lagrone (AL). Catharine, wife of Michael Kinard, relinquished dower before Jacob Roberts Brown, Justice of Newberry County, 30 July 1799. Acknowledged in open court July Term 1799. Recorded 30 July 1799.

D, 318-320: 3 Jan 1799, John Leavell of Newberry County to John Abernathy of same, for £172 s10 sterling, 345 acres on north side Bush River, part of tract granted to Isaac Williams, part of grant to Henry Demonge, and part of tract granted to Hugh Marshall. John Leavell (Seal), Wit: Thos Clark, James Leavel. Peggy Leavell (P), wife of John Leavill, relinquished dower 3 Jan 1799 before J. R. Brown, J.N.C. Plat included showing adjacent land owners: John Leavell, Charles Crow, Thomas Gary, William Reeder.

D, 321-322: 10 Jan 1799, John Abernathy of Newberry County to George McKitrick of same, for £67 s12 sterling, 169 acres on north side Bush River, part of tract granted to Henry Demonge, part of tract granted to Hugh Marshall, adj. William Reeder, Thomas Gary, John Leavell, George Clark, originally land of John Leavel and conveyed to John Abernathy 3 Jan 1799. John Abernathy (Seal), Wit: Robert McKitrick (mark), Jesse Davis (X), Wm Belton. Rhoda Abernathy (X), wife of John Abernathy, relinquished dower 30 July 1799 before J. R. Brown, J.N.C. Proved by the oath of Jesse Davis 30 July 1799 before J. R. Brown, J.N.C. Recorded 31 July 1799.

D, 322-323: 3 Jan 1799, John Abernathy of Newberry County to John Leavell of same, for £217 s10 sterling, 345 acres on Bush River, formerly called Chandlers Mill, part of tract granted to Isaac Williams, part of tract granted to Henry Demonge, part of tract granted to Hugh Marshall, and part of a tract granted to John Abernathy and John Leavel and whereon said mill now stands. John Abernathy (Seal), Wit: J. R. Brown, Thos Clark, James Leavell. Rhoda Abernathy (X), wife of John Abernathy, relinquished dower 3 Jan 1799 before J. R. Brown, J.N.C. Proved by the oath of Thomas Clark before P. Williams, J.P. Recorded 31 July 1799. Plat included showing adjacent land owners: John Leavell, Charles Crow, John Gary, Thomas Gary, John Abernathy.

D, 324-325: 30 March 1799, Susannah Caldwell, William Caldwell, David Caldwell, Daniel Dyson and Nimrod Overby of State of SC for £143 sterling, to Yourath Basket of same, 220 acres in Newberry County on Saluda River adj. James Creswell, John Caldwell. Susannah Caldwell (X) (Seal), William Caldwell (X) (Seal), David Caldwell (Seal), Da'l Dyson (Seal), Nimrod Overby (Seal), Wit: Thomas Anderson, Robt McAliester, Daniel Basketh. Plat included. Proved by the oath of Thomas Anderson 22 July 1799 before Robert Gillam, J.P. Recorded 31 July 1799.

D, 325-326: Joshua Gillam of Newberry County for £100 sterling to Robert Gillam Esq'r, 200 acres on a branch called Pages Creek by plat made by William Caldwell 9 May 1796, part of plantation whereon Robert Gilliam Senr dec'd formerly resided in his lifetime, conveyed to said Joshua Gillam by deed dated 19 July 1797 and recorded in Book D, page 353... dated 2 March 1799. Joshua Gillam (Seal), Wit: John Thomas S. M., Abram Dyson, Thomas Farrow. Alce Gillam (mark), wife of Joshua Gillam relinquished dower 22 May 1799 before J. R. Brown, J.N.C. Proved by the oath of Thomas Farrow 31 July 1799 before J. R. Brown, J.N.C. Recorded 31 July 1799.

D, 326: Joshua Gillam for $400 to Robert Gillam, one negro boy named Sam, 25 Feb 1799. Joshua Gillam (Seal), Wit: Daniel Towles, Fields Read (X). Proved by the oath of Daniel Towles 31 July 1799 before J. R. Brown, J.N.C. Recorded 31 July 1799.

D, 327-328: 7 Jan 1799, John Abernathy of Newberry County to George Clark of same, for £120 sterling, 181 acres on north side Bush River, part of several tracts granted from John Leavell to said John Abernathy 3 Jan 1799. John Abernathy (Seal), Wit: Jesse Davis (X), G. Harbirt. Plat included by Go Harbirt, D. S., 7 Jan 1799. Rhoda Abernathy (X), wife of John Abernathy, relinquished dower 30 July 1799 before J. R. Brown, J.N.C. Proved by the oath of Jesse Davis 30 July 1799 before J. R. Brown, J.N.C. Recorded 31 July 1799.

D, 328-331: Lease and release. 1 & 2 Oct 1783, Hugh Kilpatrick of Guilders Creek, Ninety Six District to Jeremiah Stark of same district, for £100 SC money, 100 acres on a small branch of Gilders Creek on south side Broad River adj. Jane Kilpatrick, originally granted to Thomas Kilpatrick 6 Feb 1773, recorded in Book FFF, page 118, and Auditor's Office, Book M. No. 12, page 318 on 23 July 1773. Hugh Kilpatrick (mark) (Seal), Wit: James Lindsey, George Speake, James Hughston. Proved 1 Nov 1784 by the oath of James Lindsey. Recorded 31 July 1799.

D, 332-336: Lease and release. 17 & 18 June 1784, Jeremiah Stark of Ninety Six District, to James Huston, planter, of same district, for £100 SC money, 100 acres on a small branch of Gilders Creek on south side Broad River adj. Jane Kilpatrick, originally granted to Thomas Kilpatrick 6 Feb 1773, recorded in Book FFF, page 118, and Auditor's Office, Book M. No. 12, page 318 on 23 July 1773, conveyed by Hugh Kilpatrick to Jeremiah Stark 2 Oct 1783. Jeremiah Stark (Seal), Wit: John Hughston, Arthur McCrackin, John Thomas S. M. Proved 1 Nov 1784 by the oath of John Huston 27 Oct 1798 before L. E. Casey, J. N. C. Recorded 31 July 1799.

D, 336-337: 27 August 1798, James Huston, planter, of Newberry County, to James Wright of same, for £60 sterling, 100 acres on a branch of Gilders Creek on south side Broad River adj. Jane Kilpatrick, originally granted to Thomas Kilpatrick 6 Feb 1773. James Huston (mark) (Seal), Wit: John Huston, George Harbirt, Joseph Hughey. Mary Huston (Hughston), wife of James Huston, relinquished dower 27 Oct 1798 before L. E. Casey, J. N. C. Proved 27 Oct 1798 by the oath of G. Harbirt 27 Oct 1798 before L. E. Casey, J. N. C. Recorded 31 July 1799.

D, 338-339: 27 August 1798, John Huston, planter, of Newberry County, to James Wright of same, for £20 sterling, 34 acres, part of tract of 107 acres granted 1 May 1786 to said John Huston on branches of Indian Creek. John Huston (Seal), Wit: James Hewston (mark). Plat included showing adjacent land owners John Hughston, James Huston, Robt Glasgow, Patrick Lowry. Mary Huston (mark), wife of John Huston, relinquished dower 27 Oct 1798 before L. E. Casey, J. N. C. Proved 27 Oct 1798 by the oath of G. Harbirt 27 Oct 1798 before L. E. Casey, J. N. C. Recorded 31 July 1799.

D, 339-340: 20 Dec 1797, James Williamson of York County, SC, to John Tinsley of Newberry County, for £73 sterling, 100 acres in Newberry County on waters of Saluda, adj. William Stuart, granted to John Williamson and conveyed by him to James Williamson 17 Dec 1797. James Williamson (Seal), Wit: James Glen, John Glen. Proved in Newberry County by the oath of John Glen 3 July 1799 before Daniel Parkins, J.P. Recorded 31 July 1799.

D, 340-341: 7 May 1799, William Hamilton of Newberry County to Charles Crenshaw of same, for $94, 23½ acres, part of 150 acres granted to William Hamilton 14 Sept 1771, recorded in Book III, page 297, adj. Finches line, on Kings Creek. Willm Hamilton (Seal), Wit: Thos Hamilton, Will'm Richards, John Ellis. Elisabeth Hamilton, wife of William Hamilton relinquished dower 7 May 1799 before L. E. Casey, J. N. C. Proved by the oath of Thomas Hamilton before Edw'd Finch, J.P. Recorded 31 July 1799.

D, 342: 9 Feb 1799, Lewis Hogg to Jesse Chandler [consideration not mentioned], 100 acres, part of 300 acres granted to Lewis Hogg in 1787, adj. Jacob Keller, Wliliam Darby, "said Darys" and John Kelly, Dickey. Lewis Hogg (Seal), Clares Hogg (mark) (Seal), Wit: William Darby (W), William

Chandler, George Pratt. Proved in Newberry County by the oath of Wm Chandler 27 July 1799 before Edw'd Finch, J.P. Recorded 31 July 1799.

D, 343-346: Lease and release. 7 & 8 June 1774, John Daugharty of Ninety Six District, gunsmith, to James Caldwell, planter, for £100 SC currency, 100 acres granted to John Doharty (alias Daugharty) 18 May 1773 in Craven County on south side of Broad River on a small branch of Second Creek adj. William Dorkins, Patrick Kelly, recorded in Book PPP, page 43. John Daugharty (Seal), Wit: John Caldwell, John M. Williams, James Maffet. Proved in Ninety Six District by the oath of John Caldwell 5 Oct 1774 before Mich'l Dickert, J.P. Recorded 31 July 1799.

D, 346-347: 9 April ____, Thomas Rutherford of Newberry County to Robert Rutherford Senr of same, for £10 sterling, 123 acres on waters of Second Creek adj. William Dawkins, Galaspie, Horsey, Col. Rutherford. Thomas Rutherford (Seal), Wit: Francis Higgins, Robert Rutherford Junr, H. Slappy. Proved 31 July 1799 by the oath of Francis Higgins before Fred Nance, J.P. Recorded 31 July 1799.

D, 347-348: Ann Williams of Newberry County for love, god will and affection to my son Thomas Williams of same, all the negroes now in my possession: one negro man named Dunkin and his wife Cate, one negro woman Let, one negro boy Dunkin, one negro boy Named Ben, only Dunkin & his wife Cate and Let, I reserve for myself during my natural life, 4 June 1799. Ann Williams (X) (Seal), Wit: Stephen McCraw, P. Williams. Proved by the oath of Providence Williams 29 July 1799 before Edw'd Finch, J.P. Recorded 31 July 1799.

D, 348-349: South Carolina, Newberry County. Personally appeared Michael Dickert before Jacob Roberts Brown, Judge for Newberry County, and saith on 5 February 1774 he did see regular conveyances from Martin Mahaffy the original grantee for 200 acres on waters of Cannons Creek to David Tenant and from said Tenant to Peter Strasingee and from Strasingee to Valentine Luttinger, done before Michael Dickert who was then acting as justice of the peace and that the conveyances were destroyed in the time of the late war, and said Valentine Lattinger has been in possession of said land ever since 1774 and in still living in the full possession of the land aforesaid, 30 July 1799. Mich'l Dickert Senr.

Also affidavits of Joseph Chapman and Jacob Buzzard, 30 July 1799 before J. R. Brown, J. N.C.

Vallentine Lattinger maketh oath that the whole of the titles of his land as before set forth were destroyed by getting wet in the time of the late war and that the mutilated pieces of paper herewith deposited is such parts of his said titles, 31 July 1799. Vallentine Luttinger (mark). Recorded 31 July 1791.

D, 349-350: 14 March 1798, Matthias Kinnard, planter, of Newberry County, to Andrew Kinnard, planter, of same, for £50 sterling, 250 acres in the fork of Broad and Saluda Rivers on a branch of Eleazers Creek, adj. Adam Summer, Samuel Kelly, Stephen Eleazer, recorded in Book M. No. 13, page 68, and is the land granted to George Fouser in 1774. Mathias Kinnard (MK) (Seal), Wit: Jas McMaster, Laurence Rickard (mark). Proved by the oath of James McMaster 31 July 1799 before Daniel Parkins, J.P. Recorded 31 July 1799.

D, 350-351: Micajah Bennett of Newberry County, planter, for $639.66 to James McMorries of same, the following negroes: one old negro woman named Nancy and her daughter also named Nanny, one other old negro woman named Hannah and her son a negro man named Will, whereas said John McMorries hath become security for the said Micajah Bennett in a note payable to Thomas Clark at two months for $150 and likewise his security in another note payable to Daniel Williams at two months for $300, and said Micajah Bennett is indebted to said John McMorries in the sum of $189.66 on a book account, mortgage of said negroes, 19 Feb 1799. M. Bennett (Seal), Wit: Richard Bennett, Daniel Lofton. Proved by the oath of Richard Bennett 25 July 1799 before John Speake, J.P. Recorded 31 July 1799.

D, 352-353: 25 July 1795, Thomas Wadsworth and William Turpin of state of SC, merchants, to Benjamin Johnson, for £40, tract on land in Newberry County called Dimond Hill, 34 acres, granted to Thomas Wadsworth, William Turpin and John Means, adj. land of Rutherford, John Montgomery, Speake, Caldwell. Thomas Wadsworth (Seal), Will'm Turpin (Seal), Wit: James Boyce, James Young, A. Cates. Proved by the oath of James Young 25 July 1799 before Thomas Wadsworth, J. L. C. Recorded 31 July 1799.

D, 353-354: William Day of Laurens County, Tavern keeper, for £28 sterling to Asa Griffin, 70 3/4 acres in Newberry County on a branch of Mill Creek, part of tract whereon I now live, 28 Sept 1797. Wm Day (Seal), Wit: Daniel Towles, Squire Lonam. Mary Day (X), wife of William Day, relinquished dower 28 Sept 1797 before J. R. Brown, J.N.C. Proved by the oath of Daniel Towles 30 July 1799 before J. R. Brown, J.N.C. Recorded 1 Aug 1799. Plat included showing adjacent land owners: Thomas Cummins, Jas Gates, Day & Boulware, Nathan Todd.

D, 355-356: 7 March 1797, Joseph Caldwell of Newberry County to Benjamin Johnson of same, for £45 sterling, 100 acres on a small branch of Second Creek, a tract granted to John Daugharty 18 May 1773 and conveyed to James Caldwell and willed by James Caldwell to his son Joseph Caldwell. Joseph Caldwell (Seal), Wit: Charles Crenshaw, Michael Lang [German signature], Henry Wicker. Mary Caldwell, wife of Joseph Caldwell, relinquished dower 9 March 1797 before L. E. Casey, J.N.C. Proved 30 July 1799 by the oath of Michael Long before P. Williams, J.P. Recorded 1 Aug 1799.

D, 356-357: 19 Sept 1798, Thomas Lake and wife Elizabeth, Joseph Lake and wife Jane, Noah Bonds and wife Fanny, of Newberry County to Nathan

Crenshaw of same, for £64 sterling, 128 acres in Newberry County on north branches of Enoree River adj. Samuel Hill, David Sims, on Bailey branch. Thomas Lake (Seal), Elizabeth Lake (X) (Seal), Joseph Lake (+) (Seal), Jane Lake (X) (Seal), Noah Bonds (Seal), Fanny Bond (X) (Seal), Wit: David Sims, William Hutchison (X), Enoch Lake. Proved by the oath of David Sims 23 July 1799 before Saml Kenner, J.P. Recorded 28 July 1799.

D, 357-360: Lease and release. 13 & 14 Jan 1778, Dorman Hanson of Ninety Six District, planter, to Zebulon Gaunt and Nebo Gaunt his son in partnership of Camden District, for £700 currency, 100 acres on a branch of Saluda River called Bush Creek now called Bush River, part of 450 acres granted to Dorman Hanson 2 Oct 1768, recorded in Book CCC, page 44. Dorman Hanson (Seal), Winneford Hanson (mark) (Seal), Wit: Israel Gauntt, Georg Hanson (mark), Solomon Hanson (mark). Proved in Ninety Six District by the affirmation of Israel Gaunt 31 May 1785 before Wm Houseal, J.P. Recorded 10 Aug 1799.

D, 360-361: 29 June 1768, Jacob Smith of Edgefield County for £100 sterling to Andrew Lee (de'd), late of county aforesaid, 300 acres in Newberry County on the waggon Road that leads from Philemon Waters Ferry on Saluda up the Country, which tract was granted to Jannet Austin 12 Jan 1769, recorded in Book DDD, page 33, which tract I never made title to said Andrew Lee for but it appears by the last will of said Andrew Lee recorded in Edgefield County 1787 that he willed the above tract to Sarah Lee his youngest daughter, dated 29 June 1798. Jacob Smith (Seal), Wit: Arthur Long (mark), William Brown (mark). Proved in Newberry County by the oath of William Brown 18 Sept 1798 before Daniel Parkins, J.P. Recorded 10 Aug 1799.

D, 361-362: Bargain made 30th day of 12th month 1796, between Walter Harbirt and Joseph Cook for part of a tract of land the said Walter Harbirt now lives on, part lying on south side of Bush River where the said Joseph Cook is now settling on, for $4 per acre and for which said Harbirt has received 68 dollars and a half and five pence half penny. Walter Harbirt (H), Wit: Henry Hollingsworth. Proved In Newberry County by the oath of Henry Hollingsworth 12 Aug 1799 before Daniel Parkins, J.P. Recorded 14 Aug 1799.

D, 362: 1 Aug 1799, Abijah Oneal and Hugh Oneal, executors of the will of William Oneal deceased, of Newberry County, to Elisha Ford of same, for £5 s10, 35 acres on waters of Bush River adj. John Duncan, John Embers, Elisha Ford, granted to said William Oneal dec'd 7 Feb 1791. Abijah Oneall (Seal), Hugh ONeall (Seal), Wit: Jess P. Pemberton, Joth'n Chandler. Proved by the oath of Jonathan Chandler 2 July 1799 before Daniel Parkins, J.P. Recorded 20 Aug 1799.

D, 363-364: 4 Sept 1798, Michael Johnston of Newberry County to Stephen Shell of same, for £140 sterling, tract in the original 298 acres but by resurvey 400 acres, granted to Robert Brooks 6 Feb 1774 and part of another tract granted to John Johnston 6 Feb 1786 on Joshua's branch, waters of Gilders

Creek. Michael Johnston (Seal), Wit: Go. Harbirt, John Johnston. Elizabeth Johnston, wife of Michael Johnston, relinquished dower 17 Oct 1798 before L. E. Casey, J.N.C. Proved by the oath of George Harbirt 27 Oct 1798 before L. E. Casey, J.N.C. Plat included, certified 3 Sept 1798 by Go. Harbirt, D. S., showing adjacent land owners: Hugh Read, William Dunlap, John Huston Ridgedell, John Kinard, Robert Brown. Recorded 26 Aug 1799.

D, 364-365: 17 June 1799, Richard Bonds of Chester County, SC, to Nathaniel Henderson of Newberry County, 160 acres on Beaver Creek on waters of Broad River, adj. William Liles, Elisha Lake. Richard Bonds (X) (Seal), Wit: Valentine Liles, Robt Powell. Proved by the oath of Robert Powell 22 June 1799 before Saml E. Kenner, J.P.

D, 366: John Griffis of Newberry County, planter, for £10 SC money, paid by John Rigard of same, mortgage one cow and calf, one heifer, one mare colt, a sorrel 2 years old, one new hunting saddle, all my bedding, two plows, 2 aces, one mattock, one iron wedge, one pot, etc., and the crop as it stands, 2 Aug 1798, for payment of £10 by 2 Feb 1799. John Griffis (Seal), Wit: Christiana Barbara Houseal (mark), Wm. Houseal, J.P. Recorded 5 Sept 1799.

D, 366-367: 27 Aug 1799, George Kinard of Newberry County to John Gragg of same, for $187, 125 acres, half of 250 acres granted to Matthias Kinard deceased on waters of Cannons Creek, adj. 250 acres to William Gragg Junr by Matthias Kinard, original plat dated 2 June 1772. George Kinard (X) (Seal), Wit: Jno B. Mitchell, William Gragg Senr, William Baird. Proved by the oath of John B. Mitchell 28 Aug 1799 before Fred Nance, J.P. Recorded 9 Sept 1799.

D, 367-368: 27 Aug 1799, Matthias Kinard of Newberry County to William Gragg Junr of same, for $187.50, 125 acres, half of 250 acres granted to Matthias Kinard deceased on waters of Cannons Creek, adj. Frederick Hogle. Mathias Kinard (mark) (Seal), Wit: Jno B. Mitchell, William Gragg Senr, William Baird. Proved by the oath of John B. Mitchell 28 Aug 1799 before Fred Nance, J.P. Recorded 9 Sept 1799.

D, 368-370: 2 Aug 1799, Elisha Ford of Newberry County to Isaac Kirk of same, merchant, for £23 sterling, 35 acres adj. Elisha Ford, John Dunkin, Joseph Furnas, tract granted to William Oneal 7 Feb 1791, recorded in Book C. No. 5, page 234, and Abijah & Hugh Oneal, exrs. of said William Oneal deceased, conveyed the land unto Elisha Ford by deed recorded in Book E, page 362. Elisha Ford (Seal), Wit: Hugh ONeall, John Meyer, Henry ONeall. Sarah Ford, wife of Elisha Ford, relinquished dower 2 Aug 1799 before J. R. Brown, J.N.C. Plat included showing tract on waters of Bush River, 14 July 1785. Proved by the affirmation of Henry Oneall 9 Sept 1799 before Fred Nance, J.P. Recorded __ Sept 1799.

D, 370-372: 2 Aug 1799, Elisha Ford of Newberry County to Isaac Kirk of same, merchant, for £160 sterling, two contiguous tracts on waters of Bush River: one tract lately sold by John Elleman to Elisha Ford adj. land of Dunkin, land granted to William Oneal decd, Matthias Elmore, 197 acres; the other tract adj. Thomas Oneal, 197 acres, part of 200 acres which David Humphrey and wife Jane on 25 Oct 1785 granted to Elisha Ford, and recorded in Newberry County Book C, page 891; tract of 11 acres and 85 perches being the same land which William Oneal deceased by his will dated 15 July 1786 did grant to his daughter Sarah Ford, wife of said Elisha Ford. Elisha Ford (Seal), Wit: Hugh ONeall, John Meyer, Henry ONeall. Sarah Ford, wife of Elisha Ford, relinquished dower 2 Aug 1799 before J. R. Brown, J.N.C. Plat included showing tract on waters of Bush River, 14 July 1785. Proved by the affirmation of Henry Oneall 9 Sept 1799 before Fred Nance, J.P. Recorded 9 Sept 1799.

D, 373: William Irby of Newberry County for £4 sterling to Merideth William Moon of same, doctor, 4 acres, part of 200 acres on north east side of Saluda River near old town, last conveyed by William Tate Esquire to said William Irby, adj. Tate, Joseph Goodman, 9 July 1799. Wm Irby (Seal), Wit: Robert Tate, John Dyson, Thomas Kay. Proved by the oath of John Dyson 13 Sept 1799 before Robert Gillam, J.P.

D, 374-377: Lease and release. 27 & 28 Aug 1790, John Palmer and wife Hannah of Newberry County to Abijah Oneal and Hugh Oneal of same, sons and executors of the estate of the late William Oneal, deceased, for themselves and in trust for their brothers William Oneal, John Oneal, Henry Oneal, and Thomas Oneal, minors, for £100 SC money, 100 acres on Bush Creek, part of 250 acres granted to Thomas Shaw 10 Sept 1765, laid off on the south east side of said tract, adj. Thomas Shaw. John Palmer (Seal), Hannah Palmer (H) (Seal), Wit: John Elleman, John Palmer Junr, Samuel Orick (X). Proved by the affirmation of John Elleman 13 Sept 1799 before Fred Nance, J.P. Recorded 18 Sept 1799.

D, 377-378: 11 June 1799, John Coppock Senr of Newberry County to Abijah Oneal and Samuel Kelly Junr, admrs. of John Kelly decd, for £89 sterling, 112 acres on Bush River of which 33½ acres is part of tract granted to Barbary Echard and conveyed to Vincent Simmons from Simmons to John Millhous and from Millhouse the said 33½ acres to Samuel Worthington and by Mercer Babb, exrs. of said Worthington, to John Coppock; the other part granted to Thomas Ryle 13 July 1770 recorded in Book EEE, page 463 and conveyed by said Ryall to Samuel Worthington and by the executors of Worthington to John Coppock, adj. Joseph Coppock, William Grimes, Israel Chandler. John Coppock (Seal), Wit: Jonathan Chandler, P. B. Waters. Proved by the oath of P. B. Waters 17 Sept 1799 before Fred Nance, J.P. Recorded 17 Sept 1799.

D, 378-379: 12 June 1799, Abijah Oneal and Samuel Kelly Junr, admrs. of John Kelly decd, of Newberry County, to John Coppock, son of Joseph Coppock of same, for £57 sterling, 80 acres on waters of Bush River, being part of three original surveys: one granted to Barbary Echard 7 Oct 1762, recorded in Book WWW, page 153, one other granted to John Millhouse 3 Dec 1766, recorded in Book FFF; one other granted to John Milhouse 29 April 1768 and recorded in Book CCC, page 76, adj. land of Joseph Coppock, William Grimes, at the high water mark of any dam that may hereafter be made at the place where Kellies mill now stands. Abijah Oneall (Seal), Saml Kelly (Seal), Wit: Israel Chandler, P. B. Waters. Proved by the oath of P. B. Waters 17 Sept 1799 before Fred Nance, J.P. Recorded 17 Sept 1799.

D, 380: 12 June 1799, Abijah Oneal and Samuel Kelly Junr, admrs. of John Kelly decd, of Newberry County, to Israel Chandler of same, for £43 sterling, 80 acres on waters of Bush River, part of 200 acres granted to Thomas Ryall 13 July 1770, recorded in Book EEE, page 463, adj. land surveyed for Barbara Echard, Jeremiah Lewis, said tract conveyed by Thomas Ryall to Samuel Worthington 14 Dec 1771 and conveyed by exrs. of Worthington to John Coppock in April 1792. Abijah Oneall (Seal), Saml Kelly (Seal), Wit: John Coppock, P. B. Waters. Proved by the oath of P. B. Waters 17 Sept 1799 before Fred Nance, J.P. Recorded 17 Sept 1799.

D, 381: 13 Sept 1799, Hugh Oneal, miller, and Abijah Oneal, planter, of Newberry County, to Joseph Thompson of same, tanner, for $40, 10 acres, part of tract of 100 acres which John Palmer and wife Hannah 28 Aug 1790 conveyed to Hugh Oneal and Abijah Oneal, sons and exrs. of William Oneal, deceased. Abijah Oneall (Seal), Hugh Oneall (Seal), Wit: John Coate, John Elleman, Charles Oneall. Proved by the affirmation of John Elleman 13 Sept 1799 before Fred Nance, J.P. Recorded 18 Sept 1799. Plat included showing adjacent land owners: George McKinny, Hugh Oneall, John Elleman.

D, 382-383: 3 Aug 1799, John Elleman of Newberry County, to Joseph Thompson of same, tanner, for $728, two tracts on waters of Bush River adj. Hugh Oneall, George McKinsey, Isaac Elmore, Matthias Elmore; one tract of 179 acres and the other three acres, the tract of 179 acres being part of 200 acres which Stephen Elmore on 13 June 1769 conveyed to said John Elleman, recorded in Newberry County Book C, page 713; three acres is part of 200 acres which David Humphrey and wife Jane conveyed 25 Oct 1785 granted to Elisha Ford, recorded in Book C, page 891, and said Elisha Ford by deed 10 July 1797 conveyed to John Elleman. John Elleman (Seal) Wit: Isaac Kirk, Hugh Oneall, William Jenkins. Plat included. Mary Elleman (X), wife of John Elleman, relinquished dower 23 Aug 1799 before J. R. Brown, J.N.C. Proved by the affirmation of Isaac Kirk 9 Sept 1799 before Fred Nance, J.P. Recorded 18 Sept 1799. Recorded 9 Sept 1799.

D, 384-385: 5 Aug 1799, John Elleman of Newberry County, yeoman, to Isaac Kirk of same, merchant, for £17 sterling, 25 acres and 130 perches, part of same tract which Stephen Elmore conveyed to John Elleman, recorded in Newberry County in Book C, page 713, on SW side Bush River adj. Elisha Ford, Thomas Oneall. John Elleman (Seal) Wit: Joseph Furnas, John Wright.

Plat included. Proved by the affirmation of Joseph Furnas 20 Sept 1799 before Fred Nance, J.P. Recorded 20 Sept 1799.

D, 385-386: Plat of 150 acres included showing adjacent land owners: John Marpot, Joseph Coppock, Samuel Inman, Samuel Taylor, Henry Steddom.

13 July 1799, Thomas Haskit of Newberry County, planter, to Isaac Kirk of same, merchant, for $450, 150 acres on waters of Bush River adj. Henry Steedom, Joseph Coppock, John Marput, Inman, Samuel Taylor, it being the tract which John Ridgdill conveyed 28 & 29 Oct 1787, recorded in Newberry County Book A, page 462-3. Thomas Haskit (Seal), Wit: Joseph Furnas, Amos Dunkin, Benjamin Evans, Ann Haskit, wife of Thomas Haskit, relinquished dower 30 July 1799 before J. R. Brown, J.N.C. Proved by the affirmation of Joseph Furnas 20 Sept 1799 before Fred Nance, J.P. Recorded 20 Sept 1799.

D, 387: 10 July 1797, Elisha Ford of Newberry County to John Elleman of same, for £1 s8 sterling, 3 acres on NE side Bush River, tract whereon said Elisha Ford now lives, originally granted to Henry LittleJohn and conveyed to David Humphrey. Elisha Ford (Seal), Wit: William Spencer, John ONeall. Proved by the affirmation of John Oneall 20 Sept 1799 before Fred Nance, J.P. Recorded 20 Sept 1799.

D, 388: 14 Aug 1799, William Dickson and wife Hannah of Pendleton County, SC, to Richard Sloan of Newberry County, for £100 sterling, the remaining part of tract of 400 acres granted to Nicholas Dickson, 150 acres on waters of Gilders Creek, adj. John Finny[?], Joshua Teague, Samuel Teague, James Spence. William Dickson (Seal), Hannah Dickson (X) (Seal), Wit: Robert Dickson (D), John Sloan. Proved by the oath of John Sloan 5 Sept 1799 before P. Williams, J.P. Recorded 25 Sept 1799.

D, 389: Received 17 May 1799 of Mr. James Devinport $350 for a negro girl named Lidda. David Coolter, Jo's Erwin, Test: Isaac Davenport, James Tomas (mark). Proved in Newberry County by the oath of Isaac Davenport 21 Aug 1799 before Charles Griffin, J.P. Recorded 1 Oct 1799.

South Carolina, Newberry County. 2 March 1799, rec'd of Robert Gillam the exr. to the estate of Robert Gillam deceased, $12, the full amt the legatees parts of the estate. Abram Dyson, James Smith (X), Saml Martin, Joshua Gillam, Test: James Dyson. Recorded 1 Oct 1799.

D, 390-392: 16 May 1773, Joseph Campbell, late of Craven County, SC, planter, to Francis Davenport of same, by grant dated 2 May 1770 to Joseph Campbell, 350 acres in Berkley County on waters of Little River adj. land of David Emery, Henry Pitts, John Monk, George Goggans, and Daniel Goggans, for £50 SC money, 100 acres, part of said grant. Joseph Campbell (+) (Seal), Wit: George Goggans, James Campbell, James Davenport. Proved in Berkely County by the oath of James Campbell 18 May 1773 before Jno Caldwell, J.P. Recorded 1 Oct 1799.

D, 392: South Carolina, Newberry County. William Frederick Houseal to give to Christina Barbary Houseal, aquits her and her property in real and personal in a marriage, 16 Sept 1799. Wm. Houseal (Seal), Wit: John Richart, Wm Stone. Proved by the oath of John Richart 11 Dec 1799 before Fred Nance, J.P. A True record of the Original Divorce 11 Oct 1799.

D, 393: Personally appeared John Pearson and on his solemn affirmation declared that some time after the decease of John Evans of Enoree he did see and read a deed of gift for 150 acres on Enoree River commonly called Wm. Hendricks Mill unto John Hendricks, son of said William Hendricks and grandson of said John Evans, 7 June 1788. John Pearson before Levi Casey, J.P.

South Carolina, Laurens County. Personally appeared Reuben Flannagan Senr and made oath that he did see John Evans sign, seal, and deliver a deed of gift to John Hendricks his grandson of a tract of land upon Enoree River of 150 acres called the mill tract whereon said John Hendricks now lives and that John Odell deceased with this deponent did subscribe their names as witnesses, 16 Aug 1798. Reuben Flannagan before Geo: Whitmore, J.P. Recorded 21 Oct 1799.

D, 393-394: Elizabeth Turner Senr of Newberry County, widow, appoints David Stephens of said county attorney to recover a negro man named Ace, 21 Oct 1799. Elizabeth Turner (Seal), Wit: Samuel Miles, Joseph Reagan, Charles Griffin. Proved by the oath of Charles Griffin, J.P. 21 Oct 1799. Recorded 22 Oct 1799.

D, 395-398: Lease and release. 9 March 1773, Peter Scott of Berkley County, SC, and wife Mary to John Regan of same, for £100 currency, 100 acres, the NW half of 200 acres granted to Peter Scott 29 April 1768 on a branch of Saluda River called the Beaverdam. Peter Scott (P) (Seal), Mary Scott (X) (Seal), Wit: William Shelly, Alexander McKelvey, William Aspenal (O). Proved by the oath of Wm Aspenal 13 March 1773 before Wm. Houseal, J.P. Proved by the oath of Wm Aspenal 18 Oct 1773 before Jno. Caldwell, J.P. Recorded 9 Oct 1799.

D, 398-401: Lease and release. 31 May and 1 June 178, John Reagan of Newberry County, and wife Elizabeth, to John Wright of same, £10 sterling, 100 acres, the NW half of 200 acres granted to Peter Scott 29 April 1768 on a branch of Saluda River called the Beaverdam, conveyed by Peter Scott to John Reagan 8 & 9 Sept 1773. John Reagin (Seal), Elizabeth Reagin (mark) (Seal), Wit: James Sutterfield, John Coats, Jesse Reagin. Proved by the oath of John Coats 9 Oct 1773 before Fred. Nance, J.P. Recorded 9 Oct 1799.

D, 401-404: Lease and release. 11 Feb 1791, James Sutterfield of Newberry County to William Gould of same, for £20 sterling, 80 acres on north side Beaverdam, a branch of Saluda, part of 200 acres granted to Peter Scott 29 April 1768, conveyed 9 March 1773 to John Reagin, and by him to John

Wright 12 June 1788 and by John Wright to James Sutterfield 11 April 1790. James Sutterfield (Seal), Elizabeth Sutterfield (X) (Seal), Wit: William King (mark), Daniel Earp, Mary Sutterfield (X). Proved by the oath of William King 9 Oct 1799 before Fred. Nance, J.P. Recorded 9 Oct 1799.

D, 404-407: Lease and release. 11 Feb 1791, James Sutterfield of Newberry County to Daniel Earp of same, for £10 sterling, 20 acres on Beaverdam Creek, waters of Saluda, adj. George Clark, William Gould, in the SW corner of a tract of 200 acres granted to Peter Scott 9 April 1768, conveyed 9 March 1773 to John Reagin, and by him to John Wright 12 June 1788 and by John Wright to James Sutterfield 11 April 1790. James Sutterfield (Seal), Elizabeth Sutterfield (X) (Seal), Wit: William King (mark), Daniel Earp, Mary Sutterfield (X). Proved by the oath of William King 9 Oct 1799 before Fred. Nance, J.P. Recorded 9 Oct 1799.

D, 407-411: Lease and release. 9 Nov 1791, William Gould of Newberry County to Daniel Earp of same, for £50 sterling, 80 acres on north side Beaverdam, a branch of Saluda, part of 200 acres granted to Peter Scott 29 April 1768, conveyed 9 March 1773 to John Reagin, and by him to John Wright 12 June 1788 and by John Wright to James Sutterfield 11 April 1790 then to William Gould 10 & 11 April 1791. William Gould (mark) (Seal), Sarah Gould (mark) (Seal), Wit: Hezekiah Riley, George Watson, Mary Camdell [Conwell] (X). Proved by the oath of Hezekiah Riley 9 Oct 1799 before Fred. Nance, J.P. Recorded 9 Oct 1799.

D, 411-413: Lease and release. 20 & 21 Dec 1784, John Kraud of Ninety Six District, to Daniel Earp of same, for £190 sterling, 100 acres on the north side of Saluda on a branch thereof called Beverdam Creek adj. Peter Scott, William Hamson, granted to said John Kraud 15 May 1774. Johannes Krauts[?] [German signature] (Seal), Wit: William Taylor, George Clark (mark). Proved by the oath of Wm Taylor 22 Dec 1784 before Wm Houseal, J.P. Recorded 9 Oct 1799.

D, 414-417: Lease and release. 9 & 10 July 1786, William Gould of ninety Six District to Daniel Earp of same, for £10 sterling, 35 acres on waters of Saluda on Beaverdam, part of 200 acres granted to Peter Scott 29 April 1768, 100 acres of which was conveyed by Peter Scott to said William Gould 2 Dec 1768. William Gould (mark) (Seal), Wit: Joseph Wright, William Satterfield (X), William King (mark). Plat by Jo's Wright, D. S., 1 July 1786 included showing adjacent land owners; William Gould, Elijah Botner, James Satterfield. Proved by the oath of William King 9 Oct 1799 before Fred Nance, J.P. Recorded 9 Oct 1799.

D, 417-419: Lease and release. 10 April 1790, John Wright of Newberry County and wife Jemima to James Sutterfield of same, for £10 sterling, 100 acres on waters of Saluda on Beaverdam Creek, part of 200 acres granted to Peter Scott 29 April 1768 and conveyed by Peter Scott to John Reagin and from John Reagin to John Wright. John Wright (Seal), Jemima Wright (Seal),

Wit: Jo's Wright, Gabriel McCoole, Jesse Wright. Proved by the oath of Gabriel McCoole 6 Nov 1799 before Fred Nance, J.P. Recorded 6 Nov 1799.

D, 420-423: Lease and release. 18 & 19 July 1777, Isaac Cook of Ninety Six District, to Margaret Gallaway and William Herbison, exrs. of the estate of Peter Galloway, deceased, of same, for £50, 150 acres in Berkley on the north side of Saluda River on a branch known as Beaverdam branch, adj. Jonathan Gilbert, granted 13 July 1770. Isaac Cook (I) (Seal), Charity Cook (Seal), Wit: Rob't Speer, James Brooks, John Galloway. Proved in Newberry County by the oath of Robert Speer 21 Oct 1799 before Fred Nance, J.P. Recorded 21 Oct 1799.

D, 423: Elizabeth Turner, widow, of Ninety Six District, for love and affection to Sarah Turner, wife to son Edward Turner of same, one negro fellow Named Isaac also one wench named Sarah, 10 June 1781. Elisabeth Turner (Seal), Wit: Saml Kelly Senr, Ben Long. Proved in Newberry County by the oath of Ben Long 21 Oct 1799 before Robert Gillam, J.P. Recorded 21 Oct 1799.

D, 424: Elizabeth Turner, widow, of Ninety Six District, for love and affection to grandson David Turner of same, one mulatto boy named Tony, 15 Oct 1792. Elisabeth Turner (Seal), Wit: Saml Kelly Senr, Ben Long. Proved in Newberry County by the oath of Ben Long 21 Oct 1799 before Robert Gillam, J.P. Recorded 21 Oct 1799.

D, 424-425: Peter Heer of Newberry County, planter, for love and affection to son Laurence Heer of same, 100 acres on a branch of Cannons Creek adj. Robert Muffet, Martain Charles, Peter Richard, 29 Dec 1790. Peter Heer [German signature], Wit: Henry Ruff, Christ'n Wedmman (mark). Proved by the oath of Henry Ruff 19 Oct 1799 before Edward Finch, J.P. Recorded 22 Oct 1799.

D, 425: Peter Heer of Newberry County, planter, for love and affection to son Peter Heer Jr. of same, 100 acres on a branch of Cannons Creek adj. Robert Muffet, George McCulloch, Laurence Richard, John Richard, 29 Dec 1790. Peter Heer [German signature], Wit: Henry Ruff, Christ'n Wedmman (mark). Proved by the oath of Henry Ruff 19 Oct 1799 before Edward Finch, J.P. Recorded 22 Oct 1799.

D, 426-427: 28 Jan 1794, John Buzard of Newberry County, planter, to Peter Hare Junr of same, for £30 sterling, 50 acres on a branch of Cannons Creek being the NE part of 250 acres granted to said John Buzard, adj. Flake, John Buzard, Elisha Anderson. John Buzart (B) (Seal), Wit: Dav'd Ruff, J.P., Frederick Davis, Elijah Anderson. Proved by the oath of Elijah Anderson 19 Oct 1799 before Edw'd Finch, J.P. Plat included 13 Jan 1794 by David Ruff, D.S. Recorded 22 Oct 1799.

D, 427-429: 17 Feb 1798, Jacob Cromer, Philip Gruber and Mary Gruber his wife, planters, for $150 to Peter Heer, 100 acres granted to Andrew Gromer recorded in Book FFF, page 343, granted 25 May 1774, and said Jacob Gromer is the son of Andrew Gromer and lawful heir to said tract of land, and with the approbation of his mother now wife to said Philip Gruber, said land adj. John Warn. Jacob Cromer (X) (Seal), Philip Gruber (Seal), Mary Gruber (X) (Seal), Wit: Laurence Hare (H), Thomas Medill. Proved in Newberry County 19 Oct 1799 by the oath of Lawrence Hare before Edw'd Finch, J.P. Recorded 22 Oct 1799.

D, 429-430: 15 June 1799, William Richardson of Edgefield County to Daniel Richardson of same, for $113, 120 acres on east line of a tract granted to David Richardson 17 Feb 1767 in Berkley County at the Beaverdam of Saluda River, an undivided portion of grant left by the will of David Richardson to his son John Richardson and thence transferred to aid William Richardson. William Richardson (Seal), Wit: Nath'l Abney, Thomas Wright, A. Eskridge. Proved by the oath of Thomas Wright 21 Oct 1799 before Charles Griffin, J.P. Recorded 22 Oct 1799.

D, 430: Newberry County. Reuben Griffin for $260 to Joseph Pitts, one negro woman named Bek about 15 years of age, 10 July 1799. Reuben Griffin (Seal), Wit: Charles Griffin. Proved by the oath of Charles Griffin 21 Oct 1799 before Robert Gillam, J.P. Recorded 22 Oct 1799.

D, 431: South Carolina, Newberry County. William Aspenell appeared and made oath that he has known Samuel Edwards (decd) this many years, that the deponant does not think for seven years past he has been of sound mind & memory to dispose of his property or to do any other business where property was concerned, and further he believes that said Edwards was the son of Joseph Edwards (decd) of Virginia & the deponant told Joseph Edwards Jun'r of Virginia if was wrong for him to enter into any contract with Saml Edwards, 22 Oct 1799. William Aspennel (mark) before Daniel Parkins, J.P.

William Summers & Thos Willoughby Waters appeared before me and makes oath that they knew the within named Samuel Edwards and it is their opinion that said Edwards for four or five years past incapable of transacting his own business any time since until his death, 22 Oct 1799, before Daniel Parkins, J.P. Recorded 22 Oct 1799.

D, 431-432: Asa Garrett of Newberry County to William Beavers of same for $350, 120 acres on waters of Indian Creek adj. Uriah Conner, part of 205 acres granted to Robert Brooks 5 Feb 1787, recorded in Book PPPP, page 643, dated 24 May 1799. Asa Garrett (Seal), Wit: William Gary, Uriah Conner. Proved by the oath of William Gary 22 Oct 1799 before Robert Gillam, J.P. Recorded 22 Oct 1799.

D, 433-434: Asa Garrett of Newberry County to William Beavers of same for $350, 50 acres on south side of Indian Creek adj. said Brooks, part of tract granted to Richard Brooks __ Feb 1768, recorded in Book 3 B, page 521, entered in Auditors Office in Book H. No. 8, page 517, 12 April 1768, dated

24 May 1799. Asa Garrett (Seal), Wit: William Gary, Uriah Conner. Proved by the oath of William Gary 22 Oct 1799 before Robert Gillam, J.P. Recorded 22 Oct 1799.

D, 434-435: 27 Nov 1797, John Geradine and Mathias Hare of Newberry County, planter, to John Eigelberger of same place, planter, for £4 s13 d4 sterling, 20 acres on a branch of Cannons Creek adj. Philip Slike, Laurence Rikard, Thomas Rikard. J. Geradine, Mathisa Hare (H), Wit: Joseph Raymond, John Raymond Peter Hare (P). Proved in Orangeburgh District by the oath of Peter Hare 6 Dec 1799 before Wilson Cook, J.P. Recorded 22 Oct 1799.

D, 435-437: 16 July 1799, Brice Prather of Laurens County for £50 sterling to John Philips of "county aforesaid," 150 acres on south fork of Dunkins Creek lying in Laurens & Newberry Counties, granted to said Brice Prather, 50 acres of which was granted 1 May 1797, recorded in Book IIII, page 482, 100 acres granted to said Brice Prather 3 March 1788, recorded Book WWWW, page 307. Brice Prather (X) (Seal), Wit: Jesse Jones, William Whitten. Proved in Laurens County by the oath of Jesse Jones 25 July 1799 before George Whitmore, J.P. Martha Prather (O), wife of Brice Prather, relinquished dower 29 July 1799 before L. E. Casey, J.N.C. Recorded 22 Oct 1799.

D, 437-438: William Oneall for $600 to Levi Hilburn of Newberry County, 24 acres on Bush River adj. land of John Oneall, Thomas Oneall, known by the name of the tract of land whereon the sawmill now stands formerly belonging to the father of the said William Oneall, part of plantation granted to Joseph Wright 13 Oct 1767 conveyed into the possession of William Oneall Sen'r dec'd who bequeathed that same to said William Oneall. William Oneall (Seal), Wit: P. B. Waters, Fred Nance, J.P. Mary Oneall, wife of William Oneall, relinquished dower 22 Oct 1799 before J. R. Brown, J.N.C. Recorded 22 Oct 1799.

D, 438-441: Lease and release. 13 & 14 Dec 1787, Michael Raccurst Junior of Newberry County, planter, to Michael Raccurst Senior, planter, for £46 sterling, 46 acres, part of 350 acres originally granted to Thomas Raccurst on Cannon Creek which was jointly left to William Raccurst, Michael Raccurst, and Peter Raccurst, joint heirs of Thomas Raccurst, and was divided amongst them accordingly 3 June 1771, now the above Peter Raccurst being dead, left the above Michael Raccurst Jun'r his sole heir at law of the 46 acres. Michel Rickert (+) (Seal), Efe Rickert (X) (Seal), Wit: Martin Charles (X), Henry Stockman (H). Proved by the oath of Henry Stockman 10 Sept 1796 before Wm Houseal, J.P. Recorded 22 Oct 1799.

D, 442-443: William Panton, merchant, copartner with John Leslie and Thomas Forbes, under the firm of Panton, Leslie, and Company, at present residing at Pensacola, in the Province of West Florida, appoint friends Edward Penman and Alexander Rose, merchants, and William Desaussure, attorneys at law, all of Charleston, SC, Esquires, to recover all things due in the states of North Carolina, South Carolina, and Georgia, sign at Mobelle 1 Feb 1790. Wm Panton (LS), Wit: John Toyce, Robt Leslie. Acknowledged in West Florida 3 Feb 1790 before Falk, Captain of the Regiment of Luescannord[?]. Wit: John Ford, John Redmond, Alexander Fraser. Recorded 29 Oct 1799.

D, 444-448: Lease and release. 18 & 19 Dec 1790, William Panton, merchant, of the Kingdom of Great Britain, to Thomas Davidson of Laurens County, SC, for £120 sterling, 300 acres in Berkley County on a branch of Saluda River called Little River adj. Thomas Green, William Burton, John Stuart, Doctor Benjamin Farar, granted 15 May 1768 to Robert Gowdey. Wm Panton by his attorneys Ed Penman, Henry Wm. Desaussure (LS), Wit: Chas I. Colcock, Wm. Robertson. Acknowledged by the said Edward Penman and Henry William Desaussure before E. H. Bay. Proved by the oath of Charles I. Colcock before E. H. Bay. Recorded 29 Oct 1799.

D, 448-451: Lease and release. 5 & 6 March 1797, Samuel Sotcher of Edgefield County, to John Leppard of Newberry County, for £60 sterling, 200 acres on waters of Bush River in the fork of Broad and Saluda Rivers, part of tract of 2000 ares granted to Henry Middleton on 19 June 1762, adj. Jacob Pennington, Thomas Gary, Henry Middleton, conveyed by said Middleton to Isaac Lindsey, then to Samuel Sotcher. Samuel Sotcher (mark) (Seal), Fanney Sotcher (X) (Seal), Wit: Jesse Forbis, Eunice Sotcher (X). Proved in Newberry County by the oath of Jesse Forbush 8 July 1799 before P. Williams, J.P. Recorded 9 Nov 1799.

D, 451-452: 9 Sept 1799, Hambelton Murdock of Ninety Six District to Levi Pitts of same, for £80 sterling, 100 acres on waters of Little River, part of 350 acres granted to Hambleton Murdock 12 Jan 1769 adj. Charles Pitts, William Pitts, Wm. Smith. Hamilton Murdock (Seal), Wit: James Murdock, William Deavenport (+). Proved in Newberry County by the oath of James Murdock 11 Sept 1799 before Charles Griffin, J.P.

D, 452-455: Lease and release. 22 & 23 Dec 1776, Jonathan Puckett and wife Mary of Ninety Six District to Levi Pitts of same, for £150, 100 acres on Little River adj. land of Hamilton Murdock, Oliver Towls, originally granted to Mary Nelley the present wife of said Jonathan Puckett 12 Jan 1768. Jonathan Pucket (Seal), Mary Pucket (O) (Seal), Wit: William Pitts, James Motes. Proved [date not indicated] in Newberry County by the oath of James Mote (mark) before P. Williams, J.P. Recorded 25 Nov 1799.

D, 456-457: 5 Feb 1798, William Tenant, Sheriff of Ninety Six District, o Benjamin Glover of Cambridge in Ninety Six District, merchant, by a writ of fieri facias from the court of common pleas at Cambridge viz't William Thompson against Philemon Waters dated 13 Nov 1795, entered in the office on 13 Nov 1795, said William Tenant did seize under said execution two tracts of land, and were struck off to the said Benjamin Glover for £13 s1, 200 acres surveyed for Philimon Waters 8 Sept 1788 on waters of Saluda River adj. Cune, Major Summers, Crapes, Sumpert [Schumpert], and also 200 acres surveyed for Philemon Waters 14 June 1792 on waters of Whites branch, Big Creek and Cannons Creek, adj. Reuben Morgan, Spencer, Thompson, David Linsey, recorded in Secretary's office in Book ZZZZ, page 32 and Book E No. 5, page 387. Wm Tennent Shff 96 District (Seal), Wit: Jno Dunlap, Ste. C. Wood. Proved in Newberry County by the oath of Jno Dunlap 27 Nov 1799 before Frederick Nance, J.P. Recorded 29 Nov 1799.

D, 458-459: 15 July 1799, Isaac Cook of Laurens County to William Jenkins of Newberry County, for £150, 200 acres on waters of Saluda River called the Beaver Dam, granted to David Motes 24 Aug 1770 and also 46 acres, part of tract granted to said David Mote from Henry Haford 23 Aug 1774 and which was granted to said Hafford 11 June 1759 from Stephen Holsen, and adj. said 200 acres and lands of John Coats, Robert Williams, David Jay, Isaac Hollingsworth. Isaac Cook (mark) (Seal), Wit: Samuel Brown, John Jay, Gabriel McCool. Proved in Newberry County by the statement of Samuel Brown 30 July 1799 before Daniel Parks, J.P. Recorded 20 Dec 1799.

D, 459: Micajah Bennett of Newberry County planter, for $450 to Thomas Clark of same, a negro boy named Sam between 20 and 23 years of age, of yellow complection, 28 Aug 1799. M. Bennett, Wit: John McCoy, Richard Bennett, Mary Bennett. Proved by the oath of John McCoy 3 Dec 1799 before Edw'd Finch, J.P. Recorded 20 Dec 1799.

D, 460-461: 2 April 1793, John Thomas of Greenville County, Sc, planter, to Philip Sleich, for £60 sterling, 250 acres in Newberry County on north side Cannons Creek adj. Bar'd Levingston. John Thomas (Seal), Wit: Ephraim Cannon, John Leitner, Christ'r Wedenman (W). Proved by the affirmation of Ephraim Cannon 2 April 1793 before Dav'd Ruff, J.P. Recorded 27 Dec 1799.

D, 461-463: March 8th 1794 by request of James Williams I have laid out unto his brother Providence Williams 169 acres on waters of Beverdam Creek. Plat included showing adjacent land owners: John Williams, James Williams.

24 March 1794, James Williams of Newberry County and settlement of the Beverdam, heir at law to James Williams deceased, to Providence Williams Junr, for £50 sterling, 169 acres, part of tract granted to said Williams 24 Oct 1771, recorded in Book IIII, page 278, and in the Auditor's Office in Book L No 11, page 86, adj. John Williams. James Williams (mark), Wit: James Lindsey, Stephen Williams, Jesse Brooks. Proved 25 March 1794 by the oath of James Lindsey before Providence Williams, J.P. Recorded 29 Dec 1799.

D, 463-464: Jacob Harman and Thomas Smith of Lexington County in the District of Orangeburgh, executors of John Harman decd, appoint our trusty friend James Johnson of Newberry District our lawful attorney to receive from James Greenlee of North Carolina a certain negro wench and four children (wench named Nann), 21 Feb 1800. Jacob Harmon (mark) (Seal), Thomas Smith (Seal), Wit: George Metz, Christian Swygert. Proved in Orangeburgh

District by the oath of George Mettz 21 Feb 1800 before John Hampton, J.P. Quo. Recorded 21 Feb 1800.

D, 464-468: Lease and release. 13 & 14 Oct 1783, Charnell Wallis of Orangeburgh District between Broad and Saluda Rivers, SC, planter, to Jacob Buchter of same, for 50 guineas, 150 acres on a branch of Broad River called Enoree, granted to Richard Kelly 8 Aug 1767 and conveyed by said Kelly to Paul Townsend, decd., who by will directed his executor Thomas Jones to sell the aforesaid land, and conveyed to Charnill Wallace 24 Nov 1779, recorded in Auditors Office in Book H No. 8, page 300. Charnell Wallis (mark) (Seal), Wit: William Manning, Samuel Rall, Wilhelm Zeagler. Proved 14 Oct 1783 by the oath of Saml Rall before Michael Leitner, J.P. Recorded 21 Feb 1800.

D, 469-473: Lease and release. 24 & 25 Sept 1784, John Green, planter, of Ninety Six District, to Jacob Bookter Senr, of District of Orangeburgh, for £100, 100 acres, part of 550 acres granted to John Green 7 June 1774 in Berkley County on waters of Enoree in the fork of Broad and Saluda Rivers adj. Awberry Noland, Richard Kelly, recorded in Book KK No 10, page 336; said 100 acres adj. Daniel Gorie, James Kelly on Enoree River. John Green (X) (Seal), Sarah Green (mark) (Seal), Wit: Daniel Gorrie, Alexander Bookter. Proved in Orangeburgh District by the oath of Alexander Bookter 27 Sept 1784 before Mich'l Leitner, J.P. Recorded 21 Feb 1800.

D, 473-477: 12 Dec 1799, John Henderson of Newberry County to Daniel Mazyck (eldest Captain of the late Second Regiment of Foot of South Carolina on Continental establishment commanded by Lieutenant Colonel Commandant Francis Marion), mortgage of 340 acres between the mouths of Tyger and Enoree River called and known by the name of Mazycks Island for the debt of £400 sterling on condition of four bonds. John Henderson (Seal), Wit: Levi Casey, James McMorries. Proved in Columbia, SC, by the oath of Levi Casey before Peter Freneau, J.P. Recorded 24 Feb 1800.

D, 477-478: 4 July 1799, William Farrow of Laurens County, SC, to Levi Pitts of Newberry County, for 241 Spanish milled dollars, one negro man slave called Harry. William Farrow (Seal), Wit: Joel Foster, James Pitts. Proved 17 Jan 1800 by the oath of James Pitts before Providence Williams, J.P. Recorded 21 Feb 1800.

D, 478-482: Lease and release. 20 & 30 Dec 1793, Isaac Davinport to Joseph Stuart, both of Newberry County, for £50 sterling, 50 acres, part of 300 acres granted to said Isaac Davinport 5 May 1773 in Berkley County, now Newberry County, on waters of Little River. Isaac Davinport (Seal), Wit: Thomas Peterson, John Stuart, Joseph Stuart. Proved by the oath of John Stuart 20 March 1794 before Mercer Babb, J.P. Recorded 22 Feb 1800.

D, 482-486: Lease and release. 26 Jan 1786, John Wright of Newberry County, planter, to Joseph Stuart of same, for £50, 150 acres in Berkley County on waters of Little River adj. Saml Nelson, granted to said John Wright 23 Dec

1771. John Wright (Seal), Jemima Wright (Seal), Wit: John Maxwell Ma't, John Douglass, William Plunket. Proved in Newberry District by the oath of William Plunket 28 Jan 1800 before Fred Nance, J.P. Recorded 22 Feb 1800.

D, 486-488: 7 Dec 1792, Thomas Brooks to Joseph Stuart, both of Newberry County, for £10 sterling, 50 acres, part of tract formerly granted to Samuel Nelson 2 June 1769 and is the NE side of said tract and conveyed to Thomas Brooks 31 Aug 1777. Thomas Brooks (Seal), Susanna Brooks (Seal), Wit: Rhoda Babb, Catharine Euts, Jude Stiddon (Stidman). Proved 27 Feb 1792 by the oath of Catharine Eutes before Mercer Babb, J.P. Recorded 22 Feb 1800.

D, 488-489: 18 March 1796, Solomon Hopkins of Laurens County to John Stuart of Newberry County, for £70 sterling, 100 acres adj. Thomas Peterson, John Mans, Benj'a Long, James Thomas, part of two tracts, one part being 66 acres, part of 100 acres granted in 1770 to John Dooly and conveyed by him to William Ellis and by William Ellis to John Newton and from John Newton to Solomon Hopkins, the other 34 acres, part of 150 acres granted to John Newton in 1771 and conveyed by him to said Solomon Hopkins. Solomon Hopkins (Seal), Wit: Robert Speer, Thomas Peterson, Joseph Stuart. Proved in Newberry District by the oath of Joseph Stuart 28 Jan 1800 before Fred Nance, J.P.

D, 490-492: Lease and release. 10 & 11 Jan 1783, Thomas Waters of Craven County, SC, planter, to Jacob Presnell of Ninety Six District, SC, planter, for £750 sterling, 300 acres granted to John Ragis 22 Feb 1771 and conveyed by him 12 Jan 1780 to said Thomas Waters, on waters of Saluda River on a branch running into Buffalow Creek. Thomas Waters (Seal), Wit: John Thos Fairchild, Abraham Fairchild, Benjamin Powell. Proved by the oath of John Thomas Fairchild 11 Jan 1784 before John Fairchild, J.P. Recorded 24 Feb 1800.

D, 493: Barbara Houseal of District of Newberry, widow, for love, god will and affection to my children John Stogman, Adam Stogman, Christena Stogman, George Stogman, and Solomon Weddingman, all my personal estate to be equally divided amongst them, 15 Feb 1800. Barbara Houseal (mark) (Seal), Wit: Barbara Charels (mark), Sebilla Fray (B). Proved by the certification of George Ruff, J. Q., 15 Feb 1800. Recorded 26 Feb 1800.

D, 494-495: 14 Feb 1800, William Stuart of Lincoln County, Georgia, to William Stuart of Edgefield County, SC, for $500, 130 acres in the District of Newberry adj. Joseph Reagan, Joshua Stuart, John Tinsley, Nathan Wright, part of 400 acres granted to William Stuart decd by an old grant dated 12 Jan 1769, 70 acres of which was sold unto George Arnold and 200 acres sold to Joseph Reagan. William Stuart (Seal), Wit: Samuel Johnson, John Stuart (X). Proved in Lincoln County, Georgia, by the oath of Samuel Thompson and John Stuart 14 Feb 1800 before Britain Lockhart, J.P. Recorded 27 Feb 1800.

D, 495-497: 15 March 1800, James Johnson of Newberry District to Benjamin Johnson for £200 sterling, 130 acres, part of tract of 300 acres granted to James Johnson 14 Aug 1770. James Johnson (Seal), Wit: George Goggans, Sarah Davinport (D), J. Davis. Rachael Johnson (O), wife of James Johnson, relinquished dower 3 April 1800 before J. R. Brown, J.Q.U. Proved by the oath of Sarah Davinport 3 April 1800 before J. R. Brown, J.Q.U. Recorded 5 April 1800.

D, 497-500: Lease and release. 7 & 8 Dec 178-, John Garrett of Newberry County and settlement of Indian Creek to Joseph Spence of Lexington County, Orangeburgh District, for £65 sterling, 140 acres, part of 148 acres granted to said John Garrett 19 Aug 1774, recorded in Book SSSS, page 4, and in the Auditor's Office in Book M. No. 13, page 263, 31 July 1775, adj. land of William Largent, eight acres being a former contract between John Garrett and Daniel McClary. John Garrett (mark) (Seal), Stace Garrett (mark) (Seal), Wit: John Lofton, Samuel Garrett, James Lindsey. Proved 11 Oct 1790 by the oath of James Lindsey before John Lindsey, J.P. Recorded 5 April 1800.

D, 501-503: 29 Dec 1791, John Johnston Junr and wife Susannah of Newberry County to Joseph Spence of same, for £15 sterling, 75 acres, part of 566 acres on Indian Creek adj. Widow Evans, John Garrett, originally granted to Thomas Lehre 4 Dec 1786, recorded in Book PPPP, page 255. John Johnston (Seal), Susannah Johnston (X) (Seal), Wit: David Spence, Charles Johnston. Proved 29 Dec 1791 by the oath of David Spence. Plat included showing 75 acres, part of 566 acres formerly surveyed for William Gray and relapsed to Thos Lehre adj. Widow Edwards, by A. Pearson, D. Surveyor. Recorded 5 April 1800.

D, 503-504: 28 Jan 1800, Joseph Stuart Sen'r of Newberry County to Joseph Stuart Jun'r for $100, 50 acres on waters of Little River, part of 300 acres granted to Isaac Devinport 5 May 1773 adj. Joseph Stuart Senr, Thomas Peterson, Volentine Braswell. Joseph Stuart (X) (Seal), Wit: William Plunket, John Stuart. Mary Stewart (X), wife of Joseph Stuart Senr, relinquished dower 28 Jan 1800 before J.R. Brown, J.Q.U. Proved by the oath of John Stewart 28 Jan 1800 before Fred Nance, J.P. Recorded 6 April 1800.

D, 505-506: 9 Feb 1792, Abraham Eddens and wife Sarah of Newberry County for £58 sterling to Richard Mansel of Fairfield County, 207 cares on a branch of Enoree River on Broad River, granted to John Chandler 5 Dec 1785 adj. William Calmes, Widow Hogg. Abraham Eddens (mark) (Seal), Sarah Eddens (+) (Seal), Wit: Joseph Hogg, Zachariah Hogg, Jonathan Pratt. Proved in Newberry County 16 March 1793 by the oath of Zachariah Hogg before Edw'd Finch, J.P. Recorded 6 April 1800.

D, 506-507: Thomas Cross of Laurens County for £37 sterling to Obed Parish of Newberry County, 150 acres granted to said Thomas Cross 6 Sept 1774 and recorded in Book SSS, page 558 adj. Simon Polston's line, Thos Cross Senr., dated 26 Feb 1799. Thomas Cross (Seal), Wit: Zimri Carter, John Tweed, Jeremiah Tucker. Martha Cross, wife of Thomas Cross, relinquished dower 31 Aug 1799 before J. R. Brown, J.N.C. Proved in Newberry County by the oath of Jeremiah Tucker 4 March 1799 before Edw'd Finch, J. P. Recorded 6 April 1800.

D, 508: State of South Carolina, Newberry District. Abraham Large of district aforesaid to Samuel Arfax of same, two brown mares, one of which is 12 years old, the other 4 years old, likewise an iron grey horse 2 years old, for $40. Abraham Large (A) (Seal), Wit: Jn Mitchel, Lewis Martin. Proved by the oath of Lewis Martin 12 March 1800 before P. Williams, J.P. Recorded 6 April 1800.

D, 508-511: Lease and release. 7 & 8 Jan 1787, James Plunkett and wife Elizabeth of Newberry County, to Benjamin Wood of same, for £100 old currency, 100 cares in Craven County on waters of Beverdam branch, waters of Saluda adj. James Jones, Gibeon Jones, granted to James Plunkett 17 March 1776. James Plunkett (Seal), Elisebeth Plunkett (Seal), Wit: William Burton, George Gibson (mark), William Burton. Proved 24 Jan 1800 by the oath of William Burton Senr before J. R. Brown, J.Q.U. Recorded 7 April 1800.

D, 512-513: Benjamin Wood of Newberry District for £50 sterling to James Cleland of same, tract on waters of Beverdam, 100 cares granted to James Plunkett and conveyed 7 Jan 1787... dated 28 Jan 1800. Benjamin Wood (mark) (LS), Wit: Saml Lindsey, Robert Cleland. Judith Wood (X), wife of Benjamin Wood, relinquished dower 28 Jan 1800 before J. R. Brown, J.Q.U. Proved by the oath of Saml Lindsey 28 Jan 1800 before J. R. Brown, J.Q.U. Recorded 7 April 1800.

D, 513-514: John Johnston of Newberry District for $85 to Stephen Bowers, tract on waters of Carls Creek, waters of Cannons Creek, 68 acres granted to said John Johnston 3 April 1797 and recorded in Book Q No. 5, page 297, dated 17 Feb 1800. John Johnston (mark) (LS), Wit: Fred Nance, John Tidmore. Elizabeth Johnston (X), wife of John Johnston, relinquished dower 17 Feb 1800 before Daniel Parkins, J.Q. Recorded 7 April 1800.

D, 514-515: 4 April 1799, John Kinard of Newberry County to George Griffice of same, for $50, 50 acres on a small branch of Camping Creek, part of 400 cares granted to John Kinard 3 Dec 1771. John Kinard (mark) (Seal), Wit: Jer McDanal, John McDanel, Henry Edwards (X). Proved by the oath of John McDanal 10 Feb 180 before Michl Dickert, J.P. Plat included (3 April 1800) showing 50 acres, part of 500 cares granted to John Kinard and adjacent land owners Henry Long, Conrad Gardener, John Kinard, by P. B. Waters, D. S. Recorded 7 April 1800.

D, 516: 27 July 1799, William Richards of Newberry County to Gideon Nelson of same, for $400, 250 acres on waters of Enoree River, also 50 acres adj.

William Shell Senr. William Richards (Seal), Wit: Jonathan Pratt, George Pratt, Joseph Jones. Proved by the oath of Jonathan Pratt 9 Sept 1799 before Edw'd Finch, J.P. Recorded 7 April 1800.

D, 517-518: 31 Jan 1799, Jeremiah Hubbard, Henry Thompson, Allen Thompson, heirs of the late Henry Thompson decd of Newberry County for £35 to Edward Hill of Newberry County, 200 acres on south side Broad River on waters of Kings Creek adj. John Steel, James Wilson, John Brown, Thomas Cross, originally granted to Henry Thompson deceased 4 May 1775. Henry Thompson (Seal), Allen Thompson (Seal), Jarate Hubbord (X) (Seal), Wit: Janet Wilson (X), Elizabeth Wilson (X), James Wilson. Proved in Newberry District by the oath of James Wilson 24 Jan 1800 before Edward Finch, J.P. Recorded 7 April 1800.

D, 518-519: 13 Nov 1799, Meek White and wife Jane of Newberry County to William Neall of same, for £93 s17 sterling, 78 acres on waters of Indian Creek, part of tract granted to Meek White 5 Feb 1787, recorded in Book SSSS, page 18, on west side Indian Creek, adj. Brown, James Wilson, William Largent, Benjamin Nerad. Meek White (Seal), Wit: Henry Jones, Jesse Forbis. Jean White (mark), wife of Meek White, relinquished dower 13 Nov 1799 before J. R. Brown, J.N.C. Proved by the oath of Jesse Forbis 13 Nov 1799 before J. R. Brown, J.N.C. Recorded 7 April 1800.

D, 520: 5 Aug 1799, Lewis Hogg and Clary Hogg of Newberry County to Benjamin Maybin of same, for $106, 100 acres adj. Marquis Littleton, John Dawkins, Robert Maybin, widow Goree. Lewis Hogg (Seal), Clary Hogg (X) (Seal), Wit: Jos Hogg, John Kelley, Robert Maybin. Proved by the oath of Robert Maybin 9 Jan 1800 before Saml Kenner, J.P. Recorded 7 April 1800.

D, 521: 8 Feb 1800, Joseph Collier of Newberry County to John Simpson, merchant, of Laurens County, for $60, tract willed to me by my father Benjamin Collier, 25 acres on Mudlick, waters of Little River, north side Saluda River in Newberry County adj. Samuel Harris, John Barlow, and land where the widow lives and John Collier, part of tract granted to Benjamin Collier. Joseph Collier (X) (Seal), Wit: John Gallegly, James Sproull. Proved by the oath of John Gallegly 25 Feb 180 before Charles Griffin, J.P. Recorded 7 April 1800.

D, 522: 3 Jan 1800, Thomas W. Waters and Danl Parkins, both of Newberry District, in consideration of the said Danl Parkins esquire having joined in a note of hand to Charles Banks, Thomas Gibson and Elizabeth Grigsby, executors of Levi Manning, for $433.33 payable 1 January next, which sum said Thomas W. Waters is owing to Charles Banks, Thomas Gibson and Elizabeth Grigsby, mortgage of negroes Daniel and Patience his wife and Hannah their daughter about 8 years old. Thos W. Waters (Seal), Wit: Hugh Oneall, Jesse Pugh. Proved by the affirmation of Hugh Oneall 11 March 1800 before Thos Brooks, J.P. Recorded 7 April 1800.

D, 523-524: John Dunkin of Newberry County for $70 to Margaret Edmondson of same, 25 acres, part of 500 acres granted to William Gilliam and conveyed by William Gilliam son and heir to the above said William Gillam, to said John Dunkin 10 & 1 Feb 1794 on waters of Bush River adj. Thomas Coppock, Taylors branch, Samuel Taylor's line, 5 Feb 18000. John Dunkin (Seal), Wit: Joseph Furnas, Sarah Carl (mark), Ann Hollingsworth (X). Elizabeth Dunkin, wife of John Dunkin, relinquished dower 10 March 1800 before Daniel Parkins, J.Q. Proved by the statement of Joseph Furnas 7 March 1800 before Thomas Brooks, J.P. Recorded 7 April 1800.

D, 524-525: Providence Williams of Newberry County for $350 to Samuel Pearson of same, 169 acres being part of 300 acres granted to James Williams deceased and conveyed by James Williams his son and heir at law to said Providence Williams, adj. John Williams, 16 Dec 1799. Providence Williams (Seal), Wit: William Belton, John Furnas, W. Cook. Mary Williams (X), wife of Providence Williams, relinquished dower 11 March 1800 before Daniel Parkins, J.Q. Proved 12 March 1800 by the affirmation of John Furnas before Thos Brooks, J.P. Recorded 7 April 1800.

D, 526-527: William Irby of Newberry District for £200 sterling to William Moore of Edgefield District, 200 acres on north side Saluda River adj. Thomas Brown, 13 March 1800. William Irby (Seal), Wit: John Satterwhite, Sampson Pope. Henrietta Irby, wife of William Irby, relinquished dower 13 March 1800 before Daniel Parkins, J.Q. Proved in Newberry District by the oath of Sampson Pope 13 March 1800 before Daniel Parkins, J.Q. Recorded 7 April 1800.

D, 527-528: 24 March 1800, Van Davis of Newberry County to Isaiah Pemberton of same, for £20, 30 acres on west side of Beaverdam, part of 171 acres granted to Van Davis 21 Jan 1785. Van Davis (Seal), Wit: Richard Pemberton, Van Davis, Charles Crow (X). Proved 27 March 1800 by the affirmation of Richard Pemberton before Thos Brooks, J.P. Recorded 7 April 1800.

D, 528-529: 12 Feb 1800, Robert Johnston and wife Sarah to Ezekiah Waldrop, both of Newberry County, for $100, 25 acres adj. Benjamin Johnston, to Robert Johnston's spring branch, James Johnson, Charles Scott. Robert Johnston (X) (Seal), Sarah Johnston (X) (Seal), Wit: George Goggans, James Toland, Isaac Davenport. Proved by the oath of George Goggans 18 March 1800 before Charles Griffin, J.P. Recorded 7 April 1800.

D, 529-530: Richard Tear of Newberry County for £35 sterling to Nathan Todd of Laurens County, 100 acres on waters of Kings Creek, part of 300 acres granted to Francis Davis and conveyed by him to John Adkins and by Adkins to Charles Wilson and by him, dated 7 Nov 1798. Richard Tear (Seal), Wit: William Spence, David Boyd. Chloe Tear (X), wife of Richard Tear, relinquished dower 8 March 1799 before J. R. Brown, J.N.C. Proved by the oath of William Spence before Providence Williams, J.P. Recorded 7 April 1800.

D, 531: David Watts of Newberry County for £32 sterling to Jeremiah McDanal, one negro boy named John, 1 Dec 1792. David Watts (Seal), Wit: Jacob Harrel (X), John McDanal. I do assign over all my right of the within Bill of Sale to John McDanal, 10 April 1799. Test: Michl Dickert Senr, Adrian Witt (A). Proved by the oath of John McDanal 7 April 1800 before Michl Dickert. Proved by the oath of Adrian Witt 7 April 1800 before Michl Dickert. Recorded 10 April 1800.

D, 532-534: Lease and release. 29 Nov 1794, John Hammons and wife Ruth of the State of North Carolina, to Jesse Anderson of Ninety Six District, South Carolina, for £100 sterling, 100 acres granted to said John Hammons 6 July 1774 in the fork of Broad and Saluda Rivers on a small draft of Second Creek adj. Samuel Lonam, Jeremiah Williams. John James Beeding Hammons (X) (Seal), Ruth Hammons, Wit: Eli Cook Anderson (X), Levi Anderson. Proved in Newberry District by the oath of Levy Anderson 13 March 1800 before Edw'd Finch, J.P. Recorded 10 April 1800.

D, 535-536: 26 March 1800, Mary Parks of Chester District, SC, to Hezekiah Jackson of Newberry District, for $60, 67 acres on waters of Cannons Creek, part of tract granted to Dederick Euts 2 March 1768, recorded in Book CCC, page 236. Mary Park (X) (Seal), Wit: John Park, William Dowes (mark), Robert Park. Proved in Newberry District by the oath of William Dowes 29 March 1800 before Fred Nance, C.C.P. Recorded 10 April 1800.

D, 536-537: 18 Oct 1798, John Johnston of Newberry County to Archabel McMullen of same, for £70 sterling, 150 acres, part of 560 acres granted to 4 Dec 1786 to Thomas Lehrie on Indian Creek, waters of Broad River. John Johnston (Seal), Wit: Go Harbirt, James Gordon, Jesse Gary. Susannah Johnston (X), wife of John Johnston, relinquished dower 6 Sept 1798 before L. E. Casey, J.N.C. Proved by the oath of James Gordon 19 Oct 1798 before John Speake, J.P. Recorded 10 April 1800.

D, 537-538: John Dennis of Newberry District to Samuel McQuerns of same, for $150, 100 acres on a small branch of Big Creek, part of 200 acres granted to Reason Ragan 31 Aug 1774, conveyed to John Dennis by Joseph Nichols adj. land sold to Ellis Pugh and Robert Yeldon of the same tract of 200 acres, 50 acres to each of them, 5 April 1800. John Dennis (Seal), Wit: Jas Johnson, Wm Presnal. Ann Dennis (mark), wife of John Dennis, relinquished dower before Daniel Parkins, J.P. Proved by the oath of Jas Johnson 5 April 1800 before Daniel Parkins, J.P. Recorded 10 April 1800.

D, 539-540: 1 Feb 1796, Adam Lagrone of Newberry County, planter, to John Kibler of same, wheel wright, for £30, 62½ acres in the fork of Saluda and Broad Rivers, part of 250 acres granted to Tobias Lagrone 10 Nov 1762 adj. Frederick Darrar, Christian Houpt, Frederick Lagrone, now the above 62 acres was lawfully transferred to Adam Lagrone from his father Tobias Lagrone 12 March 1785. Adam Lagrone (AL) (Seal), Mary Lagrone (X) (Seal), Wit: Michael Kubler [German signature], Wm Houseal, Jacob Epting. Proved by the oath of Michael Kibler 12 Feb 1796 before Wm Houseal, J.P. Recorded 10 April 1800.

D, 540-543: Lease and release. 1 & 2 May 1795, John Jacob Terrer of Orangeburgh District, SC, planter, to John Kibler of Newberry County, wheelwright, for £150, 250 acres in the fork of Broad and Saluda Rivers adj. Peter Bickle, Margaret Buckter, originally granted to Daniel Ebba 9 July 1755, recorded in Book PP, page 293 on Bounty, transferred to John Jacob Terrer 18 & 19 Nov 1766. Jacob Derer (Seal), Elizabeth Tarer (X) (Seal), Wit: Ethel'd Davis, Andrew Tarer (AT). Proved in Newberry County by the oath of Andrew Tarer 8 April 1800 before James McMaster, J.P. Recorded 11 April 1800.

D, 544-545: Plat for 62 acres included showing Bush River, and adjacent land owners James Brooks, Mary Steedham, Samuel Kelly, John Furnas, John Galbreath "formerly called James Hogs."

John Galbreath of Newberry District for $200 to John Kelly of same, 62 acres, part of tract granted 24 Nov 1767 to William Coates for 200 acres in Craven County (when surveyed) on N side Bush River, waters of Saluda River, 27 March 1800. John Galbreath (Seal), Wit: James Galbreath, Abraham Saner (X). Proved in Newberry District by the oath of James Galbreath 27 March 1800 before Geo Harbirt, J. Quo. Recorded 19 April 1800.

D, 545-546: South Carolina, Newberry County. William Hambleton has leased to Micajah Bennett one acre of land near to John Ellis it laying on the main waggon road at the place where James Hambleton begun to build and said Hambleton is to let Bennett have timber to build a house of twentyfour feet by sixteen and if said Hambleton finds shingles said Bennett is to put on a shingle roof and if not Bennett may put on a cabbin "Ruff" the logs is to be hewed down and planked above and below and a partition to be in the house, said Bennett is to have privilege of the fire wood and to have use of the house for three years beginning from 25 December next and in compensation said Bennett is to pay said Hambleton £4 per year for three years, 18 Sept 1799. William Hamilton, Wit: Jacob King, Thomas Hamilton. Proved by the oath of Jacob King 14 April 1800 before Hez. Speake, J.P. Recorded 21 April 1800.

D, 545-546: South Carolina, Newberry District. Micajah Bennett has rented to Jacob King a house and one acre of land, it being the house that said Bennett rented to William Hamilton for three years, and I do now rent to Jacob King from this date to the expiation of said term for £12, 29 March 1800. Micajah Bennett (Seal), Wit: Tho's Lindsey, Lewis Bennett. Proved by the oath of Thomas Lindsey 21 April 1800 before Fred Nance, J.P. Recorded 21 April 1800.

D, 547-548: 13 Nov 1799, Charles Crow and wife Sarah of Newberry County to Robert Stewart of same, for £49 s9 d4 sterling, 112 acres on waters of Bush River, a tract land out for Charles Crow 4 Aug 1794, recorded in Grant Book K. No. 5, page 460, which land lies on the north side of Bush River on a small branch. Charles Crow (Seal), Wit: Wm. Neel, Jesse Forbis. Sarah Crow (X), wife of Charles Crow, relinquished dower 13 Nov 1799 before J. R. Brown, J.N.C. Proved by the deposition of Jesse Forbis 13 Nov 1799 before J. R. Brown, J.N.C. Recorded 26 April 1800.

D, 549: South Carolina, Newberry County. John Thomas of county aforesaid for £8 to John Abernathy, israel Chandler, Jonathan Chandler, and Jonathan Taylor, all of same county, one bay horse about 13½ hands high, four years old next spring, with saddle spots, one blue sow & seven pigs ear marked with two under half crops, one bed and furniture, 11 Feb 1799. John Thomas (Seal), Wit: Fred Nance, J.P., Jno Thweatt. Recorded 5 May 1800.

D, 549-550: George Coon of Rutherford County, North Carolina, to Daniel Dewalt and George Gray, both of Newberry District, SC, bound to George Coon Senr of state and district aforesaid in the sum of $200, 29 Jan 1800, to exonerate the said George Coon Senr from right, title, claim, and interest which Nicholas Coon and Mary hath or ever had in the estate real and personal of Benedick Coon, father of said George Coon Senr and Nicholas Coon, late of district aforesaid, deceased. George Coon (Seal), Daniel Dewalt (Seal). Proved by the oath of Geo Ruff, J. Q. Recorded 12 May 1800.

D, 550-551: 9 Oct 1797, George Coon Senr of Newberry County, to John Coon of same, 100 acres on waters of Broad River on a branch of Crims Creek, formerly granted to Michael Colfel 22 Aug 1751 George Koon (X) (Seal), Wit: Christian Friedrich[?] Kromer [German signature], John Kinard, Jno Peter Kinard. Proved by the oath of Christian Comer 12 Feb 1800 before Mich'l Dickert, J. P. Recorded 12 May 1800.

D, 552-555: Lease and release. 23 & 24 Dec 1789, Peter Stockman of Ninety Six District, Tanner, to George Koone of same, planter, for £45 sterling, 50 acres, part of 400 acres granted 12 Feb 1755 to Andreas Meyer on a branch of Crims Creek adj. land of Andreas Rist, Benedick Kuting, Johannes Kountz, recorded in Book PP, page 366, and said Andreas Meyer transferred 100 acres of the 400 acres to Benedick Koon, and said Benedick Koon transferred 50 acres to Peter Stockman 10 & 21 June 1789. Peter Stockman [German signature] (Seal), Wit: Wm Houseal, Jacob Frey, Adam Pietenback (A). Proved in Lexington County by the oath of Adam Beatenback 21 July 1792 before John Adam Sumer, J.P. Adam Bidenbach [German signature]. Recorded 12 May 1800.

D, 555-556: South Carolina, Newberry District. George Ashford of district aforesaid appoints friend and son Michael Ashford of Union District, SC, attorney to receive from John Debell and William Debell, exrs. of Mary Johnson deceased of Louden County, Virginia, all such property or legacies due to me or bequeathed to me or my wife Sarah Ashford by my mother in law Mary Johnson deceased, dated 20 May 1800. George Ashford (Seal), Wit: Isaac Kirk, Francis Hatton. Proved in Newberry District by the oath of Francis Hatton before Edward Finch, J.P., 20 May 1800. Recorded 20 May 1800.

D, 557: 9 Oct 1799, David Richardson of Newberry County to Philemon Waters of same, for £5 sterling, 6 3/4 acres on Saluda River, part of tract granted 3 March 1788 to said David Richardson, adj. Philimon Waters. David Richardson (Seal), Wit: P. B. Waters, David Waters. Proved by the oath of Philemon B. Waters 15 May 180 before Fred Nance, C. C.P. Recorded 20 May 1800.

D, 558: 4 May 1799, Northrup Marple and Ann Marple of Fairfield County, planter, for $492 to David Cannon of Newberry County, 123 acres, being the north part of a tract of 550 acres granted to John Cannon on Cannons Creek, a branch Broad River adj. Jacob Bowers, Adam Epting, David and Samuel Cannon, Northrup Marple. Northrup Marple (Seal), Ann Marple (X) (Seal), Wit: Josias Wood, Abraham Nilance, James McGill. Proved in Fairfield County by the oath of James Mcgill 5 Dec 1799 before Benj'a May, J.P. Recorded 20 May 1800.

D, 559-560: Charles Crenshaw of Newberry District for $200 to John James of same, 23½ acres granted 14 Sept 1771 to William Hamilton and conveyed by him to Charles Crenshaw adj. Edward Finch, on Kings Creek, to the waggon road, 8 April 1800. Charles Crenshaw (Seal), Wit: Samuel Lindsey, Abner Crenshaw. Eunice Crenshaw, wife of Charles Crenshaw, relinquished dower 15 April 1800 before Levi Casey, J. Qm. Recorded 27 May 1800.

D, 560-561: 23 June 1798, Jonathan Pratt of Newberry County to William Shell of same, for £100 sterling, 355 acres, part of three different surveys adj. William Collinsworth. Jonathan Pratt (Seal), Wit: Stephen Shell, Thomas Collinsworth, George Harbirt. Elizabeth Pratt (X), wife of Jonathan Pratt, relinquished dower 2 July 1798 before Edward Finch, J.P. Proved by the oath of Stephen Shell 2 July 1798 before Edward Finch, J.P. Recorded 27 May 1800.

D, 561-562: Stephen Shell of Newberry County for $295 to William Shell of same, 131 acres, part of tract conveyed to Stephen Shell by William Finch 4 Oct 1706 [sic], all that part of said tract that lies above a certain branch which heads in the land which said William Shell purchased of Jonathan Pratt, it being a branch of Second Creek, 29 Dec 1798. Stephen Shell (Seal), Wit: Lemmon Shell, William Wright, Ira Shell. Proved 20 Jan 1800 by the oath of Ira Shell before Edw'd Finch, J.P. Recorded 27 June 1800.

D, 562-564: 7 Oct 1794, John Dunkin and wife Jeney of Newberry County to William Addington of same, for £30 sterling, 30 acres on Duncan Creek, granted to John Duncan 13 March 1788, recorded in Grant Book YYYY, page 153 adj. John Dunkin, John Clark, Levi Casey. John Duncan (I) (Seal),

168

Jen Dunkin (Seal), Wit: Moses Whitton, Phillip Whitten, P. Martch. Proved by the oath of Moses Whitten 24 May 1800 before Levi Casey, J.Q.M. Recorded 27 May 1800.

D, 565-567: 2 Aug 1768, Jacob Nortz of Craven County, SC, planter, to Jacob Bushart of same, planter, for £200 SC money, 350 acres on waters of Cannons Creek, granted to Jacob Nortz 14 May 1752. Jacob Nortz (Seal), Wit: John Martin Fridig, Jacob Bookman, Philip Pearson. Proved in Orangeburgh District by the oath of Jacob Bookman 10 May 1785 before John Kennerly, J.P. Recorded 29 May 1800.

D, 567-571: Lease and release. 10 & 11 June 1769, Abraham Nordike of Berkley County, SC, carpenter, and wife Mary, to Henry Black of same, for £100 SC money, 100 acres, part of 300 acres granted to Abraham Nordike 29 April 1768 in the fork of Broad and Saluda Rivers on a small branch of Cannons Creek, waters of Broad River, adj. Presley, Laurence Lagrone. Abraham Nordike (Seal), Mary Nordike (Seal), Wit: William Taylor, Laurence Lagrone, Philip Gradwole. Proved in Berkley County by the oath of Philip Grodwole 9 May 1771 before Mich'l Dickert, J.P. Recorded 29 May 1800.

D, 571: David Wedinmans Ear Mark as follows a crop in the right Ear and a hole in the left. Fred. Nance, R.M.C.

D, 572-573: ____ 1792, Shadrack Clavel of State of Virginia, planter, to Jacob Bushart, planter, of State of SC, for £12 sterling, 100 acres in Newberry County on a branch of Cannons Creek, granted to Abraham Nordike and not known who granted by as the plat being burnt adj. land of Martin Taylor, John Bolan, John Rice, Henry Black, and made over from Abraham Nordike to Doris Felmate and then to Frederick Feltmate and then to Shadrach Clavel by Frederick Feltmate 6 June 1790. Shadrack Clavel (X) (Seal), Wit: Jno H. Ruff, George Cromer. Proved by the oath of George Cromer 5 Jan 1794 before David Ruff, J.P. Recorded 29 May 1800.

D, 573-574: 4 Feb 1793, Adam Black of Orangeburgh District, planter, to Jacob Buzard of Newberry County, planter, for £26 sterling, 100 acres in Newberry County on a branch of Cannons Creek, granted to Abraham Nordike, part of 300 acres adj. J. Buzard, Laurence Laground, John Rice, Martin Taylor. Adam Black (X) (Seal), Wit: Jno H. Ruff, John Houseal, Rich'd Sonley. Proved in Newberry County by the oath of John Houseal 4 Feb 1793 before David Ruff, J.P. Recorded 29 May 1800.

D, 574-575: 12 Jan 1793, William Feltmate of Lexington County, planter, to Jacob Buzard of Newberry County, for £20 sterling, 100 acres in Newberry County on a branch of Cannons Creek, granted to Abraham Nordike, part of 300 acres adj. A. Black, Martin Taylor, John Rice, said Buzzard. William Feltmate (X) (Seal), Wit: Peter Stuckman, John Wendel, Joseph Caldwell. Proved in Newberry County by the oath of Peter Stuckman 23 March 1795 before David Ruff, J.P. Recorded 29 May 1800.

D, 576: Frederick Feltmate, late of South Carolina, but now of Harbour County, Province of Nova Scotia, appoints Shadrack Clavel of South Carolina my lawful attorney to recover 100 acres in the fork of Broad River on Little Saluda on Cannons Creek, 7 June 1792. Frederick Feltmate (F) (Seal), Wit: John Lefett. Acknowledged before me, Mich'l Houseal, J.P. Shadrack Clavel signed over his right to Jacob Buzard having rec'd full sattisfaction from him, 23 Oct 1792. Shadrack Clavel (X), Wit: J. H. Ruff, George Cromer. Proved in Newberry County by the oath of George Cromer 5 Jan 1793 before David Ruff, J.P. Recorded 29 May 1800.

D, 577-578: 6 June 1790, Frederick Feltmate of Sydney County, Province of Nova Scotia, to Shadrack Clavel, for £20, 100 acres in the fork of Broad River and Saluda on waters of Cannons Creek, 7 June 1792. Frederick Feltmate (F) (Seal), Wit: Matthew Gregg, Sarah Gregg, John Lefett, Mich'l Houseal, J.P. Recorded 29 May 1800.

D, 578-579: Laurence Righart of Newberry County for $141.50 to Michael Kinard of same, 50 acres on a branch of Crims Creek in the fork of Broad and Saluda Rivers adj. John Dominie, granted to Maria Margareta Stoudemoyer on bounty, 2 Jan 1754, and George Stoudemoyer her grandson and heir at law conveyed to Laurence Righard 2 & 3 Jan 1776. Laurence Righard (R) (Seal), Wit: John Pester, Michael Righard (M), Peter Righard (PR). Anistasia Righard (X), wife of Laurence Righard, relinquished dower 24 Jan 1800 before George Ruff, J.Q.U. Proved by the oath of John Piester 25 Jan 1800 before George Ruff, J.Q.U. Recorded 30 May 1800.

D, 580-581: Gibeon Burton of Newberry District for £25 to William Burton of same, two mairs, one a bay about 14 hands high branded with a round OT on the bullock and shoulder, one a sorrel mare 15 hands not branded, three feather beds and furniture, six head of cattle, two iron potts, one dutch oven, two dishes and six plates, six knives and forks, two basons, two saddles, three plows, two axes, one bag of cotton supposed to be 100 weight, five head of hogs and two smoothing irons, 29 May 1800. Gibeon Burton (Seal), Wit: William Burton Junr, Aron Burton. Proved 30 May 1800 by the oath of Aaron Burton before Thomas Brooks, J.P. Recorded 30 May 1800.

D, 581-582: John Satterwhite Jun'r of Newberry County for $300 to William Reagan, 186 by resurvey on Beaverdam Creek, granted to William Turner for 150 acres and conveyed by Samuel Saxon Esq're Sheriff of Ninety Six District under an execution, dated 25 May 1798. John Satterwhite Jun'r (Seal), Wit: Reason Reagan, Daniel Richardson, John Reagan (mark). Susannah Satterwhite, wife of John Satterwhite, relinquished dower 25 May 1798 before J. R. Brown, J.N.C. Proved by the oath of John Reagan 16 Jan 1800 before J. R. Brown, J.N.C. Recorded 16 June 1800.

D, 582-583: Hannah Gauntt of Newberry District for $100 to Jacob Gauntt of same, 2 acres of land with the house, etc., which was left to Hannah Gauntt by her late husband Israel Gauntt, part of tract of 50 acres on the head of

Palmeto branch, waters of Bush River, 20 June 1800. Hannah Gauntt (Seal), Wit: Barshaba Harris (mark), Richard Clegg, Isabella Todd. Proved by the oath of Richard Clegg 21 June 1800 before Fred Nance, C.C.P. Recorded 21 June 1800.

D, 584-585: Jonathan Chandler of Newberry District for £160 sterling to Nathan Washington Perry of same, tract on north side Bush River, part of tract granted to Abraham Cardine for 400 acres on 30 Aug 1762 and by divers transferences conveyed to me by Jacob Chandler, 9 Jan 1800. Jonathan Chandler (Seal), Wit: John Leasel, James Griffin. Ruhama Chandler, wife of Jonathan Chandler, relinquished dower 19 Jan 1800 before J. R. Brown, J.N.C. Proved by the oath of James Griffin 9 Jan 1800 before J. R. Brown, J.N.C. Recorded 21 June 1800.

D, 585-589: Lease and release. South Carolina 21 & 22 Feb 1786, Clement Davis "of the late County of Newberry" planter to William Hall of state aforesaid, for £30 Virginia money, 92 acres, part of 200 acres granted to said Clement Davis 22 Feb 1771 in Berkley County, now Newberry, on a small branch of Bush Creek called Reedy branch, adj. Marmaduke Coate, Teague. Clement Davis (mark) (Seal), Wit: William Miles, Van Davis, Abijah Davis. Proved in Newberry County by the oath of Van Davis 8 April 1800 before Stephen Williams, J.P. Recorded 27 June 1800.

D, 590-591: 28 Jan 1800, Abel Thomas of Newberry District to Thomas Jenkins of same, for £30, 100 acres adj. lands of Charles Bridges, Abel Thomas, Mozeych, part of tract granted to John Rankin 10 Jan 1775. Abel Thomas (Seal), Wit: Fred Nance, Peter Connor. Proved 1 July 1800 by the oath of Frederick Nance before Thomas Brooks, J.P. Recorded 1 July 1800.

D, 591-592: 21 Oct 1797, James Campbell of Newberry County, planter, to James Gordon of same, brick layer, 411 acres upon Pattersons Creek, a branch of Indian Creek, a water of Enoree River, the same being contained in several different surveys: one granted to William Gantonby of 100 acres, one to Michael Volmer of 50 acres, 125 acres being part of 230 acres granted to Charles King, and 34 acres granted to said James Campbell and 102 acres, part of 203 acres granted to said James Campbell. James Campbell (Seal), Wit: William Knox, J. McMorries, Edward Lindsey. Mary Campbell, wife of James Campbell, relinquished dower 7 Aug 1798 before Levi Casey, J.N.C. Proved by the oath of John McMorries 8 June 1798 before John Speak, J.P. Recorded 1 July 1800.

D, 593-594: Jonathan Taylor of Newberry County for £50 sterling to Abraham Hollinsworth of same, 100 acres on waters of the Beaverdam, adj. William Nelson, James Brooks, granted 31 Aug 1774, recorded in Auditor Genls Office in Book M. No. 13, page 319, to Matthew Brooks and conveyed by him to said Jonathan Taylor 1 & 2 June 1786. Jonathan Taylor (Seal), Wit: Henry Stiddom, John Stiddom, Martha Steddom. Proved 27 June 1800 by the oath of Henry Steddom before Thomas Brooks, J.P. Recorded 2 July 1800.

D, 594-595: 8 Nov 1799, William Belton of Newberry County for £20 sterling to John Belton of same, 50 acres, part of 200 acres granted to said William Belton in the fork between Broad and Saluda rivers adj. Thomas Clark, William Belton, James Coates. Wm Belton (Seal), Wit: Thomas Clark, Charity Clark, Priscilla Clark. Susannah Belton (M), wife of William Belton, relinquished dower 3 July 1800 before George Harbirt, J. Q. Proved by the oath of Thomas Clark 3 July 1800 before George Harbirt, J. Quo. Recorded 3 July 1800.

D, 595-596: South Carolina, Newberry District. I have undertaken to build the Goal [gaol, jail] of Newberry District and William Summers, Thomas Mills, Levi Hilburn, Henry Bates, Hezekiah Riley and John Worthington have become my security for the true performance of my contract, and I do indemnify my securities by mortgage of Jesse a fellow about 26 years old and his wife Peggy about 25 years old and her son William about 5 years old and Bet her daughter about one year old, Ben a lad about 14 and his brother Harry about 10, Dick a boy about 5 years old, Rachael a girl about 13 years of age, Judy a wench about 26 years old and her two sons Sigh about 4 and John about 2, Thomas Waters shall give good counter security, ___ July 1800. Thos M. Waters (Seal), Wit: Isaac Kirk. Proved by the affirmation of Isaac Kirk 5 July 1800 before Fred Nance, C.C.P. Recorded 5 July 1800.

D, 597-598: 10 Jan 1800, Thomas and Elizabeth Lake of Newberry County to Elijah Lake of same, for $300, 133 acres adj. Elisha Lake, widow Gories, James C. Young, Nathan Grainshaw [Crenshaw]. Thomas Lake (Seal), Elizabeth Lake (X) (Seal), Wit: Wm Morries, Elisha Lake, Wm. Lake. Proved by the oath of Elisha Lake 18 July 1800 before Samuel E. Kenner, J. P. Recorded 19 July 1800.

D, 598-599: 5 July 1800, Samuel Crumley of Newberry District to John Abernathy of same, for $500, 222½ acres in Newberry County adj. Robert Richardson, John Crumley, Samuel Hughens, Robert Plunk, Onslow Barret, part of tract granted to William Thompson and part of tract granted to John Crumley and devolving to said Samuel Crumley by heirship. Samuel Crumley (Seal), Wit: Susannah Belton (M), Alexander Dunlap, Wm. Belton. Ann Crumley (X), wife of Samuel Crumley, relinquished dower 7 July 1800 before George Harbirt, J. Q. Proved by the oath of Alexander Dunlap 7 July 1800 before George Harbirt, J. Quo. Recorded 19 July 1800.

D, 600-601: Plat for 46 acres by P. B. Waters, D. S., showing adj. land owners: Thos Brooks, Saml Pearson, John Coats, Rosanah Russell.

John Coate of Newberry County for $230 to Frederick Nance of same, 46 acres on Scotch Creek, waters of Bush River adj. Thomas Brooks, Samuel Pearson, John Coats, Rosanah Russell, 11 Jan 1800. Jno Coate (Seal), Wit: Wm. Satterwhite, P. B. Waters. Susanna Coate, wife of John Coate, relinquished dower 21 June 1800 before George Harbirt, J. Quo. Recorded 19 July 1800.

D, 602: 9 April 1800, William Collier of Newberry District to John Simpson, merchant, of Laurens District, for $85.65, one black mare about 4 years old, 14 hands high, no brand visible, one saddle, feather bed and furniture, William Collier (X) (Seal), Wit: Jas Sproull, John Gallegly. Proved in Newberry District by the oath of John Gallegly 17 July 1800 before Charles Griffin, J.P. Recorded 20 July 1800.

D, 603-608: Lease and release. 2 & 3 Aug 1776, John Scott and wife Easther of Craven County, Ninety Six District, SC, to Samuel Feere of the province aforesaid, for £95 SC money, 150 acres in Craven County on N side Saluda on waters of Bush River adj. Jeremiah Ham, Michael Cromer. John Scott (I) (Seal), Esther Scott (E) (Seal), Wit: James Young, William Barlow, Jeremiah Ham. Proved by the oath of James Young 1 March 1777 before William Houseal, J.P. Recorded 28 July 1800.

D, 608-610: 18 Oct 1797, Jonathan Reeder of Newberry County, SC, planter, to Charles Crow Junr of same, for £53 sterling, 238 acres on beaver dam, a branch of Bush River adj. William Reeder, David Williams, Robert McKeterick, grant recorded in Book E. No. 5, page 405. Jonathan Reeder (Seal), Wit: Jonathan Chandler, Squire Lonam. Rebekah Reeder, wife of Jonathan Reeder, relinquished dower 18 Oct 1797 before J. R. Brown, J.N.C. Proved by the oath of Squire Lonam 18 Oct 1797 before J. R. Brown, J.N.C. Recorded 4 Aug 1800.

D, 610-611: 25 July 1796, Peter Stuckman of Ninety Six District and wife Cathorina to George Rittlehover of same, for £20 sterling, 50 acres, part of 166 acres granted to said Stockman 2 Oct 1786, recorded in Book OOOO, page 24, on waters of Crims Creek adj. said Ritlehover. Peter Stockman (Seal), Catherina Stockman (X) (Seal), Wit: J. A. Houseal, George Adam Summer, Adam Rish (X). Proved in Newberry District by the oath of Adam Rish 1 Aug 1800 before Mich'l Dickert, J.P. Recorded 4 Aug 1800.

D, 612-613: Peter Stockman of Newberry County to John Adam Rish for £15, 79 acres granted to said Stockman 2 Oct 1786, recorded in Book OOOO, page 24, on waters of Crims Creek adj. said Jacob Epting, by plat dated 16 Feb 1798. Peter Stockman (LS), Wit: John A. Setzler, William Fullmer, George Setzler. Proved in Newberry District by the oath of John Adam Setzler 13 March 1800 before Mich'l Dickert, J.P. Recorded 4 Aug 1800.

D, 614-617: Lease and release. South Carolina, Ninety Six District, 7 & 8 Nov 1785, Thomas Eastland of district aforesaid to William Stripling of same, for £500 sterling, 150 acres granted to Thomas Eastland 27 Nov 1770, on waters of Saluda River adj. Coleman Brown. Thomas Eastland (Seal), Wit: George Goggans, William Irby, William Bladon. Lucy Eastland, wife of Thomas Eastland, relinquished dower 14 March 1800 before Daniel Parkins, J.Q. Recorded 4 Aug 1800.

D, 617-618: 26 Aug 1799, Samuel Yeargan of Newberry County to James Spence of same, tract of 12 3/4 acres adj. said Spence, Daniel Reider, in the fork of Kings Creek, part of tract granted to James Cato 23 June 1774, recorded in Book QQQ, page 518. Samuel Yeargain (Seal), Wit: Daniel Reider (X), Mary Yeargain, Bartlett Yeargain. Proved by the oath of Daniel Reider 9 Aug 1800 before Edw'd Finch, J.P. Recorded 11 Aug 1800.

D, 618-619: 16 Aug 1798, Wallis Jones of Greenville County, SC, for £40 sterling, to Isaac Mills of Newberry County, 75 acres in Newberry County, granted to me on 6 May 1771, on east side Bush River adj. land of Wallis Jones Junr, James Pugh. Wallis Jones Senr (Seal), Elizabeth Jones (X) (Seal), Wit: Wallis Jones Junr, Henry Jones. Elizabeth Jones (X), wife of Wallis Jones Senr, relinquished dower in Greenville District before Daniel Parkins, J. Q. Proved in Newberry District by the oath of Wallis Jones Junr 11 Aug 1800 before Jacob Beiller, J.P. Recorded 11 Aug 1800.

D, 619-620: 29 Aug 1798, Wallis Jones Junr of Newberry County, for £30 sterling, to Isaac Mills of same, 150 acres in Newberry County on east side Bush River adj. land of Jacob Beiller and Philimon Waters, James Patty's estate, James Pugh, Wallis Jones Senr, granted to Wallis Jones Junr 20 Nov 1784. Wallis Jones Junr (Seal), Rachel Jones (X) (Seal), Wit: Wm Conwill, Daniel Parkins. Rachel Jones (X), wife of Wallis Jones Junr, relinquished dower in before J. R. Brown, J.N.C. Proved by the oath of Daniel Parkins Esqr 11 Aug 1800 before Jacob Beiller, J.P. Recorded 11 Aug 1800.

D, 621-623: Lease and release. 17 & 18 July 1789, John Riley of Newberry County to Jeremiah Riley of same, for £20 sterling, 150 acres, part of tract granted to said John Riley 31 Aug 1774 on Palmeto Branch, waters of Bush River. John Riley (X) (Seal), Wit: Joseph Summers, Zacheriah Riley (mark). Acknowledged in Newberry County by said John Riley before Thomas W. Waters, J. P. Recorded 12 Aug 1800.

D, 623-624: 22 Aug 1798, John Woodall and Joseph Woodall of Pendleton County, SC, three & twenty mile Creek, to Robert McAlees, for £40 sterling, tract on waters of Gilders Creek granted to William Woodall 31 Aug 1774.. John Wooddall (Seal), Hannah Hobson (mark), Joseph Wooddall (Seal), Anney Wooddall (mark), Wit: Joseph Caldwell, Joseph Elliott, John Bennen. Proved in Newberry District 16 Aug 1800 by the oath of John Benning before T. Brooks, J.P. Recorded 16 Aug 1800.

D, 625-626: William Burgess of Newberry District for £54 s6 sterling to William Moore of Edgefield District, 140 acres in Newberry District, north side Saluda River being the land I now live up, adj. John Atkerson and others, 19 June 1800. William Burgess (Seal), Wit: Gilson Yarbrough, James Little (X). Proved in Edgefield District by the oath of James Little 7 July 1800 before Nath'l Abney, J.P. Recorded 19 Aug 1800.

D, 626-629: Lease and release. 23 & 24 Dec 1768, George Hollingsworth of Berkley County, SC, planter, to Jacob Hoge of same, planter, for £100, 150 acres on Bush Creek granted 28 Aug 1767 to George Hollingsworth. George Hollingsworth (Seal), Jane Hollingsworth (Seal), Wit: Jacob Brooks (I), William Downs, William Gary. Proved in Berkley County by the oath of Jacob Brooks 21 July 1769 before James Lindley, J.P. Recorded 19 Aug 1800.

D, 629-633: Lease and release. 8 & 9 Dec 1772, Jacob Hoge of Craven County, SC, planter, to William Hoge of same, planter, for £100, 150 acres on Bush Creek granted 28 Aug 1767 to George Hollingsworth and conveyed by him to Jacob Hoge. Jacob Hoge (Seal), Mary Hoge (X) (Seal), Wit: Jonath'n Downs, William Graydon Junr. Proved in Ninety Six District 27 May 1773 by the oath of Jonathan Downs before Ja's Lindley, J.P. Recorded 19 Aug 1800.

D, 633-634: 8 Sept 1800, James and Nancy Vessells and Ridley Vessels his mother of Newberry County, to Elijah Lake of same, for $130, 110 cares adj. James C. Young, Crenshaw, Robert and Mary Mabin. James Vessells (mark) (Seal), Nancy Vessels (mark) (Seal), Ridley Vessels (X) (Seal), Wit: Benjamin Maybin, Elizabeth Kelley, Patience Hannah Burell (X). Proved in Newberry District by the oath of Benjamin Maybin 8 Sept 1800 before Saml E. Kenner, J.P.

D, 635-638: Lease and release. 8 & 9 Feb 1775, Samuel Coate of Ninety Six District, farmer, to James Gardner of same, farmer, for £200 sterling, 150 acres on waters of Bush River granted 28 Aug 1767 to George Hollingsworth, recorded in Book BBB, page 227, and conveyed 24 Dec 1768 to Jacob Hoge, and said Hoge 9 Dec 1772 to William Hoge, and William Hoge 7 Dec 1774 to Samuel Coate. Samuel Coate (X), Wit: Richard Level (X), Jno Furnas, Simon Quinn. Proved 7 Sept 1789 by the deposition of Richard Leavell before Mercer Babb, J.P. Recorded 8 Sept 1800.

D, 638-642: Lease and release. 30 & 31 Dec 1787, James Gardner of Winton County, Orrangeburgh District, SC, and wife Mary, to Samuel Miles of Newberry County, 96 district, planter, for £79, 150 acres on waters of Bush River granted 28 Aug 1767 to George Hollingsworth, and conveyed 23 & 24 Dec 1768 to Jacob Hoge, and said Hoge 9 Dec 1772 to William Hoge, and William Hoge 6 & 7 Dec 1774 to Samuel Coate, and Samuel Coate conveyed to said James Gardner 8 & 9 Feb 1775. James Garner (Seal), Mary Garner (X) (Seal), Wit: Richard Leavell, Edward Leavell, Eleanor Leavell. Proved 7 Sept 1789 by the deposition of Richard Leavell before Mercer Babb, J.P. Recorded 8 Sept 1800.

D, 642-643: Plat for 5 acres on Road to Charleston adj. Robert Floyd, Eliphaz Davis.

Eliphaz Davis of Newberry District for $100 to Charles Jones and Joshua Jones of state of SC, five acres, part of 167 acres granted to Charles Crow on waters of Bush River. Eliphaz Davis (Seal), Wit: John Jones, Go. Harbert, J.

Quo. Martha Davis, wife of Eliphaz Davis, relinquished dower 2 Sept 1800 before Geo. Harbert J. Quo. Recorded 8 Sept 1800.

D, 643-644: South Carolina, Newberry District. John Wadlington of State of Kentucky, for $500 to Daniel Parkins, Esquire, of State of SC, a negro man Toney of a black complexion about 37 years of age, stout and well maid, 1 Sept 1800. John Wadlington (Seal), Wit: Jesse B. Pemberton, Fred Nance. Proved in Newberry District by the oath of Frederick Nance 1 Sept 1800 before Thomas Brooks, J. Peace. Recorded 8 Sept 1800.

D, 644: Received from Gary Davis in cash $260 in sundry other debts of mine he has paid in the whole amount of $1976.66 for which I sell negroes viz., Jesse, Ben, Paul, Peggy and her two children, Nan an old wench and Lilly her daughter, 15 March 1800. Thomas W. Waters, Wit: Benjamin Gregory (X). Proved in Newberry District by the oath of Benjamin Gregory before Jacob Bieller, J.P. Recorded 8 Sept 1800.

D, 645-646: James Burnes of Newberry [County] for £165 sterling to John Blackburn, 150 acres, a tract granted 23 June 1774 to Benjamin Norwood on a small branch of Indian Creek, south side of Enoree, 7 Aug 1798. James Burnes (X) (Seal), Wit: Wm Blackburn, Isaac Cannon, Geo. Harbert. Proved by the oath of George Harbert 27 Oct 1798 before L. E. Casey, J.N.Ct. Mary Burnes (mark), wife of James Burnes, relinquished dower 17 Oct 1798 L. E. Casey, J.N.Ct. Recorded 29 Sept 1800.

D, 646-648: John King of Newberry County for 100 guineas to John Bell of same, 50 acres on north side Saluda River on waters of Hawlick Creek, part of tract of 230 acres granted to John Waits and by said John Waits conveyed to John King; also a tract of 19 acres on north side Saluda River on a branch of Hawlick Creek, part of tract granted to Nehemiah Rotton 5 March 1787 adj. McDougles' line, John Waites line, Henry Creek's line, conveyed from Nehemiah Rotton to James Harpe then to Henry Creke and from Henry Creek to John King; also 128 acres, part of tract of 500 acres granted to William Mazyck and conveyed to Col. Phillimon Waters and by said Phillimon Waters to Henry Creek and by H. Creek to John King, adj. John Waits, William Taylor; also 150 acres on Musgroves Creek, waters of Big Saluda granted to Henry Creek adj. John Waits, Jacob Smith, John Caleys, Col. Philemon Waters, Maidows; another tract of 60 acres, part of tract to John Waits adj. Henry Creek, Henry Jotes[?], whereon said Waits formerly lived and conveyed by John Waits to Henry Creek and by Creek to John King; also 100 acres adj. lands of said John King, Beverly Borum, Dr. Cains, on which said Caines now lives, John Ryals, dated 5 Feb 1799. John King (Seal), Mary King (X) (Seal), Wit: Chr Caines, Caleb Caines (mark), Mary Caines (mark). Proved in Newberry District 11 April 1800 by the oath of Christopher Caines before Jacob Bieller, J.P. Recorded 8 Oct 1800.

D, 649: Jonothan Taylor of Newberry District for £4 sterling to Joseph Furnas of same, one sorrel mare about 4 years old, about 15 hands high, branded RG,

3rd day of the 10th month 1800. Jonothan Talor (Seal), Wit: Edward Benbow, John Coppock. Proved by the affirmation of Edward Benbow 11 Oct 1800 before Fred Nance, C. C. Pls. Recorded 11 Oct 1800.

END OF DEED BOOK D

179

Botner, Elijah 23, 153
Bottner, Ludwig 137
Bottoms, John 111
Bough/t, Eva Susanah (Wayman) 40
    Leonard 40
Boulware 146
    James 56
Bounds, Dudley 93
Bounetheau, Peter 100, 115
Bouzart, Jacob 14
Bower/s, Andrew 119
    George 83, 87
    Jacob 83, 168
    Stephen 162
Bowie, George 101
Bowler, Rutherford 110
Boyakin, Francis 18
Boyce, James 91, 146
Boyd 133
    David 6, 16, 57, 61, 98, 113, 124, 126,
        127, 164
    Eleanor/Ellinor 98
    Hugh 1, 19, 46, 48, 77, 85
    James 65
    John 6, 16, 46, 51, 69, 90, 91, 93
Boyes, James 64
Boykin, Francis 123
Boys, John 108, 141
    Robert 141
Bozeman, David 43
    John 43
    Philimon 43
    Susannah 43
Bozier, Isaac 48
Bozman, David 113
Bradford, Charles D. 105
Bradley, Michael 113
Bradshaw, Henry 75
    James 75
    Samuel 137
    South 23
Brandon 51
    Thomas 51
Brannon, Robert 30
Braselman/n 126
    Peter 5, 94
Brasilman, John David 94
    Peter 5, 28, 35, 42, 63, 94
Braswell, Valintine 97, 98
    Volentine 161
    Voluntine 87, 88
Breshter, Margaret 79
Bridges, Ann 87, 96
    Charles 62, 89, 171
    George 39, 41, 86, 87, 96, 98, 125
    Nancy 96
Brit, John 53
Brooks, Ann 84
    B. 91

Bartlett 12, 65
    Daniel 103
    David 120
    Dudly/ey 1, 32, 37, 56
    Elisha 37, 96, 97, 118, 138, 141
    Elizabeth 47
    Jacob 9, 49, 107, 114, 175
    James 154, 166, 171
    Jesse 158
    John 58, 59, 73, 118
    Mary 25, 49
    Mat(t)hew 91, 129, 171
    Nancy 25, 96, 97
    Richard 25, 36, 37, 155
    Robert 25, 147, 155
    Sarah 25, 37
    Susanna/h 49, 160
    T. 174
    Thomas 45, 49, 59, 73, 160, 163, 164,
        170-172, 176
    William 36, 37, 84
    Zachariah Smith 32, 37, 47
Brown 133, 163
    Christian 80
    Coleman 56, 173
    Elizabeth 29, 129
    George 18
    J. 5
    J. R. 11, 13, 15, 16, 30, 31, 35, 38, 40,
        58, 62, 67, 71, 72, 74, 80, 83, 85,
        91-93, 97, 99, 103, 109, 110, 111, 113,
        118, 122, 127, 131-133, 137, 138, 140,
        141, 143, 146, 148-151, 156, 161-164,
        167, 170, 171, 173, 174
    Jacob 28, 112
    Jacob R. 55, 56, 81, 112, 142
    Jacob Roberts 19, 33, 34, 52, 57, 73,
        142, 145
    James 13, 101
    Jeremiah 119
    John 30, 163
    Joseph 41
    Larkin 110
    Misibeth 89
    Nathan 108
    R. 22, 23, 25, 27, 51, 70
    Robert 29, 52, 89, 129, 148
    Samuel 14, 86, 119, 122, 158
    Sims 8, 9, 29, 93
    Thomas 77, 164
    William 147
Brukten, Margaret 78
Brummit, Nancy H. 57
Buchan(n)an, Alex M. 99
    Benjamin 142
    James 10, 37
    Jesse 114
    John 99, 114
    Joseph 5

180

Duford, Francis 67
Dugall, James 6
Dugan, Robert 19
Duglas/s, John 70, 94
  Lydia 70
Duke, Henry 65
Dukeras, Michael 125
Duncan, Amos 23, 45, 78
  Elizabeth 45, 78
  James 11
  John 11, 22, 86, 106, 147, 168
  Samuel 22, 45, 78, 85, 111
  Sarah 22
Dunkin 76, 149
  Amos 45, 78, 129-131, 151
  Elisabeth 45, 164
  Jeney 168, 169
  John 50, 51, 148, 164, 168
  March 51
  Nelson 76
  Rachel 97
  Samuel 72, 119
Dunlap, Alexander 172
  John 66, 158
  William 27, 51, 88, 148
Dunn, Andrew 62, 63
  David 62
  Henry 80, 90
Dunnon, Robert 16
Duraux, J. D. 123
Dyson, Abraham 81, 140, 143, 151
  Daniel 26, 27, 109, 129, 143
  Isaac 27
  James 27, 109, 138, 140, 141, 151
  John 27, 138, 140, 149
Eaney, Ulrigh 72
Earp, Daniel 153
Eastland, John 90
  Lucy 173
  Thomas 34, 56, 90, 173
Eaynes, Ulrage 27
Ebb/a, Daniel 4, 166
Echard, Barbara/y 22, 149, 150
Eddens, Abraham 161
  Sarah 161
Ed(d)erington, Henry 90, 101
Edinborough 79
Edmondson, Margaret 164
Edwards, David 55
  Edward 118
  Hannah 17
  Henry 162
  John 56, 57, 72, 118
  Joseph 155
  Joshua 83
  Mary 55
  Mary (Turner) 118
  Obediah 51
  Samuel 17, 55, 155

Widow 161
Egnar/er, George 80
  Rachael 80
Ehney-- see Eaney
Eigelberger, John 156
  Michael 130
Eiglebarger, Barbara/y 9, 106
  Catharine (Sheely) 67
  Christian 67
  George 50, 67
  John 4, 9, 53, 54, 67, 68, 106
  Maria Ursula 67
  Ursula 50
Eigner, George 80
Eleazer, Stephen 146
Eliot, Josiah 30
Elleman/on, Abner 16, 76-78
  Catharine 76, 77
  Elizabeth 119
  Enos 4, 22, 45, 71, 77, 98, 119, 136
  Jean 71
  John 4, 45, 76, 78, 84, 149, 150, 151
  Mary 150
  Susannah 4
  William 4, 71, 78, 84
Ellenwyers, Hans George 101
Ellermon, Abner 45
Elliman, Abner 78
  William 78
Elliot/t, George 43, 117
  Joseph 174
  Josiah 27, 51
  Mary 117
  Salley 117
  Sarah 117
  William 41, 43, 117
Ellis, Edmond 26
  Elizabeth 53
  John 5, 14, 53, 144, 166
  Simeon 49, 50, 132
  William 33, 160
Elmore, Charity 45
  Isaac 12, 16, 22, 84, 150
  John 85
  Joseph 78
  Mat(t)hias 12, 16, 28, 45, 48, 56, 76, 91,
    104, 136, 149, 150
  Rachael 85
  Ridgeway 78, 84
  Sarah 45
  Stephen 17, 28, 36, 45, 48, 56, 85, 90,
    91, 101, 103, 114, 131, 136, 150
  Thomas 78
  William 45, 78, 91, 104
Elton, Ant'y 57
Embers, John 147
Embree, John 100, 101, 103, 104, 129, 131
  Jonathan 131
  Moses 80, 100, 131, 136

188

190

(Hare), John 29, 136
  Laurence 155
  Mathias 125, 136, 156
  Michael 125
  Peter 28, 29, 125, 136, 154, 156
  William 120
Harling, Jacob 30
Harlock, Daniel 68
  Jasper 68
  Margaret 68
  Mary (Epp) 68
  Thomas 68
Harlocken, Jasper 68
Harman/on, Jacob 158
  John 1, 63, 86, 98, 111, 158
  John Leonard 142
  Mary 98
Harpe, James 176
Harps, Daniel 133
Harrel, Jacob 165
  William 111
Harrington, John 75
  Rhoda 90
Harris, Barshaba 171
  Berry 43
  Clough 12
  George 52
  Little Berry 12
  Micajah 8, 65
  Mosely 12
  Nathaniel 12
  Rees 12
  Samuel 12, 99, 163
  Victor 88
Harrison, John 78, 84, 85, 124
Hart, Adam 118
  Delilah 15, 54
  George 15, 54
Hartell, George 30
Hartle, George 83
Harwin, James E. 109
Hasket, Thomas 125, 131
Haskit/t, Ann 151
  Thomas 3, 5, 104, 151
Hatcher, Seth 89
Hathorn, David 115
  James 115
Hattale, George 125
Hattel/l, George 131
  Saraha 131
  Sharlot 131
Hatton, David 86
  Francis 168
  James 86
Hausihl, Wm 131
Hawkins, Peter 17, 34, 74, 135
Ha(y)worth, Nathaniel 6, 53, 88
Hayne, William 126
Hays/es, James 94, 115

Joseph 115
  Robert 115
  William 105
Hazel, Henry 26
Hazle, Henry 138, 140, 141
Hazlet, John 129
Healter, Andrew 87
Heard, John 94
  Stephen 21
Heaton, Benjamin 76, 77, 95, 127
Heep, George 21
Heer, Laurence 154
  Peter 154
Heller, John 66, 67
  Margaret 18
Hencock, Barber 35
Henderson, A. 21
  David 64, 108
  John 47, 64, 82, 109, 159
  Nally 57
  Nathaniel 109, 123, 148
  Samuel 18, 19
Hendrick/s, Charity (Sarvarris) 106
  Isaac 106
  John 106, 152
  Margaret 106
  Obediah 42
  Patience 42
  Rebeccah 106
  Thomas 106
  William 106, 152
Hendrix, Henry 44
  Jane 44
  Jean 44
  John 82
  John Linvell 14
  William 51
Henning, Danl 94
Henry, James 129
  Robert 123
  Robert H. 18
Herbison, William 154
Herndon, Benjamin 50, 51, 82, 135
  Joseph 14, 51, 121
  Stephen 51
Herron, Thomas 129
Hertel, Daniel 83
  George 83, 87
Hewett, Francis 60
Hewit, Charles 2
  Francis 83
Hews, George 117
Hicker, John Andrew 130
Hiett, G. Adam 59
Higdon, John 118
Higgins, Francis 63, 64, 69, 73, 76, 133, 145
High, John 64
Hilbirn, Wm. 76

194

196

Mansil, John 101
Mantz, George 128
Marbutt, John 2
Marchant, Richard 80
Mares[?], John 135
Margin, William 14
Marion, Francis 159
Markley, Abraham 67, 68
Marple, Ann 168
   Northrup 168
Marpot/Marput, John 151
Mars, Robert 19, 82, 135
Marshall/ell, George 134
   Hugh 32, 74, 126, 133, 134, 142
   James 120
   Mary 32, 74, 126, 133, 134
Martch, P. 169
Martin, David 33, 75
   Lewis 162
   Martha 75
   Patrick 83, 111
   Saml 94, 151
Mason, David 79, 97
   Jacob 125
Matox, Lydia 63
Matthews, James 91
   Mark 109
Mattocks, Lydia 63
Maxedon, John 13, 111
   Martha 13
Maxedun, John 66
Maxwell, Andrew 63
   James 96, 97, 140
   John 140, 160
   John Butler 140
May, Benj'a 168
   James 107
   John 61
Maybin, Benjamin 163, 175
   Robert 163
Mayer, Benedict/k 40, 68
Mays, Samuel 140
Mayson, Archey 137
   Archey G. 95
   Elizabeth (Swift) 137
   Henrietta 137
   James 3, 56, 65, 72, 77, 94, 95, 114, 137
   James Robert 77, 137
   Joab 97
   Robert 53
   William 33, 65
Mazyck, Daniel 159
   Isaac 7
   William 7, 97, 176
McAdam, Robert 134
McAlees, Robert 174
McAliester, Robt 143
McBurney, John 89
McCart, James 47, 79

McCary-- see MacCary
McCinsey, Elizabeth 84
McCiterick, Robert 88
McClary, Daniel 161
McClel(l)and, 24
   David 82
   William 82
McClure, Charles 105
   Robert 57, 122, 138
McColah, John 89
McCombs, Robert 86, 140
McConnel, Samuel 14
McCool, 37
   Gabriel 154, 158
   James 80, 120, 122, 135
McCoombs, R. 101
   R. M. 140
McCoy, John 158
McCrackin/en 135
   Arthur 44, 104, 144
   James 44
   John 134
   Thomas 44
   William 8
McCraw, Edward 122
   Stephen 89, 145
   William 83, 111
McCreary, Samuel 29
McCulloch, George 154
McDanal, Jeremiah 106, 135, 136, 162, 165
   John 125, 135, 136, 162, 165
McDaniel, Andrew 48
   Daniel 12
   Elendar 109
   Elenor 109
   Elizabeth 46
   Hambleton 46
   Jeremiah 28, 29, 83, 125
   John 28, 29, 78, 92, 109, 125
   Roderick 115
McDonald, Donald 74
   Elizabeth 41
   Joseph 39
   Roderick 115
McDonold, John 109
McDougles, 176
McDowall/ell, Susanna 119
   William 9, 106, 119
McDugal/l, Patrick 109
   Ralph 12
McElduff, Thomas 13
McElhaney, John 31
McGill, James 118, 132, 168
McGlamery/ie, Andrew 116
   Samuel 54
   William 29, 41, 101, 116
McGrigor, Alexander 38

197

McKee-- see also Mackie, McKie
  Robert 103, 104
McKelvey, Alexander 152
McKetchen, D. 18
McKeterick, Robert 173
McKie-- see also McKee, Mackie
  Alexander 1, 5, 11, 17
  Daniel 5, 11, 15-17, 19, 21, 25, 55, 73,
    99
  Fanny 17
  Michael 57
  William 33
McKinny/ey, George 76, 150
  Saml 16
McKinsey, George 150
McKinzey, Elizabeth 84
McKit(e)rick, George 142
  Robert 110, 142
McLang, James 127
McLear(e)n, David 66
McLees, Robert 113
McLin[?], Widow 63
McLonan, James 127
McMaster, James 109, 146, 166
  Margaret 109
McMeen, James 109
McMichael, Elizabeth 24
  Patrick 24
McMillan, W. 94
McMor(r)ies, James 146, 159
  John 71, 74, 84, 85, 88, 101, 102, 105,
    115, 120, 123, 136, 146, 171
  Nancy (Morgan) 136
  William 32, 74
McMullen/in, Archabel 165
  Arch'd 1
McNeel, Thomas 24
McNees/e, James 69
  Thomas 1
McNeil/McNiel, James 36, 96
McNure, Thomas 24
McQuanling, Arthur 35
McQueenling, Arthur 56
  Saml 56
McQuerns, Samuel 87, 112, 116, 125, 165
Means, John 75, 146
Medill, Thomas 155
Menneweather, William 6
Merchant, Richard 59
Mereweather, William 6
Met(t)z, George 158, 159
Metzcur, Henry 38
  Margaret (Farbarn) 38
Metzger, Henry 76
Metzgon, Henry 76
Metzker, Henry 20, 64
  Margaret 20
Mexedon, Martha 111
Meyer, Andreas 167

John 148, 149
Michel, Matt 140
Mick, Margaret (Clarendon) 69
  Margaret (Clarondon) 69
Mid(d)leton, Henry 49, 69, 93, 101, 157
Miles, David 3, 45, 46, 86, 131
  Samuel 45, 58, 100, 103, 131, 152, 175
  William 45, 171
Mil(l)hous/e, John 17, 22, 125, 149, 150
  Robert 114, 115
  Sarah (Cook) 114, 115
Miller, E. 119
  John 119, 121
Mills, Alex'r 15, 62
  Charity 2
  Henry 107
  Isaac 12, 87, 174
  John 3
  Rebekah 2
  Thomas 15, 172
  William 17, 62, 76
Millwee, William 70
Minick, Bartholomew 42
Mink/s, John 10, 33, 42, 107
  Jacob 107
Mitchel/l, Daniel 69
  Isaac 26, 33, 34, 43
  John B. 14, 16, 41, 61, 96, 112, 148
  Jn 162
  William 92
Mits, Adam 35
Moncrieff, John 112
Monk, John 1, 11, 19, 151
  Thomas 106
Monro, Daniel 20
Montgomery, Andrew 101
  George 37, 84, 122
  John 146
  Robert 84
  Saml 101
  William 101
Montz, George 128
Moon, M. W. 2, 85
  Meredith William 129, 149
Mooney, Joseph 15
Moor/e, Elizabeth 33
  James 136
  James Walker 118
  John 24, 37, 99
  Robert 33, 39, 79, 105, 122, 123, 128
  William 33, 77, 122, 164, 174
Morans, Widow 126
More, John 37, 99
  Robert 24
Morehead 22
  James 50
Morgan, Asbell 124
  Christian 65
  Deborah 131

198

201

Rikert, Laurence 119
Riley, Alese 61
  Hezekiah 107, 153, 172
  Jeremiah 85, 174
  John 20, 63, 65, 174
  Patrick 61, 65
  Tarrance 61, 87
  Terrel 87
  Thomas 37
  William 29
  Zacheriah 174
Rilly, Elender 60
Riser, George 117
Rish, Adam 173
  John Adam 173
Risinger, Fight 123
  Jacob 139
Risner, George 113
Rist, Andreas 167
Ritchey, John 120
  Margret 120
Ritter, Lewis 121
  Ludwick 121
  Mary 121
Rittlehover, George 173
Rivers, Jonah 56
  Sarah 56
Roach, James 12
Road/s, Conasad[?] 54
  Nathan 67
Robbin, John 81
Roberson, Allen 98
  John 52
Roberts, George 38
  Henry 1, 126
  Obadiah 1
Robertson, John 52, 81, 83
  Richard 83
  Wm. 157
Robin, John 81, 83
Robinson, Basil 11
  John 13, 55
  Mark 13
  Richard 81, 83
Robison, Allin 7
Robtogal, Jacob 13
Rogers, Daniel 11, 12
  Gassaway 21
  Gassiway 66
  John 42
  Robert 134
  Thomas 10
Rose, Alexander 156
Ross, William 19
Rotan, Nehemiah 29
Rotes, Conrad 78
Rotton, Nehemiah 176
Rowan, Mathew 110
Royal, John 109

Royston, John C. 54
  John Cary 15
  Robt 15, 59
Rub, Peter 106
Ruble, Peter 119
Ruchman, Joseph 76, 95
Ruff, Barbara 61, 94
  Christian 27
  David 18, 22, 33, 35, 39, 43, 50, 52, 57,
    61, 63-65, 67, 70, 71, 75, 79, 80, 84, 96,
    100, 101, 105, 106, 113, 114, 122, 124,
    126, 128, 139, 142, 154, 158, 169, 170
  Elizabeth 100, 124
  Elizabeth (Rutherford) 22
  George 22, 33, 61, 63, 64, 79, 94, 124,
    128, 160, 167, 170
  Henry 79, 124, 154
  J. H. 170
  John H. 35, 65, 169
  John Henry 64, 79
  Sally (Pester) 124
Runnels, Thomas 43
Russel/l, Andrew 101, 123
  Robert 91, 141
  Rosan(n)ah 25, 56, 58, 59, 78, 172
  Samuel 73
Ruth, John 118
Rutherford 146
  Col. 145
  Elizabeth (Ruff) 22
  Robert 13, 23, 75, 90, 95, 101, 104, 122,
    125, 126, 145
  Thomas 52, 145
  William 112
Rutledge, E. 24
  Edward 49, 66, 69, 93, 101
Ryall, Thomas 149, 150
Ryals, John 176
  Thomas 46
Ryle, Thomas 149
Samsam, John 43
Sanders, John 57, 109
  Massa/Massy 109
  Michael 48
Saner, Abraham 166
Sarvarris, Charity (Hendricks) 106
Satterfield, William 66, 153
Satterwhite, B. 11, 21, 28
  Bartlett 1, 6, 32, 34-36, 38, 55, 73, 84
  Catherine 34
  Catherine (Floyd) 35
  Drury 5, 28, 55, 56, 73
  Frances 6
  John 6, 11, 15, 22, 55, 56, 70, 73, 85, 91,
    164, 170
  Mary 55, 56
  Susannah 73, 170
  William 1, 5, 28, 45, 55, 58, 59, 69, 72,
    82, 85, 88, 91, 98, 110, 114, 133, 172

(Smith), Mathew 124
Moses 3, 36, 89
Peter 11
Robert 63
Samuel 21
Sarah 57
Susanna 63
Thomas 15, 158
William 5, 21, 118, 157
Smyley, John 71
Margaret 71
Smyth, Andrew 9, 11, 79, 83
Elizabeth Ann 9
Somer/s, Adam 40
George Adam 40
Heinrich 23
Susana 40
Son, Jacob 113
Sonley, Rich'd 169
Sotcher, Eunice 157
Fanney 157
Samuel 157
Sou(l)ter, George 50
John 101
Martin 101, 128, 139
Sparks, George 51
John 13
Margaret 13, 52
Stephen 49, 104
William 134
Speak/e 146
George 143
Hezekiah 115, 166
John 1, 2, 5, 9, 12-14, 17, 20, 21, 36, 37,
43, 44, 51, 52, 55, 65, 71, 74, 77, 84,
85, 93, 97-99, 101, 102, 104, 105, 108,
115-117, 120, 123, 131, 133, 134, 139,
146, 165, 171
Richard 6, 123
Speakman, Thomas 36, 37
William 25, 35
Spearman/on, Edmond 62, 47, 95
James 32, 47, 95, 114, 133, 138
Thomas 32, 57, 133
Speer/s, David 9
Robert 7, 15, 49, 120, 131, 154, 160
William 15
Speir, David 97
Robert 14
Spence, Andrew 51, 58, 61, 124, 126, 134
David 131, 133, 161
Elizabeth 42, 46, 48
James 42, 46, 48, 51, 61, 113, 126, 151,
174
Joseph 46, 48, 131, 161
Martha 131
Robert 42, 46, 48, 64
William 58, 61, 164, 165
Spencer 158

Andrew 61
William 55, 76, 151
Spereman, James 125
Spiller, John 56
Spragins, Orsamus 44, 45
Spray, Thomas 16
Spro(u)ll, James 141, 163, 173
Stalley, Peter 5
Stamock, 37
Stark/s, Jeremiah 143, 144
Thomas 59, 102
Stearley, George Michael 78
Steddom 53
Henry 53, 100, 101, 151, 171
Martha 171
Steedham, Mary 166
Steedom, Henry 151
Steel, John 61, 65, 163
Stegall, John 114
Stephens, Adam 86
David 152
Sterling, John 138
Stevenson, John 56
Stewart, Alexander 6, 14
Daniel 49
James 127
Jennet 7
John 13, 14, 48, 57, 97, 103
Joshua 7, 49, 94
Mary 14, 161
Robert 7, 94, 167
William 7, 14
Stiddom, Henry 171
John 171
Stiddon, Jude 160
Stidman, Henry 49
Jude 160
Stockman 70
Catherina 173
Henry 156
Johannes 130
John Adam 62
John George 62
Peter 129, 167, 173
Stogman, Adam 160
Christena 160
George 160
John 160
Stone 70
Burgess 140
John William 125
William 23, 125, 152
Stoudemayer, George 115
Margaret 115
Stoudemire, George 115
Stoudemoyer, George 170
Maria Margareta 170
Stoudenmyer, George 115
Margaret 115

Stoudmire, George 54, 91
Stoudmyer, Anne Margaret 78
  George 78
Stowdmyer, Anna Margaret 78
  George 78
  John 78
Strahan, James 82, 83
  Moses 82, 83
Strasingee, Peter 145
Strawbell, Daniel 68
Strawhan/on, James 21, 82
  Moses 21
Strawn, George 105
Strawther 73
  Francis 10
  James 8, 9
  Richard 27, 28, 72, 100
  Susannah 10
  William 10
Stripling, Jesse 95
  William 56, 173
Strobel, Daniel 68
Strogman, Barbara (Houseal) (Wedding-
man) 160
Strother-- see also Strawther
  Delila 100, 114
  Jas. 64
  Richard 100, 113, 114
Strozer, Peter 119
Stuart, Alexander 77
  John 139, 157, 159-161
  Joseph 159-161
  Joshua 160
  William 74, 144, 160
Stub, Samson S. 129
Stuckman, Cathorina 173
  Peter 69, 70, 169, 173
Suber-- see also Zuber
  Conrad 130
  George Henry 47
  Michael 27
  Mike 67
Sum(m)er/s, Adam 40, 146
  Anne Maria 42
  George 40
  George Adam 173
  Henry 23, 59, 62
  John 59, 74
  John Adam 40, 42, 64, 65, 70, 112, 113,
    130, 167
  Joseph 136, 174
  Major 157
  Mary 42
  William 15, 23, 75, 127, 136, 155, 172
Sumpert 157
Sunford, John 21
Sutliff, William 140
Sutterfield, Elizabeth 153
  James 152, 153

Mary 153
Swan, Andrew 4, 101
  John 16
Sweetenburgh, Abrahart 70
  Anna\e Catharine 70
  John 114
Swetman, John 49
Swettenburgh, John 64
Swift, Elizabeth 77, 137
  Elizabeth (Mayson) 137
  Jonathan 137
  William 77, 95, 137
Swigart, George 47
Swightenbergh, John 40
  John 40
Swinford, John 82
Swygert, Christian 158
Symmes, Daniel 15
Taggart, Nancy 50, 63
Talor, Jonothan 176
Tamrey, William 61
Tar(r)er, Andrew 166
  Elizabeth 166
  Frederick 79
  Jacob 79
  Johan Jacob 79
Tate, Ann 29
  Henry 29, 98
  James 30, 126, 132
  Jesse 30
  Nathan 71
  Robert 18, 126, 149
  Samuel 30, 126
  William 41, 132, 149
Taylor, Isaac 69
  Jacob 102
  John 47
  Jonathan 77, 97, 116, 129, 167, 171, 176
  Martin 169
  Polley 53
  Rhoda 116
  Samuel 151, 164
  William 1, 9, 22, 46, 48, 106, 153, 169,
    176
Teague 171
  Abner 87
  Abraham 5
  Ailse 23
  Elijah 16, 23, 38, 132
  James 43, 70
  Joshua 70, 130, 132, 151
  Samuel 5, 23, 45, 57, 130-132, 151
Tear, Chloe 164
  Richard 29, 41, 60, 83, 111, 164
  Stephen 111
Teasdale, Isaac 16
Teer, John 1
  Robert 61
  William 53

Ten(n)ant, David 145
  William 33, 67-69, 86, 94, 157, 158
Terrer, John Jacob 166
Thomas, Abel 125, 171
  Ann 20, 28
  Edward 34
  Isaac 28
  James 160
  John 12, 14, 20, 23, 28, 38, 44, 45, 46,
    86, 90, 97, 143, 144, 158, 167
  Martha 97
  Mary 28
  Nathan 31
  Timothy 15, 34, 76
Thomerson, William 133
Thom(p)son 158
  Abraham 24, 36, 96
  Allen 163
  Charles 24, 87
  Elizabeth 56
  Farley 127
  Henry 52, 163
  Joseph 23, 49, 140, 150
  Lewis 49
  Richard 16, 33, 54, 119
  William 6, 22, 24, 49, 53, 55, 73, 157,
    172
Thweatt, Edward 100
  Jno 167
Tidmore, John 162
Timberman[?], Martin 61
Tinney, William 51, 61
Tinsley, James 33
  John 122, 144, 160
Todd, Isabella 171
  Nathan 146, 164
Toland, Elizabeth 124
  Isaac 75
  James 138, 164
  John 85
Tolbert, John 63
  Robert 63
Tolbirt, Daniel 83
Tolleson, John 41, 51, 58
Tomas, James 151
Torbet, John 63
Towles, Daniel 26, 143, 146
  Joseph 56, 57, 100
Towling, Elizabeth 26
Towls, Oliver 157
Townsen/d, James 66
  Moses 79, 80
  Paul 13, 80, 159
Toyce, John 157
Trayer, Godfrey 125
Trotter, John 28, 70, 72
  Joseph 133
Troup, John 20
Tucker, Harbirt 44

Jeremiah 162
Tull(e)y, Mat(t)hew 52, 139
Tune, John 6
Turke, Thomas 141
Turner, Alexander 32, 74, 84, 134
  David 44, 154
  Edward 26, 154
  Elisabeth 10, 44, 45, 68, 69, 73, 152, 154
  Francis 37
  John 16, 32, 37, 44, 62, 85, 90, 91, 108
  Mary 20, 59
  Mary (Davenport) 70
  Mary (Edwards) 118
  Polly 44
  Robert 84
  Sarah 154
  Susannah 133
  Thomas 15, 49, 80, 91
  Widow 6
  William 39, 44, 56, 59, 70, 80, 118, 125,
    133, 170
Turpin 55
  William 15, 63, 65, 69, 91, 133, 146
Tutt, Benjamin 6
Tweed, David 36
  John 162
  William 36
Tygart, John 46
Tyger, William 64
Vanderhorst, Arnoldus 130
  John 130
Vardeman, James 66, 75
  Jean 66
Vardiman, Bridget 105
  James 13, 65, 66, 105
  Jean 66, 105
  William 105
Verden, James 2
  Sarah 2
Vessel(l)s, James 175
  Nancy 175
  Ridley 175
Vetito, Stephen 3
Virden, Edenia/h 2, 46, 47
  James 2
  Sarah 2
Vitlook[?], Elisabeth 50
Volentine, John 19
Volmer, Michael 171
Voluntine 41
  John 47
Waddleton, Edward 64
  William 30, 64
Wade, Susannah 15
Wadlington, Edward 86
  George B. 107, 108, 110
  James 9, 10, 49, 95, 98, 131
  John 13, 176
  Marg(a)ret 10, 131

PLACE INDEX

PLACE INDEX

PLACE INDEX

www.ingramcontent.com/pod-product-compliance
Lightning Source LLC
Chambersburg PA
CBHW060459290526
45791CB00001B/184